The Self
in Transition

The John D. and Catherine T. MacArthur Foundation
Series on Mental Health and Development

THE SELF IN TRANSITION

Infancy to Childhood

Edited by

Dante Cicchetti and
Marjorie Beeghly

THE UNIVERSITY OF CHICAGO PRESS / CHICAGO AND LONDON

Dante Cicchetti is professor of psychology and psychiatry at the University of Rochester and director of the Mt. Hope Family Center. Marjorie Beeghly is research associate in the Child Development Unit of the Children's Hospital in Boston.

The University of Chicago Press, Chicago 60637
The University of Chicago Press, Ltd., London
© 1990 by The University of Chicago
All rights reserved. Published 1990
Printed in the United States of America
99 98 97 96 95 94 93 92 91 90   5 4 3 2 1

Library of Congress Cataloging in Publication Data

The Self in transition : infancy to childhood / edited by Dante
  Cicchetti and Marjorie Beeghly.
        p.   cm.—(The John D. and Catherine T. MacArthur Foundation
  series on mental health and development)
    Includes bibliographical references.
    ISBN 0-226-10662-4 (alk. paper)
    1. Self in children.   2. Self in infants.   I. Cicchetti, Dante.
  II. Beeghly, Marjorie.   III. Series.
  BF723.S24S44   1990
  155.4'1825—dc20
                                                                    90-35059
                                                                    CIP

The University of Chicago Press gratefully acknowledges a subvention from the John D. and Catherine T. MacArthur Foundation in partial support of the costs of production of this volume.

⊗ The paper used in this publication meets the minimum requirements of the American National Standard for Information Sciences—Permanence of Paper for Printed Library Materials, ANSI Z39.48-1984.

This volume is dedicated to the memory of
Lawrence Kohlberg and Henry A. Murray

Contents

Acknowledgments

We wish to thank the John D. and Catherine T. MacArthur Foundation for making the conference and the compilation of this volume possible. We also wish to thank Robert Emde, who directs the network, and Jerome Kagan, head of the New England node, for their guidance and support. Moreover, we wish to thank Nancy Reisman for her administrative support during the preparation of the conference and Victoria Gill for typing this manuscript and for her superb efforts in helping bring this work to fruition.

Dante Cicchetti also would like to thank Norman Garmezy, Paul Meehl, Alex Siegel, Alan Sroufe, and Edward Zigler for their friendship, support, and inspiration. In addition, Dante wishes to extend his appreciation to his mother Dolores, his grandmother Josephine Butch, his sisters Eugenia and Candace, and his colleagues and friends Heidi Mitke, Sheree Toth, and Jennifer White for their concern, supportive presence, and insightful contributions. Finally, Dante wishes to acknowledge Aimee Mann for her creative and personal inspiration.

Marjorie Beeghly extends her appreciation to her colleagues and mentors Inge Bretherton and Elizabeth Bates for their intellectual stimulation, support, and friendship and to her husband Glenn K. Wasek for his love, patience, and support.

Contributors

Elizabeth Bates   University of California, San Diego
Marjorie Beeghly   The Children's Hospital, Boston
Barbara Belmont   National Institute of Mental Health
Leslie Bottomly   National Institute of Mental Health
Helen K. Buchsbaum   The University of Colorado Health
   Sciences Center
George Butterworth   University of Sterling, Scotland
Vicki Carlson   Washington University School of Medicine
Dante Cicchetti   University of Rochester, Mt. Hope Family
   Center
James P. Connell   University of Rochester
Robert N. Emde   The University of Colorado Health Sciences
   Center
Jerome Kagan   Harvard University
Robert A. LeVine   Harvard University
Andrew N. Meltzoff   University of Washington
Editha Nottelmann   National Institute of Mental Health
Sandra Pipp   University of Colorado
Marian Radke-Yarrow   National Institute of Mental Health
Catherine E. Snow   Harvard University
L. Alan Sroufe   University of Minnesota
Gerald Stechler   Boston University, School of Medicine
Sheree L. Toth   University of Rochester, Mt. Hope Family
   Center
Malcolm Watson   Brandeis University
Dennie Palmer Wolf   Harvard University

1 Perspectives on the Study of the Self in Transition

Dante Cicchetti and Marjorie Beeghly

A long and illustrious history accompanies the study of the self. In fact, the quest to understand the interrelations of the soul, the mind, and the self has been a primary concern of philosophers since the pre-Socratic period. Aristotle's (1965) *de Anima* contains a summation of much early thinking on the self, both through his questioning of the existence of a unitary entity which could embody both soul and mind and through his efforts to address how the soul, conceptualized as pure function, and the body, conceptualized as pure substance, could coexist. A common thread of concern regarding the origins and functions of the self and of the role of perception, feeling, cognition, and will has its origins in Aristotelian thought and pervades much of Western philosophy. This quest for the essence of the self has continued into the psychoanalytic tradition (Stechler, in this volume) and, most recently, has captured the attention of researchers in developmental psychology and developmental psychopathology (Baron-Cohen 1989; Cohen 1980; Harter 1983).

Now that the study of the self has gained ascendancy in these developmental perspectives, researchers have found increasingly ingenious ways to operationalize this elusive construct (Kagan, in this volume; Lewis and Brooks-Gunn 1979). Consequently, much exciting work has occurred; for example, investigating the ontogenesis of the self system, the relation between the study of the self and other domains of the human mind (e.g., emotion, social-cognition, morality, language/representation), and the ways in which the functioning of the self system can be disrupted or break down (see, for example, Adler and Buie 1979; Baker and Baker 1987; Butterworth, in this volume; Cicchetti et al., in this volume; Connell, in this volume; Damon and Hart 1982, 1988; Emde and Buchsbaum, in this volume; Harter 1983; Lewis and Brooks-Gunn 1979; Meltzoff, in this volume; Pipp, in this volume; Selman 1980; Snow, in this volume; Sroufe, in this volume; Watson, in this volume).

1

Although various theoretical approaches to the self have been taken, the majority of philosophers, phenomenologists, and psychologists have emphasized the duality of the self; that is, the self has been conceptualized both as subject (the "I") and as object (the "me") (cf. Wylie 1961, 1979). This view was first articulated by William James in 1890. Cooley (1902) and Mead (1934) also recognized these two components of the self, choosing to focus on the me aspect ("self as known"). Cooley thought that knowledge of self and other developed simultaneously. Moreover, he conceived of the self as a reflective "looking glass" wherein the self is reflected through others—that is, other people are the "looking glass" for oneself (see Lewis and Brooks-Gunn 1979).

Drawing upon James' and Cooley's notions of the self, Mead (1934) proffered the first systematic description of the development of the self. Mead believed that the self was constructed actively by the infant. He stated that language development was linked intimately to the ontogenesis of the self system (in this volume, see Bates; Cicchetti et al.; Radke-Yarrow et al.; Snow; Wolf). Specifically, Mead contended that language provided the means of interaction to take the perspective of others, to perceive the self as an object in its own right, and to differentiate between self and others. In essence, Mead conceptualized the self as a cognitive structure that arose out of interaction with the world.

Many other prominent historical thinkers have likewise argued that the self develops through relationships with others (see, for example, Baldwin 1897; Emde, Gaensbauer, and Harmon 1976; Erikson 1950; Heider 1958; Kelly 1955; Merleau-Ponty 1964; Sander 1975; Spitz 1959; Sullivan 1953; Vygotsky 1962; Wallon 1949). Despite this extensive historical tradition, the validity of the self as a psychological construct has been disputed periodically (see also Kagan, in this volume). In fact, during the height of the behaviorist tradition, intrapsychic constructs, such as the self, largely were banished from scholarly circles (see Cicchetti and Pogge-Hesse 1981).

Nonetheless, the role of the self in numerous theories of development and the resurgence of research on its course and vicissitudes emphasize its importance. Unfortunately, theoretical and research attention toward the self largely has failed to approach this important construct from a developmental perspective (Harter 1983). Not surprisingly, due to the emphasis of developmental psychology, whatever work has been done has focused on normal development. Moreover, even less attention has been directed toward the self during the transition from infancy to early childhood. It is this pivotal period to which the authors in this volume have imparted a developmental perspective.

Psychoanalytic theory (in this volume see Pipp; Sroufe; Stechler) has provided one of the most important and richest developmental perspectives on the self. Although Freud (1950) first described the process whereby the infant comes to recognize himself or herself as a being separate from the mother, the work of Margaret Mahler and her colleagues has been the most influential in applying a psychoanalytic developmental approach to the emergence of the self (Mahler 1963, 1967; Mahler, Pine, and Bergman 1975). Mahler describes the process of separation-individuation, which is seen as signaling the beginning of identity formation (in this volume, see also Emde and Buchsbaum; Pipp; Stechler). In effect, the infant progresses from a normal state of symbiosis in which the child has not differentiated from the mother, through a series of phases concluding with the development of a sense of self as separate from the mother. While the role of this process in self development is clear, Mahler focuses on the role of the mother and minimizes both the mechanisms by which the child achieves a sense of self and the child's role in the process (Harter 1983; see also Winnicott [1953] 1971).

This theoretical approach, with its focus upon the internalization of interpersonal relations (Kernberg 1976) and its relevance for the development of the self, continues to be evidenced in the theorizing of Heinz Kohut (1971, 1977). According to Kohut and other object relations theorists, parental empathic failure during childhood results in the inability of the child to develop intrapsychic structures which can effectively regulate self-esteem and soothe the self. Consequently, the child depends on the environment to provide those functions (Baker and Baker 1987). Although Kohut defines the self simply as "the center of the individual's psychological universe" (1984, 311), implications for the development of a healthy or unhealthy self are emphasized throughout his theorizing.

As can be seen, the psychoanalytic and object relations schools present a significant theoretical base upon which to build a further theoretical and empirical developmental understanding of the self (Greenberg and Mitchell 1983). Specifically, the object relations approach has underscored and highlighted the importance of good-quality parent-child interaction for healthy self development and future adaptive socioemotional functioning.

Attachment theorists contribute yet another important thread in the evolution of the study of the self. During the formative years, attachment holds a central role in the development of identity and self-knowledge. Especially relevant is the concept of internal working models both of attachment figures and of the self in relation to others. While internal working models have only recently reached ascendancy within attachment theory, their psychoanalytic roots of self and object representations have been integral to object relations theory since its inception (Fairbairn 1952; Guntrip 1961; Klein 1932). According to Bowlby (1980), internal working models are the product of experiences with significant caregivers in early childhood. Although working models are subject to change over time, they are thought to be relatively enduring representations which persist over the life span. If the caregiver is emotionally responsive and available, a secure attachment relationship develops (Ainsworth 1969). This, in turn, results in positive internal working models of both self and others (Bretherton 1985, 1987; Cicchetti et al., in press; Main, Kaplan, and Cassidy 1985). In recent years, developmentalists have extended the study of representational models of attachment figures and the self into the period of transition from infancy to childhood (Greenberg, Cicchetti, and Cummings, 1990).

Of note in examining the historical roots of the development of the self is yet another theoretical approach, evidenced in the cognitive-developmental schools of Piaget (1962) and Werner (1957; Werner and Kaplan 1963). Piaget thought knowledge of the self and of other people as independent from object knowledge did not occur until the end of the sensorimotor period. Guided by the orthogenetic principle, Werner and Kaplan theorized that the "primordial sharing experience" between the mother, child (self), and object of reference proceeded from a state of relative undifferentiation to one characterized by increasing differentiation and hierarchic integration. Moreover, Werner and Kaplan claimed that the motivation to engage in symbolic activity emanated from the desire to share experiences with the other social partner (see, in this volume, Cicchetti et al.; Watson; Wolf).

Additionally, research in the domain of moral development has enhanced the understanding of the self system. Kohlberg's (1981, 1984) stages of moral reasoning and Selman's (1976) stages of social perspective-taking, as elaborations of Baldwin's (1897) and Mead's (1934) theories about the social construction of reality and the self, describe some of the competence characteristics of the moral domain relevant to self development. Morality has been conceived of as the reasoning about the regulation of social interactions—in particular, social conflicts. Moral situations cannot be conceived of unless people act and get into conflicts with each other due to their actions. More recent work by Dunn (1987); Emde, Johnson, and Easterbrooks (1987); and Gilligan and Wiggins (1987; see also Gilligan 1982) on the development of morality during the transition period further elucidates the processes whereby social interactions impact on the development of moral reasoning, self-definition, and self-understanding.

While turning from the study of normal development to the domain of developmental psychopathology, object relations theorists have continued to make significant contributions to refining further the concept of the self (Kernberg 1975; Kohut 1971, 1977). For example, the core of self pathology stems from the individual's failure to develop internal resources adequate to meet the adult's needs for self-soothing (Adler 1985). When empathic failures are extensive during early childhood, a variety of self disorders may occur. These include a self prone to fragmentation, a depleted self, a rigid self, an unempathic self, an overstimulated/overindulged self, and a grandiose self. For the borderline, the root cause of anxiety is the threat of the loss of self through psychological disintegration due to being abandoned (Bemporad et al. 1982; Cicchetti and Olsen 1990; Kernberg 1975; Kohut 1971, 1977). When a disruption of a self-object relationship occurs, depression also may emerge (Kegan 1982; Kohut 1984). In depression, the child also may selectively recall or recognize information which confirms the belief that the self has been rejected (Cicchetti and Schneider-Rosen 1986; Guidano and Liotti 1983; Cummings and Cicchetti, 1990).

Attachment theorists have extended the object relations tradition and are beginning to elucidate the role of inadequate internal working models of attachment figures and the self in relation to others in the emergence of various psychopathological conditions (Cicchetti et al., 1990). Specifically, attachment dysfunctions have been linked to the etiology of conduct disorders (Greenberg and Speltz 1988) and mood disorders (Cummings and Cicchetti, in press), as well as to future emotional and behavioral disorders (Bowlby 1988; Guidano 1987; Rutter and Garmezy 1983; Sroufe and Fleeson 1986).

In recent years, researchers have increasingly begun to investigate the self system from a developmental perspective across the major periods of life (Connell, in this volume; Damon and Hart 1982, 1988; Harter 1983). Much of this work has focused on self development during infancy (see, for reviews, Butterworth, in this volume; Meltzoff, in this volume), childhood, and adolescence (Broughton 1978; Damon and Hart 1982, 1988; Harter 1983; Selman 1980). However, surprisingly little work has appeared on the ontogenesis of the self from infancy through early childhood. Despite the integral role of the self construct in both normal and pathological development, theoreticians and researchers have all too often neglected the etiological roots of the self and the role which it exerts on development across the life span (see Connell, in this volume; Damon and Hart 1988; Harter 1983). The relative dearth of research on the self in transition makes those studies which have been conducted especially significant.

Lewis and Brooks-Gunn (1979) have carried out a series of seminal systematic investigations of visual self-recognition in infancy (see also Amsterdam 1972; Darwin [1872] 1965; Dixon 1957; Gallup 1977; Preyer 1893). Lewis and Brooks-Gunn postulate that there are four major advances in the development of self-knowledge during the first two years of life. Infants are conceived as displaying an unlearned attraction to images of other infants before three months of age. From three to eight months, infants develop the ability to recognize their own images in a mirror by means of contingency clues—that is, from observed correspondences between the infant's own movement, known by proprioceptive feedback (see Butterworth, in this volume), and the movements of the mirror-image, known visually. After age eight months, infants begin to discriminate their own images from those of opposite-sex babies and of older children and adults. During this period, infants associate particular stable categorical features with the self. After twelve or thirteen months of age, infants begin to develop the ability to recognize their own images on the basis of the features of the image alone, not relying solely on contingency clues. Finally, from approximately twenty to twenty-four months onward, behaviors and expressions emerge that imply that toddlers are aware not only of their appearance but also of their activities; thus, self-admiring behaviors (such as strutting and preening), embarrassment, and coyness may be observed (Cicchetti et al., in this volume; Lewis et al. 1989; Schneider-Rosen and Cicchetti 1990).

Also at approximately this age, as Kagan (1981) has demonstrated, the frequency of a child's self-descriptive statements increases dramatically. In addition, Bretherton and Beeghly (1982) have demonstrated that toddlers talk about the emotions of others before they discuss their own internal states (see also Cicchetti et al., in this volume). Interestingly, the findings of Kagan and of Bretherton and Beeghly are congruent with Cooley's (1908) and Bain's (1936) earlier work. Both Cooley and Bain concluded that children master self and other words between $2\frac{1}{2}$ and 3 years of age and that they acquire a sense of other prior to acquiring a sense of self.

Kagan (1981) reports that during the transition period, children cry after watching a strange adult experimenter perform a task that they feel incapable of doing, perhaps implying that children have developed a "sense of standards" by early toddlerhood. Cicchetti and Aber (1986) have suggested that the affective reaction accompanying childrens' recognition of their own limitations also may reveal the beginnings of shame and guilt.

The Papers

We next present a brief description of the contributions to this volume. Where possible, we highlight the links between the historical approaches and the current contributions to the study of the self. The theoretical and empirical work of the contributors to this volume conveys the exciting progress made toward understanding the development of the self, as well as the challenges which continue to exist given the paucity of work on the self system during the transition from infancy to early childhood.

The impetus for the current volume grew out of a conference, held at Harvard University in November 1985, on the development of the self during the transition from infancy to childhood. The conference, organized by the two of us and hosted by the New England node of the John D. and Catherine T. MacArthur Foundation Network on Early Childhood, was one of a series of meetings sponsored by the MacArthur Foundation, which in 1982 recognized the importance of and pledged support to the study of the psychological, cultural, and biological processes which mediate the transition from infancy to childhood. Preparation of a volume addressing the self in transition was a logical extension of the energy and thought-provoking discussions which were generated during the conference. Contributions were solicited both from speakers at the conference and from individuals commissioned to write about critical issues not addressed at the Harvard meeting.

In chapter 2, Gerald Stechler discusses the historical progression of the psychoanalytic study of the self and relates his analysis to the transition from infancy to childhood. The goal of Stechler's chapter is to review some of the key positions of the concept of the self as arranged along a chronological pattern of the development of psychoanalysis. Parallel to this chronological path is a conceptual path which traces the evolution of the self from a drive- or instinct-dominated model to one in which drive aspects are subservient to interpersonal and experiential factors (cf. Loevinger 1976; Sroufe, in this volume). Stechler also speculates about some of the current issues related to the development of the self. An intriguing idea he puts forth is that the self combines both self-created and adult-modeled solutions (in this volume, see also Snow; Sroufe; Wolf). Furthermore, Stechler addresses several questions central to furthering the understanding of the ontogenesis of the self system: (1) How can there be an interplay between contemporaneously collected data on the self system and retrospective views (see also Snow, in this volume)? (2) With a decreasing reliance on drive theory, are there models of affect which can be useful (in this volume, see Cicchetti et al.; Emde and Buchsbaum; Pipp; Sroufe)? (3) What new understanding of gender identity can be contributed by self psychology (see Gilligan 1982; Watson, in this volume)?

Robert Emde and Helen Buchsbaum break new ground in their empirical work on autonomy *and* connectedness during the transition period (in this volume, see Cicchetti et al.; Connell; Pipp; Sroufe). In contrast to the extant polarized views concerning autonomy versus connectedness, Emde and Buchsbaum postulate that in early self development, processes of autonomy are concurrent with processes of connectedness. Emde and Buchsbaum first review the psychoanalytic perspective on the self arising from a developmental systems view (see Stechler, in this volume). Next they outline a theory of an affective self (see Sroufe, in this volume; Stechler, in this volume), based in part on findings from their longitudinal research on how early self-awareness is accompanied by a sense of moral awareness.

Couched within a motivational framework, James Connell defines self-system processes as appraisals of the self in relation to ongoing activity in the areas of competence, autonomy, and relatedness. (For a psychoanalytic developmental perspective on these issues, see Emde and Buchsbaum, in this volume; Pipp, in this volume.) Connell puts together a model, derived from self theory and supported by empirical findings, in which the context, self, and patterns of action are linked together. Based on the individual's experiencing of the environment, the self evaluates the degree to which needs for competence, autonomy, and relatedness are being met. These self appraisals, in turn, influence the manner in which the individual engages in specific enterprises. Of particular note for this volume are the impressive data

Connell brings to bear in support of his claims concerning the needs of competence, autonomy, and relatedness during the transition period and the life-span developmental analysis which he proposes.

Writing from a biosocial perspective, Robert LeVine proposes that enculturation and the representation of the self are key concepts for understanding cultural diversity in childhood experience and for analyzing the nature of psychological development in any setting. LeVine presents convincing evidence that consideration of the psychological effects of childhood experience from a population perspective results in conclusions which differ from those based on an examination of individual differences. In addition, LeVine notes that mother-infant conversation is a population-specific phenomenon and that it rarely occurs among non-Western agricultural societies (in this volume, see Bates; Cicchetti et al.; Radke-Yarrow et al.; Snow; Wolf). Research must be conducted in these non-Western societies to ascertain any negative consequences for self development and to determine if any alternate pathways to self growth are undertaken.

George Butterworth argues that when studying the development of the self it is important to consider the interaction of various ontogenetic systems (e.g., perceptual, cognitive, and motor development) rather than to treat these domains in isolation. Butterworth's views are congruent with the organizational framework presented by Sroufe and by Cicchetti and his colleagues in this volume. In his chapter, Butterworth advocates the acknowledgment of perceptual and motor processes in particular. He illustrates through a series of fascinating experiments how self-specification through perception can be understood in terms of Gibson's (1982) assertion that proprioception is best conceived as a general form of self sensitivity, regardless of the modality in which information arrives. Butterworth begins by asking if the self-concept has its roots in processes of sensory perception. He determines that, in fact, perception provides information relevant for the self. However, he goes on to stress the importance of developing a theory which can transform the product and processes of self-perception into a form of self-conception.

Andrew Meltzoff, through a carefully devised set of programmatic investigations, examines some fascinating aspects of social phenomena that contribute to an infant's sense of self. Meltzoff stresses the criticality of exploring self-concept through the use of a range of techniques which address various domains of development (in this volume, see Butterworth; Cicchetti et al.; Kagan; Sroufe). For Meltzoff, the social mirror notion is a more apt analogue of the actual processes that occur in self development than is the physical mirror. According to Meltzoff, inferences that a rudimentary self does not emerge before eighteen to twenty-four months of age may be incorrect due to the nature of the self paradigms which have been utilized (see also Butterworth, in this volume; Pipp, in this volume; Stern 1985; Trevarthen 1979).

Meltzoff's observations are especially important when exploring the development of the self during the transition period. His belief in the possible earlier emergence of the self is underscored by the work of Elizabeth Bates, who argues that the acquisition of any natural language requires a preexisting "theory of self." Bates provides an interesting and informative account of the processes underlying the acquisition of pronominal reference language. As we see in the work of Butterworth and Meltzoff, the focus on another domain of experience (i.e., language) reveals important information about the unfolding of the self during the transition period.

In extending a linguistic approach into early childhood, Dennie Wolf suggests that one defining characteristic of selfhood resides in a movement from unity to the utilization of many voices and versions of internal experience. Changes in child discourse are measured to gauge this progression. Through the use of excellent case examples, Wolf utilizes children's narratives to put forth a fascinating account of the various roles and linguistic functions that are adopted in naturally occurring speech and in story form.

In further studies illustrating how the study of language can inform our knowledge of self-system processes, Catherine Snow utilizes a unique approach in considering mechanisms by which adults might contribute to the development of the self in children. Snow examines cases in which conversations between parents and children contribute to the child's self development. She argues that careful attention to parental communication with children reveals the difficulty of distinguishing between a self-constructed self and an other-constructed self (see Stechler, in this volume; Watson, in this volume). Snow's work places the development of some aspects of the self firmly in the interpersonal sphere where parent and child work together. As have many of the great systematizers in the history of the study of the self, Snow argues that *self* is a social construct. That is, its definition, development, and maintenance depend on social interaction and require interpersonal work (see also Damon and Hart 1988; Erikson 1950; LeVine, in this volume; Meltzoff, in this volume; Sroufe, in this volume).

Similarly recognizing the importance of relationships in the development of the self, Sandra Pipp believes that more precise statements about the nature of the self can be made by comparing domains in which the sense of self arises in the context of other with domains in which it arises in the context of the relationship. In the psychoanalytic tradition, Pipp employs the metaphor of separation and connection to explore the development of the relation among infants' developing senses of self, other, and relationships (see Emde and Buchsbaum, in this volume; Sroufe, in this volume). Pipp, like Sroufe, underscores the point that in both object relations and attachment theory perspectives the infant's sense of self is said to derive from relationships with significant others (Ainsworth et al. 1978; Mahler et al. 1975).

Malcolm Watson also explores self development in relation to social contexts. He contends that an understanding of complex role intersections defines the self in relation to others. Watson further argues that this ability is not yet present during the transition years. Watson's work nicely illustrates the developmental sequences that define children's differentiation of self from other, as well as their understanding of social roles.

Alan Sroufe approaches the study of the self from an organizational perspective (see also Cicchetti et al., in this volume). He addresses three central problems: (1) how to conceptualize the self, (2) how to account for the emergence of the self, and (3) how to understand the significance of variations of self development. For Sroufe, like Bowlby ([1969] 1982), the self is conceived as emerging from the history of attachment relationships in conjunction with the ongoing significance of early self-representations. As is true for Stechler, LeVine, Connell, Pipp, Cicchetti, and other contributors to this volume, Sroufe emphasizes the role of early care in self development.

Dante Cicchetti, Marjorie Beeghly, Vicki Carlson, and Sheree Toth also adopt an organizational perspective in their studies of the development of the self system in children with Down syndrome and in children who have been maltreated. In the tradition of developmental psychopathology (Cicchetti 1984, 1989, 1990; Rutter 1986), Cicchetti and his colleagues examine the development of several domains of self development in these populations (e.g., internal working models of attachment figures and of the self in relation to others, visual self-recognition, internal state language, symbolic play, and perceived competence). Following the tenets of an organizational approach (see Cicchetti and Wagner, 1990), Cicchetti and his collaborators employ several different measures of self development (e.g., self-reports, observations of interactions, experiments). The use of multiple measurement strategies, coupled with the investigation of a broad array of domains of the self, enables these researchers to formulate a more comprehensive understanding of the self system in these two groups of "high-risk" children. Cicchetti and his colleagues argue convincingly that, just as with the study of different cultures (LeVine, in this volume), the study of these atypical populations can enhance our understanding of the self during the transition from infancy to childhood, primarily by affirming and challenging existing theories derived from the study of normal populations.

Marian Radke-Yarrow, Barbara Belmont, Editha Nottelmann, and Leslie Bottomly further explore psychopathological conditions and self development. Radke-Yarrow and her colleagues assessed the offspring of depressed mothers in efforts to examine mothers' verbal behavior as a potentially important contributor to the self-knowledge and self-conceptions of young children. They conclude that mothers convey a significant amount of "self-relevant" data to their toddlers. Given the role which the self plays in various theories of depression (Abramson et al. 1978; Cicchetti and

Schneider-Rosen 1986; Kegan 1982), the work of Radke-Yarrow and her collaborators provides a possible mechanism whereby negative self-attributions may be socialized.

In the final contribution to the volume, Jerome Kagan presents a fictionalized dialogue that recaps the controversies which have accompanied the study of the self. Specifically, he questions the wisdom of relying on self-reports and addresses concepts such as free will, the existence of a unitary self, and subjective versus objective experience. Even though Kagan's dialogue is focused on adult-self issues, his chapter is an appropriate conclusion to the volume, as current researchers addressing the self from a developmental perspective continue to struggle with these ancient questions.

These exciting contributions demonstrate that a developmental approach, both historically and contemporaneously, has resulted in significant progress in our understanding of the self during this important transition period in early ontogenesis. In addition, these chapters make it apparent that issues related to the self require an examination of interactions among biological, psychological, and social factors, as well as multidomain assessments of functioning. It is our hope that this volume will facilitate empirical work in this direction.

References

Abramson, L. Y., M. E. P. Seligman, and J. D. Teasdale. 1978. Learned helplessness in humans: Critique and reformulation. *Journal of Abnormal Psychology* 87: 49–74.

Adler, G. 1985. *Borderline psychopathology and its treatment.* New York: Aronson.

Adler, G., and D. H. Buie. 1979. Aloneness and borderline psychopathology: The possible relevance of child development issues. *International Journal of Psycho-Analysis* 60:83–96.

Ainsworth, M. D. S. 1969. Object relations, dependency and attachment: A theoretical review of the infant-mother relationship. *Child Development* 40:969–1025.

Ainsworth, M. D. S., M. Blehar, E. Waters, and S. Wall. 1978. *Patterns of attachment.* Hillsdale, N.J.: Erlbaum.

Amsterdam, B. K. 1972. Mirror self-image reactions before age two. *Developmental Psychology* 5:297–305.

Aristotle. 1965. *de Anima.* New Haven, Conn.: Yale University Press.

Bain, R. 1936. The self-and-other words of a child. *American Journal of Sociology*: 767–75.

Baker, H., and M. Baker. 1987. Heinz Kohut's self psychology: An overview. *American Journal of Psychiatry* 144:1–9.

Baldwin, J. M. 1897. *Social and ethical interpretations in mental development.* New York: Macmillan.

Baron-Cohen, S. 1989. The autistic child's theory of mind: A case of specific developmental delay. *Journal of Child Psychology and Psychiatry* 30:285–97.

Bemporad, J., H. Smith, C. Hanson, and D. Cicchetti. 1982. Borderline syndromes in childhood: Criteria for diagnosis. *American Journal of Psychiatry* 139:596–602.

Bowlby, J. [1969] 1982. *Attachment and loss*. vol. 1. New York: Basic.

Bowlby, J. 1980. *Attachment and loss*. Vol. 3, *Loss, sadness, and depression*. New York: Basic.

———. 1988. Developmental psychiatry comes of age. *American Journal of Psychiatry* 145:1–10.

Bretherton, I. 1985. Attachment theory: Retrospect and prospect. In *Growing points of attachment theory and research*. Edited by I. Bretherton and E. Waters. Monographs of the Society for Research in Child Development, vol. 50, nos. 1–2, serial no. 209:3–38.

———. 1987. New perspectives on attachment relations. In *Handbook of infancy*. 2d ed. Edited by J. Osofsky. New York: Wiley, 1061–100.

Bretherton, I., and M. Beeghly. 1982. Talking about internal states: The acquisition of an explicit theory of mind. *Developmental Psychology* 18:906–21.

Broughton, J. 1978. Development of concepts of self, mind, reality, and knowledge. In *Social Cognition*. Edited by W. Damon. San Francisco: Jossey-Bass.

Cicchetti, D. 1984. The emergence of developmental psychopathology. *Child Development* 55:1–7.

———. 1989. Developmental psychopathology: Some thoughts on its evolution. *Development and Psychopathology*:1–4.

———. 1990. The organization and coherence of socioemotional, cognitive, and representational development: Illustrations through a developmental psychopathology perspective on Down syndrome and child maltreatment. In *Socioemotional development*. Edited by R. Thompson, Nebraska Symposium on Motivation, vol. 36. Lincoln: University of Nebraska Press, 275–382.

Cicchetti, D., and J. L. Aber. 1986. Early precursors to later depression: An organizational perspective. In *Advances in infancy*, vol. 4. Edited by L. Lipsitt and C. Rovee-Collier. Norwood, N.J.: Ablex, 87–137.

Cicchetti, D., M. Cummings, M. Greenberg, and R. Marvin. 1990. An organizational perspective on attachment beyond infancy: Implications for theory, measurement, and research. In *Attachment during the preschool years*. Edited by M. T. Greenberg, D. Cicchetti, and M. Cummings. Chicago: University of Chicago Press, 3–49.

Cicchetti, D., and K. Olsen. 1990. Borderline disorders in childhood. In *Handbook of developmental psychopathology*. Edited by M. Lewis and S. Miller. New York: Plenum.

Cicchetti, D., and P. Pogge-Hesse. 1981. The relation between emotion and cognition in infant development: Past, present, and future perspectives. In *Infant social cognition*. Edited by M. Lamb and L. Sherrod, 205–271. Hillsdale, N.J.: Erlbaum.

Cicchetti, D., and K. Schneider-Rosen. 1986. An organizational approach to childhood depression. In *Depression in young people: Clinical and developmental perspectives*. Edited by M. Rutter, C. Izard, and P. Read. New York: Guilford, 71–134.

Cicchetti, D., and S. Wagner. 1990. Alternative assessment strategies for the evaluation of infants and toddlers: An organizational perspective. In *Handbook of early intervention*. Edited by S. Meisels and J. Shonkoff, 246–277. New York: Cambridge University Press.

Cohen, D. 1980. The pathology of the self in primary childhood autism and Gilles de la Tourette syndrome. *Pediatric Clinics of North America* 3:383–402.

Cooley, C. H. 1902. *Human nature and the social order*. New York: Scribner.

———. 1908. A study of the early use of the self-words by a child. *Psychological Review* 15:339–57.

Cummings, E. M., and D. Cicchetti. 1990. Attachment, depression, and the transmission of depression. In *Attachment during the preschool years*. Edited by M. T. Greenberg, D. Cicchetti, and E. M. Cummings. Chicago: University of Chicago Press.

Damon, W., and D. Hart. 1982. The development of self-understanding from infancy through adolescence. *Child Development* 53:841–64.

———. 1988. *Self-understanding in childhood and adolescence*. New York: Cambridge University Press.

Darwin, C. [1872] 1965. *The expression of the emotions in man and animals*. Chicago: University of Chicago Press.

Dixon, J. C. 1957. Development of self recognition. *Journal of Genetic Psychology* 91:251–56.

Dunn, J. 1987. The beginnings of moral understanding: Development in the second year. In *The emergence of morality in young children*. Edited by J. Kagan and S. Lamb. Chicago: University of Chicago Press.

Emde, R. N., T. Gaensbauer, and R. Harmon. 1976. *Emotional expression in infancy: A biobehavioral study*. New York: International Universities Press.

Emde, R. N., W. Johnson, and M. A. Easterbrooks. 1987. The do's and don'ts of early moral development: Psychoanalytic tradition and current research. In *The emergence of morality in young children*. Edited by J. Kagan and S. Lamb. Chicago: University of Chicago Press.

Erikson, E. H. 1950. *Childhood and society*. New York: Norton.

Fairbairn, W. 1952. *An object relations theory of the personality*. New York: Basic.

Freud, S. 1950. Instincts and their vicissitudes. *Collected papers*. London: Hogarth.

Gallup, G. C. 1977. Self-recognition in primates: A comparative approach to the bidirectional properties of consciousness. *American Psychologist* 32:329–38.

Gibson, J. 1982. The uses of proprioception and the detection of propriospecific information. In *Reasons for realism: Selected essays of James J. Gibson*. Edited by E. Reed and R. Jones. Hillsdale, N.J.: Erlbaum.

Gilligan, C. 1982. *In a different voice*. Cambridge, Mass.: Harvard University Press.

Gilligan, C., and G. Wiggins. 1987. The origins of morality in early childhood relationships. In *The emergence of morality in young children*. Edited by J. Kagan and S. Lamb. Chicago: University of Chicago Press.

Greenberg, J., and S. Mitchell. 1983. *Object relations in psychoanalytic theory*. Cambridge, Mass.: Harvard University Press.

Greenberg, M., D. Cicchetti, and E. M. Cummings, eds. 1990. *Attachment beyond infancy*. Chicago: University of Chicago Press.

Greenberg, M., and M. Speltz. 1988. Attachment and the ontogeny of conduct problems. In *Clinical implications of attachment*. Edited by J. Belsky and T. Nezworski. Hillsdale, N.J.: Erlbaum, 177–218.

Guidano, V. F. 1987. *Complexity of the self*. New York: Guilford.

Guidano, V. F., and G. Liotti. 1983. *Cognitive processes and emotional disorders: A structural approach to psychotherapy*. New York: Guilford.

Guntrip, H. 1961. *Personality structure and human interaction: The developing synthesis of psychodynamic theory*. New York: International Universities Press.

Harter, S. 1983. Developmental perspectives on the self system. In *Handbook of child psychology*. Edited by E. M. Hetherington. New York: Wiley.

Heider, F. 1958. *The psychology of interpersonal relations*. New York: Wiley.

James, W. [1890] 1963. *Psychology*. New York: Fawcett.

Kagan, J. 1981. *The second year: The emergence of self-awareness*. Cambridge, Mass.: Harvard University Press.

Kegan, R. 1982. *The evolving self*. Cambridge, Mass.: Harvard University Press.

Kelly, G. 1955. *Theory of personality: The psychology of personal constructs*. New York: Norton.

Kernberg, O. F. 1975. *Borderline conditions and pathological narcissism*. New York: Aronson.

_____. 1976. *Object relations theory and clinical psychoanalysis*. New York: Aronson.

Klein, M. 1932. *The psychoanalysis of children*. London: Hogarth.

Kohlberg, L. 1981. *Essays on moral development*. Vol. 1, *The philosophy of moral development*. San Francisco: Harper & Row.

_____. 1984. *Essays on moral development*. Vol. 2, *The psychology of moral development*. San Francisco: Harper & Row.

Kohut, H. 1971. *The analysis of the self*. New York: International Universities Press.

_____. 1977. *The restoration of the self*. New York: International Universities Press.

_____. 1984. *How does analysis cure?* Chicago: University of Chicago Press.

Lewis, M., and J. Brooks-Gunn. 1979. *Social cognition and the acquisition of self*. New York: Plenum.

Lewis, M., M. W. Sullivan, C. Stanger, and M. Weiss. 1989. Self-development and self-conscious emotions. *Child Development* 59:146–56.

Loevinger, J. 1976. *Ego development*. San Francisco: Jossey-Bass.

Mahler, M. S. 1963. Thoughts about development and individuation. *Psychoanalytic Study of the Child,* vol. 18. New York: International Universities Press, 307–24.

_____. 1967. On human symbiosis and the vicissitudes of individuation. *Journal of the American Psychoanalytic Association* 15:740–63.

Mahler, M. S., F. Pine, and A. Bergman. 1975. *The psychological birth of the human infant*. New York: Basic.

Main, M., N. Kaplan, and J. C. Cassidy. 1985. Security in infancy, childhood and adulthood: A move to the level of representation. In *Growing points of attachment theory and research*. Edited by I. Bretherton and E. Waters. Monographs of the Society for Research in Child Development, vol. 50, nos. 1–2, serial no. 209:66–104.

Mead, G. H. 1934. *Mind, self, and society.* Chicago: University of Chicago Press.

Merleau-Ponty, M. 1964. *Primacy of perception.* Translated by W. Cobb. Evanston, Ill.: Northwestern University Press.

Piaget, J. 1962. *Play, dreams and imitation in childhood.* New York: Norton.

Preyer, W. 1893. *Mind of the child.* Vol. 2, *Development of the intellect.* New York: Appleton.

Rutter, M. 1986. The developmental psychopathology of depression: Issues and perspectives. In *Depression in children: Clinical and developmental perspectives.* Edited by M. Rutter, C. Izard, and P. Read. New York: Guilford.

Rutter, M., and N. Garmezy. 1983. Developmental psychopathology. In *Handbook of child psychology.* Edited by P. Mussen, vol. 4. New York: Wiley, 775–911.

Sander, L. W. 1975. Infant and caretaking environment: Investigation and conceptualization of adaptive behavior in systems of increasing complexity. In *Explorations in child psychiatry.* Edited by E. J. Anthony. New York: Plenum.

Schneider-Rosen, K., and D. Cicchetti. 1990. Early self-knowledge and emotional development: Visual self-recognition and affective reactions to mirror self-images in maltreated and nonmaltreated toddlers. Submitted for publication.

Selman, R. 1980. *The growth of interpersonal understanding: Developmental and clinical analyses.* New York: Academic.

Selman, R. 1976. Social cognitive understanding. In *Moral development and behavior.* Edited by T. Lickona. New York: Holt, Rinehart & Winston.

Spitz, R. 1959. *A genetic field theory of ego formation.* New York: International Universities Press.

Sroufe, L. A., and J. Fleeson. 1986. Attachment and the construction of relationships. In *Relationships and development.* Edited by W. Hartup and Z. Rubin. Hillsdale, N.J.: Erlbaum.

Stern, D. 1985. *The interpersonal world of the infant: A view from psychoanalysis and developmental psychology.* New York: Basic.

Sullivan, H. 1953. *The interpersonal theory of psychiatry.* New York: Norton.

Trevarthen, C. 1979. Communication and cooperation in early infancy: A description of primary intersubjectivity. In *Before speech: The beginnings of human communication.* Edited by M. Bullowa. London: Cambridge University Press.

Vygotsky, L. 1962. *Thought and language.* New York: Wiley.

Wallon, H. 1949. *Les origines du caractere chez l'enfant: Les precludes du sentiment de personalite.* 2d ed. Paris: Presses Universitaires de France.

Werner, H. 1957. The concept of development from a comparative and organismic point of view. In *The concept of development.* Edited by D. B. Harris. Minneapolis: University of Minnesota Press.

Werner, H., and B. Kaplan. 1963. *Symbol formation: An organismic-developmental approach to language and the expression of thought.* New York: Wiley.

Winnicott, D. [1953] 1971. Transitional objects and transitional phenomena. In *Playing and reality.* Middlesex, England: Penguin.

Wylie, R. (1961). *The self-concept: A critical survey of pertinent research literature.* Lincoln: University of Nebraska Press.

———. 1979. *The self-concept.* Vol. 2, *Theory and research on selected topics.* Lincoln: University of Nebraska Press.

2 Psychoanalytic Perspectives on the Self during the Transition Period

GERALD STECHLER

When I hear the phrase *transition period,* it calls to mind one of my favorite cartoons, which appeared in *The New Yorker* a number of years ago. Adam and Eve are standing hand in hand as they are about to leave the Garden of Eden. One is saying to the other, "This is a time of great transition." In the beginning, when God told Moses the story of the transgression and expulsion, either he was anticipating psychoanalysis or else Sigmund Freud, a number of years later, was using certain uncited references.

The part of psychoanalysis anticipated in that portion of Genesis is the powerful theme of transition from the assumed innocence of infancy to the sentience and responsibility of childhood and later development. Many threads are woven in. First, there is the image of boundless nurturance: all is granted and available for the picking, without labor and without limit. However, the nurturance is not entirely boundless. There is one prohibition: the fruit of the Tree of Knowledge may not be eaten. If God had been a strategic family therapist, one could say that he virtually paradoxed Adam and Eve into the transgression. The second aspect of the theme is the conflict about obedience and the array of defenses erected against obedience and justifying disobedience; in short, the story of autonomy and separation-individuation with all its Sturm und Drang. Responsibility is avoided at all costs. When God asks, "Where are you?" Adam doesn't answer. Then, variously, Eve and the serpent are blamed. In psychoanalytic terminology, denial, repression, and projection are everywhere. And finally, what are gained and lost by virtue of this disobedience? Gained is not just knowledge in its most general sense but, more specifically, knowledge of good and evil, implying a rudimentary sense of morality, and, most specifically, knowledge of sexuality with the concomitant shame and guilt. And what is lost by virtue of this disobedience? The garden itself is lost, although further contact with

This work was supported in part by grants from the John D. and Catherine T. MacArthur Foundation, the Spencer Foundation, and the Jack Spivack Child Development Fund.

17

God is possible through hard work and redemption. Margaret Mahler would say that it is rapprochement that remains possible.

Psychoanalysis is often credited with being a general theory of psychology and then is immediately criticized for leaving out certain very important areas, such as cognitive development. It would be easier from the outset if we were more clear about what is central to psychoanalysis and what is more at the periphery. At its foundation, psychoanalysis deals with the stormy side of life. No matter how much discussion takes place about the more cerebral, more ethereal, or even the more adapted sides of existence, interest in those aspects arises because Freud saw the direct connection between gut-level forces and those more elevated aspects of life.

In *Beyond the Pleasure Principle,* Freud (1920) stated that the most ubiquitous psychological mechanism for healthy adaptation was the tendency to turn passively experienced anxiety into a situation of active mastery. One of the examples he cited in relation to this principle was the only infant observation he ever published. An eighteen-month-old infant was observed with a simple toy, a wooden spool on the end of a string. The toddler was seen repeatedly throwing the spool under a sofa and retrieving it by pulling on the string. Freud interpreted this play as an act of mastery over the passively experienced separation anxiety that was important in the child's life at that time. The child was now in control of the comings and goings rather than being the recipient of such events. Freud thought, however, that this tendency was so universal and so well accepted that he would not spend any more time on it. Rather, he was interested in those instances in which this mechanism failed and in which, no matter how many times the person engaged in repetitive attempts to master the trauma, mastery was not achieved. Thus, he left for nonanalytic psychologists the immense realm of smoother adaptation.

We must be careful here not to equate *turbulent* with *pathological.* Many parts of our being start out in a cauldron of conflict and turmoil. That does not necessarily mean that those parts will end up as unhealthy aspects of us. Quite the contrary. With appropriate resolution and ultimate mastery, those elements which arise from the most conflictual origins may end up being our strongest, most resilient parts.

The concept of the self stands in an unusual position within psychoanalysis. Sometimes it is not present at all. Sometimes it seems like the vessel within which the dynamic events are occurring. Yet, at other times, it is both the vessel and the contents of the vessel. One of the aims of this chapter will be to review some of the key positions of the concept of the self as arranged along a more or less chronological pattern of the development of psychoanalysis. Parallel to this chronological path is a more conceptual one which traces the evolution from a drive- or instinct-dominated model, to one in which the drive aspects are quite subservient to interpersonal and experiential factors. As this framework shifts, so does the meaning of the term *self.* A second aim, addressed at the end of the chapter, is to carry the thinking beyond a review of various historic positions and engage in speculation about some current issues related to self.

Freud himself did not emphasize the term *self,* although much of his thinking about the structural point of view and the interaction of the tripartite components of the psychic apparatus can be seen as related to that concept. Within the structural model, the ego has been the part most closely allied with the idea of self. But that poses some very thorny theoretical problems that will be elaborated below.

Later authors who did start to refer directly to the idea of self introduced it under a number of different theoretical perspectives or routes. Perhaps the most general classification of these routes is the division between those who introduced self within the more traditional, drive-dominated theory of psychoanalysis and those for whom the centrality of the idea of self was part of an evolutionary process that was taking them away from the psychoanalytic drive theory. Edith Jacobson and Margaret Mahler are two leading examples of psychoanalysts who became intensely interested in questions about the development of the self, while remaining steadfast in their adherence to classic drive theory. D. W. Winnicott and Erik Erikson also focused on issues of self and identity; and while not seeking to overthrow drive theory as part of their creative thinking, they tended to downplay its importance. They did this by giving greater emphasis to other factors. In Winnicott's case, it was object relations; for Erikson, psychosocial and cultural influences were ascendant. In the last category, one finds the work of George Klein and Heinz Kohut. For these two psychoanalysts, the idea of the self was of central importance, but was only part of a systematic examination of psychoanalytic metapsychology and of drive theory in particular. Both of them, in somewhat different ways, were led to an ultimate rejection of drive theory.

What is perhaps most remarkable about all these authors is that, although they represent widely divergent approaches within the general framework of psychoanalysis, there is much greater congruity among them when they get down to the more descriptive, clinical level of infant and toddler development. Jacobson (1964) speaks of the initial wavering state of mind in which self and object world may become fused and confused. She also emphasizes the influence of the infantile defenses of denial and repression on the formation of our images of the self and the object world. Insofar as these defenses cut out unpleasurable memories, they eliminate unacceptable aspects of both the self and the outside world. "The defects caused by the work of repression may be filled in by screen elements, by distortions or by embellishments produced by the elaborate maneuvers of the ego's defense system" (p. 20). Regarding the transition period, Jacobson notes that, even with the enormous development of the sense of identity in connection with the bodily and mental self-images during the toddler period, conscious fantasies of merger with the love object remain quite normal in the three-year-old. Not wishing to reify self, Jacobson, along with Greenacre (1958), considers identity a flexible and functional term rather than one with absolute meaning.

Mahler (Mahler, Pine, and Bergman 1975) devotes a great deal of attention to the normal and abnormal development of the self during infancy, toddlerhood, and beyond. She points out that at roughly eighteen months of age the child is at the height of "the ideal state of self" (a term coined by Joffe and Sandler [1965]). This is a complex representation of the "symbiotic dual unity," with its inflated sense of omnipotence now augmented by the toddler's feeling of his or her own magic power as the result of a spurt in autonomous functioning. The next period is one of great vulnerability, for the child must "return to earth," with a more realistic, less delusional sense of self. But this return must be sufficiently gentle and free from narcissistic injury so that a reasonable level of self-esteem can be maintained. Available, empathic parents are the key to a healthy transformation. When the parents function in a suboptimal way by being unavailable or by thwarting or ridiculing the child's efforts to be close or to be away, the child will develop considerable anxiety around both closeness and separateness, as well as with respect to autonomous actions. As would be expected, self-esteem will also be impaired. Mahler considers the achievement of rapprochement to be the final phase of the process of separation-individuation. This highly vulnerable period marks the transition from toddlerhood into later childhood. She, along with others, sees the multiple potentiality for the introduction of pathological patterns at this transition point.

In discussing the young infant, Winnicott (1965) spoke of the baby's Being (which he spelled with a capital B) almost as if he were talking about an innate soul. One of his central postulates is that when the Being is respected by an empathic parent, it enlarges and strengthens and promotes the development of a true self. Conversely, if the parents impose their own external agenda on the baby in a way that does not respect the essential quality of the baby, a reasonable external adaptation may take place, but the fragile infantile Being will be crushed, and in its place will arise a false self. This false self, which is entirely dedicated to external validation and the pleasing of others, is seen by some as the early ontogenesis of the borderline personality or the narcissistic character disorder.

Erikson, next to Freud, is perhaps the psychoanalytic figure most familiar to developmental psychologists and therefore needs the least elaboration. For our purposes, it will suffice to note that the affective-cognitive states of shame and doubt were central in Erikson's (1950) formulation of the transition period. The core conflict of the period is that of autonomy versus shame and doubt. Following Freud's structural model, Erikson assigns to the ego the task of resolving this conflict.

With the introduction of ego psychology into psychoanalysis, the attempt was made to address the issues of adaptation and of integrative functioning. The synthesis of the parts into a functional whole was accounted for by expanding the ego so that it became an integrator. But while one problem was being solved, another was being created. Ego now had two different meanings within the theory and, even more confusing, was positioned at two different levels within the psychic apparatus. In its older, more restricted meaning, ego was a coequal structure in the tripartite model along with id and superego. In its new expanded role, it was also the coordinator of all functions, serving the overall aim of adaptation.

In reaction to this ambiguity, Klein (1976) introduced a clarification by adopting the term *self* to specify the synthetic function, with ego relegated to its original position as one of the three structures of the psychic apparatus. Klein, of course, did not stop with this fairly simple semantic distinction. He proposed a model of the self and its development that was directly tied in to the clinical theory of psychoanalysis. Conflict, its ramifications and its resolution, is at the heart of the clinical theory, and conflict became the basis for his theory of the construction of the self.

From birth onward, infants are faced with incompatibilities. Klein called these incompatibilities breaches of expectancy and breaches of integration. As has now been well demonstrated within developmental psychology, expectancy schemata are established very early in life. The inevitable violations of these expectancies create the breaches. In very short order, a rudimentary self is established around the expectancies, so that the violations are a challenge to that self and its integration. Each challenge creates the dual possibilities of mastery and failure. Mastery is more likely when the size of the challenge is regulated by the parent so as to be within the capacity of the child. Under those circumstances, a resolution of the incompatibility is achieved, and the self structure is augmented. It is, in fact, augmented in a specific way. The manner or mode by which the child resolves the conflict becomes part of the self. It is by this process that we can be said to develop our own style or character.

Of course, not all solutions are invented de novo by the toddler in the course of conflict resolution. Just as often, the parent will model or impose a solution. Thus, the self, or character, combines self-created and adult-modeled solutions. At the other pole, when the magnitude of the challenge is too great and mastery is not possible, a repressive process which diminishes the self takes place. The failures also become incorporated as part of our self, although consciously we most often regard them as not self and then project them outward. In short, the self as well as the not self is the integrated summation of all our solutions and failures.

This constructionist point of view is distinctly different in its assumptions than the drive model. Yet, one of the wonders of psychoanalytic thinking is that the whole theory is so loosely knit and constituted of such diverse elements, containing both mechanistic and systemic approaches, that opposing theorists such as Mahler and Klein can make such similar statements so long as they remain close to the clinical or observational data.

One important difference between Mahler and Klein has to do precisely with the issue of separation-individuation and the development of the self during the transition period. Unlike Mahler, Klein saw the move toward autonomous functioning and the move toward togetherness as coexisting from the very beginning of life. In agreement with Piaget, he saw the fundamental proactive tendencies in babies. As they reach out and act upon the world and receive perceptual verification of the effect of their acts, they develop a component of the constructed self which Klein called the "I" self. From very early on, first in momentary and then in more sustained ways, they begin to operate as separate beings. The other part of the self, the "we" self, is built out of the interpersonal shared experiences, which contain both harmonious and conflicted aspects. As Klein sees it, what is incorporated in the we self is not the other person per se as much as it is the interaction between the baby and the other. The I and the we are the foundations, respectively, of later autonomous and affiliative tendencies.

One clear implication of the parallel development of the two lines is that there is no necessary polarization between the two. As we have shown in other work, well-functioning families simultaneously support both aspects of the development of the self much of the time (Stechler and Kaplan 1980). In these contexts, the development of the I self and the we self can be mutually facilitative. At times, however, children must experience conflict, as their assertions test the limits of parental rules and patience. This may be seen as yet another challenge, this time a challenge concerning integration, or (in more traditional psychoanalytic terminology) a struggle with ambivalence. This particular struggle, to unify self-assertive acts and motives with the incorporated limitations and prohibitions of the parents, varies greatly in quality and in intensity from child to child. As mentioned above, one of the propositions in Klein's model is that our adaptive style or character is the integrated summation of our solutions to the interpersonal and impersonal challenges that have confronted us, along with the holes and sealed-off areas which represent our failures at mastery in the face of overwhelming challenges. Distortions can occur in either the I or the we self depending on how the family system may promote or impair development in very specific areas, and in very specific ways.

Recent additions to a psychoanalytic theory of the self have been made by Heinz Kohut. From his clinical work, Kohut (1977) saw that technically and theoretically the developmental epoch we are discussing lay at the heart of psychoanalysis. More and more, patients appeared with pregenital character disturbances and were found to be intractable to the classical analysis, which focused on the interpretation of oedipal conflicts. Not only was the content of the interpretation often far from the mark because the disturbances arose from an earlier developmental period; more important, the technique of interpretation per se was misguided because the patient's subjective state was one not of unresolved conflict but rather of a threatened and fragmented self which could not receive the interpretation as anything other than an assault or a withdrawal of empathy by the analyst. In short, there was not a sufficiently cohesive self organization present to even hear or assimilate an interpretation.

This discovery had major impact on both the technique of psychoanalytic treatment and the developmental model. If, despite the appearances of occupational and even social success, the aspect of self organization that Kohut called the narcissistic line of development was so fragilely organized that the patient could not tolerate the analyst's neutral and interpretive stance, then a different mode of communication was needed. If the interpretation of oedipal-level conflicts not only fell on deaf ears but was perceived by the patient as critical and rejecting, then a way must be found to be with the patient in a mode that represented the more infantile forms of relationship. Furthermore, the analyst's stance with respect to these earliest patterns of relationship must be one which allows for the recapture of the storms of the original developmental periods but clearly does not recapitulate the failings of those early and primary parent-infant and parent-toddler relationships. In order to accomplish this, Kohut extended the empathic mode, which had always been an aspect of analytic practice, into a full-blown technical approach.

This must be distinguished from a gratifying or seductive attitude. Empathy is a complex topic in itself, but at the very least it should imply an attentive, open connection with the patient. It does not mean approving of or gratifying the patient's acts or wishes, which is always dangerous and leads to explosive transference and countertransference manifestations. Rather, empathy validates whatever the subjective position of the patient may be at any given moment—validates it in the sense of it being knowable and shareable by the analyst, whether that be at a cognitive or purely affective level. Thus, empathy becomes the validation and is the vehicle by which the patient can feel known and held by the analyst in a way that the evidence would suggest was lacking the first time around. When the empathic approach is properly used by an analyst, a more cohesive self eventually starts to appear in the patient. In the technical terminology employed by Kohut, the analyst becomes a self-object for the patient. Then, by a process of transmuting internalization, this self-object restores the previously fragile or fragmented self into a state of greater cohesiveness.

The original developmental condition which led to this form of self pathology is thought to be severe empathic failure by the parents during the infantile and transitional periods. In the same way that the empathic analyst can offer herself or himself as a self-object, leading to a restoration of the self, the empathic parents from the outset become the original self-object that is the sustaining structure for the narcissistic line of development. If, because of their own depression, character pathology, addiction, and so on, their empathic availability is sporadic or unpredictable, the baby will not be able to use them as a sustaining self-object. Kohut perceived the ways in which patients sought to use him as a sustaining self-object, and he further refined his developmental model based on that perception. He delineated two early stages of development, the mirroring phase and the idealization phase:

> When the child's self-assertive presence is not responded to by
> the mirroring self-object, his healthy exhibitionism—
> experientially a broad psychological configuration even when
> single body parts, or single mental functions, are conspicuously
> involved as representatives of the total self—will be given up,
> and isolated sexualized exhibitionistic preoccupations concern-
> ing single symbols of greatness (the urinary stream, feces,
> phallus) will take over. And similarly, when the child's search
> for the idealized omnipotent self-object with whose power he
> wants to merge fails, owing either to its weakness or its refusal
> to permit a merger with its greatness and power, then again,
> the child's healthy and happy wide-eyed admiration will cease,
> the broad psychological configuration will break up, and iso-
> lated sexualized voyeuristic preoccupations with isolated sym-
> bols of the adult's power (the penis, the breast) will take over
> (Kohut 1977, 171–72).

Central to these hypotheses is the distinction between an integrated, total representation of the self and isolated, partial representations. The latter are taken to be the preconditions for the development of self pathology. The parents' contribution to health and pathology is pivotal. While events such as births, deaths, illnesses, and family breakups unquestionably can play an important role in the development of psychopathology, the critical factor resides in the repetition of empathic failures. There is, nevertheless, a distinctly optimistic note to this model. Parents do not have to be perfect. Far from it. In Kohut's formulation, two important protective factors incline development toward health. First, the infant possesses a sort of magnet or radar directed toward health. It may simply represent the fact that empathic interactions feel better than nonempathic ones, so that is where the infant's attention and energy will be directed. Second, the threshold for the amount of mirroring needed to create a fairly cohesive self may be fairly low.

Taken together, these points imply that the baby will seek that aspect of relationship or self-object which will provide the organizational matrix for the development of a cohesive self. This perhaps goes beyond what Kohut has actually stated, but it seems clear that he implies a very systemic notion similar to Klein's: namely, that the overriding motivation is to maintain organization. The therapist can make substantial use of this assumption by ensuring that all parts of the patient are mirrored. An excessive focus on the pathological aspects distorts the picture, as would a reluctance to empathize with the parts of the self that the patient feels are awful.

Another major protective factor is that the criteria for parental empathy are not at all stringent. Kohut is not talking about the finely tuned validating interaction sought in psychoanalysis. Rather, he is referring to fairly basic attention to the infant. Even if the parent mistakes the baby's intentions and misresponds, or goes so far as to thwart the baby's acts, deliberately or unintentionally, this is not necessarily experienced by the infant as an empathic failure. Fundamentally, it is the parents' lack of attention to the baby and his or her wishes that represents the empathic failure.

The mirroring phase focuses both on the vegetative and on the self-assertive stages of infantile development. During these phases, the understanding and facilitation of the infant's aims by the parent are the key to establishment of a sustaining self-object. Repeated empathic failure during the mirroring phase leads to a deficit in the self. Deficits are seen as the basis of the most severe primary disorders of the self, including psychoses, borderline states, and schizoid and paranoid personalities. Repeated empathic failures starting later, during the succeeding idealization phase, lead to a somewhat stronger self, with compensations becoming the central feature. The person is still subject to primary disorders of the self in later life, but they are of a much more analyzable variety, specifically the narcissistic personality disorders, such as hypochondriasis and depression, or the narcissistic behavior disorders, such as perversion, delinquency, or addiction.

Some of the differences between Kohut and Freud are differences in emphasis. Both see the more severe pathologies as arising from the earlier, pre-oedipal phases of development. Kohut puts less weight on the endogenous unfolding of the drives and more on the empathic versus unempathic nature of the primary objects, but that is also true of most post-Freudian analysts. One point of more distinct disagreement is around the concepts of deficit and conflict. As has been just mentioned, Kohut views repeated empathic failure as producing a deficit in the organization of the self. It is a hole, a weakening of structure that leaves the person vulnerable to fragmentation. The transference neurosis that is the sine qua non of a Freudian analysis is not within the developmental capacity of that person. Interpretations that would clarify conflicts for those with adequate self development not only fall on deaf ears for the patient with self pathology but are in fact experienced by them as further empathic failures and as criticisms coming from the analyst.

Klein's work suggests a way to resolve even this difference. His concept of incompatibilities does, in fact, bridge both conflict and deficit. Kohut recognizes both clinically and theoretically that the existence of sustained intrapsychic conflict requires a sufficiently intact psychic structure within which such conflict can exist. That is the traditional psychoanalytic view. Klein broadens the framework and notes that even the youngest baby is capable of experiencing incompatibilities and begins to build psychic structure—self—out of the mastery or resolution of those incompatibilities. One can speculate that if Freud had pursued his conjectures about active mastery over passively experienced anxiety, his theory would have arrived much sooner at the place where one now finds psychoanalysis.

Emphasis on the organizational aspects of the self has led Kohut away from drive theory. He believes that in these disorders, what the analyst finds when he or she comes to the bedrock of the infantile experience is the emptiness, the depression, the yearning, and the rage stemming from the repeated empathic failure and narcissistic injury. Drive manifestations are not primary but are the residual phenomena secondary to the disintegration of the self. When the self is functioning in a cohesive, integrated manner, it appears seamless and drive manifestations are not seen. This particularly applies to classical analytic theory's aggressive instinct. For Kohut, aggression is a reaction to narcissistic threat rather than a primordial drive.

At this point, although much more could be said about the psychoanalytic view of the self in the transition period, it might be useful to take stock by looking at some of the questions which face the psychoanalytic theory of the self and which are far from being fully answered:

1. How can the movement from a more mechanistic to a more systemic psychoanalytic model be continued and advanced, particularly in looking at those developmental epochs that clearly form a watershed in the life span, such as the transition period we are discussing?

2. Given the self psychologies of Klein and Kohut, how can there be an interplay between the contemporaneous data we can gather in infancy and childhood and the retrospective view of these periods that emerges through psychoanalysis?

3. Psychoanalytic theory spends an extraordinary amount of time talking about the emotional side of life and, paradoxically, lacks a systematic model of affect. With drives now assuming a much diminished position in the psychoanalytic understanding of motivation, are there models of affect that may be useful?

4. The transition period is clearly pivotal for gender identity. What new understanding of gender identity can be offered by self psychology?

Some directions for seeking the answers and some examples of specific attempts will be given.

General systems theory and, more recently, the theory of self-organizing systems (Prigogine 1978) offer more than new metaphors for psychological data. They offer new ways of ordering the data. Instead of thinking of the self as divided into classical categories (e.g., perception, cognition, affect, motivation, and actions), we can seek coherence around functional subsystems, which are then integrated into more global systems. For example, under the classic Freudian position, aggression was considered one of the two primary instincts or drives; and assertive acts, motives, and fantasies were considered to be derivatives of this primordial instinct. (The other primary drive, of course, is libido.) Kohut, Klein, and others have rejected this model, and Kohut has proposed that aggression is a reaction to a threat or injury to the self. Assertion is considered to be an aspect of the infant's functioning, starting in the mirroring phase, but Kohut's psychology does not elaborate upon it, probably because he is not a developmentalist.

In our own thinking, we have separated assertion and aggression as action components of two distinctly different biopsychological systems (Stechler and Halton 1987). They are equally primordial, and neither derives from the other. Of course, in a fully integrated living organism, it is somewhat of an abstraction to speak of an independent subsystem. Obviously, they work only when they are part of a whole. But each subsystem can be considered to be complete insofar as it contains a full complement of perceptual, cognitive, motivational, actional, and affective components. The assertive action pattern so prominent in older infants and toddlers is seen to be part of the fundamental proactive, searching, engaging, acting-upon system. The actions of this subsystem are self-generated and usually alloplastic; and the affects generally associated with the activities of this system are on the euphoric end of the spectrum: specifically, interest, excitement, and joy.

In contrast, aggression is seen as one part of a totally different biopsychological subsystem that is dedicated to the self-protection of the organism. Normally dormant, it becomes activated only in the context of perceived threat. It may be autoplastic or alloplastic, although the aggressive component of the self-protective system is usually directed outward. And finally, its activities are usually associated with the dysphoric affects of fear, distress, and anger.

This systemic view of assertion and aggression is relevant to the transition period because it has enabled us to understand better the ways in which some two-year-old children can be free in the expression of their assertive aims—elaborating their play and their relationships, sometimes pushing limits, but being able to deal with prohibitions with reasonable equanimity—while others are often caught up in constant battles, sterile repetitive play, or pervasive inhibitions. Tracing the longitudinal development of these children, we have been able to see how family patterns have created greater or lesser contamination between assertion and aggression. These two subsystems, which have such independent origins, can become mutually contaminated via experiences in which the normal assertive aims are constantly thwarted or are treated as if they were aggressive assaults on others. If the child's assertive acts are thwarted and punished, the child feels threatened, self-protective mechanisms are mobilized, and the assertive intents become contaminated with aggressive reactions. This model has suggested a new approach for one of the pivotal issues of self development during the transition.

This same model, although incomplete and admittedly dealing with only one of a large number of complex issues being negotiated around the transition, is nevertheless an example of how we can address the second question raised above: the question of relating child development research to psychoanalysis. Frequent taped interviews with young mothers, and many observations of mothers and children in their homes and at our clinic during developmental tests and free-play sessions, gave us the data from which this model evolved (Sander 1962). Since the infants and toddlers could not really be in psychoanalysis, it is frivolous to ask if that perspective would present a different view. But it is not frivolous to claim that we are making inferences about intrapsychic processes that are in the same realm as those that come out of psychoanalysis proper.

The clinical application of this model has been explored (Stechler 1987a) in psychodynamic outpatient therapy and has also been used extensively in the inpatient treatment of severely disturbed adolescents and their families. It is useful to have a clear and coherent understanding of the relationship between assertion and aggression and to have a concise model of the treatment methods and goals with respect to disturbances in these areas. Succinctly stated, an aim of the treatment is to restore the healthy differentiation between assertion and aggression, a distinction that had become contaminated as part of a pathological developmental process. Since this view of aggression in its natural state is as a reactive protective device, one does not have to control, suppress, modify, modulate, or neutralize it. Once it has been differentiated from assertion, the vehement, easily provoked aggression that may have been quite prominent will fade dramatically. At the same time, assertion itself is restored to its natural proactive fulfilling condition. This approach is different than one which attempts to treat aggressive behavior by invoking some form of inhibition. That inhibitory method rarely succeeds; and when it does, it is likely to have the unfortunate consequence of simultaneously inhibiting assertion.

The third question about affect and motivation can be touched on here in only the briefest way. Other contributors to this volume elaborate on this issue in more detail (see in this volume, for example, Cicchetti et al.; Emde and Buchsbaum; Sroufe). For the moment, it is sufficient to say that after having been almost totally neglected for decades—perhaps because it was too messy—careful and imaginative studies of infant and toddler affect have opened a new world of ideas. Over twenty-five years ago, Silvan Tomkins (1962, 1963) presented a theory of affect, which at the time was based primarily on his perceptive observations as well as his personality testing of patients. Differentiated affects, present in rudimentary form from birth onward, serve as the powerful amplifiers and symbolizers of the less differentiated, less mobile, and usually less impelling physiological drive states. Infant studies have added important substance to this original thinking. It is certainly the model that has informed the way we try to view affect in our work.

One affect of particular relevance to the transition period is shame. The grandiose and exhibitionistic self of the young child is brought back to earth through the exercise of shame. Its action is unique because it is the only fundamental affect that is reflexive in nature; that is, it is directed toward the self. Tomkins' theory lists shame as one of the initially differentiated affects. Observers such as Izard (1982) have shown that in rudimentary form the shame face is present starting in early infancy. One sees the typical sideward and downward casting of the eyes along with a sideward and downward turning of the head, burying the chin in the shoulder, so to speak. Furthermore, the primary stimulus that elicits this expression is the breaking of an active social contact.

The paleontologist Richard Leakey (Leakey and Lewin 1983) has advanced a model of hominid evolution in which shame, and not aggression, is invoked as the key mechanism whereby prosocial, cooperative behavior is maintained within the small, wandering, food-sharing groups from whom we have descended. An individual's refusal to share is met by ostracism rather than attack from the group, triggering shame and resulting in eventual compliance. In our longitudinal observations, the toddler in the transition period, like Adam, hides in shame and can be seen as part of a developing tendency to inhibit defiant behavior. Shame is thus a normal affect but clearly one which can be overused by parents. It can also be blended with fear or other affects, even joy or excitement, leading to the kinds of deviations in self development we see clinically. This argument does not make the distinction between shame and guilt. That distinction has been the subject of much discussion in both the psychological and cultural anthropological literature. For our purposes, we are speaking only of the more primordial state. According to Tomkins' theory of affect, it is shame that is observable from earliest infancy. Leakey also uses the term *shame* in its most elemental sense, as does Erikson (1950).

Still in a speculative frame of mind, I would also add that Edmund Wilson, the sociobiologist, has now completed the loop in which he first showed how genetic patterns influence culture (Wilson 1983). The second half of the loop describes how cultural patterns influence the gene pool. He maintains that in relatively small, segregated breeding groups, such as have characterized the hominid species up until recent times, any substantially advantageous behavioral pattern, no matter how complex, will become well represented in the gene pool within thirty to forty generations. In the human reproductive cycle, this is less than a thousand years, a mere nothing in our evolutionary history. If, as Leakey said, a group which shamed its deviant members rather than beating them up was more adaptable and more successful, the shame affect would in time become part of the genetic makeup. Then, it is reasonable to expect that babies would behave as they do when social approval is withdrawn. It also makes sense in understanding how the socialization process of the transition period is so laden with shame.

The last question on the list has to do with the relationship between self and gender development. This too is particularly germane to the transition period because although there is some ambiguity about the centrality of gender in the young infant and even in the older infant, there is no such doubt regarding the young child. One way to operationalize the question is to ask how important the issues of gender are in the initial development of the self over the first two years. An answer was suggested by the reanalysis of the data from our longitudinal study. For methodological reasons, we decided to abstract and analyze the records, deleting all references to the sex of the child. After we had done this for a dozen or so cases, we noticed that even these very detailed records did not appear to contain any clear phenomenological evidence as to the sex of the child. There might, of course, be some fairly superficial cues, such as whether dolls or trucks appeared as the prominent toys. But if one eliminated or disregarded that sort of information, then neither the behavior of the parents nor the behavior of the child would indicate boy or girl. Presenting the censored material to fairly sophisticated audiences produced random judgments. It is not a firm finding and is one that suffers from trying to prove a null hypothesis.

Nevertheless, in contrast to some authors (such as Chodorow 1978) who have emphasized the merging in mother-daughter pairs in the first year of life, we have found that maternal personality, rather than sex of child, is the more important determinant of merger (Stechler 1987b). The first two years are caught up with the powerful issues of self development. It should be assumed that the parents, with their images of each sex, are coloring the ways in which they negotiate these issues. But based on the evidence we have thus far, the coloration would appear to be quite individualized for each mother rather than being uniform across families. Some mothers seem to rejoice in their daughters' feistiness and independence, while others encourage daintiness and self-control. For parents of boys, the same differences appear. Some are delighted with feistiness, and others are threatened by it. For many parents, both feelings are there at the same time. The primary issues are tied to the universal human themes of self development. How they are played out is a combination of or interaction between the child's gender and the family's personality and culture. It is not simply a matter of the child's gender.

The issues of the first two years may well reverberate differentially once a gender identity is fairly well established. For example, with respect to the model of assertion and aggression described above, we have no clear evidence that the degree of contamination between the two is likely to be greater for either sex up until age two. However, the effect of a high level of contamination may well start to chart different life courses for the two sexes after age two, when gender identity becomes such an important part of the self. If assertion has become highly aggressivized in a child by age two, it might not matter at that age whether the child is a boy or a girl. But later on, the girl may suffer a much more global inhibition of assertive functions because she is a girl. The reasoning behind this speculation is that in our culture it is much easier for a boy to accept and function with an aggressive image of the self and therefore not have to inhibit his assertions. The girl, on the other hand, will be likely to find her contaminated assertion-aggression incompatible with the overriding feminine goal of what Miller (1976) calls "the maintenance of relationship." Giving priority to this latter goal, the girl will inhibit the assertion along with the aggression. But, as has already been indicated, this inhibition will set in only after the girl knows she is a girl, and is operating under the rules she believes to apply to her sex.

Just how the definition of self as a self-in-relationship becomes a primary feminine quality remains something of a mystery. Returning to Klein's dual definition of self as containing both I and we components, we can see that the we self, or self-in-relationship, is a universal aspect of early development, common to both boys and girls. The shift away from that balanced position may reside in the discovery by the boy, probably sometime during the latter part of the second year or the early part of the third year, that he and his mother are of opposite sex. One can imagine that a revolution in the boy's we self takes place at that time. Since major elements of the we self are built from the mother-child interaction, the boy cannot simply continue to invest in that part of himself, given the newly discovered gender divergence.

One can visit a day-care center and see boys up to a certain age prancing around in high heels, carrying pocketbooks, and wearing necklaces. Their exhibitionism seems to be completely unself-conscious. Some brief, finite time after that, these same boys would be totally humiliated to be seen that way in public, although more private dressing may continue. Presumably, the discovery of gender divergence between self and mother has taken place, and that part of the we self representing mother must be put in hiding. Since that feminine part may constitute the bulk of the boy's we self, there may be a more global turning away from the self-in-relationship and a greater reliance on the I—the achieving, autonomous self—from that point onward. Thus, the salient question about self-in-relationship may not be "How do girls get that way?" but rather, "How do boys stop being that way?"

At this point, we have two distinct factors leading to a separation of personality development for the two sexes. One is a suppression of assertion by girls for whom assertion and aggression have been more highly contaminated. The other is a suppression of the self-in-relationship by boys when they discover that their mother is a female and they are not. Thus, even for boys and girls who may negotiate the first year or so with relatively well balanced

I and we selves, quite inexorable pressures may drive that apart during the second and third year, so that boys end up with a predominance of I self and girls with a predominance of we self.

Clearly, this last set of points has been speculative and any one of them may or may not prove valid or fruitful. They have been introduced not to convince any one of the truthfulness of the positions but merely to indicate some current controversy and to show how much work lies ahead of us.

Self as a concept seems to have become more and more central within psychoanalysis and is particularly pertinent to understanding the transition from toddlerhood to childhood. Caution is always advisable because this kind of concept can easily become reified or become so global that it explains everything and nothing at the same time. As psychoanalysis becomes more systemic and constructionistic, however, there does seem to be a valid and useful place for a summary term that refers both to the status of a complex developmental process and to a subjective core that is the touchstone by which experiences and acts are evaluated and organized.

References

Chodorow, N. 1978. *The reproduction of mothering.* Berkeley: University of California Press.

Erikson, E. 1950. *Childhood and society.* New York: Norton.

Freud, S. 1920. *Beyond the pleasure principle.* Standard edition, vol. 18.

Greenacre, P. 1958. Early psychical determinants in the development of the sense of identity. *Journal of the American Psychoanalytic Association* 6:612–27.

Izard, C. 1982. *Measuring emotions in infants and children.* New York: Cambridge University Press.

Jacobson, E. 1964. *The self and the object world.* New York: International Universities Press.

Joffe, W., and J. Sandler. 1965. Notes on pain, depression, and individuation. *Psychoanalytic Study of the Child* 20:394–424.

Klein, G. 1976. *Psychoanalytic theory.* New York: International Universities Press.

Kohut, H. 1977. *The restoration of the self.* New York: International Universities Press.

Leakey, R., and R. Lewin. 1983. *People of the lake.* New York: Avon.

Mahler, M., F. Pine, and A. Bergman. 1975. *The psychological birth of the human infant.* New York: Basic.

Miller, J. B. 1976. *Toward a new psychology of women.* Boston: Beacon.

Prigogine, I. 1978. Time, structure, and fluctuations. *Science* 201:777–85.

Sander, L. 1962. Issues in early mother-child interaction. *Journal of the American Academy Child Psychiatry* 1:141–66.

Stechler, G. 1987a. Clinical applications of a psychoanalytic systems model of assertion and aggression. *Psychoanalytic Inquiry* 7:348–63.

Stechler, G. 1987b. Gender and self: Developmental aspects. *Annual of Psychoanalysis* 14:345–55.

Stechler, G., and A. Halton. 1987. The emergence of assertion and aggression during infancy: A psychoanalytic systems approach. *Journal of the American Psychoanalytic Association* 35:821–38.

Stechler, G., and S. Kaplan. 1980. The development of the self: A psychoanalytic perspective. *Psychoanalytic Study of the Child* 35:85–105.

Tomkins, S. S. 1962. *Affect, imagery, consciousness*. Vol. 1, *The positive affects*. New York: Springer.

Tomkins, S. S. 1963. *Affect, imagery, consciousness*. Vol. 2, *The negative affects*. New York: Springer.

Wilson, E. O. 1983, March. Invited address at the meeting of the American Psychoanalytic Association. Boston.

Winnicott, D. 1965. *The maturational process and the facilitating environment*. New York: International Universities Press.

3 "Didn't You Hear My Mommy?" Autonomy *with* Connectedness in Moral Self Emergence

ROBERT N. EMDE AND HELEN K. BUCHSBAUM

Psychoanalytic thinking has traditionally emphasized the importance of the early caregiving relationship for the optimal development of ego and self (see Sroufe, in this volume; Stechler, in this volume). Two different perspectives are noteworthy. One is longitudinal and has its origins in Freud's (1921) theorizing about a "primary identification" with mother occurring in infancy. An assumption contained within this is that infancy experience is characterized by a form of undifferentiated connectedness with mother which is a prerequisite for subsequent autonomous function; in other words, there is a necessary developmental sequence from connectedness to autonomy (Erikson 1950; Hartmann [1939] 1958; Loewald 1971; Mahler, Pine, and Bergman 1975). Another perspective, which is more recent, will be reviewed in this essay. Based on observations of children, it draws its orientation from a developmental systems approach and postulates that in early self development, processes of autonomy are concurrent with processes of connectedness (see also Connell, in this volume).

This chapter is divided into three parts. First, we will review the psychoanalytic perspective arising from a developmental systems view. Second, we will outline our theory of an affective self, which includes autonomy with connectedness. Third we will present some recent longitudinal research observations. Our theory of self development includes processes of shared meaning within the context of the infant-caregiver relationship. These lead to an executive, autonomous sense of "we" as part of self. Social referencing, a form of emotional signaling, will be discussed in terms of developmental changes which are important for self, for early negotiations with another person, and for early moral internalization. It is our emergent view that early self-awareness carries with it a sense of moral awareness. This has roots both in biological preparedness and in the particular experiences within the caregiving relationship.

Psychoanalytic Perspectives from a Developmental Systems View

Freud's Beginning Systems Theory

Freud's theory was, in the main, a mechanistic one. Still, some aspects show the beginnings of a systems theory. Freud's (1905) theory of psychosexual development emphasized early pregenital stages which retain an organization but become inhibited at around five to seven years of age, when superego formation is prominent and latency is entered. In his *Three Essays on the Theory of Sexuality,* the third essay is entitled "The Transformations of Puberty." The earlier psychosexual stages are reorganized during puberty under a still higher level of organization, and, in the normative instance, genital primacy is achieved as earlier phases are subordinated. Although Freud's language may seem somewhat different, it can be read today in developmental systems theory terms: over the course of development, there is increasing organization and transformation; this includes both hierarchization and integration (cf. Sameroff 1983; Werner 1948).

Nearly two decades ago, Klein (1969) pointed to the fact that there were two kinds of theories of sexuality embedded in Freud's psychoanalysis. One was Freud's metapsychology—abstract, formal, largely mechanistic, and based on energy metaphors. The other was Freud's clinical theory, and it was of a different sort—less systematized, with inferences at a lower level of abstraction, and changing with knowledge gained from clinical experience. The clinical theory continues to change with accumulated knowledge and is becoming more open and oriented to developing systems and change (Emde 1980; Gedo and Goldberg 1973; Stolorow 1980).

An analogous review pointed to a clinical theory of affect which had been initiated by Freud (Emde and Gaensbauer 1980). Freud's later clinical model of affects, like his clinical theory of sexuality, was also unsystematized, and it changed. By drawing together diverse elements of this line of thinking, one can portray a picture in which affects were considered active organizing principles and inseparable from cognition. Unconscious guilt (Freud 1923) and unconscious anxiety (Freud 1926) were considered to be agencies which could organize and monitor activity, thought, defenses, and symptoms. In this line of thinking, they were signals, no longer intimately connected with drive states but located in the ego (or superego) and acknowledged as organizing and motivating factors. Freud's later organizational model of affects can be stated as follows: Affects are composite states including motoric aspects, perceptions, and direct feelings of pleasure and unpleasure; they are rooted in biology, and they include cognition and evaluative aspects; they are seen to function unconsciously as well as consciously and to organize mental functioning and behavior. In this later formulation, affects are signals, seated in the ego.

This line of thinking about affects has grown in the clinical literature of psychoanalysis since Freud. Propositions from a review of this literature include the following: (*a*) Affects are central in clinical psychoanalysis, where they are good guides for understanding motivation and states of mind. (*b*) Affects are adaptive; they are autonomous ego structures as well as being immersed in conflict. (*c*) Affects are continuous aspects of our lives. (*d*) Affects are vital ingredients for human biological relatedness. (*e*) There are signal affects other than anxiety.

Psychoanalytic Theories of Self Based on Childhood Observation

The more recent line of psychoanalytic systems thinking about early self is based on childhood observation. Relevant theories include those of Spitz, Bowlby, Sander, Stern, and ourselves. In many ways, these theories build on each other, and all emphasize the interdependence of connectedness and autonomy in the child's increasing sense of other and of self. This interdependence is not generally appreciated by many psychoanalytic theorist, who instead see connectedness and autonomy as successive phases or parallel developmental lines.

Spitz (1957) theorized that the development of self is a differentiating process beginning early in infancy. Nodal points in the organization of self were described in terms of a differentiation of ''I'' from ''non-I'' at three months (marked by the smiling response), a discrimination of love objects from strangers at eight months (marked by stranger anxiety), and a culminating sense of self-awareness beginning at around fifteen months (marked by the child's use of ''no'' in gesture and word). Throughout this developmental process, there are both ''centripetal and centrifugal trends,'' as Spitz put it. In other words, corresponding to the child's growing autonomy and wish for independence is a growing sense of separateness in which an emotional tie to the caregiver is replacing close bodily proximity and contact.

Spitz emphasized that the objectification of the self goes hand in hand with the objectification of the other and that there is, in the toddler's acquisition of the no, a new level of autonomy in which a new awareness of the other goes along with the new awareness of the self. The child internalizes the no gesture from the parent and thereafter is able to use the no against the parent as well as others. The internalization process occurs because the child hears ''no'' from the parent, repeated many times, and experiences repeated frustrations, which strengthens the recall of such experiences—due to the Zeigarnik effect, where incomplete actions are better remembered. Such internalization of the no then contributes to an ''identification with the aggressor,'' where the child is seen to use prohibition against the self in play, as well as against others.

Spitz, following Freud, emphasizes the gain in mastery that occurs in this process.

With clashes of will and with the internalization of no, the child comes to learn the boundaries of his/her will and of self. This is considered a "momentous step," for there is now an alternative in which discussion replaces attack, a distinctly human achievement. The child has a beginning capacity for judgment or accomplishment, which will eventually form the basis for self-criticism. Thus, Spitz links the beginning of awareness of self and of growing autonomy with a corresponding sense of social consciousness and the inception of verbal discussion. After this time, discourse with the other and with the "generalized other," as conceptualized by Mead (1934), becomes possible (Spitz 1957).

In a scheme based on his extensive observations of caregiver-child interactions, Sander (1962, 1964, 1980) has made explicit his developmental systems view of early self emergence. Adaptive regulation is a central concept. The ontogeny of self is seen as a differentiation of basic self-regulatory mechanisms which are common to living systems. This development parallels an ontogeny of adaptive negotiations seen from the interpersonal perspective. Thus, self-regulation emerges within the context of the infant-caregiver relationship. Organizing processes in development are seen in terms of polarities that exist in dynamic opposition but proceed along together in the course of a trajectory. Integrative mechanisms are highlighted in Sander's scheme, for they bring about new coordinations between organism and environment at nodal points in development. Polarities which exist at all phases of development include those of differentiation/integration, perturbation/stability, and *autonomy/connectedness*.

Many of Sander's interactional observations were based on the period of early infancy, which he refers to as that of "initial regulation," when basic infant physiological activities become coordinated with maternal activities. However, Sander's longitudinal studies with Pavenstedt extended beyond the early infancy period and consequently led to an enumeration over time of a series of adaptive issues negotiated between infant and caregiver. The emergence of self is considered against a background of a regulatory developmental process, with certain issues being salient at different ages. Sander's scheme can be thought of as extending Spitz's scheme while providing more detail at the interpersonal level. With the beginning of the infant's social smile, initial regulation gives way to "reciprocal exchange" issues, followed by "initiative" and "focalization," the latter referring to the infant's focusing need— meeting demands on the mother and developing increasing initiatives that depend on the availability of mother. "Self-assertion" is an issue which emerges at around fourteen to twenty months. Now the toddler's newly developed awareness of intentions and motivational states serves to consolidate a sense of separateness in the midst of restrictions and opposition on the part of caregivers. Toward the end of this time, the child begins to infer intentions of the other from contextual cues and to match those intentions with his or her own willfulness, sometimes taking a contrary position. This development leads to the issue called "recognition" in eighteen- to thirty-six-month-olds. The toddler experiences an enhanced awareness within himself/herself, and this "self-recognition" enhances shared awareness. This kind of self-recognition depends on being recognized by the other and provides a new resource, for the toddler can now begin to rely on the awareness of his or her own inner states and of shared meaning.

Bowlby's (1958, 1969, 1973, 1980) theory of attachment offers a major contribution to a developmental systems perspective. The child's affiliation to the caregiver is seen as a developmental subsystem of separate motivating importance, distinguishable from the subsystems concerning feeding and sexuality. After six months of age, the child normally becomes attached to one or more specific caregivers, so that an "attachment figure" now provides a sense of security which fosters exploration; furthermore, separation now causes pain and, if prolonged, may lead to disorganization and devastation for the child. Bowlby's theorizing has led to extensive observations and research by virtue of the "Strange Situation" designed by Ainsworth and her colleagues (Ainsworth et al. 1978), which has been used to assess security of attachment at one year of age. Several studies have shown that the mother's sensitivity and responsiveness to infant cues, observed during the first year at home, is predictive of the infant's security of attachment as observed later in the Strange Situation laboratory assessment (see review in Bowlby 1988).

Bowlby's theory gives additional emphasis to the complementarity of the developmental emergence of autonomy with connectedness. An infant's emerging self reflects both. Security of attachment enables exploration and autonomy, while anxious attachment results in less autonomy and a sense of restriction. The latter points have received ample empirical validation by the work of Sroufe and colleagues and others, as summarized by Bretherton (1985). This complementarity may be further understood from the vantage point of inner experience. As the child develops working models of attachment figures, he or she also develops corresponding working models of self (see Cicchetti et al., in this volume; Gersten et al. 1986; Schneider-Rosen and Cicchetti 1984). Previous caregiving experiences in which the caregiver responded appropriately to the child's attachment behavior contribute to a working model of a loving attachment figure and has a corresponding working model of a self who is loved and can love. In the case of anxious attachment, previous caregiving experiences are likely to consist of inadequate or inappropriate responses to the child's attachment behavior. The child then comes to base forecasts about attachment figures on the premise that they are unlikely to be available, with corresponding negative outcomes for a working model of the self. In addition, such a child is apt to struggle with anger, avoidance, reproaches, and other affects which guide coping mechanisms for dealing with distrust and pain, as opposed to having a sense of security that comes from secure attachment experiences.

Bowlby's model of psychopathology places particular emphasis on the multiple models of self and attachment figures which emerge during the transition age period. He emphasizes a particular kind of disjuncture between models that can take place because of deviance in the family environment. If primary caregivers are unavailable, rejecting, or too frustrating, the infant may come to exclude information defensively because of too much pain (Bowlby 1980). This tendency is seen in anxious behavioral patterns in the Strange Situation, wherein infants avoid or angrily resist their mothers on reunion after a brief separation. Such reactions are based on the child's everyday experience, which is largely nonverbal and is cumulative during the latter part of infancy.

During the second year, with the advent of language and greater representational capacity, children begin to assimilate parental formulations and interpretations of their experiences; they add semantic memory to their earlier episodic memory (cf. Tulving 1972). In deviant families, a disjuncture in experience occurs at this age because parents tend to verbally disconfirm the child's painful experience. They tell the child he/she is not rejected, that he/she is happy, or that he/she is not supposed to express unhappiness. Thus, there is a constriction of experience, and multiple models of self and of attachment figures may develop—some based on earlier autobiographical, nonverbal episodic memory and others based on semantic generalization and what the child is told he/she is supposed to experience. It is relevant to our discussion that this can only occur after a point in development when self-awareness, negation, language, and a sufficient degree of shared meaning in the midst of opposing tendencies become significant in the child's experience. Bowlby relates his notions of psychopathology to Winnicott's concept of the "false self" (Bowlby 1972) and discusses problems such children have with later expectations of abandonment by attachment figures; these restrict autonomy.

Stern's (1985) theory of self emergence is directly concerned with the interpersonal world, one in which a developing sense of self occurs along with a developing sense of other. The theory has four successively ordered developmental "senses of self," each characterized by an organizing, subjective perspective about self and other. During the first two postnatal months, there is a "sense of an emergent self," characterized by a physical self in which the very young infant is experiencing some sense of organization, coherence, and agency in beginning interactions with the caregiver. A "sense of core self," from age two to six months, is one in which there exists an organizing subjective perspective based on the many interpersonal capacities which have now developed. During this period, there is a "domain of core relatedness" in which infants begin to sense they are physically separate from the caregiver. Infants also begin to gain a sense of agency and coherence with distinct affective experiences. The next subjective perspective is that of ''a sense of subjective self,'' with a corresponding ''domain of inter-subjective relatedness.'' This occurs in the seven- to nine-month age period and is considered a quantum step since there is now a matching of mental states between infant and caregiver. This sense of subjective self and other depends upon a set of newly developed interpersonal capacities. These include the infant's ability to share a focus of attention, to share intentionally with another, and to attribute the existence of feelings in others and sense when they are congruent with his or her own feelings. The fourth sense of self, which begins around fifteen to eighteen months, involves a fundamentally different organizing, subjective perspective about self and other. The toddler now has a vast store of personal experience which can be rendered as symbols; these convey meanings which can be communicated and which can be negotiated with another. This enables a perspective referred to as ''the sense of a verbal self,'' and it operates in the ''domain of verbal relatedness.''

As with the other psychoanalytic theorists reviewed, the verbal domain represents a watershed in development of self and other for Stern. It is important not only because of new capacities for symbolism, which make possible new intentions and counterintentions (i.e., conflict), but also because of language, which paradoxically makes parts of experience less shareable. Stern's assumption is that the three earlier, preverbal subjective perspectives of self persist and to some extent cannot be expressed in language. In a discussion reminiscent of Bowlby's use of the semantic-versus episodic-memory distinction, Stern (1985) discusses how language transforms the child's experience and separates the new form of experience from an original global experience. Another important feature of this new level of self and other is that it makes possible mutually negotiated ''we meanings'' in the context of language. Many of these we meanings are covert and unique and become hard to rediscover—the latter often being a task of psychotherapy.

From the point of view of autonomy and connectedness, Stern's theory is important in that he introduces the development of, in addition to a sense of self, and a sense of other, a third aspect of the infant's subjective world: a sense of ''self-with-other.'' Stern speaks of, early in infancy, the ''self-regulating other'' who is the caregiver, an essential part of the infant's self-regulation. This aspect of self-with-other continues as shared meaning increases in complexity with the development of the child's intersubjective world. The new level of the we sense with the onset of language was noted above. In other words, throughout the process of self emergence, the emotional availability of the caregiver involves satisfaction of an *intersubjective developmental need;*

even after the development of verbal relatedness, there is a need for the caregiver to reaffirm a shared sense of we. It is important to acknowledge that an intersubjective state has been understood.

It seems noteworthy that the psychoanalytic theorists reviewed here present child observations which lead them to a convergent description of a developmental progression and that there are agreed-upon landmarks indicating times of transformation. The theory of an "affective self" which emerged from our laboratory (Emde 1983) began with observations of these same landmarks in which a broad array of behavioral and physiological phenomena where taken into account. The times of transformation were conceptualized as those of biobehavioral shift (Emde, Gaensbauer, and Harmon 1976). Such times of shift involve sleep-wakefulness, perceptual, cognitive, motor, and affective changes in organization. Shift times that occur at age two months and at seven–nine months were the focus of initial study, and shift times at twelve–thirteen months and eighteen–twenty-one months were a focus of later work (Emde 1984; McCall 1979).

To the observer, the affective changes at each shift are especially salient. These are what originally drew Spitz's attention to these times of developmental change; he highlighted affective changes such as the onset of the social smile, the onset of stranger anxiety, and the affective no as indicators of successive "organizers of the psyche" (Spitz 1959). In our work, we have documented that these affective developmental changes have been seen to occur toward the end of changes in other sectors; we therefore conceptualize them as integrative factors, promoting consolidation of adaptive functioning at a higher level of organization. Consolidation appears to occur through two modes: one through social feedback (what is attended to and rewarded) and the other through internal feedback (what is experienced as new, interesting, and pleasurably mastered). Both of these modes provide incentives for engagement with a world at a new level; it can be said that they promote a wider world of being and of interaction.

In addition to promoting developmental consolidation, affects are seen to have a more pervasive role both in development and in everyday experience. They are seen to be active, ongoing, and adaptive features of our lives, serving both motivational and evaluative functions. At any given time, affects allow us to monitor ourselves, our states of being, and engagement with the world. They also allow us to monitor others and their needs, intentions, and states of being.

The theory of affective self adds still another dimension to these adaptive functions. The theory is based on research that has shown that emotions are biologically patterned, with a similar organization throughout the life span. Its major tenet is that our emotions provide us with a core of continuity for our self-experience throughout development. An affective self is adaptive in two ways. First, because we can get in touch with our own consistent feelings, we know we are the same in spite of the many ways we change. Second, because of the specieswide biological consistency of our human "affective core," we are able to get in touch with the feelings of others and be empathic.

An affective self is seen to have its roots in earliest infancy and indeed seems based on three biological principles which permeate development. These principles are important to highlight in this discussion, for they involve both autonomy and connectedness. The first biological principle is that of *self-regulation,* a principle basic for all living systems and as true for behavior as for physiology. The young infant not only regulates attentiveness and sleep-wakefulness cycles but also evidences self-regulation of longer-term developmental functions. The infant maintains a behavioral integrity during major environmental changes, often in spite of considerable handicap. Recent observations of developmental resiliency illustrate self-righting tendencies for important developmental functions when an adequate environment is restored following early deficit or trauma (Clarke and Clarke 1976; Sameroff and Seifer 1983; Werner 1948).

Social fittedness is a second biological principle operating throughout life. The human infant is born preadapted for participating in human interaction, with organized capacities for initiating, maintaining, and terminating interactions with other humans. Recent research has elucidated an array of automatic and specialized social capacities which are present not only in the infant but in the parent of the young infant (see Brazelton and Als 1979; Papousek and Papousek 1982; Sander 1975; Stern 1977; Tronick 1980).

Affective monitoring is the third biological principle. The self-regulating, social being in infancy monitors experience according to what is pleasurable and unpleasurable, indicating a preadapted, organized basis in the central nervous system for guiding behavior on the basis of affective valence. In early infancy, such monitoring is preeminently social in purpose in that infants' affective expressions are used to guide caregiving responses. A mother hears a cry and relieves the presumed cause of distress. She sees a smile with cooing and cannot resist a playful interaction. Later in development, infants make use of affective monitoring for guiding their own behavior, whether mother intervenes or not.

These three biological principles are separable in theory only. Within the individual, they are inseparable. They are intertwined, in some respects illustrating complementarity from the observer's point of view, and together they enable both developmental consistency and change.

When looked at from the point of view of the third principle, which has to do with emotional monitoring, the first two principles have to do with autonomy and connectedness. From earliest infancy, emotions provide some sense of coherence for self-regulatory experience. But this can occur only if there is "a self-regulating other," as Stern and Sander have graphically illustrated. In terms of the second principle of social fittedness, which involves connectedness, there is from the beginning a coherence provided by emotional availability of the caregiver in the presence of the emotional or interactional infant, a process sometimes referred to as emotional resonance, or "attunement" (Stern 1984). After the middle of the first year, emotional signaling becomes more complex. By seven months, the infant seeks out emotional signals of others to guide behavior in terms of "social referencing" phenomena (Klinnert et al. 1983). Still later, in the middle of the second year, evidence for the coherence function of social fittedness is evident as empathy for another develops. Empathy enhances a new level of connectedness in the midst of autonomy by virtue of emotional monitoring of another's experience, which differs from one's own. We believe empathy has major roots in biology as well as in the experiences with the caregiver. In the next section, we will build further on our theory of affective self, in terms of its involving the affective monitoring of a new sense of mutuality, with the caregiver represented along with the child's self or a guiding influence which we refer to as an executive sense of we.

The idea of an affective core of continuity for self is supported by evidence from several sources. In addition to clinical practice and everyday experience, wherein we use our emotions to get in touch with another's humanity and then appreciate what is of core concern, there are other sets of evidence from research. One concerns the similar organization of emotional expressions in infants, children, and adults, from research programs which have used a variety of scaling techniques. (Studies of adults and children as well as infancy studies from our laboratory are summarized in Emde 1983). There is also evidence for the cross-cultural presence of discrete emotions—happiness, surprise, anger, sadness, fear, disgust, and, to some extent, interest (Ekman, Friesen, and Ellsworth 1972; Izard 1971). This evidence involves a universality of both expression and recognition of these emotions from facial expressions and the specification of facial movements involved in each of these patterns of emotion (for review, see Ekman 1982; Izard 1982). Another line of evidence concerns the presence of discrete patterns of emotional expression in infancy; research has shown that infant patterns of facial expression fit the theoretical patterns suggested from emotion research on adults (for review, see Campos, Emde, and Caplovitz 1984). Evidence also exists for consistency in vocalic expression of emotion, both in adults (Johnson et al. 1986; Scherer 1979) and in children. Finally, evidence for continuity in our affective life comes from the recognized importance of emotional availability and emotional referencing in infancy research and clinical work (Bowlby 1973; Feinman 1987; Feinman and Lewis 1981; Mahler et al. 1975; Sorce and Emde 1981). Indeed, it may be mother's emotional availability during the child's infancy which enables infant exploration, learning, and play.

Autonomy with Connectedness in the Transition from Infancy

As we proceed in our theorizing, we must watch out for misleading metaphors. While they can capture our imagination and draw our attention to unappreciated similarities, metaphors can also capture us in another way. They can imprison us within the narrow confines of the images presented. We worry about this latter aspect more with some metaphors than others. Thus, to speak of the toddler's self as grandiose or exhibitionistic, as some have, is more misleading than helpful. The prideful, delightful toddler who is mastering new patterns of motor activity and rules about behaving—who is finding pleasure in feedback (current and anticipated) from both self and others—is neither grandiose nor exhibitionistic. These words are misleading because they carry connotations which are adultlike, pejorative, and pathological.

Similarly, some may be tempted to think of parallel developmental lines of an ''I self'' and of a ''we self.'' But these are not parallel developmental lines, because parallel lines never meet; nor is development well symbolized as linear in either its process or its outcome. Moreover, an I self, containing an attribute or autonomous functioning, and a we self, containing an attribute or a move toward togetherness and affiliation, although conceptually separable, are interdependent. In fact, as will become evident, one enables the other in terms of both theory and child observation.

A View of the ''We-go''

In a posthumously published essay, Klein (1976) asserted that psychoanalysis had need of a theory of a ''we-go'' to correspond to its theory of ego. The child's developing sense of we and of the interpersonal world of shared meaning is now becoming the increasing focus of research attention among developmentalists and psycholinguists (Bretherton 1985; Bruner 1982; Kaye 1982; Mueller, 1989; Rommetveit 1974; Stern 1985). A historical base for this work has origins in the social psychology of Mead (1934) and Vygotsky (1962)—thinking which now seems to be receiving a new appreciation.

It is perhaps a paradoxical influence that in our age, so preoccupied with narcissism and self, we are impelled to begin seeing a different aspect of psychology, a we psychology in addition to a self psychology. This represents a profound change in our world view. To appreciate it, one only has to be reminded that much of our thinking in psychology has been dominated by I-you or I-thou dialectics. As a variant, Piagetian developmental psychology, which has been so influential, has emphasized the inanimate aspect of the environment in the child's constructions of the world. As such, it has dealt with an I-it epistemology.

There appear to be conceptually separable pathways in development for a sense of I and a sense of we. Extending the thinking of the psychoanalytic theorists reviewed thus far, however, we seem to see *three* interacting pathways of self and of shared meaning, not two. These include the sense of I, of other, and of we. Together they constitute what might be considered a "discourse frame" for self and for social interaction. Prior inattention to the realm of the we in developmental psychology is all the more striking when we consider the universality of pronoun schemes. Not only are there a first person (I), a second person (you), and a third person (he/she/it), there is the plural form. From the perspective of interpersonal psychology, a sense of the we involves a most profound shift of self perspective—a shift to an active experiencing of shared reality with another. As adults, we have not only I-thou dialogues but I-we dialogues.[1]

The three biological principles of affective self (self-regulation, social fittedness, affective monitoring) underlie the formation of the we discourse. A beginning sense of we is present after the age seven- to nine-month biobehavioral shift, during the phase of what Stern (1985) refers to as the "intersubjective self." The infant can now experience intentions and plans beyond the immediate action and can match intentions with the caregiver in the context of joint attention and feeling. Toward the end of the first year, the situation is such that Bretherton and Beeghly (1982) have described it as "an interfacing of minds." Communications, gestures, and actions now involve a matching of intentions with another. It is worth noting that emotional signaling changes, so that the infant not only expresses simple motivational states through emotion but also uses emotional expressions in a process of negotiation with another person. One often sees that graded and blended signals are presented in order to begin a discourse of emotional signaling. In this process, emotional expressions have a purpose of eliciting a set of responses from the other. Responses are not reflexive but instead are goal directed, subjected to modification in the course of achieving an end point.

This development is highlighted by the form of emotional signaling we refer to as social referencing. Social referencing, the seeking out of an emotional signal from another in a situation of uncertainty in order to regulate behavior, can be considered to have three phases of dyadic progression in infancy. In all phases, there is a regulation of behavior within the caregiver-infant relationship.

The earliest phase, that of *maternal social referencing,* occurs during the first six months. The infant presents emotional expressions of need states, and

---

1. Dialogues involving third persons, often in the role of the observer or critic, are the stuff of role relationship themes. The plural forms of you and of they enter into an inner discourse of self with "generalized other." As such, they can also be considered aspects of the developing child's articulation of role relationship themes and of "objectification" or categorization of social norms.

mother references the infant in order to decrease her uncertainty about caregiving and then guides her behavior accordingly. She looks to the infant and meets the infant's expressed need. The infant has a clear and perhaps a high-intensity signal. The next phase of this dyadic progression begins during the second half of the first year, with the addition of *infant social referencing*. The infant encounters uncertain situations and seeks out clear emotional expressions from the significant other (usually mother) in order to resolve the uncertainty. This is the level of social referencing which has been most researched by our group and by others. The third phase of dyadic progression in social referencing, *social referencing in negotiation*, begins in the second year. There is now back and forth emotional signaling in a situation of dyadic uncertainty. The uncertainty involves expectations about the response of the other in relation to one's need or intention. Over the course of social referencing in such interactions, modifications of intentional states take place. As noted above, the infant increasingly uses emotional expressions which are not necessarily related to simple motivational states.

We have hypothesized that infant social referencing, which is especially prominent from age six to eighteen months, has an important adaptive function in facilitating self development—that is, in promoting, sustaining, and enlarging working models of the three dynamic aspects of the self system: (*a*) the experience of self, (*b*) the experience of the other (e.g., attachment figure), and (*c*) the experience of self with other, or we. Shared meaning, in the sense of checking the other to match one's intentions with the other and enlarging a sense of the we becomes especially important during the second and third years. To dramatize this point, one only needs to be reminded of observations of "emotional refueling" and of "checking back" by Mahler and her colleagues (1975) and Ainsworth's concept of "using the mother as a secure base for exploration" (Ainsworth et al. 1978), as well as experimental studies which have demonstrated an association between the infant's ability to look at mother's face and the level of exploration and play (Carr, Dabbs, and Carr 1975; Sorce and Emde 1981).

Self-Awareness and Early Moral Development

Our longitudinal observations (Emde, Johnson, and Easterbrooks 1988) have convinced us that social referencing has an important role in mediating early moral development as well as early self-awareness. In toddlerhood, there are uncertainties of standards, rules, and prohibitions, and the adaptive functions of social referencing seem concerned with facilitating the new sense of self in relation to an early moral sense. Situations of prohibition are among the most salient situations involving uncertainty. The toddler seems uncertain about the shared meaning of the prohibition and about its consequences and looks to the parent's face by way of checking for more information.

Social referencing has been seen to occur at the onset of the prohibition (which is usually vocal). It may also occur as the toddler begins a prohibited act, or it may occur when the child completes a prohibited act and checks for a reaction by looking to the face of the parent. Interestingly, corresponding to what appears to be the time of emergence of self-awareness in the middle of the second year, there is sometimes an enhanced self-conscious quality to this checking process. The infant's facial expression may have a positive affective tone (sometimes interpreted by parents as pride) or a negative affective tone (sometimes interpreted by parents as shame or as a "hurt feelings" look).

This draws attention to yet another aspect of autonomy with connectedness; namely, that self-awareness and early morality occur in an integrated manner. Both seem to emerge at the same time in development. Both depend on a consistent, emotionally available sense of self, other, and we, and both are mediated by social referencing.

Further, these domains have a logical interrelatedness. Competence in one domain enables competence in the other; deficit or deviance in one is likely to produce deficit or deviance in the other. If a child carries out rules, whether for do's or for don'ts, and receives acknowledgment of that form of shared meaning from parents, the child is likely to feel a solid sense of self in the midst of the other and beyond. Correspondingly, if a child has a solid sense of self and of other in the midst of the we, there will be a naturalness and pleasure in the mastering of new rules within an ordered social context.

Biological Preparedness

We would like to say a bit more about the biological preparedness for early self-awareness and moral development. Both aspects of self have an important basis in caregiving experiences (e.g., see Cicchetti et al, in this volume; Gersten et al. 1986; Schneider-Rosen and Cicchetti 1984; Sroufe 1983; Waters, Wippman, and Sroufe 1979). Less evident, however, has been the importance of biological preparedness for these domains. Kagan (1981) has summarized arguments for the role of maturation and biology in the emergence of self-awareness. We would like to array some evidence for a similar background for early morality.

We believe such a biological background has a number of features. First, there is evidence for a basic reciprocity built into fittedness for human social interaction. This operates (as we have reviewed in our discussion of "three biological principles") from earliest infancy, and there is every reason to believe that a child's sense of fairness about reciprocity between humans—whether in play, school, or work—may grow out of the regulatory principle of social fittedness. It is also true that a supportive caregiving environment is needed to support the biological preparedness for reciprocity. As Bruner (1982) has playfully put it for language development, the child requires a family environment which as a language acquisition support system (LASS) to complement Chomsky's postulated language acquisition device (LADD). As with all of these biological preparedness features, the bulk of individual developmental variation may arise from family environment influences.

The second feature of biological preparedness for early morality may have to do with empathy. Empathic arousal as a prosocial motivater has been seen by Hoffman (1977) to have an important role in morality. The emergence of comforting responses during the middle of the second year, along with helping and sharing behaviors, has been documented in studies by Radke-Yarrow, Zahn-Waxler, and their colleagues (Radke-Yarrow, Zahn-Waxler, and Chapman 1983; Zahn-Waxler and Radke-Yarrow 1982). It has provided evidence for empathy as a normative developmental acquisition. Kagan (1984) has argued for a strong maturational basis of empathy and has speculated that the empathic human potential for certain feeling states may act as a natural constraint for the toddler's aggression against others and thus be a ''non-relativistic platform upon which a set of universal, or principled, moral standards can be built'' (p. 123).

Most recently, the work of Matsumoto and associates (1986) has indicated that four-year-olds engage in a version of the ''prisoner's dilemma'' game in such a way that they show the same elements of reciprocity, sharing, and fairness as do college students playing a similar game. One is also impressed by the research of Goodnow (1987), which indicates the pervasiveness of household rules having to do with reciprocity and fairness in different family cultures in Australia. Results of these research programs suggest that the young child operates according to a sense of reciprocity and fairness if given the context to demonstrate that understanding and to perform according to it.

Some Observations of Early Morality and Self

An earlier essay (Emde, Johnson, and Easterbrooks 1988) reported some preliminary observations from an ongoing longitudinal study of middle-class families with normal infants seen in both the home and the laboratory at six-month intervals. Although individual differences were considerable by age twenty-four months, all observed infants presented evidence of internalized rules concerning don'ts as well as do's. This was true providing a parent was present and could be referenced. We are now in a position to extend those preliminary observations.

Earlier in this chapter, we speculated that the toddler's social referencing of the parent might be especially frequent during prohibitions and during the developmental onset of self-awareness. Further we speculated that there might be a ''self-conscious'' quality to the child's looking under these circumstances and that there might be considerable positive emotion as well as negative emotion. Analyses of coded videotapes from an ongoing longitudinal study of middle-class families, with parents and infants seen together, support these speculations. In a variable coded as infant "emotion sharing," which refers to the child looking to either parent, there was a dramatic inverted-U–shaped function. Across the thirty-three families observed, the children evidenced moderate amounts of such looking and sharing at twelve and twenty-four months, but there were high levels at eighteen months ($p < .001$ on repeated measures ANOVA). It was also noteworthy that negative emotion sharing (with distress) was rare in this middle-class sample; almost all instances of looking to parent involved a positive emotion (smiling or interest) on the infant's face. Interestingly, the frequency of parental prohibitions showed the same inverted-U function, with highly significant results and a peak at the eighteen-month age. As predicted, toddler compliance to parental prohibitions increased to the end of the second year (Easterbrooks and Emde 1985b).

Longitudinal observations during the child's second year provided convincing evidence of internalization of don'ts (prohibitions) under "the watchful eyes of the caregiver." A developmental sequence emerged involving uncertainty, social referencing, emotional exchanges, and increasing restraint. We did not systematically test for internalization of prohibitions without the parents present, but informal observations and parental reports suggested infants at this age would be unable to maintain a prohibition without an emotionally available significant other being present.

Current longitudinal observations at thirty-six months of age indicate the situation is different. Preliminary results strongly suggest that parental prohibitions are internalized such that they are followed even when parents are absent or when they are challenged by another in the context of play. Further, the child's behavior in the prohibition situation at this age provides an opportunity to see what kind of evidence exists for the main theme of this chapter. Internalized rules, without the parent being present, carry with them a sense of the "other"; and to the extent they are activated in a new social context, they carry with them an autonomous sense of the we. (We will return to this point in our conclusion.)

At age thirty-six months, in the prohibition situation, the child's mother enters with two very appealing toys. She tells the child not to play with the toys as they are special. Mother then leaves the child and interviewer alone. After allowing a brief period of spontaneous play, the interviewer engages the child in doll play and, in effect, challenges the child's adherence to the prohibition by having a bunny puppet invite the child to play with the prohibited toys. If the child does play with the toys, the interviewer reminds the child of the prohibition. Upon her return, the mother asks the child if he/she played with the toys.

Twenty of the twenty-five children observed in this situation showed clear restraint with mother out of the room. Four of these children did not touch the prohibited toys at all; sixteen others delayed touching until after temptations came from the experimenter; five children played with the toys soon after mother left the room.

During our playroom observation of children at age thirty-six months, they also participated in telling narratives designed to probe for their representations of situations involving early morality. Each narrative presented a different situation in which the main character was involved with some moral issue. The narratives were each introduced by the experimenter, who established the situation and then, by asking "Show me what happens now?" prompted the child to enact a resolution. Each story involved a doll of the same gender as the child being tested. Any peer involved was also of the same designated gender and age. Mother and father dolls were used in some stories. Many narratives were presented to the child; for purposes of this discussion, four narratives, administered in our laboratory playroom with mother and father absent from the room, will be enumerated. These include a nap story to probe for adherence to a rule in the face of a temptation; a new-horse story to probe for reciprocity in the midst of peer aggression; an ice cream story to probe for a sense of empathy; and a moral dilemma story to probe for the child's resolution of a conflict posed by a prosocial inclination versus a prohibited behavior.

The last story could also be considered a probe for the child's representation of an early moral self, since the child was confronted with choice between two moral possibilities. The story rests on the child's understanding of other domains we have been discussing (namely, empathy and the adherence to rules in the face of a temptation).

Overall, our idea is that the children's representations of these themes provide insights into the early moral self because that mental structure is based on the child's relationship experiences with significant others. Representations of relationships in narrative themes can therefore be used to explore the child's growing sense of both autonomy and connectedness.

Narratives and Responses

We will now describe each narrative and present the children's responses. You will note that for some stories only twenty-four of the twenty-five children's responses are reported, due to one child's refusal to respond to a number of the stories presented.

A Rule Given by Mother: Nap Story

Props: Bed, toy box (open with two toys in it—a doll and a truck).
Mother doll: Jane, it's time for your nap. Go upstairs to your room now.
Child doll: I don't want to take a nap.

Mother doll: [*firmly*] Listen to me. Go up now! [*Child goes to room and is placed between bed and toy box.*]

Experimenter: [*Hands child doll to subject and says*] Show me what happens now.

RESULTS.   The extent to which children adhered to the rule to nap differed. Only three of the twenty-four children accepted the rule and napped without ever playing. Thirteen children first obeyed and then followed the nap with play. Six children played first and later obeyed. Two children never obeyed.

Children who both napped and played used a variety of approaches to reconcile the rule with the temptation. Some asked the mother doll if the nap time was over. Others had the child doll in bed with the toys. Still others had the mother doll reiterate the rule. Several children rearranged roles via symbolic play, so that the child doll became the mother who put a toy doll to bed. This clever solution made it so one "child" was napping while the other child (identified with the subject child) could play by assuming the role of the mother.

Reciprocity in the Midst of Peer Aggression: New-Horse Story

Props include a toy horse. The characters include two dolls, Jane and Susan, who are the same sex as the child, as well as mother and father dolls. Mother and father dolls watch the following exchange.

Jane: This is my brand new horse. I can ride it all around the room. Watch me!

Susan: I want a turn! [*Pushes Jane off toy and hits Jane.*] Let *me* ride it!

Jane: Ouch! That hurt! I want my toy back!

Experimenter: [*Hands Jane to subject and says*] "Show me what happens now."

RESULTS.   We were especially interested in children's responses that represented reciprocity, since we regarded such exchanges as an index of the child's moral understanding of social rules. Seven of the twenty-five children enacted reciprocity, with turn-taking established. One of the children did this with aggression (i.e., with the dolls hitting each other) prior to each turn-taking episode. Twelve children enacted aggression with no reciprocity. Forms of aggression included the child dolls hitting each other, the parent dolls hitting the child doll, and the subject hitting the child dolls. Six children displayed neither aggression nor reciprocity.

Consequences for aggression varied. Two children informed the parents of the aggressive behavior, and one child had the parents comfort the children. Four children enacted punishments by the parents. Another three children reinforced the notion of sharing. One child had the new horse run over the family. Four children had the injured child reciprocate aggressively against the attacker. Three children had no consequences follow the aggressive behavior. The remaining seven children's narrative responses did not include any aggression.

Empathy: Ice Cream Story

Props include appropriate dolls and a toy bicycle. The characters are mother, father, and two children of the same gender.

> *Experimenter:* Here's Mommy and Daddy, Jane and Susan. They're walking to the store to get ice cream. Susan is riding her bike. On no, she fell off!
>
> *Susan:* [*cries*] Ow, I hurt my knee, I fell off my bike.
>
> *Experimenter:* [*hands Jane to subject and says*] "Show me what happens now."

RESULTS.   Fifteen of the twenty-four children enacted prosocial responses, usually by enlisting the aid of an adult (mother, father, doctor). Two children had the peer doll help. Seven children had no one help.

Morality in the Midst of Challenge: Moral Dilemma Story

Our last narrative may be seen by some as similar to the classic "Heinz dilemma" used by Kohlberg and colleagues to study moral judgments in school-age children (see Colby et al. 1983). The narrative stem is intended to place a prosocial inclination in conflict with a binding internalized rule. The child is thus presented with a moral-conflict situation and must choose. The experimenter inquires about the child's reasons for his/her choice.

> *Susan:* Ow! I hurt my leg! My owie's bleeding! Get me a Band-Aid! It hurts!
>
> *Jane:* Okay . . . Oh, but Mommy says we can't touch stuff on the bathroom shelf. [*Jane walks over to an older child who is of the same gender and is in a different room.*]
>
> *Jane:* I need a Band-Aid for Susan. Her leg is bleeding.
>
> *Older child:* Mom says you can't take things off the bathroom shelf, and I need to go now! [*Older child leaves.*]
>
> *Experimenter:* Why did Jane do that? [*Then adds objection from the point of view of the other issue (e.g., What is Mom going to say? What's going to happen to Susan?).*]

RESULTS.   Nineteen of the twenty-five children showed clear evidence of grappling with the dilemma. Only four children did not engage in a prosocial response, and two of those reiterated the rule. The remaining twenty-one children enacted a variety of prosocial responses. Twelve children got a Band-Aid, and seven discovered an alternative prosocial response (e.g., kissed the leg, removed the owie, got antiseptic, or waited for the owie to get better). One child found another way to enlist the absent mother's help (namely, by waiting for mother's return), and one child both engaged in an alternative prosocial response and enlisted help from the absent mother.

We also looked for evidence of moral responses as a result of our inquiry following the child's story completion. These responses also gave further evidence of grappling with the dilemma. To justify their solutions, seven children reiterated mother's prohibition about not getting the Band-Aid. Ten children offered some justification for having engaged in either the prosocial behavior of getting a Band-Aid or an alternative prosocial response. Five children who engaged in an alternative prosocial response provided no additional explicit discussion of their reasons for not getting a Band-Aid. Only three children offered no explanation at all for their behaviors; two of these did not engage in any prosocial response, and one got a Band-Aid.

Narrative Representations of the We

The children's responses to these four narratives revealed varying degrees of a sense of both autonomy and connectedness. We believe that the more sophisticated narrative responses provide evidence for a new sense of autonomy (with enhanced control and power) that emerges from the connectedness. This is what we have referred to as an executive sense of we. Other forms of integration between these two senses suggest possible precursors of the we.

Several children resolved the dilemma between napping and obeying mother or playing with toys by having the child doll become a mother who was putting her baby (the toy doll) to bed. This solution seems a poignant example of the interplay between the child's sense of autonomy and of connectedness in resolving moral issues. The child takes the role of another with whom there is a close connection (mother) in order to gain an enhanced sense of control and power. We can take note that this psychological process does not yet make use of a sense of "we-ness" but instead makes use of a role assumption. Is it a precursor of an executive sense of we? Is it an early form or precursor of identification? Do the positive aspects of identification and of a sense of an executive we have common origins? More investigation is needed to answer these questions.

Most of the children's responses to the new-horse narrative give evidence of another aspect of autonomy with connectedness. Seven children demonstrated good internalization of rules about reciprocity. Although the children who enacted aggressive interactions did not as clearly demonstrate an internalization of rules regarding the restraint of aggression, the majority of these children responded with clear representations of the parent's responses to the aggressive behavior of the initiator child and/or of the one who reciprocated. Only five of these children presented no consequences for this aggression. Such representations of parental punishments, comforting behaviors, and statements about sharing suggest that children employ models from their parents' behaviors in discovering solutions to moral conflicts.

The children's responses to the ice cream (or empathy) story seem the least developed of the narrative responses with respect to having the child doll enact an autonomous response that is reflective of parental models. Only two children had the doll child become the helper. The majority had the child doll seek help from an adult. This distribution of responses suggests that empathic responses may be an early component of moral internalization, perhaps only when parents or other adults can be counted upon. The child does not yet seem represented as being connected with the other so as to share the more mature and powerful role.

The children's responses to the moral dilemma reveal the struggles that can be engaged at this early age. These involve representations of two different kinds of connectedness experiences (internalized prohibitions and prosocial inclinations). They also involve representations of the children's autonomous judgments and actions. As mentioned earlier, nineteen of the twenty-five children evidenced a struggle about whether or not to engage in a prohibited social behavior. More than half of the children who resolved the story by getting a Band-Aid for the hurt child showed indications of an internalized sense of the other, as evidenced by their expressed need to justify their behavior (for example, "I had to, his owie was bleeding"), to punish the behavior, or to avoid breaking the rule by discovering an alternative prosocial response.

Examples of the Executive We in Action

Moral decisions in narratives take place at the representational level of the children's experience. How do such decisions look when observed in the realm of behavioral challenges? We examined this question by observing our thirty-six-month-olds' responses to a prohibition paradigm that we briefly mentioned earlier. It is in this latter domain that we learned most poignantly about the we.

The prohibition paradigm described earlier involves having the mother enter the room holding two appealing toys, which she tells the child not to touch. The mother then leaves for three minutes, and the interviewer has a bunny puppet progressively tempt the child to transgress the rule.

In response to the first temptation from the bunny puppet, child A says, "Let's wait till Mommy's here." The experimenter asks, "Why?" Child A replies, "I want her to be here." Child A then briefly touches the toy and says, "Let's wait for Mommy. I can play with it when Mommy comes back."

Child B approaches the nonprohibited toys in the playroom. The child is interested in the bunny. When the bunny asks about the prohibited toys, the child indignantly says, "Couldn't! Couldn't because real special." In response to the next temptation, the child says, "Maybe he could." And after the third temptation, the child agrees temporarily to play with the rabbit and the prohibited toys but quickly asserts, "I couldn't play with her (the doll) now. Mom says I could pretty soon." The child never does play with the prohibited toys during mother's absence.

Before leaving the room, the mother of child C tells the child, "It's real important that *we* don't touch these toys. They're not ours." After mother leaves, the child tells the interviewer, "If we touch these, they will break. They're dangerous." In response to the next series of temptations, the child says, "We can't touch these because they're somebody's. They'll break. The rabbit will cry, and there'll be a fire." The child then touches a loose piece of the transformer to show the experimenter how it could break. He starts picking up parts of the transformer. When asked about this, he says, "We can't play with 'em." Then the experimenter says, "But you are playing with them," to which the child responds, "No, I'm not, because they're dangerous." When next asked about mother's return, the child says, "Okay, I won't play with it. I won't play with it again because they're somebody's." Mother returns, and the child tells her, "I didn't play with it . . . little bit played with it." He then tells mother he wants to play with the special toys and he'll share the toys with other kids.

Child D plays with the blocks and engages the experimenter in a game with a toy truck in the playroom. In response to the first temptation, the child says, "I don't know. What did my mom say? She said not to play with those, didn't she? So I better not play with those."

By virtue of voice, posture, and look, the last child gives emphasis to a message other three-year-olds also communicated. "Didn't you hear my mommy? I better not play with those toys. We had better not either." We are being told there is autonomy *with* connectedness in an emerging moral self.

References

Ainsworth, M. D. S., M. Blehar, E. Waters, and S. Wall. 1978. *Patterns of attachment.* Hillsdale, N.J.: Erlbaum.

Bowlby, J. 1958. The nature of the child's tie to his mother. *International Journal of Psycho-Analysis* 39:350–73.

———. 1969. *Attachment and loss,* vol. 1. New York: Basic.

————. 1973. *Attachment and loss,* vol. 2. New York: Basic.

————. 1980. *Attachment and loss,* vol. 3. New York: Basic.

————. 1988. Developmental psychiatry comes of age. *American Journal of Psychiatry* 145(no. 1): 1–10.

Brazelton, T. B., and H. Als. 1979. Four early stages in the development of mother-infant interaction. *Psychoanalytic Study of the Child* 34:349–69.

Bretherton, I. 1985. Attachment theory: Retrospect and prospect. In *Growing points of attachment theory and research.* Edited by I. Bretherton and E. Waters. Monographs of the Society for Research in Child Development, vol. *50,* nos. 1–2, serial no. 209.

Bretherton, I., and M. Beeghly. 1982. Talking about internal states: The acquisition of an explicit theory of mind. *Developmental Psychology* 18:906–21.

Bruner, J. 1982. *Child's talk: Learning to use language.* New York: Norton.

Campos, J., R. N. Emde, and K. Caplovitz. 1984. Emotional development. In *The encyclopedia dictionary of psychology.* Edited by R. Harre and R. Lamb. Oxford: Basil Blackwell.

Carr, S. J., J. M. Dabbs, and T. S. Carr. 1975. Mother-infant attachment: The importance of the mother's visual field. *Child Development* 46:331–38.

Clarke, A. M., and A. D. B. Clarke. 1976. *Early experience: Myth and evidence.* London: Open Books. New York: Free Press, 1977.

Colby, A., L. Kohlberg, J. Gibbs, and M. Liberman. 1983. *A longitudinal study of moral development.* Chicago: University of Chicago Press for the Society for Research in Child Development.

Easterbrooks, M. A., and R. N. Emde. 1985. Assessing emotional availability in early development. In *Early identification of children at risk: An international perspective.* Edited by W. K. Frankenburg, R. N. Emde, and J. W. Sullivan. New York: Plenum, 79–101.

————. (1985b). When mommy and daddy say no: A longitudinal study of toddler compliance. Paper presented at the meeting of the Society for Research in Child Development. Toronto.

Ekman, P., ed. 1982. *Emotion in the human face.* 2d ed. Cambridge: Cambridge University Press.

Ekman, P., W. Friesen, and P. Ellsworth. 1972. *Emotion in the human face.* New York: Pergamon.

Emde, R. N. 1980. Toward a psychoanalytic theory of affect: I. The organizational model and its propositions. In *The course of life: Psychoanalytic contributions toward understanding personality development.* Edited by S. Greenspan and G. Pollock. Vol. 1, *Infancy and early childhood.* Washington D.C.: U.S. Government Printing Office, 63–83.

————. 1983. The prerepresentational self and its affective core. *Psychoanalytic Study of the Child* 38:165–92.

————. 1984. The affective self: Continuities and transformations from infancy. In *Frontiers of infant psychiatry,* vol. 2. Edited by J. D. Call, E. Galenson, and R. L. Tyson. New York: Basic, 38–54.

Emde, R. N., and T. J. Gaensbauer. 1980. Modeling emotion in human infancy. In *Behavioral development: The Bielefeld interdisciplinary project.* Edited by K. Immelmann, G. Barlow, M. Main, and L. Petrinovich. New York: Cambridge University Press, 568–588.

Emde, R. N., T. J. Gaensbauer, and R. J. Harmon. 1976. Emotional expression in infancy: A biobehavioral study. *Psychological Issues.* Monograph series, vol. 10, no. 37.

Emde, R. N., W. F. Johnson, and M. A. Easterbrooks. 1988. The do's and don'ts of early moral development: Psychoanalytic tradition and current research. In *Issues in moral development.* Edited by J. Kagan. Chicago: University of Chicago Press.

Erickson, E. 1950. *Childhood and society.* New York: Norton.

Feinman, S. 1987. A critical review of theory and research on infant social referencing. Paper presented at the meeting of the Society for Research in Child Development. Baltimore, Maryland.

Feinman, S., and M. Lewis. 1981. *Social referencing and second order effects in ten-month-old infants.* Paper presented at the meeting of the Society for Research in Child Development. Boston.

Freud, S. 1905. *Three essays on the theory of sexuality.* Standard edition, vol. 7. Reprinted in 1953. London: Hogarth.

_____. (1921). *Group psychology and the analysis of the ego.* Standard edition, vol. 18. London: Hogarth, 67–145.

_____. 1923. *The ego and the id.* Standard edition, vol. 19. Reprinted in 1961. London: Hogarth.

_____. 1926. *Inhibitions, symptoms and anxiety.* Standard edition, vol. 20. Reprinted in 1959. London: Hogarth.

Gedo, J., and A. Goldberg. 1973. *Models of the mind: A psychoanalytic theory.* Chicago and London: University of Chicago Press.

Gersten, M., W. Coster, K. Schneider-Rosen, V. Carlson, and D. Cicchetti. 1986. The socio-emotional bases of communicative functioning: Quality of attachment, language development, and early maltreatment. In *Advances in developmental psychology,* vol. 4. Edited by M. E. Lamb, A. L. Brown, and B. Rosoff. Hillsdale, N.J.: Erlbaum.

Goodnow, J. J. 1987. Parents' ideas, actions, feelings: Models from developmental and social psychology. Paper presented at the meeting of the Society for Research in Child Development. Baltimore, Maryland.

Hartmann, H. [1939] 1958. *The ego and the problem of adaptation.* New York: International Universities Press.

Hoffman, M. L. 1977. Moral internalization: Current theory and research. In *Advances in experimental social psychology,* vol. 10. Edited by L. Berkowitz. New York: Academic.

Izard, C. 1971. *The face of emotion.* New York: Meredith and Appleton-Century-Crofts.

_____, ed. 1982. *Measuring emotions in infants and children.* Cambridge: Cambridge University Press.

Johnson, W. F., R. N. Emde, K. R. Scherer, and M. D. Klinnert. 1986. Recognition of emotion from vocal cues. *Archives of General Psychiatry* 43:280–83.

Kagan, J. 1981. *The second year: The emergence of self-awareness.* Cambridge, Mass.: Harvard University Press.

_____. 1984. *The nature of the child.* New York: Basic.

Kaye, K. 1982. *The mental and social life of babies: How parents create persons.* Chicago: University of Chicago Press.

Klein, G. S. 1969. Freud's two theories of sexuality. In *Clinical-cognitive psychology: models and integrations.* Edited by L. Bregar. Englewood Cliffs, N.J.: Prentice-Hall, 136–81.

————. 1976. *Psychoanalytic theory: An exploration of essentials.* New York: International Universities Press.

Klinnert, M. D., J. J. Campos, F. J. Sorce, R. N. Emde, M. J. Svedja. 1983. Social referencing: Emotional expressions as behavior regulators. In *Emotion: Theory, research and experience.* Edited by R. Plutchik and H. Kellerman. (Vol. 2, *Emotions in early development.*) New York: Academic, 57–86.

Loewald, H. W. 1971. On motivation and instinct theory. *Psychoanalytic Study of the Child* 26:91–128.

Mahler, M. S., F. Pine, and A. Bergman. 1975. *The psychological birth of the human infant: Symbiosis and individuation.* New York: Basic.

Matsumoto, D., W. Haan, G. Yabrove, P. Theodorov, and C. Cooke-Carney. 1986. Preschoolers' moral actions and emotions in prisoner's dilemma. *Developmental Psychology* 22(no. 5): 663–70.

Mead, G. H. 1934. In *Mind, self and society.* Edited by C. Morris. Chicago: University of Chicago Press.

McCall, R. B. 1979. The development of intellectual functioning in infancy and the prediction of later I.Q. In *Handbook of infant development.* Edited by J. Osofsky. New York: Wiley.

Mueller, E. Toddlers' peer relations: Shared meaning and semantics. 1989. In *Child development today and tomorrow.* Edited by W. Damon. San Francisco: Jossey Bass.

Papousek, H., and M. Papousek. 1982. Integration into the social world. In *Psychobiology of the human newborn.* Edited by P. M. Stratoon. New York: Wiley, 367–90.

Radke-Yarrow, M., C. Zahn-Waxler, and M. Chapman. 1983. Children's prosocial dispositions and behavior. In *Handbook of child psychology.* 4th ed. Edited by W. Kessen. Vol. 4, *Socialization, Personality and Social Development.* Edited by P. H. Mussen and E. M. Hetherington. New York: Wiley, 469–545.

Rommetveit, R. 1974. *On message structure.* New York: Wiley.

Sameroff, A. J. 1983. Developmental systems: Contexts and evolution. In *Handbook of child psychology.* 4th ed. Edited by W. Kessen. Vol. 1, *History, Theories and Methods.* Edited by P. H. Mussen. New York: Wiley.

Sander, L. 1962. Issues in early mother-child interaction. *Journal of the American Academy of Child Psychiatry* 1:141–66.

————. 1964. Adaptive relationships in early mother-child interaction. *Journal of the American Academy of Child Psychiatry* 3:231–64.

————. 1975. Infant and caretaking environment: Investigation and conceptualization of adaptive behavior in a series of increasing complexity. In *Explorations in child psychiatry.* Edited by E. J. Anthony. New York: Plenum, 129–66.

————. 1980. Polarity, paradox and the organizing process in development. Presentation at First World Conference on Infant Psychiatry. Cascais, Portugal.

Scherer, K. R. 1979. Acoustic concomitants of emotional dimensions: Judging affect from synthesized tone segments. In *Nonverbal communication: Readings with commentary.* Edited by S. Weitz. New York: Oxford University Press, 105–11.

Schneider-Rosen, K., and D. Cicchetti. 1984. The relationship between affect and cognition in maltreated infants: Quality of attachment and the development of visual self recognition. *Child Development* 55:648–58.

Sorce, J. F., and R. N. Emde. 1981. Mother's presence is not enough: The effect of emotional availability on infant exploration. *Developmental Psychology* 17(no. 6): 737–45.

Spitz, R. A. 1957. *No and yes: On the genesis of human communication.* New York: International Universities Press.

————. 1959. *A generic field theory of ego formation.* New York: International Universities Press.

Sroufe, L. A. 1983. Infant-caregiver attachment and adaptation in the preschool: The roots of competence and maladaptation. In *Development of cognition, affect, and social relations.* Edited by M. Perlmutter. *Minnesota Symposium on Child Psychology,* vol. 16. Hillsdale, N.J.: Erlbaum, 46–81.

Stern, D. N. 1977. *The first relationship: Mother and infant.* Cambridge, Mass.: Harvard University Press.

————. 1984. Affect attunement. In *Frontiers of infant psychiatry,* vol. 2. Edited by E. Galenson and R. Tyson. New York: Basic.

————. 1985. *The interpersonal world of the infant.* New York: Basic.

Stolorow, R., and B. M. Lochman. 1980. *Psychoanalysis of developmental arrests: Theory and treatment.* New York: International Universities Press.

Tronick, E. 1980. The primacy of social skills in infancy. In *Exceptional infant,* vol. 4. Edited by D. B. Sawin, R. C. Hawkins, L. O. Walker, and J. H. Penticuff. New York: Brunner/Mazel, 144–58.

Tulving, E. 1971. Episodic and semantic memory. In *Organization of memory.* Edited by E. Tulving and W. Donaldson. New York: Academic, 382–403.

Vygotsky, L. S. 1962. *Thought and language.* Cambridge, Mass.: MIT Press.

Waters, E., J. Wippman, and L. A. Sroufe. Attachment, positive affect, and competence in the peer group: Two studies in construct validation. *Child Development* 50(no. 3): 821–29.

Werner, H. 1948. *Comparative psychology of mental development.* New York: International Universities Press.

Zahn-Waxler, C., and M. Radke-Yarrow. 1982. The development of altruism: Alternative research strategies. In *The development of prosocial behavior.* Edited by N. Eisenberg. New York: Academic.

4 Context, Self, and Action: A Motivational Analysis of Self-System Processes across the Life Span

JAMES P. CONNELL

This chapter presents a motivational analysis of self-system processes that can be applied across the life span. Self-system processes from this perspective are defined as appraisals of self in relation to ongoing activity, specifically with regard to the meeting of three fundamental psychological needs: competence, autonomy, and relatedness. The motivational analysis targets specific self-system processes for investigation and organizes these processes according to which of the three fundamental needs is most centrally involved. Next, characteristics of the social context are derived that should individually and jointly facilitate (and inhibit) the meeting of these needs and thus provide the intersubjective basis for the development of self-system processes. Finally, given that the self-system processes are, by the above definition, appraisals of self in relation to *activity,* the analysis concludes with a description of six patterns of activity within cultural enterprises such as school, home, and work. These different patterns of activity are thought to be a function of variation in the self-system processes within the specific enterprise.

In part 1 of the chapter, I flesh out the theoretical background of the motivational analysis as it now stands. Parts 2 and 3 contain an empirical agenda for the study of self-system processes in infancy and in middle childhood. Finally, in part 4, I discuss the implications of the motivational analysis for the study of self-system processes in the transition between infancy and childhood.

Part 1: Theoretical Analysis

Self-System Processes Defined: A Dialectical View

In the dialectical view, self-system processes are neither a property of the individual nor an output of the social or material context. These appraisals of self in relation to particular activities are understood as the product of a dialectical relation between individual psychological needs at one pole and patterns of social relationships and contingencies at the other (Connell and Ryan 1987). At the most general level, this dialectical relation, this intersubjectivity, represents the common definitional feature of self-system processes across the life span. However, depending on the developmental period and the cultural enterprise in which the self-system processes are examined, distinctive forms are expected.

A second definitional feature common across the life span is the set of individual needs assumed to be at work in the dialectical relation—specifically, the needs for competence, autonomy, and relatedness (Connell and Ryan 1987). By specifying these three fundamental needs, the analysis can proceed to deduce the self-system processes generated as the individual seeks to meet these needs. Once identified, inter- and intra-individual variation in these self-system processes is seen as a function of these needs being fulfilled or frustrated in interactions with the social surround. The selection of these particular needs as the motivational bases for the development of self-system processes represents, in many ways, a ''leap of faith'' inspired by the three major theoretical traditions in the study of human motivation.

Organismic motivation theorists' emphasis on experiencing oneself as competent in one's interaction with the physical and social surround (e.g., Deci 1975; White 1959) led to the identification of *competence* as a basic human need. The competence need is fulfilled when the person experiences himself or herself as being able to produce specific outcomes, in the sense both of achieving positive ends and of avoiding negative outcomes. Modern learning theories, such as Rotter (1966), also emphasized the importance of expectancies about having control over culturally and/or individually defined outcomes. In Bandura's (1977) self-efficacy theory and Abramson, Seligman, and Teasdale's (1978) reformulated learned helplessness model, expectancy of control includes both beliefs that outcomes are reliably related to behaviors and beliefs that one is able to access the necessary behaviors. Although these expectancy theorists and other more recent formulations (e.g., Skinner, Chapman, and Baltes, 1988) do not speak of the *need* for competence; their emphasis on competence beliefs as important for effective behavior is consistent with the assumption that competence is a basic psychological need.

Deci and Ryan's (1985) theory of self-determination assumes that *autonomy* is also a fundamental psychological need. While not specifying autonomy as a fundamental psychological need, ego analytic theorists such as Angyal (1941) and Loevinger (1976), along with deCharms' (1968) theory of personal causation, incorporate similar notions into their general frameworks. Following this work, autonomy is defined as the experience of choice in the initiation, maintenance, and regulation of behavior, and the experience of connectedness between one's actions and personal goals and values.

Finally, the object relations theory of Mahler, Pine, and Bergman (1975) and the attachment theories of Bowlby (1969) and Ainsworth and associates (1978) have led to *relatedness* being included as the third fundamental need in this tripartite motivational analysis. Relatedness, as represented here, encompasses the need to feel securely connected to the social surround and the need to experience oneself as worthy and capable of love (in this volume, see also Cicchetti et al.; Pipp; Sroufe). This latter aspect of the need for relatedness can also be referred to as a need for high self-esteem.

Subsuming relatedness to oneself under the more general construct of relatedness and positing it as a psychological need in its own right are consistent with the developmental thrusts of the object relations and attachment views that emphasize the social roots of self-esteem. The motivational centrality of *self*-esteem is also consistent with work such as that of Covington and Beery (1976) and Harter (1983a, 1983b), who also view self-esteem as a central motivational construct in its own right.

The assumption of three fundamental psychological needs is neither unique nor wholly original; it derives from a variegated set of theoretical roots. The interplay of autonomy and competence needs has been extensively studied by Deci and Ryan (1985), and the trio of achievement, power, and affiliative needs studied by McClelland (1965) has considerable intersection with the present formulation. Emde and Buchsbaum (in this volume), Pipp (in this volume), and Ryan (in press) discuss the developmental unfolding of autonomy and connectedness. Notably, Freud captures the essence of the relatedness and competence constructs in his famous statement on the markers of healthy adaptation, "to love and to work."

The current motivational analysis could make a unique contribution in that the three "motivational primitives" direct us to particular self-system processes to be studied and then to hypotheses regarding relations between these processes and individuals' experience of the social surround and their patterns of activity within particular cultural enterprises.

Self-System Processes Associated with Competence,
Autonomy, and Relatedness

From the postulation of three fundamental psychological needs, two questions arise: (1) *What* self-system processes would be relevant to the fulfillment of these particular needs within various cultural enterprises? (2) Depending on the fit or lack thereof between individual needs and social contexts, what self-system processes would be expected to show inter- and intra-individual variation within and across different developmental periods? Addressing the first question allows for specifying which self-system processes are of most motivational significance across the life span. Addressing the latter question regarding individual variation in self-system processes allows for putative linkages to be specified between individuals' appraisals of self, their social surround, and what they actually do within particular cultural enterprises (e.g., home, work, school).

The forthcoming definitions of these self-system processes will be left intentionally broad, reserving specific operationalizations for the subsequent discussion of these processes within particular developmental periods and cultural enterprises. Presenting them at this point serves only to demonstrate the theoretical linkages between the three psychological needs and self-system processes.

Competence

In order for the individual to experience a sense of competence within a particular enterprise, two component self-system processes are proposed as central: *perceived strategy* (knowledge of how to go about achieving particular outcomes) and *perceived capacity* (beliefs in one's ability to execute the operative strategy). A very similar distinction between means-end and agency beliefs is made by Skinner and associates (1988).

Skinner and I have referred to both of these self-system processes under the general rubric of "control understanding" and have extensively reviewed other theoretical and empirical treatments of similar distinctions (Skinner and Connell 1986). The unique aspects of the current formulation are the selection of these specific self-system processes on the basis of their motivational significance, and the assertion that these processes develop out of the interaction between the need for competence and environmental contingencies and feedback.

Autonomy

The self-system processes associated with autonomy are referred to as *self-regulation processes* (Connell and Ryan 1984, 1987; Ryan and Connell 1989; Ryan, Connell, and Deci 1985). These processes involve the initiation, inhibition, maintenance, and redirection of activity. Although intentionally broadly conceived, self-regulation is more specifically understood in terms of the degree of autonomy experienced in the regulation of activity. These self-regulation processes are conceptually distinct from the self-system processes associated with the competence motive in that the latter concerns the person's strategies and capacities for producing or avoiding particular *outcomes* of activity, whereas self-regulation processes involve appraisals of the locus of causality for the activity itself (Ryan and Connell, 1989).

Relatedness

Self-system processes associated with relatedness involve the appraised security of one's relationships with significant others in the social surround, and the experience of oneself as worthy and capable of affection and positive regard. These processes are drawn from the attachment literature (e.g., Bretherton 1985; Sroufe and Waters 1977), where the notion of felt security is cited as the central affective experience of a secure relationship with one's caretaker, and from classic theoretical literature on the self (e.g., Cooley 1902; James 1890), where self-related affect is linked closely to the experience of oneself in relation to significant others.

The self-system processes associated with each of the three psychological needs are summarized in figure 1.

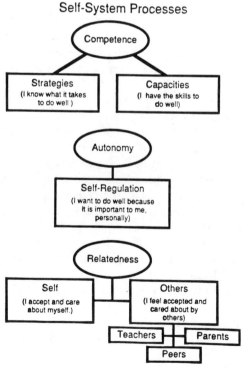

Figure 4.1. Self-system processes associated with three psychological needs.

Social Bases of Self-System Processes

Patterns of social contingencies and relationships make up the other pole of the dialectical relation between individual needs and social context. Three specific dimensions are thought to be central to the development of self-system processes across the life span: specifically, the structure, autonomy support, and involvement afforded the individual by the social surround (Connell and Ryan 1984; Deci and Ryan 1985; Grolnick and Ryan 1987b). The individual's experiences of structure, autonomy support, and involvement (or lack thereof) are the intersubjective aliments for the emergence and differentiation of self-system processes associated with each of the three fundamental needs. From this motivational perspective, these three characteristics of social relations are descriptions of the individual's *experience* of the information embodied in verbal and non-verbal interpersonal communications—whether these communications occur in a one-on-one interaction or are embedded in cultural systems such as institutional regulations and incentive systems, role-related expectations, or other modes of symbolic communication, such as the mass media.

Structure refers to clearly communicated and optimally challenging expectations for and consequences of individual action, to consistent administration of these consequences, and to the provision of competence-relevant feedback. In lay terms, "I know what is expected of me and what will happen if I succeed or fail; I expect these consequences to occur in a consistent fashion; and I expect to receive useful information about my performance." These assertions suggest that the person is experiencing optimal structure within a particular enterprise. *Autonomy support* refers to the communication of choice, room for initiative, recognition of feelings, and a sense that activity is connected to personal goals and values. In lay terms, "I feel that I have choices about what to do, that my feelings are understood, and that I am being supported in doing something that is connected to my own personal goals or values." *Involvement* has to do with the communication of interest in the individual through the dedication of natural and psychological resources and with the enjoyment of the individual by those in the social surround. The experience of involvement is captured in the following statement: "I think people like me, know and care about me (as a person), and enjoy being with me" (Grolnick and Ryan 1987b).

These three facilitative capacities of the social surround can be inhibitory forces as well. Lack of structure is experienced as inconsistency, noncontingency, or overly difficult requirements; lack of autonomy support as being controlled and pressured toward particular goals; lack of involvement as being isolated, neglected, and ignored.

The descriptions of these motivationally relevant aspects of the social surround are, at this point, broad-based and adevelopmental. Later in this chapter, these same general descriptions will be applied to the developmental periods of infancy and childhood, at which point the overlap between these descriptions and other researchers' formulations of similar issues will be presented.

Patterns of Activity within *Cultural Enterprises*

As discussed earlier, the final component of this motivational analysis is an attempt to describe what people actually do when they experience particular configurations of the self-system processes associated with the three psychological needs. There are at least two reasons for pursuing this analysis of patterns of activity. First, the fulfillment (or lack thereof) of the three needs, as reflected in the self-system processes associated with each, is only understandable in relation to the individual's ongoing activity within cultural enterprises; thus, a central theoretical concern is the process by which appraisals of self translate into patterns of activity (and vice versa). Second, appraisals of self are relatively inaccessible to the social surround. This limited access may result from both the incapacity or unwillingness of the individual to *communicate* and/or the social surround to *interpret*. Thus, the individual's patterns of *activity* within the cultural enterprise and the culturally salient *outcomes* of these patterns of activity (e.g., economic status, school performance, social acceptance) are important data upon which social contingencies and relationships are calibrated. For these two reasons, it becomes necessary to invoke a description of individual activity within cultural enterprises; this description can then be linked theoretically and empirically both to the self-system processes described earlier and eventually to the degree of structure, autonomy support, and involvement afforded the individual by the social context.

As a starting point for this analysis of activity in cultural enterprises, the concepts *engagement* and *disaffection* were adopted. These constructs originate with Merton's (1953) seminal analysis of individual adaptation to the experience of what he called ''anomie'' (specifically, as this experience was promulgated by social structures within a capitalist economy). Although his analysis was in reference to economic enterprises and its developmental focus was restricted to adulthood, its relevance for the current work is threefold: (1) Merton's description begins with the individual's appraisal of self in relation to goals and to the means to those goals within a social context. (2) The description extends to a broad pattern of activity, including cognitive, emotional, and behavioral concomitants of these appraisal processes. (3) Merton looked to the social surround (in his case, to macrostructural features such as social stratification) for the contextual aliments of the individual's self-appraisals. With these three features as shared points of departure, Merton's work seemed an appropriate resource for addressing this final aspect of the motivational analysis: patterns of engagement and disaffection within cultural enterprises. (See also Wellborn, in preparation, for a more complete theoretical explication of these constructs.)

Engagement and disaffection are qualities of motivated action that are distinct from the motivational sources of the actions (i.e., the fulfillment or frustration of the needs for competence, autonomy, and relatedness) but are thought to be both outcomes of and inputs to these experiences. Our original formulation of engagement and disaffection, and that of other investigators, was to treat these descriptors as two ends of a bipolar dimension (Connell, Wexler, and Dannefer 1987). The current conceptualization of engagement and disaffected patterns of action (Connell and Wellborn 1987) retains a dimensional aspect—that is, engaged versus disaffected patterns of activity—but also includes differentiation among various types of engaged and disaffected patterns, as did Merton (1953). Figure 2 presents a model of engagement and disaffection that we are currently applying in our work on self-system processes in educational and family contexts.

As can be seen in figure 2, three forms of engagement are specified. To borrow from Merton's analysis, all three forms are characterized by an

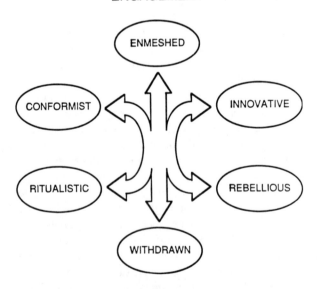

ENGAGED AND DISAFFECTED PATTERNS OF ACTION

ENGAGEMENT

ENMESHED

CONFORMIST

INNOVATIVE

RITUALISTIC

REBELLIOUS

WITHDRAWN

DISAFFECTION

Figure 4.2. Patterns of engagement and disaffection in cultural institutions, adapted from Merton 1953.

acceptance of and commitment to the goals of the cultural enterprise (e.g., to be a good student, to be a good parent). Conformist and innovative patterns are differentiated analytically by the degree of conformity to the culturally/ institutionally prescribed *means* for achieving those goals, with conformist patterns showing closer adherence to these means than innovative patterns. Here, this description departs from Merton's in that innovative patterns are viewed as being creative, idiosyncratic, but not necessarily counter to the prescribed means of the cultural institution.[1] Again departing from Merton's description, an enmeshed pattern of activity is proposed. Enmeshed forms of engagement differ from the other two forms in that greater overlap and lack of differentiation exist between the individual's *entire* set of personal goals and those of a particular institutional enterprise (e.g., "I *am* my job" versus "I *do* my job").

The three forms of disaffection are all characterized by lack of acceptance and/or withdrawal of commitment to the goals of the institutional enterprise. *Ritualistic* patterns are best characterized as "going through the motions"— that is, superficially adopting the prescribed patterns of means without accepting the goals. *Withdrawn* patterns combine suspension of commitment to the goals with no attempt even to appear engaged in the enterprise. *Rebellious* forms of disaffection are apparent when actions are directed toward a different set of goals than those of the institutional enterprise (e.g., students committed to peer acceptance in opposition to academic success) and when the means for achieving those goals are at odds with those prescribed by the institution (e.g., disrupting class versus paying attention). Rebellious and withdrawn patterns may also include leaving the enterprise altogether.

These analytic distinctions among various forms of engagement and disaffection have inspired recent empirical attempts to specify cognitive, behavioral, and emotional markers of each of these patterns within different institutional contexts and developmental periods.

Summary of the Model

Self-system processes are defined as appraisals of self in relation to activities within particular cultural enterprises. These appraisals and their subsequent consequences in individual patterns of activity are a product of the dialectic between the individual's experience of three fundamental psychological needs (competence, autonomy, and relatedness) and the experience of the social contingencies brought to bear by individuals and social groups that make up the social surround. Two other definitional features of self-system processes cut across all developmental periods: (1) the aspects of the social surround that

---

1. In contrast, Merton's (1953, 187) example of the innovative pattern was the entrepreneur who broke whatever rules necessary to achieve the cultural goal of wealth.

are seen as relevant to the fulfillment of the three fundamental needs (autonomy support, structure, and involvement) and (2) the notion that self-system processes are translated into patterns of engaged and disaffected action within particular cultural enterprises. Age differences and intra-individual change are expected (*a*) in the salience of the three individual needs; (*b*) in the phenomenological character of the self-system processes, particularly as a function of the individual's changing verbal-reflective capacities; (*c*) in the empirical markers of the perceived social context, self-system processes, and patterns of engagement and disaffection; and (*d*) in the predictive relations among these three sets of variables.

Based on the motivational analysis just described, parts 2 and 3 of this chapter present an empirical agenda for the study of self-system processes in infancy and middle childhood. Part 3 includes a more detailed operational-ization, of the constructs emerging from the motivational analysis than does part 2. The final section of the chapter focuses on the transition from infancy to early childhood. A set of theoretical and empirical issues concerning the development of self-system processes across this transition is also presented.

Part 2: Self-System Processes in the Infant-Caretaker Relationship

The application of the general model in the infancy period draws heavily on Bowlby (1969) and on Ainsworth and her colleagues' work on attachment security (e.g., Ainsworth et al. 1978; Sroufe and Waters 1977). Recent writings by Bretherton (1985) concerning the development of a working model of self, and the object relations theory of Mahler and associates (1975), also inform this application of the general model (see Sroufe, in this volume). Generally, the current work shares these theorists' assumption that the developing rela-tionship between caretaker(s) and infants during this period is of central importance to the development of self-system processes. A third line of theory and research relevant to this application of the motivational analysis is the work of my colleagues and myself on attachment system functioning, using what we refer to as a "component process approach" (e.g., Connell 1985a; Connell, Bridges, and Grolnick 1989; Connell and Thompson 1986). Using this ap-proach, we have attempted to identify sources of intra- and interindividual variation that are components of overall attachment system functioning. Thus far, we have focused on infant emotional reactions to stress and infant social interactive strategies for regulating emotion.

In the next section, I will describe how the three needs proposed in the general model can be conceptualized during the period from approximately eight months to two years of age and within the "enterprise" of the infant-caretaker relationship. This description will, in essence, elaborate the rudimentary self-system processes within the context of the infant-caretaker relationship. Of central importance to this analysis will be the *meaning* of security of attachment vis-à-vis the three fundamental needs. Next, I will apply the three-dimensional description of social context from the general model to caretaking during this period. The goal of that analysis is to "unpack" Ainsworth and her colleagues' notion of "caretaker sensitivity" into the three dimensions: caretaker provision of structure, autonomy support, and involvement to the infant. Finally, I will discuss engagement versus disaffection as the notion applies to characteristic patterns of infant behavior with their caretakers, such as those patterns included in the Ainsworth and associates (1978) system for classifying infants' behavior in the "Strange Situation" procedure.

Competence, Autonomy, and Relatedness during Infancy

My general discussion of definitional issues suggested that three psychological needs—competence, autonomy, and relatedness—are the organismic basis for the development of self-system processes across the life span. How can these three needs be conceptualized in the first two years of life, with regard to the infant-caretaker relationship?

Relatedness

The attachment theories of Bowlby (1969) and Ainsworth and associates (1978) provide the clearest explication of the nature and importance of relatedness during this period. In fact, the inclusion of relatedness in the general model stems in part from the work of these theorists. Sroufe and Waters (1977) refer to this psychological need as a need for "felt security." How can this need be expressed by infants in the first two years of life, and what self-system processes develop out of social interactive episodes in which this need is expressed and responded to by the social surround?

The infant's need for relatedness may be seen most vividly in infants' attempts to gain proximity to and contact with their caretakers. When this need for relatedness is salient, the infant's bids for proximity and contact and the responsiveness (or lack thereof) of the social surround to these bids may result in the infant appraising his or her caretakers' "availability." I will refer to the infant's appraisal of caretakers' emotional and physical availability as "emotional security." Thus, perceived emotional security is defined as the self-system process associated with the infant's need for relatedness.

Bretherton (1985), in her elaboration of Bowlby's (1969) notions of working model, discusses a more narrowly defined version of this self-system process—that is, the infant's expectations regarding the caretaker's availability and ability to relieve physical need states. Bretherton's view of emotional security is reminiscent of the psychological dilemma of "trust versus mistrust" that Erikson (1968) cites as salient during this developmental period. The view of emotional security offered in the self-system processes model is meant to reflect a broader motivational definition of relatedness that includes the infant's need for connectedness to the caretaker across the full range of positive and negative states.

This broader view of the relatedness need is consistent with evidence presented by Gaensbauer, Connell, and Schultz (1983), who demonstrated that infants' increased orientation to their mothers was predicted both by the degree of *negative* emotionality in high-stress situations and by *positive* emotionality in low-stress situations. Thus, if we can assume that the infant's orientation toward mother reflects the relatedness need, then this study suggests that the expression of this need is systematically linked to positive as well as negative emotional states. Still unresolved is how individual variation in emotional security (the self-system process associated with the infant's need for relatedness) can be operationalized. I will return to this issue briefly in the last section of this part of the chapter.

Competence

The infant's need for competence vis-à-vis the caretaker has not been as thoroughly explored as relatedness, either theoretically or empirically. Most of the work on infant competence examines the infant's attempts and capacities to master the physical surround, focusing either on psychophysical skills—for example, Haith's (1980) work on infant perceptual development, Stenberg and Campos' (1983) work on the emergence of discrete emotions, Bower's (1974) work on early concept development—or on the sources of individual differences in "mastery motivation" (e.g., Jennings et al. 1979). Recently, my colleagues at the University of Rochester have attempted to link individual differences in mastery motivation to differences in quality of attachment (Frodi, Bridges, and Grolnick 1986). However, little theoretical or empirical work exists on how infants express their need for competence *within* the caretaker-infant relationship.

I am deliberately attempting to maintain conceptual independence between the infant's competence needs as experienced in the caretaker-infant relationship and as experienced in interactions with the physical surround. However, *very* early on (perhaps before three months and the onset of the social smile), these two enterprises are indistinguishable; and even when they become distinguishable, the caretakers play an important role in the development of the child's self-system processes and patterns of engagement and disaffection in contexts other than the caretaker-infant interaction. (Refer to the discussion of parents' influence on children's self-system processes in educational contexts in part 3 of this chapter.)

What are the self-system processes that are linked to competence needs expressed in the caretaker-infant interaction? Speculatively, there is some appeal to the idea that, by the end of the first year, the infant develops *perceived strategies* to produce "caretaker outcomes." However, the limitations of infants' cognitive abilities would appear to preclude a meaningful application of the "perceived capacity" construct from the general model to this age span. When we can observe twelve-month-old infants' systematic and modifiable use of communicative signals to effect some interpersonal goal such as reaching to be picked up or crying to regain proximity, we are on firmer inferential ground vis-à-vis the perceived-strategy construct.

Here again, the social surround's responsivity to infants' bids to produce caretaker outcomes would make up the contextual end of the dialectical relation between the infants' competence needs and the social context. The product of these interactions would be interindividual variation in the presence and flexibility of infant strategies for achieving interpersonal goals and, more speculatively, in the infants' subsequent beliefs about their capacities to execute these interpersonal strategies. Again, Bretherton's (1985) description of the working model of self informs this analysis, in that part of the model may be infants' developing sense of "how to get what one wants from the social surround" and, subsequently, "the perceived capacity to execute these strategies."

Autonomy

Both Mahler et al. (1975) and Erikson (1968) discuss the importance of individuation and autonomy during the first and second years of life. (Emde and Buchsbaum, in this volume, also explore this theme.) These researchers' treatments of autonomy and individuation fit closely with the definition of autonomy presented earlier in this chapter (i.e., as the need to experience oneself on the locus of initiation, maintenance, and regulation of activity). Both works delineate the process whereby the child moves away from the caretaker physically through locomotion and psychologically through the growing awareness of the caretaker's separateness and of the power to negate the actions of others. According to these theorists, the need for autonomy is present and salient by late in the first year.

One approach to identifying the self-system processes associated with this autonomy need is to ask how and when the infant experiences fulfillment and/or frustration of this need. Again, this conceptual task is made more difficult by the infant's limited repertoire of behaviors. Recent collaborative work using a "component process approach" to studying attachment system functioning has led us to focus on "emotional self-regulation" as the self-system process associated with the autonomy need in the domain of the caretaker-infant relationship (Connell, Bridges, and Grolnick 1989). These self-regulatory processes are understood as the infant's capacities to initiate, maintain, and regulate positive and negative affect.

Vaughn, Kopp, and Krakow (1984) have investigated self-control in infancy, but their focus is almost solely on the *inhibition* of behavior (emotional and otherwise). My admittedly speculative treatment of self-regulation is broader in meaning in that it incorporates initiation as well as inhibition of behavior and positive as well as negative behavior; but it is also narrower in focus in that I restrict the behavioral content to emotionality. In our most recent work, we have offered a tentative developmental sequence of emotional self-regulation strategies across the periods of infancy and early toddlerhood (Connell et al. 1989).

As with the self-system processes associated with the other two psychological needs, the dialectical relation between the need for autonomy and the social context (specifically, the responsivity or lack thereof of the social surround to the infant in situations where the autonomy need is salient) results in the emergence and elaboration of self-regulatory processes and in interindividual variation in these processes.

Figure 3 summarizes the definitional issues regarding self-system processes in late infancy within the context of the infant-caretaker relationship. As can be seen in figure 3, I have also attempted to be more specific as to behavioral markers of these self-system processes. Perceived capacity is not defined, because the infants would be required to reflect upon their ability to execute perceived strategies, a cognitive skill presumably beyond the developmental level of infants in their first two years.

As I stated in the overview of this section, the description of self-system processes can be understood as a recasting of attachment security into motivational terms—secure infants feel competent, autonomous, and related with regard to their caretaker. This motivational recasting then allows us to identify self-system processes associated with these three needs: *perceived strategies and capacities* with competence, *emotional self-regulation* with autonomy, and *emotional security* with relatedness. With these self-system processes in hand, we can then ask, "What are the social contextual factors that could facilitate and inhibit the development of these rudimentary self-system processes within the infant-caretaker relationship?" This is the topic of the next section.

Dimensions of Social Context in Infancy

The social contextual variable most often associated with positive infant outcomes both in the attachment literature (e.g., Ainsworth et al. 1978) and in the infant-parent literature more generally (e.g., Lewis et al. 1984) is caretaker responsivity or sensitivity. Sensitivity is defined as the caretaker's

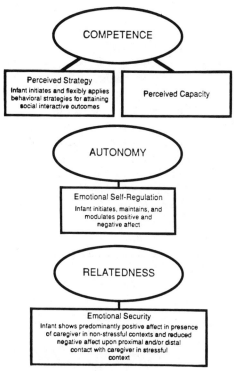

Figure 4.3. Self-system processes associated with three psychological needs in infancy.

ability to read and appropriately respond to infant signals (e.g., Ainsworth and Bell 1969). This construct has received empirical and theoretical support, and some criticism, as being the most central predictor of security of attachment at age twelve months (cf. Ainsworth et al. 1978; Lamb et al. 1985).

Definitional issues regarding this construct also pervade the infancy literature. As Lamb and Easterbrooks (1981) and Skinner and Connell (1986) point out, there appear to be at least two components to the infant's experience of a "sensitive" social surround: perceived contingency (i.e., the infants' perception that their actions lead to predictable outcomes) and appropriateness (i.e., infants perceive the outcome as responsive to their signal). For example, infants raise their arms (presumably to be picked up). A contingent response would be any response that occurs consistently following this signal (e.g., smiling at the infant). An appropriate response is to pick the child up. However, for infants to experience the caretaker as sensitive, both components must be present. The infants expect, when they signal to be picked up, that this event will occur, because most of the time it does. Believing that it will occur, then, presumably allows them potentially to forgo *immediate* responsiveness in the future.

These two dimensions of social context (contingency and appropriateness) within the infant-caretaker relationship correspond nicely to the dimensions of structure and autonomy support discussed earlier. Specifically, the infant's experience of structure is one of consistent and clear consequences of actions by the social surround. The experience of autonomy support by the infant is one of an internal locus of causality ("something about my intentions/goals led to this person's response to me"). This is different, albeit subtly, from the experience of structure whereby the infant comes to "know" what will happen following a particular action. Autonomy support results in the infant experiencing others as responsive to the particular needs that instigated the action.

Finally, the sensitive caretaker, in addition to providing structure and autonomy support, can also be characterized as involved. Involvement, as a dimension of social context in infancy, is defined as the infant's experience of the caretaker as physically and emotionally proximate when needed and predominantly positive in emotional tone.

With the addition of involvement to structure and autonomy support, the conceptual unpacking of caretaker sensitivity is complete. Figure 4 summarizes these three dimensions of social context. Efforts to operationalize each of the three dimensions have begun in our work on the development of emotional self-regulation in infancy and early childhood (Connell et al. 1989). The goal of these investigations is to relate specific dimensions of the infant's social context to inter- and intra-individual differences in emotional self-regulation in order to more fully elaborate how parents can facilitate or inhibit the development of more autonomous forms of this self-system process. At a more theoretical level, the proposed linkages between social context and the self-system processes may provide more detailed information regarding the early social interactive roots of childhood personality as manifested in interindividual variations in the self-system processes associated with all three psychological needs.

Finally, as will be detailed in the next section, the motivational recasting of attachment security and caretaker sensitivity generates a more elaborate set of antecedents from which to predict infants' actual patterns of engagement and disaffection with their caretaker.

Patterns of Engagement and Disaffection in Infancy

As with the analyses of self-system processes and social context, the attachment literature provides a starting point from which to apply the general model's notion of engagement versus disaffection to the infant-caretaker relationship. In the infancy period and within the enterprise of the infant-caretaker relationship, the predominant methodological and conceptual frame-

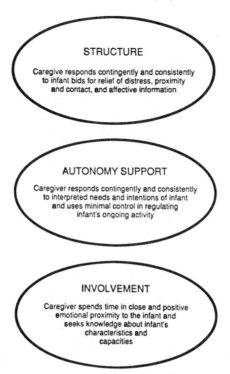

Figure 4.4.   Dimensions of social context in infancy.

work for the study of individual differences in quality of caretaker-infant relations is the ABC classification system as it is applied in Ainsworth and Wittig's (1969) Strange Situation paradigm. The classification system used to form the A, B, and C attachment types is based on a clinical rating of infants' patterns of behavior within and across the seven episodes of the Strange Situation paradigm, with the most important of these episodes being the first and second reunions with the caretaker following separation. For example, avoidant, or A, infants eschew interaction with the caretaker upon his/her return after separation. They turn away and appear to ignore the caretaker.

My intent here is to recast these and other patterns of infant social interactive and emotional behavior as patterns of engagement and disaffection with the caretaker, as discussed in part 1 of this chapter. For example, securely attached infants show engaged patterns of action and insecure infants disaffected patterns. Whether the particular classifications and subclassifications of attachment quality derived from the Ainsworth and associates (1978) system match up isomorphically with the patterns of engagement and disaffection described in part 1 of this chapter is an issue we are currently examining.

How does this recasting of the above-mentioned attachment classifications into engaged and disaffected patterns of action change our view of what these patterns of behavior represent? First, it allows us to continue interpreting these patterns of action as being a function of security and insecurity in the infant-caretaker relationship. In addition, with the defining of the self-system processes underlying attachment security and insecurity and with the social contextual nutriments of these self-system processes specified, provision of structure, autonomy support, and/or involvement affects engagement and disaffection with the caretaker *indirectly* through the self-system processes. Social interactions, then, either facilitate or inhibit the development and "firming up" of the self-system processes associated with the three fundamental needs—that is, the infants' perceived strategies for obtaining interpersonal outcomes, their self-regulation of affect, and their emotional security. These self-system processes individually and interactively then produce the characteristic patterns of engaged or disaffected behavior.

Empirical Next Steps

This initial application of the general model to self-system processes within the infant-caretaker relationship leaves a daunting set of empirical challenges for future research. We have begun our empirical efforts with studies of emotional self-regulation (Connell et al. 1989) by examining, in laboratory settings, infants' and toddlers' strategies for regulating both positive and negative emotions, with parents present and absent. We will be assessing infants' social interaction and nonsocial behavioral strategies as well as their emotional behavior in these lab settings. In the parent-present situation, observer ratings of mothers' and fathers' provision of autonomy support, structure, and involvement will also be obtained. Parent reports of these dimensions in the home and of the infant's emotional behavior at home will also be obtained. As we begin this empirical work on self-system processes in infancy, the motivational analysis reflected in the general model allows us to examine more fully the intersubjective aspects of infants' emerging social interactive and emotional characteristics.

Part 3: Self-System Processes in Educational Contexts

An extensive literature exists in the fields of education, psychology, and sociology on the relations between student self-perceptions (broadly defined) and academic performance. A review of this empirical literature is inappropriate, given the more focused theoretical agenda of this chapter. References to the literature will be made primarily to sharpen and historically integrate theoretical points being made here. The primary purpose of part 3 is to describe an assessment device that has emerged from the motivational analysis of self-system processes described in part 1 and, in so doing, to demonstrate how theoretical notions regarding the development of self-system processes can be examined in situ, within the everyday life of children in school. More specifically, I will present the variables and the item content included in the Rochester Assessment Package for Schools—Student Report Form (RAPS-S) (Wellborn and Connell 1987). These variables are derived directly from the theoretical model presented in part 1.[2]

Competence, Autonomy, and Relatedness in School

According to Erikson (1968), the period of middle childhood is marked by children's efforts to maintain a sense of industry while struggling with feelings of inferiority. One important arena in which this struggle is played out, at least in Western cultures, is school. Following Erikson and other developmental theorists such as White (1959), considerable attention has been given to the issue of school-related perceptions of competence (e.g., Harter 1982; Phillips 1984). These investigators and others have examined how individual differences in children's perceptions of their school-related competence relate both to school performance and to other self-perceptions such as self-esteem and attributional styles. Other lines of research related to children's sense of competence in school are studies of children's locus of control over success and failure in school (e.g., Crandall, Katkovsky, and Crandall 1965; Connell 1985b), attributions for achievement outcomes (e.g., Nicholls 1984; Weiner 1986), understanding of academic ability and intelligence (e.g., Nicholls 1984), and expectancies for success and failure in the academic domain (e.g., Dweck and Elliott 1983).

What ties these research traditions together under the single rubric of "competence" is their common focus on children's cognitions regarding academic outcomes. In other words, perceptions of competence, locus of control, causal attribution, and expectancies for success and failure involve either children's perceived capacities (or incapacities) to produce outcomes (perceived competence), their understanding of causes of outcomes (locus of control, causal attribution), or their beliefs about the probabilities of outcomes (expectancies).

A second overlapping theoretical tradition has emphasized that, in addition to developing a sense of competence, children need to experience a sense of autonomy in their interactions with the social surround (Ryan and Connell

---

2. For the sake of clarity, I will describe only the student report forms of the RAPS, used for elementary, junior high, and high school students. However, teacher report forms (RAPS-T) and parent report forms (RAPS-P) have also been developed to assess these same variables. An observational/interview form of the RAPS (RAPS-O) is now being developed.

1989; Ryan et al. 1985). As stated earlier, the experience of autonomy is one of choice in executing actions and experiencing oneself as the locus of initiative of those actions. Thus, autonomy involves cognitions and affects regarding one's role (or lack thereof) in initiating and maintaining behavior, as distinct from one's role in producing success or failure outcomes (i.e., competence).

A third and less thoroughly examined motivational issue involved in children's lives in school is the quality of their relationships with their social partners in the educational enterprise. These social partners include teachers, parents, and peers. One aspect of their relationships that we have identified is emotional security. Presumably, secure relationships with these social partners should enhance students' engagement in the pursuit of learning and indeed may facilitate engagement in school in the face of threats to the other two psychological needs just described, that is, competence and autonomy.

In the next section, I will flesh out the self-system processes thought to be associated with each of these three needs as experienced in the world of school, specifically with regard to the academic aspects of life in schools. The self-system processes, and their operationalization by the new assessment package, do not encompass the full set of enterprises that characterize the world of school (e.g., peer interaction, athletics). The focus here is on students' appraisals of themselves in relation to school/academic learning and achievement.

Self-System Processes Associated with the Need for Competence

As stated earlier, the two self-system processes associated with the need for competence are thought to be perceived strategies for producing success and avoiding failure outcomes, and perceived capacities to execute these strategies.

In the student report form of the Rochester Assessment Package for Schools, children are asked to endorse, on four-point scales, statements about possible strategies for doing well in school and for avoiding poor performance in school. Specifically, we ask about the following five possible strategies: unknown ("I don't know how to do well/avoid failure in school"), powerful others ("I have to get teachers to like me to do well/avoid failure in school"), luck ("I have to be lucky to do well/avoid failure in school"), effort ("Working hard is the best way for me to do well/avoid failure in school"), and ability ("I have to be smart to do well/avoid failure in school"). The specific strategies assessed were derived from open-ended interviews with children in this age range and from previous research conducted by our group and others on children's "control understanding" (e.g., Connell 1985b; Nicholls 1984; Skinner and Connell 1986; Skinner, Wellborn, and Connell 1990).

The perceived capacity and incapacity statements flow directly from the strategy statements. We ask children to endorse the degree to which they believe they have or don't have the capacity to execute only the latter four strategies. (The capacity to execute unknown strategies did not seem logically feasible.) For example, "I can (cannot) get the teacher to like me" is a capacity statement tied to the powerful-others strategy statement. Figure 5 provides examples of the items used on the RAPS-S to assess these self-system processes.

This assessment of elementary and high school students' competence-related self-system processes also draws on previous researchers' efforts (most recently and notably the work of Skinner et al. 1988) to conceptualize and assess children's beliefs about the causes of academic successes and failures and their own role as agents in producing these outcomes. The assessment device they used elaborated on earlier domain-specific models and assessments of locus of control within the achievement domain (e.g., Connell 1985b; Crandall et al. 1965), as well as theories and measures of control-

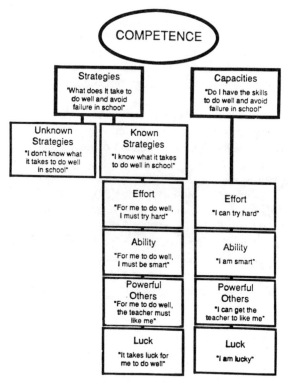

Figure 4.5.   Sample items from the RAPS-S which tap strategies and capacities associated with the need for competence.

related beliefs associated with Weisz and his colleagues (e.g., Weisz and Stipek 1982) and Abramson and her colleagues (e.g., Abramson et al. 1978). (See Skinner and Connell 1986, for a review of these positions.)

Self-System Processes Associated with the Need for Autonomy

The self-system processes associated with the need for autonomy were defined as "self-regulation processes" having to do with the initiation, maintenance, and redirection of activity within a cultural enterprise and, more specifically, with the degree to which individuals experience choice in the regulation of these activities. Within educational contexts, we have examined the regulation of three specific activities suggested to us by classroom teachers as being important to successful performance in school: doing homework, doing classwork, and answering questions in class. We also have examined the regulation of the more general activity of "trying to do well in school."

The empirical window for examining "self-regulation" in school has been children's self-reported reasons for engaging in these academic activities (Connell and Ryan 1984, 1987; Ryan and Connell 1989). When we asked children, "Why do you do your homework?" some of the reasons they gave emphasized external pressures or forces compelling them to behave, while others highlighted internal initiators such as values or self-determined goals. By examining these answers, we could assess the phenomenologically salient motivators of action. (A similar strategy has been used by Eisenberg et al. [1985] in the domain of prosocial behaviors and by Chandler and Connell [1987] for liked and disliked behaviors.)

The next step was to theoretically classify reasons for engaging in school-related behaviors along a continuum of increasing autonomy marked by four self-regulatory styles: external (e.g., "I do my homework because the teacher will yell at me if I don't"), introjected (e.g., "I do my classwork because I feel ashamed of myself if I don't"), identified (e.g., "I answer questions in class because I want to understand the subject"), and intrinsic (e.g., "I do my homework because it's fun").

External regulation is viewed as the least autonomous form of self-regulation in that the initiation and maintenance of behavior is controlled by the child's fears of external retribution or expectations of external reward and, presumably, achievement behaviors would not occur in the absence of such expected contingencies. *Introjected* regulation marks an increment along the autonomy continuum in that the regulatory source is "within the child" (i.e., the child engages in achievement behaviors to protect against loss of self-esteem). However, the regulation is still not fully autonomous in that internalized pressure is now being brought to bear to initiate and maintain activity. This notion of introjected regulation shares some conceptual features with what Nicholls (1984) and Ryan (1982) have termed *ego involvement*. *Identified* regulation is the first truly autonomous form of self-regulation in that the activity (homework, classwork, etc.) is perceived as leading to a goal that the child deems important in its own right (e.g., "to learn and understand," "because homework is important to my learning"). Finally, *intrinsic* regulation is, in effect, the sine qua non of autonomous functioning, whereby the child engages in the activity out of interest and because of the pleasure experienced in doing so.

The labeling and interpretation of these four self-regulatory styles draw heavily from theories of internalization, which is the process through which external regulations are transformed into inner regulations (English and English 1958). For example, internalization theories suggest that a continuum exists from heteronomous forms of control to active self-regulation, with identifiable gradations within that continuum (e.g., Meissner 1981; Schafer, 1968). These distinctions and sample item content are presented in Figure 6.

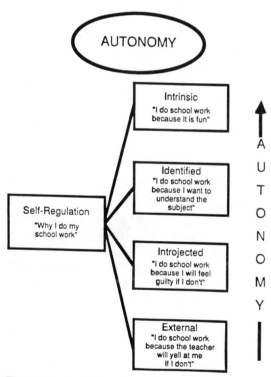

Figure 4.6.   Sample items from the RAPS-S which tap the self-regulatory processes associated with the need for autonomy.

Self-System Processes Associated with Relatedness

Relatedness to Others

Current versions of the RAPS include items exploring two dimensions of children's relationships with their parent(s), teacher(s), and peers: the emotional security of the relationship and the reported need for a closer relationship. The first dimension, emotional security, is tapped by items such as "I like being with my classmates," as well as individual emotional descriptors following the statement "When I'm with my classmates, I feel _____." These descriptors include relaxed, ignored, happy, mad, bored, important, and unhappy. A single positive to negative dimension of "emotional security versus insecurity" is derived from these items, in this case the items focus on the emotional security of relationships with classmates.

In order to tap the second dimension, reported need for closer relationships, children are also asked to endorse statements of the type: "I wish I was closer to my father; I wish my father spent more time with me; I wish my father knew me better." These items are combined into a single composite thought to reflect, in this case, the degree to which children want to have closer relationships with their fathers. From the RAPS measure of relatedness to others, children receive two scores with regard to classmates, teacher(s), mother, and father: an emotional security score, and a score on reported need for a closer relationship. We are currently working on a scoring system that combines these two dimensions into a prototypical patterns of relatedness representing a more qualitative description of the relationships the student has with teachers, peers, and parents (Connell, Lynch, and Wellborn, in preparation).

Relatedness to Self

As discussed earlier, general self-esteem is the self-system process associated with the need for relatedness with regard to self. To tap this variable, the RAPS includes six items from Harter's (1982) measure of children's general self-esteem. These items are presented in the original "structured alternative" format used successfully by Harter (1982) to assess children's general feelings of self-worth. In addition, we have included items very similar to those used to measure emotional security with others, except we ask, "When I'm *by myself,* I feel _____," and then ask children to endorse the various emotion descriptors (Wellborn and Connell 1987). The assessments of "relatedness to others" and "relatedness to self" are summarized in Figure 7.

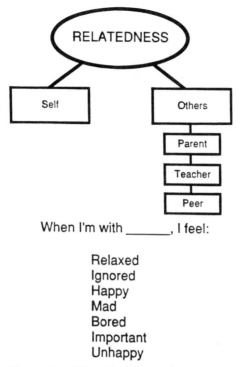

Figure 4.7. Schematic diagram of relationships measured in the RAPS-S with sample items used to assess emotional security.

Dimensions of School and Family Context

As discussed earlier, three dimensions of the social context—provision of structure, autonomy support, and involvement—are thought to be important nutriments for the needs for competence, autonomy, and relatedness within cultural enterprises. The RAPS includes items tapping the degree to which parents (separately and jointly) and teachers in school provide their children/ students with these interpersonal nutriments.

Provision of Structure at Home and in School

Positive *structure* items on the RAPS are behavioral descriptions of parents communicating clear expectations for performance (e.g., "My parents let me know what the rules are about homework"), clear consequences of less-than-adequate performance (e.g., "If I do something my parents don't like, I know what my parents will do"), and consistent application of consequences (e.g., "My parents always do what they say they're going to do"). Items designed to tap provision of structure by teachers refer to clarity of expectations as well as consistency of consequences (e.g., "I know what my teacher(s) expect of me"; "My teacher(s) do what they say they're going to do").

Lack of structure in the home and school context refers to students' experience of confusion about adult expectations, and unpredictable consequences—for example, in the home, "I never know what my parents are going to do when I do something they don't like"; "It's not clear to me what my parents expect of me in school." Lack of structure in the school context is tapped by items such as "My teacher(s) don't make it clear what they expect on school assignments"; "When I don't do well on a test, I never know how my teacher(s) will act."

The dimension of structure is expected to be most closely related to students' understanding (or lack thereof) of what strategies are effective in achieving school success. Recent research by Grolnick and Ryan (1987b) has demonstrated that lack of structure in the home context, as rated by clinical interviews of elementary school children's parents, significantly and uniquely predicts children's reports of higher unknown strategies for obtaining successful school outcomes on Connell's (1985b) measure of perceived control. With the new RAPS-S measure, we will be able to examine how students' perceptions of the degree and quality of structure at home and in school influence their specific perceived strategies for doing well in school and their perceived capacities to execute these strategies.

Autonomy Support at Home and in School

The RAPS includes items that focus on two aspects of autonomy support in the student's home and school contexts. The first is the provision of choice (e.g., "My parents let me decide when to do my homework"; "My teacher(s) let us make some of the decisions about our schoolwork"). The second is acknowledgment of feelings and opinions (e.g., "My parents/teachers respect my opinion and listen to my side of the story before deciding what to do"). Lack of autonomy support, or being controlled by others, is assessed by items such as "My mother/father tries to control everything I do" and (for school/teacher) "When I'm in school, I feel controlled; My teacher(s) try to control everything I do in class."

Extensive research demonstrates the salutory effects of autonomy-supportive interpersonal contexts on a wide variety of child outcomes. This includes our own research showing relations between school competence and autonomy support in the home (Grolnick and Ryan 1987a; Ryan, Deci, and

Grolnick 1987) and autonomy support in the classroom (Connell and Ryan 1987; Deci et al. 1981; Ryan and Connell 1989). Baumrind's (1971) work on authoritative parenting styles and deCharms' (1976) work on origin and pawn classroom environments also provide empirical and theoretical support for the notion that autonomy support is an important contextual influence on children's motivation and performance in school. Guided by our own research and these other research traditions, we have hypothesized a strong linkage between students' perceptions of autonomy support in the home and school and increased autonomy in their regulation of school activities as assessed by the RAPS.

Involvement of Teachers and Parents

The involvement dimension includes three components as delineated by Grolnick and Ryan (1987b): knowledge about, active engagement with, and positive affect toward the student. The RAPS assesses each of these components with regard to teachers and parents. In items designed to tap these three components of involvement, students are asked if their parents/teachers "know a lot about what happens to me in school"; "spend time helping me do better in school"; and "seem to enjoy being with me."

Our expectations, based again on our own and others' work in this area, are that involvement would show its primary linkages to the relatedness variables, particularly the emotional security of relationships with teacher and parents, and with relatedness to self or general self-esteem. Previous empirical work by Grolnick and Ryan (1987b) suggests that parental involvement also affects children's beliefs about their academic competence. It may be that parental and teacher involvement provides an interpersonal foundation for all three of the psychological needs upon which autonomy support and provision of structure then have their unique and more specific motivational impact. Addressing theoretical and applied issues such as these will be utmost on our empirical agenda using the new RAPS measure. Sample item contents for the three dimensions of home and school context are presented in Figure 8.

Student Engagement and Disaffection

Included in the RAPS are items designed to tap multiple aspects of the general construct "engagement versus disaffection." As previously defined, engagement is viewed as patterns of action reflecting acceptance of and commitment to the goals of learning and successful school performance. Disaffection is defined as patterns of action reflecting a lack of commitment to these goals.

88   James P. Connell

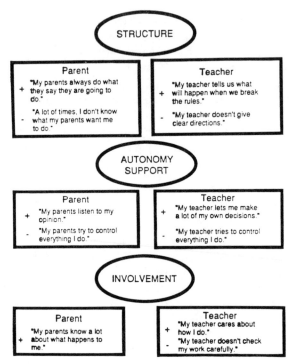

Figure 4.8.   Sample items from the RAPS-S measuring the three dimensions of home and school context.

In our view, patterns of action include, cognition, emotion, and behavior. Figure 9 summarizes variables assessed in the RAPS related to engagement and disaffection. The cognitive versus emotional versus behavioral distinctions helped guide our selection of the initial item pool for measuring engagement and disaffection and reflect the breadth of what is included under the general construct.

Another set of theoretical distinctions guiding our measurement strategy was a typology of engaged and disaffected patterns of action, inspired by Merton (1953) and shown in figure 2. In addition to tapping cognitive, emotional, and behavioral aspects of the engagement construct, we wanted to include items that could potentially discriminate between the six different forms of engagement and disaffection. The dimensions presented in Figure 9 were designed to meet both of these measurement goals. Results relating self-system processes and these patterns of engagement and disaffection are presented in Connell and Wellborn (1990).

Cognitive
- Flexible vs. Rigid Problem Solving
- Active vs. Passive Coping with Failure
- Independent vs. Dependent Work Styles
- Independent vs. Dependent Judgement
- Preference for Hard Work vs. Preference for Easy Work

Behavioral
- Class Participation vs. Uninvolvement
- On-task vs. Off-task Behavior
- Extra-curricular Academically Oriented vs. Extra-curricular Non-academically Oriented
- Career Plans
- Classes Skipped
- Tardiness

Emotional

-Anger	-Interest	-Nervousness
-Happiness	-Sadness	-Curiosity
-Boredom	-Discouragement	-Excitement

Figure 4.9. Cognitive, behavioral, and emotional aspects of engagement versus disaffection measured by the RAPS-S.

Summary

A new assessment package based on the general model presented in part 1 was described in order to demonstrate how the general model can be applied within another cultural enterprise (school) and within a different developmental period (middle childhood). Data supporting the hypothesized linkages among the context, self-system processes, and action variables have recently been presented in Connell and Wellborn (1990) and Skinner, Wellborn, and Connell (1990). We may also expect changes in the relations among the three needs across developmental periods. For example, in early development, the needs for competence and relatedness may complement each other in the child's play with caretakers, whereas, in later development, the need to be competent in the eyes of the caretakers competes with the need for relatedness (Connell and Wellborn, 1990).

Part 4: The Transition from Infancy to Childhood

The motivational analyses of self-system processes in infancy and middle childhood reveal clear commonalities across these different developmental periods at the level of the constructs in the general model—specifically, the three fundamental needs, the three dimensions of social context thought to facilitate the meeting of the three needs, and engaged and disaffected patterns of action. However, marked differences exist between these two developmental periods in the cognitive sophistication of the self-system processes, the enterprises in which infants and school children are engaged, and thus the specific pattern of actions thought to reflect engagement and disaffection within these enterprises. Perhaps a less obvious developmental difference is the shift in the relative centrality of the three psychological needs. For example, relatedness to others may be more salient in infancy, while the competence and autonomy needs may be more salient in middle childhood within the enterprise of school.

The central premise of this section is that the transition from infancy to early childhood should also be marked by *commonalities* at the level of the broad constructs guiding the motivational analyses and by *change* in (*a*) the cognitive sophistication of the self-system processes, (*b*) the nature of the cultural enterprises and patterns of actions observed within those enterprises, and (*c*) the relative salience and dynamic interrelations of the three needs. Consideration of potential developmental differences between infancy and early childhood in the interpersonal context is not included in the discussion of this transition. In theory, autonomy support, structure, and involvement should cooperatively facilitate the meeting and balancing of the three fundamental needs across the life span. However, because the needs themselves may shift in their salience and dynamic interrelations, the role of context in producing these shifts will need to be examined.

The presumption of continuity in the interpersonal nutriments of the three needs still allows for shifts in *who* provides these nutriments (e.g., caretakers to peers to spouses); for calibrations *within* interpersonal networks (such as the family) in the ways in which involvement, autonomy support, and structure are communicated, depending on the developmental level of the child; and for cultural variation in the modes and salience of these communications. Studies examining these issues are currently under way in our research group (Grolnick, Wellborn, and Connell, in preparation). Intraindividual changes in the self-system processes are also expected to be influenced by change in the social context. Indeed, this is a central tenet of the general model.

In this final section of the chapter, I will speculate as to how these three aspects of change in self-system processes (cognitive sophistication, cultural enterprises, and salience of needs) are played out over the second and third years of life, with the hope that an empirical agenda will emerge for the study of self-system processes across this transition.

Self-system Processes Associated with the Needs for Competence, Autonomy, and Relatedness

Vaughn et al. (1984) and, earlier, Kopp (1982) have tied cognitive development and language acquisition to the increased capacities of eighteen- to thirty-month-olds to regulate their own behavior and to show cross-situationally stable individual differences in this capacity. Kagan (1984) and others (e.g., Amsterdam and Greenberg 1977) have pointed theoretically and empirically to the importance of toddlers' recognition of discrepancies between their desired ends and obtained outcomes, as precursors of a well-articulated sense of self. In contrast, the motivational analysis presented up to this point does not directly address the role played by cognitive factors in the development of self-system processes. The emphasis has been on the social context's role in facilitating the development of the self-system processes associated with the three psychological needs (e.g., autonomy support for self-regulation, optimal structure for perceived capacities and strategies, involvement for emotional security). In fact, variation in social context is seen not only as a *predictor* of inter- and intra-individual variation in these self-system processes but, more in line with a Vygotskian perspective, as a constituent part of the emergence and development of these self-system processes, which are themselves cognitive *and* emotional in nature.

From this point of view, the young child's emerging abilities to symbolically generate interpersonal goals, to hold in mind these goals, to communicate to the social surround the nature of these goals, and to use symbolic (versus behavioral) information to regulate the emotions associated with these goals are all seen as a function of social exchange. Thus, the dialectical relations between the young toddlers' needs for competence, autonomy, and relatedness and the matrix of social communications *produce* the cognitive advances manifested in verbal/reflective versions of self-system processes. For example, the struggle to individuate (to be autonomous) within the context of a dependent relationship brings to the fore the challenge of behaviorally and cognitively regulating strong emotion. This interplay between social and cognitive factors in the development of self-system processes is also evident in Mahler et al.'s (1975) suggestion that it is the young toddlers' increasing *awareness* and *understanding* of the caretakers' separateness that "kicks off" the need to individuate (see also Cicchetti et al., in this volume; Sroufe, in this volume).

An object relations perspective also informs the analysis of self-system processes associated with the need for relatedness across this transition (see

Stechler, in this volume). Obviously, appraisals of emotional security will continue to be a central self-system process, as it was earlier in infancy. But, according to Mahler and her colleagues, (Mahler et al. 1975) we should expect to see increased lability in the child's appraisals by late in the second year, due to uncertainty about the caretakers' continued availability and permanence. This lability has important ramifications for the developing self-regulatory capacities. For example, the child begins to experience himself/herself directing negative affect (particularly anger) toward caretakers and others. However, such displays should not, according to these theorists, be interpreted as indicators of insecure relationships with significant others. Rather, they are markers of important developmental advances in the child's sense of self in relation to the other and in his or her own self-regulatory capacities. In our current work (Connell et al. 1989), emotional self-regulation entails both the capacity to *modulate* positive and negative emotion and the capacity to *initiate* positive and negative emotion. In fact, our own empirical work with eighteen- to twenty-two-month-olds lends initial support to the notion that moderate levels of resistant/angry behavior toward the mother in this age period may indicate precocious development of self-system processes (see Connell 1985a).

Shifts and Commonalities in Cultural Enterprises across the Transition

The broadening social world of the two- to three-year-old child, at least in American culture, expands and redefines the cultural enterprises within which the self-system processes are constituted. Within the interpersonal domain, peers, siblings, and extrafamilial adults (day-care workers, baby-sitters) are beginning to articulate their unique relationship histories with the young toddler. These new interpersonal relationships, with their distinctive matrixes of motivational nutriments and frustrations, may provide the aliments for increased differentiation and integration of the young child's perceived strategies for achieving social outcomes. Such multiple relationships may also instigate beliefs regarding personal capacities to achieve these social outcomes—that is, generalized feelings of competence in the social domain. Regulation of affect in the context of different social partners again provides opportunities for differentiation and integration of these self-system processes as well.

Recent theoretical writings concerning working models of self and other (e.g., Bretherton 1985) include speculations about whether and when separate models are constructed for different social partners. In our recent work on attachment system functioning within mother-infant and father-infant relationships, distinctive organizational characteristics and patterns of predictive claims for each relationship have been confirmed (Bridges, Connell, and

Belsky 1988). The idea that each relationship is a distinctive enterprise, with its own set of social contextual dimensions, self-system processes, and patterns of action, is guiding our current work as we assess mother- and father-infant interactions separately and examine infants' and toddlers' emotional self-regulatory strategies as well as their parents' behavior, along the three dimensions of autonomy support, structure, and involvement. By assessing the constructs from the self-system processes model within each relationship, the patterns of influence *across* these relationships can also be investigated.

Finally, although the infant to toddler transition will entail ever-widening social networks, the family (albeit nontraditional in more and more cases) is the central enterprise for most infants and young children in this culture. Due in part to an expanding social network, the young child's needs for competence, autonomy, and relatedness, as experienced within the family context, are shifting in their salience and dynamic interrelations. During this transition, it may be the dynamic interrelation per se—the fluctuating synergy and competition among these organismic needs—that is most indicative of self-system processes' development. The simultaneous expression of the needs to be close and to be free can, depending on the moment, be a source of immense pleasure or pain to the child and the caretaker—pleasure, as in the toddler's first ride on his or her tricycle with the caretaker close by; pain, as in the 2½-year-old's angry reprisals against the babysitter upon the caretaker's departure. A central theoretical and empirical issue to be addressed is how these needs and their corresponding self-system processes and social contextual nutriments become synergistically and competitively intertwined over this transition from infancy to middle childhood.

Conclusion

The uniquely human struggles to attain socially defined and valued outcomes, to experience oneself as the initiator of one's actions, and to feel loved and cared for by self and others express themselves across the life span and in the multitude of human enterprises. By postulating these needs and their social nutriments as the bases for the development of self-system processes, I hope to inform the theoretical and empirical study of these processes.

References

Abramson, L. Y., M. E. P. Seligman, and J. D. Teasdale. 1978. Learned helplessness in humans: Critique and reformulation. *Journal of Abnormal Psychology* 87:49–74.

Ainsworth, M. D. S., and S. M. Bell. 1969. Some contemporary patterns of mother-infant interaction in the feeding situation. In *Stimulation in early infancy*. Edited by A. Ambrose. New York: Academic.

Ainsworth, M. D. S., M. C. Blehar, E. Waters, and S. Wall. 1978. *Patterns of attachment*. Hillsdale, N.J.: Erlbaum.

Ainsworth, M. D. S., and B. A. Wittig. 1969. Attachment and exploratory behavior of one year olds in a strange situation. In *Determinants of infant behavior,* vol. 4. Edited by B. M. Foss. London: Methuen.

Amsterdam, B., and C. M. Greenberg. 1977. Self-conscious behavior of infants: A videotape study. *Developmental Psychobiology* 10:106.

Angyal, A. 1941. *Foundations for a science of personality*. New York: Commonwealth.

Bandura, A. 1977. Self-efficacy: Toward a unifying theory of behavioral change. *Psychological Review* 84:191–15.

Baumrind, D. 1971. *Current patterns of parental authority*. Developmental Psychology Monographs, vol. 4:1–102.

Bower, T. G. R. 1974. *Development in infancy*. San Francisco: Freeman.

Bowlby, J. 1969. *Attachment*. New York: Basic Books.

Bretherton, I. 1985. Attachment theory: Retrospect and prospect. In *Growing points in attachment theory and research. Edited by I. Bretherton and E. Waters. Monographs of the Society for Research in Child Development. Chicago: University of Chicago Press.*

Bridges, L., J. P. Connell, and J. Belsky. 1988. Infant-mother and infant-father interaction in the strange situation: A component process analysis. *Developmental Psychology* 24:92–100.

Chandler, C. L., and J. P. Connell. 1987. Children's intrinsic, extrinsic and internalized motivation: A developmental study of behavioral regulation. *British Journal of Developmental Psychology* 5:357–65.

Connell, J. P. 1985a. A component process approach to the study of individual differences and developmental change in attachment system functioning. In *Mother-infant attachment*. Edited by M. Lamb, R. Thompson, W. Gardner, and E. Charnov. Hillsdale, N.J.: Erlbaum.

———. 1985b. A new multidimensional measure of children's perceptions of control. *Child Development* 56:1018–41.

Connell, J. P., L. J. Bridges, and W. S. Grolnick. 1989. The development of emotional self-regulation. 1R01BH44449–01A1. Funded by the National Institute of Mental Health. 1989–1993.

Connell, J. P., M. Lynch, and J. G. Wellborn. In preparation. Patterns and prototypes of relatedness in middle childhood. Manuscript.

Connell, J. P., and R. M. Ryan. 1984, Fall. A developmental theory of motivation in the classroom. *Teacher Education Quarterly,* 64–77.

———. 1987. Autonomy in the classroom: A theory and assessment of children's self-regulatory styles in the academic domain. Manuscript, University of Rochester.

———. 1987, fall. Motivation development within the context of schools. *International Society for the Study of Behavioral Development Newsletter,* no. 2, serial no. 12.

Connell, J. P., and R. Thompson. 1986. Emotion and social interaction in the strange situation: Consistencies and asymmetric influences in the second year. *Child Development* 57:733–45.

Connell, J. P., and J. G. Wellborn. 1987. Patterns of engagement and disaffection in school: Contextual and self-system influences. Manuscript, University of Rochester.

———. 1990. Competence, autonomy and relatedness: A motivational analysis of self-system processes. In *Minnesota Symposium on Child Psychology*, vol. 22. Edited by M. Gunnar and L. A. Sroufe. Hillsdale, N.J.: Erlbaum.

Connell, J. P., P. Wexler, and W. D. Dannefer. 1987, April. A theory and assessment of engagement and disaffection in high school. Paper presented at the meetings of the American Educational Research Association, Washington, D.C.

Cooley, C. 1902. *Human nature and the social order*. New York: Scribner.

Covington, M. V., and R. Beery. 1976. *Self-worth and school learning*. New York: Holt, Rinehart & Winston.

Crandall, V. C., W. Katkovsky, and V. S. Crandall. 1965. Children's beliefs in their control of reinforcements in intellectual academic achievement situations. *Child Development* 36:91–109.

deCharms, R. 1968. *Personal causation: The internal affective determinants of behavior.* New York: Academic.

———. 1976. *Enhancing motivation: Change in the classroom.* New York: Irvington.

Deci, E. L. 1975. *Intrinsic motivation*. New York: Plenum.

Deci, E. L., and R. M. Ryan. 1985. *Intrinsic motivation and self-determination in human behavior*. New York: Plenum.

Deci, E. L., A. J. Schwartz, L. Sheinman, and R. M. Ryan. 1981. An instrument to assess adults' orientations toward control versus autonomy with children: Reflections on intrinsic motivation and perceived competence. *Journal of Educational Psychology* 73:642–50.

Dweck, C. S., and E. S. Elliot. 1983. Achievement motivation. In *Handbook of child psychology.* 4th ed., vol. 4. Edited by P. H. Mussen. New York: Wiley, 643–91.

Eisenberg, N., T. Lundy, R. Shell, and K. Roth. 1985. Children's justifications for their adult and peer-directed compliant (prosocial and nonprosocial) behaviors. *Developmental Psychology* 21:325–31.

English, H., and A. C. English. 1958. *A comprehensive dictionary of psychological and psychoanalytic terms.* New York: McKay.

Erikson, E. H. 1968. *Identity: Youth and crisis.* New York: Norton.

Frodi, A., L. Bridges, and W. S. Grolnick. 1986. Correlates of mastery-related behavior: A short term longitudinal study of infants in their second year. *Child Development* 56:1291–98.

Gaensbauer, T., J. P. Connell, and L. Schultz. 1983. Emotion and attachment: Interrelationships in a structured laboratory paradigm. *Developmental Psychology* 19:815–31.

Grolnick, W. S., and R. M. Ryan. 1987a. Autonomy in children's learning: An experimental and individual difference investigation. *Journal of Personality and Social Psychology* 52:890–98.

———. 1987b. The facilitating environment: Parent styles associated with children's school-related competence and adjustment. Manuscript, University of Rochester.

———. 1988. Autonomy support in education: Creating the facilitating environment. In *New directions in educational psychology.* Edited by N. Hastings & J. Schwieso. Vol. 2, *Behaviour and motivation*. London: Falmer.

Grolnick, W. S., J. G. Wellborn, and J. P. Connell. In preparation. A motivational analysis of self-system processes in educational contexts: Parental influences.

Haith, M. 1980. *Rules that babies look by.* Hillsdale, N.J.: Erlbaum.

Harter, S. 1982. The perceived competence scale for children. *Child Development* 53:87–97.

———. 1983a. Developmental perspectives on the self-system. In *Handbook of child psychology.* 4th ed. Edited by E. M. Hetherington. Vol. 4, *Socialization, personality and social development.* New York: Wiley, 275–386.

———. 1983b. Competence as a dimension of self-evaluation: Toward a comprehensive model of self-worth. In *The development of self.* Edited by R. Leahy. New York: Academic, 55–121.

James, W. 1890. *The principles of psychology.* New York: Holt.

Jennings, K. D., R. J. Harmon, G. A. Morgan, J. L. Gaiter, and L. J. Yarrow. 1979. Exploratory play as an index of mastery motivation: Relationships to persistence, cognitive functioning, and environmental measures. *Developmental Psychology* 15:386–94.

Kagan, J. 1984. The idea of emotion in human development. In *Emotions, cognition, and behavior.* Edited by C. E. Izard, J. Kagan, and R. Zajonc. New York: Cambridge University Press, 38–72.

Kopp, C. B. 1982. Antecedents of self-regulation: A developmental perspective. *Developmental Psychology* 18:199–214.

Lamb, M. E., and M. A. Easterbrooks. 1981. Individual differences in parental sensitivity: Origins, components, and consequences. In *Infant social cognition: Empirical and theoretical considerations.* Edited by M. E. Lamb and L. R. Sherrod. Hillsdale, N.J.: Erlbaum.

Lamb, M. E., R. Thompson, W. Gardner, and E. Charnov. 1985. *Infant-mother attachment.* Hillsdale, N.J.: Erlbaum.

Lewis, M., C. Felring, C. McGuffog, and J. Jaskir. 1984. Predicting psychopathology in six year olds from early social relations. *Child Development* 55:123–26.

Loevinger, J. 1976. *Ego development.* San Francisco: Jossey-Bass.

Mahler, M. S., F. Pine, and A. Bergman. 1975. *The psychological birth of the human infant.* New York: Basic.

McClelland, D. C. 1965. Toward a theory of motive acquisition. *American Psychologist* 20:321–33.

Meissner, W. W. 1981. *Internalization in psychoanalysis.* New York: International Universities Press.

Merton, R. 1953. *Social theory and social structure.* London: Free Press of Glendale.

Nicholls, J. G. 1984. Achievement motivation: Conceptions of ability, subjective experience, task choice, and performance. *Psychological Review* 91:328–46.

Phillips, D. 1984. The illusion of incompetence among academically competent children. *Child Development* 55:2000–2016.

Rotter, J. B. 1966. *Generalized expectancies for internal versus external control of reinforcement.* Psychological Monographs, vol. 80, no. 1, whole no. 609: 1–28.

Ryan, R. M. 1982. Control and information in the intrapersonal sphere: An extension of cognitive evaluation theory. *Journal of Personality and Social Psychology* 43:450–61.

Ryan, R. M. In press. The nature of the self in autonomy and relatedness. In *Interdisciplinary perspectives on the self*. Edited by G. Goethals and J. Strauss. New York: Springer-Verlag.

Ryan, R. M., and J. P. Connell. 1989. Perceived locus of causality and internalization: Examining reasons for acting in two domains. *Journal of Personality and Social Psychology* 57:749–61.

Ryan, R. M., J. P. Connell, and E. L. Deci. 1985. A motivational analysis of self-determination and self-regulation in education. In *Research on motivation in education: The classroom milieu*. Edited by C. Ames and R. E. Ames. New York: Academic.

Ryan, R. M., E. L. Deci, and W. S. Grolnick. 1987. Children's perceptions of parental involvement and autonomy-support. Manuscript, University of Rochester.

Schafer, R. 1968. *Aspects of internalization*. New York: International Universities Press.

Skinner, E. A., M. Chapman, and P. Baltes. 1988. Control, means-ends and agency beliefs: A new conceptualization and its measurement during childhood. *Journal of Personality and Social Psychology* 54:117–33.

Skinner, E., and J. P. Connell. 1986. Control understanding: Suggestions for a developmental framework. In *Aging and the psychology of control*. Edited by M. M. Baltes and P. B. Baltes. Hillsdale, N.J.: Erlbaum, 35–61.

Skinner, E. A., J. G. Wellborn, and J. P. Connell. 1990. What it takes to do well in school and whether I've got it: A process model of perceived control and children's engagement and achievement in school. *Journal of Educational Psychology* 82 (no. 1).

Sroufe, L. A., and E. Waters. 1977. Attachment as an organizational construct. *Child Development* 48:1184–99.

Stenberg, C., and J. Campos. 1983. The development of the expression of anger in human infants. In *The socialization of affect*. Edited by M. Lewis and C. Saarni. New York: Plenum.

Vaughn, B. E., C. G. Kopp, and J. B. Krakow. 1984. The emergence and consolidation of self-control from eighteen to thirty months of age: Normative trends and individual differences. *Child Development* 55:990–1004.

Weiner, B. 1986. *An attributional theory of motivation and emotion*. New York: Springer-Verlag.

Weisz, J., and D. Stipek. 1982. Competence, contingency and the development of perceived control. *Human Development* 25:250–81.

Wellborn, J. G. In preparation. A theoretical and empirical analysis of motivated activity. Doctoral dissertation, University of Rochester, Rochester, New York.

Wellborn, J., and J. P. Connell. 1987. Relatedness to self and others: Working models of self and significant others in middle childhood and adolescence. Manuscript, University of Rochester.

White, R. W. 1959. Motivation reconsidered: The concept of competence. *Psychological Review* 66:297–333.

5 Enculturation: A Biosocial Perspective on the Development of Self

ROBERT A. LEVINE

Enculturation here refers to the acquisition of cultural representations, including representations of self, by the human organism. The term was coined by Herskovits (1948; 1955, 326–33) and adopted by Mead (1963) in the context of a relativistic conception of culture, but its use is not bound to their theoretical position. On the contrary, I shall argue in this chapter that a concept of enculturation is required by any understanding of human ontogeny consistent with existing knowledge in anthropology and human biology. This claim has been made many times in a variety of terms over the past sixty years; translating it into empirical research, however, has not proved simple or straightforward. The importance of investigating how children acquire culture, and the psychological and social consequences of that process, mandates the continued search for methodological foundations and motivates the conceptualization proposed in this chapter.

In what follows, I consider the psychological effects of childhood experience from a population perspective grounded in human ecology, arriving at conclusions contrasting with those based on the psychology of individual differences. Enculturation and the representation of self are proposed as key concepts for understanding cultural diversity in childhood experience and analyzing the shape of psychological development in any setting. Recent ethnographic and developmental evidence is offered to illustrate the theoretical arguments advanced.

The idea that childhood experience exerts lasting psychological effects has drawn heavy criticism from developmental psychologists (e.g., Brim and Kagan 1980; Clarke and Clarke 1976; Kagan 1984) and anthropologists (Riesman 1982; Shweder 1979) over the past decade. The critics' central point is that the idea—sometimes referred to as the early-experience hypothesis—stands in contradiction to the empirical evidence. They base this conclusion on their interpretations of the evidence emerging from a myriad of developmental studies. However, according to the alternative framework I advance below for interpreting the evidence, it is possible to arrive at a different conclusion: namely, that empirical studies have not contradicted the idea of lasting childhood influences and that theoretical models which include such influences continue to represent our best hope for understanding human development. There is, of course, no single early-experience hypothesis but a variety of theoretical perspectives in which environmental encounters in the early years are posited as exerting an influence on some aspect of later behavior or personality—normal, abnormal, or supernormal. The critics have cast doubt on all of these perspectives, whether the outcomes are conceived of as educational achievement, psychopathology, or normal social and personality development. Thus, the argument must be conducted in general as well as specific terms.

This is not simply a neutral scientific discussion but a highly charged controversy characterized by pendulum swings in the opinions of specialists, who are often as biased as the general public about what to believe. My own biases favor the idea that early experience is influential (LeVine 1981, 1982), but I believe that only empirical research can specify the pathways and magnitudes of influence. Meanwhile, there is a need for new theoretical models consistent with the available evidence.

The argument of the critics can be summarized as follows: Theories advancing the idea that childhood experience has a lasting impact gain plausibility in our society from the prescientific folk beliefs and philosophical traditions of our culture. Thus, we are predisposed to accept this idea before considering empirical evidence brought to light through scientific investigation. Developmental studies, longitudinal and cross-sectional, have not shown a consistent pattern of evidence supporting the idea that early experience has long-term effects. On the contrary, they have found numerous instances in which children have, with age, overcome earlier deprivation, deficits, and pathologies hypothetically predictive of permanent abnormalities. The overall pattern of evidence as the critics see it favors either a stronger environmentalism in which personality is quite malleable after childhood, with the early years given no privileged place as a critical period for psychological development, or a stronger position of innatism in which individual differences in child behavior and personality are more attributable to inborn temperament and less attributable to early experience than had been thought. Persistent belief in early experience as formative or injurious is due to a prevalent orthodoxy of thought, reflecting the influence of persuasive clinicians such as Freud and Bowlby and our ideological heritage of child-rearing determinism and egalitarianism. This indictment takes a variety of forms in the analyses of different critics, but its central tendency is, I believe, fairly captured in this brief summary.

Although every element in this critical attack has some validity, it does not lead inevitably to the conclusions drawn by critics. For example, child-rearing determinism can be traced back to prescientific doctrines in Western philosophy and popular culture but so can alternative explanatory formulations based on ideas of innatism, situationalism, or adult malleability. Our culture as intellectual tradition and folk belief does not speak with a single voice about matters of psychological plasticity but generates opposing, often contradictory lines of thought. Contemporary Americans have been exposed to an extensive popular literature that claims not only that parents can mold their children's intellectual and emotional development but also that adults can remold themselves psychologically during the middle years and beyond. Innatist psychological ideas have enjoyed periodic vogues in England and the United States since the 1840s, long before genuine empirical evidence was available (Curtin 1964; Gould 1981; Kamin 1974). All of these viewpoints have had their spokespersons, scientific and ideological, and have attracted adherents. Thus, the idea of childhood influence, far from being uniquely flawed in deriving its plausibility from a nonempirical cultural tradition, shares that condition with other concepts of psychological development.

As for the evidence from developmental research, its implications are far from straightforward. If, as many of the critics have, one interprets the early-experience idea as implying irreversible effects on development, then any evidence of later recovery or delayed acquisition falsifies the hypothesis. But if one posits early experience as one influence among others, which most important theorists in this field have, then such evidence is not necessarily damaging to the hypothesis. Similarly, if one assumes that the psychological evidence collected and analyzed to date is of high enough quality to match the complexity of the problem, then its mixed findings concerning long-term effects can reflect negatively on the validity of the hypothesis. But if one believes that many of the studies were flawed and that definitive evidence will only be forthcoming in the future, then the critics seem to be making hasty judgments based on inadequate evidence.

In this chapter, I do not attempt to review and analyze the arguments and evidence brought to bear by the critics. My focus is on an unspoken assumption they share with most developmentalists: namely, that the place to look for evidence concerning the effects of early experience is in the psychology of individual differences. I shall show that this assumption diverts attention from an important body of evidence bearing on this hypothesis, that is, the results of cross-cultural research. To clarify the implications of that research, I shall examine human ontogeny from a biosocial perspective in which organisms are seen as members of populations.

A Population Perspective

Investigators of child development have concerned themselves primarily with *species-specific* and *person-specific* characteristics. The general theories (e.g., of Freud, Erikson, Piaget, and Bowlby) have been offered as formulations about the human species as a whole, positing stages and processes connected directly and indirectly with the maturation of the central nervous system during childhood. Empirical research on child development has focused largely on individual differences within relatively homogeneous populations, to identify person-specific environmental or temperamental variables that predict person-specific behavioral outcomes. *Population-specific* characteristics have usually been regarded merely as an extension of individual differences, if they are taken into account at all. From a biological point of view, however, population-specific characteristics are of central significance in the analysis of human adaptation.

Population-level variation in social organization and social behavior is a characteristic of the human species (Wilson 1975, 548–49). Fundamental adaptive patterns such as subsistence, reproduction, communication, and social hierarchy, far from being simply replicated across human populations, are highly variable. Mating arrangements (e.g., monogamy versus polygamy) and emotional display rules, which vary across *species* in much of the animal kingdom, vary across *populations* in homo sapiens.

Population units are not as clearly defined or as stable as organisms and species, but they constitute the level at which much of human adaptation is organized (Miller 1978). Despite their variability in scale, complexity, and stability of boundaries, all units we would term *populations* are interactional networks within which mating and other communicative processes tend to be concentrated. Such networks form local associations, endogamous groups and speech communities, at national and subnational levels in the contemporary world. A population tends to share an environment, a symbol system for encoding it, and an organization for adapting to it. Its boundary markers are usually recognized in local belief, reinforcing its centripetal tendencies in reproduction and communicative processes and propagating a population-specific code of conduct that reduces random variation in the ways members live their lives (LeVine and Campbell 1972, 104–9). It is through the enactment of these codes in locally organized practices that human adaptation occurs.

Human adaptation, in other words, is largely attributable to the operation of specific social organizations (e.g., families, communities, empires) following culturally prescribed scripts (normative models) in subsistence, reproduction, communication, and other domains of animal behavior. The description and analysis of these organizations and scripts are the primary tasks of social anthropology. Adaptive organization at the population level may seem ephemeral compared to neural organization; history tells us that from an evolutionary perspective particular cultures and social structures do not last long. But that instability is their strength; insofar as they change in response to environmental pressures and opportunities, they provide an adaptive flexibility that fosters survival under varied conditions.

No account of ontogeny in human adaptation could be adequate without inclusion of the population-specific patterns that establish pathways for the behavioral development of children. All too often, however, child development theorists have leaped from species-specific determinants to person-specific behaviors without sufficient attention to the intervening contexts created by social and cultural systems, and investigators have studied individual differences without examining their ecological relationships. Seeking to identify the neuropsychological "hardware" of human development, they have frequently overlooked the cultural "software" that gives it direction.

Variation *across* populations in reproductive behavior and parental care is characteristic of the human species. Sexual behavior, for example, varies widely by population in age of onset for males and females, the frequency and conditions of occurrence through the life span, composition and stability of unions, and other factors related to reproduction and child care. Lactation is another example: it varies in intensity and duration from one population to another, creating variable nutritional and social environments during infancy. In this article, I shall examine variations among populations in three aspects of human adaptation that bear on the psychological development of children: reproductive rates, communication, and the maintenance of a rule-governed order in face-to-face relations.

Birth and Death Rates

Human reproductive anatomy and physiology do not vary significantly within the species, but human population parameters such as birth and death rates do. At present, crude birth rates calculated by country vary from ten births per thousand population in Denmark and West Germany to fifty-four in Kenya. Infant mortality rates range more widely, from 6 per thousand live births in Sweden and Japan to 175 in some West African countries such as Sierra Leone and Mali—a factor worldwide of almost thirty as compared with five for crude birth rates (World Bank 1987). The magnitude of these variations is great and gradually increasing. Even before modern health and nutrition practices and contraceptive technology made their impact in the industrial world, however, there were major differences at the cross-national level in fertility, due largely to variations in socially organized practices such as birth spacing, age of marriage, and celibacy. Infant and child mortality also varied across populations in earlier centuries, due largely to greater risk of infection and malnutrition in some local areas than in others. Furthermore, these population parameters have shown a good deal of historical stability, remaining at similar levels for generations, even centuries, before and after transition periods.

What demographic differences mean for parents can be roughly estimated by examining variations in total fertility rates (TFRs), equivalent to the lifetime fertility of the average woman in a population, if she bears children at current age-specific fertility rates as she moves through her reproductive span (see table 1). Comparing regions, the highest TFR is more than 3.5 times that of the lowest, whereas for countries the highest is almost 5 times that of the lowest (Sivard 1985, 35–37).

The TFR does not accurately reflect the average number of children raised by a married woman, however, because it averages in childless women (thus underestimating sibling group size) and takes no account of losses through infant death (thus inflating it). Even allowing for those factors, variations in mean sibling group size across contemporary populations are very wide.

The average married woman among the Gusii, a people numbering approximately one million in southwestern Kenya, bears 8.7 children (median = 10), one of whom is likely to die during infancy. By contrast, the average middle-class American married woman (or her European counterpart) bears 1 or 2 children, with a high probability that all will survive. The effective sibling group size of a child born to the average Gusii is still about four times that of the middle-class American. Most other human populations fall between these two poles.

Psychological studies of individual differences have been conducted largely in the United States, Great Britain, and Canada and most often among middle-class families. In these studies, birth order has emerged as one of the few indicators of childhood experience that is consistently associated with later differences in behavior and personality (Dunn 1983; Feiring and Lewis 1984; Lamb and Sutton-Smith 1982). Research has not entirely resolved the meaning of this finding, but the observations of Dunn and her colleagues in England (Dunn and Kendrick 1982) have suggested that a child's place in the sibling order establishes, during the early years, a long-term interpersonal context for the emotional development of that child. In Dunn's (1983) view, the sibling relationship combines the reciprocity of peer relations with the complementarity of the parent-child relationship in a unique experience for

Table 1.   Total Fertility Rates (TFRs): Lifetime Fertility of Average Woman in Selected Populations

Selected Region	TFR	Country within Region	TFR
Western Europe	1.8	West Germany	1.5
North America	2.0	United States	2.1
Latin America	3.9	Mexico	4.3
South Asia	4.3	Bangladesh	5.7
Sub-Saharan Africa	6.6	Kenya	7.9

the child. Individual responses to sibling position are dependent on temperamental as well as child-rearing factors and are relatively stable in early childhood.

If we adopt the view that sibling position defines those aspects of the early environment most likely to have a long-term effect on interpersonal expectations and other aspects of behavior, then the magnitude of population differences in sibling group size by itself suggests great variation in psychological development. In some populations (e.g., U.S. middle-class), about half of all children grow up as firstborns or only-borns of their mothers, whereas the comparable figure for contemporary high-fertility peoples like the Gusii is no more than 12 to 16 percent and a large proportion of the rest are fourth- or later-borns. Without any further information and on the assumption that birth order is an important influence, we would expect to find a corresponding divergence in average patterns of personality development.

Additional information, however, suggests that cultural factors in the interpersonal environment of the child tend to magnify differences in early social experience far beyond what we might expect based on the figures of sibling group size alone.

First, the American middle-class family is a residential and social isolate compared with the domestic groups of high-fertility agrarian societies. Its living spaces (i.e., sleeping, cooking, eating, and recreational quarters) have sharp physical boundaries and are not shared with other families. Thus, the number of children born to the mother is directly translated into the number of persons using living space and in regular domestic contact with the growing child. If a child is the firstborn, there will normally be no other children living there; if the second-born, one other child; and so forth. In many high-fertility agrarian settings, on the other hand, several husband-wife units and their children share domestic space within a compound—particularly cooking, eating, and recreational quarters—so that the children of several mothers are raised together much of the time. The firstborn of a mother has regular domestic contact with several older children who in many respects are like siblings. In those agrarian societies where multifamily compounds are not the prevailing form of domestic organization, firstborn and only children are often raised with others anyway. This may happen because their young parents have not yet formed a domestic unit separate from one set of their own parents, whose home contains older children, or because mothers find it convenient and desirable to place an only child with the children of neighboring kin so the mother can devote herself to trade or cultivation and the child will not feel more lonely and isolated than other children. One way or another, in terms of regular contact with other children, the early social experience of only- or firstborn children in agrarian societies is rarely as differentiated from that of later-borns as it is in middle-class America.

Second, the norms governing access of children in general, regardless of birth order, to family resources (including parental attention) tend to be quite different in agrarian societies of high fertility. Unlike their middle-class American counterparts, these children do not have rooms, toys, or other possessions of their own, and they are often trained to maintain a respectful distance from their parents. In the social hierarchy of the domestic group, children are at the bottom—first to be assigned menial tasks, last to be allowed favors and privileges. This general situation of children vis-à-vis adults forms the background to relations among siblings.

Third, in addition to the status gap between adults and children in the domestic group, the experience of children in agrarian societies is specified by norms governing relations with each of their primary kin, namely, father, mother, and siblings. Fathers in many agrarian societies have little or no contact with infants and often hardly any with children under the age of five or six, after which they may restrict their contact to the sons. The norms that provide for differentiation and distance between men and women may be related to a cultural concept in which children are classified as part of the women's world and thus to be avoided by men.

Mothers everywhere have primary responsibility for their children and are usually the primary caretakers, but their patterns of attention in high-fertility populations differ from those of middle-class Americans. Our comparative studies suggest that in the high-fertility agrarian settings, mothers tend to give more attention during infancy than later, with the goal of soothing and protecting rather than communicating. Firstborns may receive no more maternal attention than later-borns. In sub-Saharan Africa, it is widely believed that the child who receives the most maternal attention is the *last-born,* since the mother can prolong breast-feeding, and therefore the intensive care of infancy, without concern about its termination by the next pregnancy. This belief, accurate or not, indicates how differently the mother's role is defined there than in middle-class America.

Sibling relationships are also subject to normative variation in high-fertility societies. In some settings (much of sub-Saharan Africa), young girls regularly take care of their infant siblings, developing lifelong mutual attachments. In others (traditional China, Yoruba of Nigeria) a traditional ranking of siblings (or brothers) by birth order specifies a hierarchy of statuses that endows these relationships with formal authority and respect. In contrast with the relative spontaneity of sibling relationships in middle-class American families, parents in these agrarian settings deliberately impose a structure designed to provide permanent meanings for the relationships among siblings.

These variations mean that birth rates do not translate directly into the interpersonal experience of children; norms (governing residential arrangements, the status of children, and kin relationships) intervene, creating the proximal social environments of infancy and childhood. The connections between demographic parameters, such as birth and death rates, and early interpersonal experience are to be found in traditional premises of high or low fertility and mortality underlying child-care customs among peoples at different stages of the demographic transition (LeVine 1983). At each stage, culturally organized parental investment strategies define the ends and means of reproductive and parental behavior in terms consistent with the birth and death rates of recent generations; these cultural formulas lead parents to expect certain demographic outcomes and to pursue goals predicated on such expectations for themselves and their children.

Thus, parents in high-fertility, high-mortality agrarian societies are characterized by the goal of maximizing the number of surviving children, who contribute more than they cost to the domestic group (Caldwell 1982). In low-fertility, low-mortality industrial societies, where the costs of children outweigh their contributions, parents try to optimize the development of a few children in preparation for a competitive, bureaucratic adult environment. These parental goals and strategies, organized at the population level, inform the early environment of the child and provide diverse meanings to the sibling experience in different human societies.

Communication

Communication is essential to animal survival, and a most remarkable achievement of modern zoology has been the deciphering of the codes through which species—ranging from bees to baboons—communicate for adaptive ends (Wilson 1975, 176–241). The human capacity for *symbolic* forms of communication distinguishes our species from others but has not resulted in the primary use of a single specieswide code. On the contrary, human symbolic codes tend to be population specific, normally operating to facilitate social communication at the population level but to divide the species into separate speech communities characterized by mutually unintelligible languages. The tendency for languages to diversify over time—first into dialects, then into tongues that are no longer interintelligible—when populations are socially isolated from each other is as much a human species characteristic as are the universals of phonology and syntax. Human individuals everywhere are identical in their basic capacities for communication and overall pattern of first language acquisition, but they vary by population in the linguistic codes through which normal communication is carried on.

Such variations are by no means limited to language. The facial expression of emotion, an important medium of human communication, is rooted in a universal neuromuscular program but operates according to cultural display rules that are population specific, as Ekman (1984) has demonstrated. The neural "hardware," according to which a smile is a friendly act, is modified by cultural "software," according to which a smile can be a devastating insult, an imbecilic faux pas, or a sign of personal discomfort. Social conventions may require the masking of certain emotions by a still face in specified situations. Until they learn the code, outsiders will be misled by these signals. Children within the community will be expected to learn the rules for displaying emotion and to master the code by which it can be comprehended when others display it. This process of socialization during childhood helps maintain communicative boundaries between populations. Ekman states:

> Display rules are overlearned habits about who can show what emotion to whom and when they can show it. Examples of display rules in many Western cultures are: males should not cry; females (except in a maternal role) should not show anger; losers should not cry in public and winners should not look too happy about winning. We presume that these display rules are learned early in childhood as well as later, that they vary with social class and ethnic background within cultures, as well as across cultures. (1984, 320)

Students of child language have reached beyond the study of acquisition of vocabulary and grammar among linguistically diverse peoples to examine codes of gestural communication and language use as they affect the early environment of the child. They find cross-cultural differences in patterns previously thought to be uniform for the human species. Conversational interaction between mothers and infants, for example, treated by some American observers as a requisite for normal child development, is in fact highly variable across human populations. This was first suggested by Konner (1977, 299–302), who showed that frequency of vocalization between mother and infant varied widely across samples drawn from the Kalahari San, Guatemala, and Boston. More recently, Ochs and Schieffelin (1984, 199) have claimed that the kind of extended mock conversations or play dialogues found among middle-class American mothers interacting with their babies is virtually absent among the Kaluli of Papua New Guinea and the Samoans of Polynesia. Frequency data collected by our own research group (Richman et al. 1988) in Kenya, Mexico, Western Europe, and the United States support the conclusion that mother-infant conversation is a population-specific pattern and is particularly rare among non-Western agricultural societies. Children in the latter contexts acquire different sets of understandings about communicating with their caretakers than those in societies in which face-to-face conversation as we know it is the primary mode.

Conversation in middle-class Anglo-American families is conceptualized as a series of reciprocal exchanges accompanied by eye contact. When babies are engaged in mock conversations, they learn to expect being treated as conversational equals in a visually engaged interaction. These expectations come to define interpersonal relationships in a way that is consistent with broad cultural values such as equality, independence, and honesty. In some non-Western societies such as the Gusii, however, the prevailing values are radically different, and so is the normative meaning of conversation. Eye contact is to be avoided as signifying excessive intimacy, and verbal exchange (as distinct from unilateral commanding and scolding) is largely restricted to persons whose kin relationship defines them as social equals. Parents and children are considered inherently unequal even in adulthood and ideally distant as communicative partners. Gusii parents do not engage young children in mock conversation, partly because they would experience its implications for interpersonal relations as contradicting the terms of the parent-child relationship. Their own code emphasizes the child's communicating its physical needs during infancy and responding appropriately to parental commands during early childhood. In this context, verbal exchange can mean disrespect, and mutual gaze means an uncomfortably assertive closeness. Gusii children accommodate to the parental code and learn to communicate without experiencing conversation in the Western sense of the term.

One consequence of this early communicative experience is that Gusii children are not as responsive as their American counterparts to psychological test and interview techniques, a point made (concerning children of the Kipsigis, who live near the Gusii) by Harkness and Super (1977). The question-and-answer format of psychological assessment, which seems continuous with normal interaction to middle-class Americans, is utterly alien to the experience of a child from rural Kenya and is likely to be taken as menacing or incomprehensible when an adult is conducting the assessment. A similar point has been made by Lewis (1984, 82), who found that in Tokyo nursery schools, where teachers call attention to misbehavior by asking naive questions like "Why are you doing that?" the Japanese children responded to an investigator's nonrhetorical questioning with silence, thinking (apparently) they must have done something wrong to warrant investigation. Thus, the meanings of speech acts acquired in one cultural context can hinder communication in a different context. When children learn to speak according to a cultural code, they acquire social and emotional attitudes along with linguistic forms.

In her work among the Kaluli of Papua New Guinea, Schieffelin (1984) has shown how the learning of speech routines by young children can endow sibling relationships with emotional meanings likely to outlast childhood. Speaking is highly valued among the Kaluli (Ochs and Schieffelin 1984, 288), and mothers deliberately teach their two- to three-year-old children what to say to others, primarily siblings, in certain face-to-face situations. Children are taught to defend themselves against and be assertive to older siblings, and to "feel sorry for" and be helpful to younger ones. Mothers use a particular term of address, *ade,* to model an attitude of pity toward, or concern for, the younger sibling, particularly on the part of older sisters; and that term is used by younger siblings to make appeals to their older siblings throughout their adult lives. Schieffelin emphasizes that when Kaluli use the term *ade* as adults, they do so to evoke the feelings of pity and concern first experienced when they were small children.

This New Guinea example indicates how a cultural formula—that is, a term of address used between siblings in a situation expected to elicit sympathetic concern—can mediate feelings from situations first experienced in childhood to adult situations. In learning the Kaluli language, the child also acquires feelings about persons in situations; these feelings can be summoned up through subsequent use of the verbal formula. Maternal teaching in other cultures may be less explicit and verbal formulas more subtle, but the acquisition of culture-specific feelings along with language during the second and third years of life is likely to prove influential in the emotional development of all humans.

The Maintenance of Order in Face-to-Face Relations

Animal societies regulate the activities of their members in order to prevent disruptive conflict between individuals and to promote adaptive forms of cooperation. There must be regulation of access to resources—food, water, females, and offspring—so that competition does not interfere with group and individual survival. Social organization varies greatly from one species to another, but the minimum common requirement is the maintenance of a rule-governed order in face-to-face relations. Dominance hierarchies that establish precedence and deference rankings among the adult animals of a group operate as the most prevalent form of regulation in primate societies. In humans, however, order in face-to-face relations is achieved through a wider variety of rules specified not only by social rank but by situational context and symbolic medium of communication (e.g., words, behavior, facial expressions). Rules are incorporated in more complex, population-specific codes of conduct.

Human social life owes much of its comfortable predictability to the codes of etiquette by which face-to-face behavior is channeled into conventional forms. Cultural variations in these customs of greeting, conversing, and giving and receiving deference and hospitality have been documented by anthropologists and sociolinguists. From a comparative perspective, all of these forms can be seen as means of controlling potentially disruptive displays of aggression, self-assertion, and sexuality in routine interaction (LeVine 1982, 297–98). From the perspective of each culture, however, its own forms constitute the universal standard of decency, civility, even humanity; the behavior of other peoples following other customs seems uncouth, even animalistic, sometimes justifying their treatment as nonhumans. Erikson (1966) termed as *pseudospeciation* this tendency of humans to treat each other at the population level as other animals do only at the interspecies level. Indeed, one of the greatest ironies of human society is that the very conventions that prevent conflict and promote solidarity within interactional communities tend to divide them from each other (LeVine and Campbell 1972).

Population-specific codes of conduct encompass not only rules for regulating potentially antisocial behavior but also models of virtuous behavior in face-to-face interaction that accord with local standards of morality. These models provide goals toward which parents shape the social behavior of their children. Parents, in other words, want their children to approximate during childhood cultural standards of moral virtue—such as obedience, cooperation, independence, self-assertiveness—according to the particular culture. On the whole, children do so. Differences in the social behavior of school-age children by nation, ethnic group, and social class are, as Kagan (1984, 276) recently stated, among the most robust findings of developmental research. In many cases, these population-specific differences correspond to variations in cultural values.

In the naturalistic behavior observations of the "Six Cultures" study, for example, Whiting and Whiting (1975, 64) found that attention-seeking was more than twice as frequent among American children as among children from agrarian communities in Okinawa, the Philippines, India, Mexico, and Kenya. Studies using the Madsen cooperation board task, which rewards cooperation, have shown Anglo-American and white New Zealand children of primary school age to be less cooperative and more competitive than Mexican-American, Blackfoot Indian, Australian aborigine, Polynesian (Maori and Cook Islands), and Kikuyu children (see Munroe and Munroe 1977; Thomas 1978). Thomas (1978) also found that rural Maori were more cooperative than urban Maori, suggesting that the influence of Western culture is a critical factor. The National Institute of Mental Health study by Caudill (Caudill and Schooler 1973, 331–33) showed that American children at 2½ and 6 years of age engage in more vocal and physical activity and display more positive and negative emotion than their Japanese counterparts. Caudill's hypothesis that the American children would exhibit more independence-related behavior and the Japanese more interdependent behavior of the type called *amae* in the Japanese language was confirmed by the statistical findings (333–34). In sum, systematic research indicates that significant population differences exist in the observable social and emotional behavior of preschool and school-age children.

This research shows that samples of American middle-class children and children of closely related cultures seek attention, act competitive instead of cooperative, are vocally and physically active, express emotion, and behave independently—all consistent with American values—more frequently than samples of children of diverse non-Western cultures. There are indications (Caudill and Schooler 1973, 335; Thomas 1978) that some of these differences are diminishing as non-Western communities are influenced by Western values. This body of evidence as a whole is consistent with the hypothesis that child behavior is shaped toward population-specific models of virtue.

The importance of these findings does not depend on an assumption that the child behavior patterns observed are fixed psychological dispositions that will maintain themselves regardless of environmental support. Rather, the findings indicate that the directions of child development, and the behavioral contexts of early experience, vary by culture according to adult standards of conduct. They also show that children of different cultures acquire differing interpersonal skills and strategies, differing rules for emotional expression, and differing standards by which to judge their own behavior.

The behavioral evidence from cross-cultural research conducted so far is only the tip of the iceberg of culturally divergent personality development. For an example of what deeper investigation might show, one has only to examine Doi's (1981) treatment of *amae* as an aspect of personality development in Japan. He argues in effect that the behavioral expressions of dependence and independence Caudill found to differentiate Japanese from American children have their counterparts in behavior patterns manifesting themselves in adult work, family, and psychotherapy settings, profoundly affecting the ways in which interpersonal relations are experienced. The investigation of hypotheses at this deeper level represents a serious challenge for future research.

Conclusions from the Population-Level Evidence

I have argued that adaptive patterns of reproduction, communication, and face-to-face relations in the human species are organized primarily at the population level as demographic regimes, linguistic codes, and social conventions. These normative codes, cultural models *for* behavior, constitute the proximate environment in which children are raised, operating to shape the distribution of parental and child behavior around central tendencies within a population. The evidence for cross-population variation in these central tendencies is abundant and strong. It suggests not that population-specific behavior is uniform but that it has been influenced toward the common ideals of a local community or people. There is a smaller but equally consistent body of evidence suggesting that these factors deeply affect the meanings of the child's relationships with siblings and parents, the rules forbidding certain emotional expressions, and parental expectations for child behavior and that these cultural meanings, rules, and expectations in turn affect the overt behavior of children.

At the population level, then, existing empirical evidence supports rather than discredits the influence of early experience on behavior and development. Those who have reached the opposite conclusion have focused on individual differences within populations and have made restrictive assumptions such as irreversibility a central part of the hypothesis. They have, in my opinion, underestimated the theoretical significance of the cross-cultural evidence and overestimated the power of available research tools for validly identifying individual differences in relatively homogeneous samples. We are currently at a stage in research on this problem at which it might be said that our methods work at the epidemiological level but not in the prediction of individual cases.

No critical period for the enculturation of the child has been identified in the research conducted so far. We are not in a position to specify the age at which children must acquire population-specific competencies or behavioral dispositions or to indicate what would happen to children raised for their first two or three years in one cultural environment and then changed to another. But the evidence reviewed above indicates that central tendencies in observed behavior vary in accordance with cultural values even in the first years and continue to do so as children grow up in their respective, relatively consistent cultural environments. The exact contributions of early and later learning to culturally valued mature performance may be clarified through future research, but it is not too early to claim that learning during the transition from infancy to early childhood makes a difference.

The Self and Its Development

The human organism acquires a mental organization that corresponds in many ways to the population-specific cultural codes of conduct discussed above, regulating behavior at the individual level as culture does at the population level. This mental organization is partly constituted by its cultural environment—particularly in its conceptual lexicon, images and models, rules and standards—but it is not simply a reflection of culture. The mental organization uniquely operates from the perspective of the self, regulating the behavior of a particular person who is socially recognized as responsible for his or her actions and who subjectively experiences himself or herself as the source of intentions and feelings. Public representations are translated by social communication into personal ones (Sperber 1985), but in the process they are transformed by their relevance to the self of a particular person at a specific stage of development, with a unique history, in a distinctive situation. Thus, enculturation contributes to the formation and constitution of self-representations but does not fully determine how they will be used by individuals.

The self as culturally constituted is a topic of current anthropological interest. Following the lead of Hallowell (1955), anthropologists have taken the self to be a universal of human psychology, representing personal continuity in experience, memory, and social identity while varying in its contents across cultures. As I have stated· elsewhere, "However collectivist the ideology of a group may be, the subjective experience of adults distinguishes between actions of the self as opposed to another, and the affects of pride and shame are distributed accordingly" (LeVine 1982, 295). At the same time, "Cultures vary in the attributes of the ideal self over the life course, in the actions with which pride and shame are associated and in expectancies for autonomy or interdependence in the domains of social action" (1982, 295).

The ethnographic literature on the self emerging in recent years has been summarized by LeVine and White (1986, 36–43). Some of the most important findings are relevant here. The dualisms of Western thought are rarely encountered in non-Western belief systems. More specifically, many non-Western cultures do not recognize the traditional (Western) psychological dichotomies of mind and body, thought and feeling, morality and intelligence, person and situation. Thus, emotional reactions may be viewed as located in bodily organs or social situations rather than attributed to psychological states (Lutz and White 1986). Intelligence may be seen as a product of moral virtue, impossible in a bad person. Smooth social relations may be seen as a prerequisite to good health. Religion, psychotherapy, and medicine may be virtually indistinguishable in theory and practice. In such a context, the self cannot be represented as it is in Western societies.

A second major finding is that autonomy is rarely considered the prime goal of personal development among non-Western peoples and that various forms of interdependence and connectedness are taken for granted as desirable end points for the self at many stages of life. Here, the gap between modern Western thought and that of many others, ranging from Japanese to Africans, is so great that detailed ethnographic explication is needed to prove the point to Western readers that for people of other cultures, the embeddedness of the self in a social matrix is prior to and more valued than the pursuit of personal self-interest and may preclude the desirability of a self that transcends social relations (Shweder and Bourne 1984).

Related to the other two is a third general finding: given the absence of Western dualism and the presence of a sociocentric definition of self, a separate domain of psychological discourse—including a vocabulary of subjective mental states and processes—is often missing (see White and Kirkpatrick 1985). From data such as these, anthropologists have concluded that the experience of self among the peoples they have studied, although difficult to comprehend fully, is radically different from that of Westerners. Just *how* different is a matter of some dispute (Spiro 1984), but there is little doubt that difference pervades a wide range of preferences, aversions, defense mechanisms, emotional responses, self-evaluations, and moral feelings.

Even lacking direct evidence, we can assert that the early acquisition of population-specific social and communicative behaviors in children (reviewed above) is symptomatic of divergent trends in the development of self. Caudill and Schooler (1973) drew this conclusion from their comparison of Japanese and American children, and it is consistent with the findings on cross-cultural differences in cooperation, attention-seeking, and emotional expressions— namely, that the overt social behaviors indicate an early acquisition of self-representations that are as varied at the population level as their observable counterparts. Cultural models define the goals for personal development, and each population normally provides a series of age-graded experiences guided toward those goals, permitting the acquisition of cultural representations as part of the self. The process of enculturation is goal corrected in that the child may spontaneously behave in accordance with the cultural norms for a particular age; if he or she does not, parents and others provide the corrective feedback, pressure, or instruction to facilitate age-appropriate performance in accordance with cultural standards. There may be several alternative pathways through which a child acquires the behavioral performance and the aspect of self-representation that goes with it. The transition from infancy to early childhood, in which speech and codes for affective expression are just being acquired, is an important period for the development of the self in any population. The contextual study of children at this age should be high on the future research agenda in the child development field.

References

Brim, O. G., and J. Kagan, eds. 1980. *Constancy and change in human development.* Cambridge, Mass.: Harvard University Press.

Caldwell, J. C. 1982. *Theory of fertility decline.* New York: Academic.

Caudill, W., and C. Schooler. 1973. Child behavior and child rearing in Japan and the United States: An interim report. *Journal of Nervous and Mental Disease* 157:323–38.

Clarke, A. M., and A. D. Clarke. 1976. *Early experience: Myth and evidence.* New York: Free Press.

Curtin, P. 1964. *The image of Africa: British ideas and action, 1780–1850.* Madison: University of Wisconsin Press.

Doi, T. 1981. *The anatomy of dependence.* 2d ed. New York: Harper & Row.

Dunn, J. 1983. Sibling relationships in early childhood. *Child Development* 54:787–811.

Dunn, J., and C. Kendrick. 1982. *Siblings: Love, envy and understanding.* Cambridge, Mass.: Harvard University Press.

Ekman, P. 1984. Expression and the nature of emotion. In *Approaches to emotion.* Edited by K. Scherer and P. Ekman. Hillsdale, N.J.: Erlbaum.

Erikson, E. 1966. *Ontogeny of ritualization in man*. Philosophical Transactions of the Royal Society of London, vol. 251, series B: 337–49.

Feiring, C., and M. Lewis. 1984. Changing characteristics of the U.S. family: Implications for family networks, relationships and child development. In *Beyond the dyad*. Edited by M. Lewis. New York: Plenum.

Gould, S. 1981. *The mismeasure of man*. New York: Norton.

Hallowell, A. I. 1955. *Culture and experience*. Philadelphia: University of Pennsylvania Press.

Harkness, S., and C. Super. 1977. Why African children are so hard to test. In *Issues in cross-cultural research*. Edited by L. Adler. *Annals of the New York Academy of Sciences* 285:326–31.

Herskovits, M. 1948. *Man and his works*. New York: Knopf.

———. 1955. *Cultural anthropology*. New York: Knopf.

Kagan, J. 1984. *The nature of the child*. New York: Basic Books.

Kamin, L. 1974. *The science and politics of IQ*. Hillsdale, N.J.: Erlbaum.

Konner, M. 1977. Infancy among the Kalahari Desert San. In *Culture and infancy*. Edited by P. Leiderman, S. Tulkin, and A. Rosenfeld. New York: Academic.

Lamb, M., and B. Sutton-Smith. 1982. *Sibling relationships: Their nature and significance across the lifespan*. Hillsdale, N.J.: Erlbaum.

LeVine, R. 1981. Psychoanalytic theory and the comparative study of human development. In *Handbook of cross-cultural human development*. Edited by R. Munroe, R. Munroe, and B. Whiting. New York: Garland.

———. 1982. *Culture, behavior and personality*. New York: Aldine.

———. 1983. Fertility and child development: An anthropological approach. In *Child Development and International Development*. Edited by D. Wagener. *New Directions for Child Development* 20. San Francisco: Jossey-Bass.

LeVine, R., and D. Campbell, 1972. *Ethnocentrism*. New York: Wiley.

LeVine, R., and M. White. 1986. *Human conditions: The cultural basis of educational development*. London: Routledge & Kegan Paul.

Lewis, G. 1984. Cooperation and control in Japanese nursery schools. *Comparative Education Review* 28:69–84.

Lutz, C., and G. White. 1986. The anthropology of emotions. *Annual Review of Anthropology* 15:405–36.

Mead, M. 1963. Socialization and enculturation. *Current Anthropology* 4:184–188.

Miller, J. G. 1978. *Living systems*. New York: McGraw-Hill.

Munroe, R. L., and R. H. Munroe. 1977. Cooperation and competition among East African and American children. *Journal of Social Psychology* 101:145–46.

Ochs, S., and B. Schieffelin. 1984. Language acquisition and socialization: Three developmental stories and their implications. In *Culture theory*. Edited by R. Shweder and R. LeVine. Cambridge: Cambridge University Press.

Richman, A., R. A. LeVine, R. S. New, G. A. Howrigan, B. Welles-Nystrom, and S. E. LeVine. 1988. Maternal behavior to infants in five cultures. In *Parental behavior in diverse societies*. Edited by R. A. LeVine, P. M. Miller, and M. M. West. *New Directions for Child Development* 40. San Francisco: Jossey-Bass.

Riesman, P. 1982. On the irrelevance of child rearing methods for the formation of personality: An analysis of childhood, personality and values in two African communities. *Culture, Medicine and Psychiatry* 7:103–29.

Schieffelin, B. 1984. Ade: A sociolinguistic analysis of a relationship. In *Language in use*. Edited by J. Baughman and J. Scherzer. Englewood Cliffs, N.J.: Prentice-Hall.

Shweder, R. 1979. Rethinking culture and personality theory. Part 1, A critical examination of two classical postulates. *Ethos* 7:255–78.

Shweder, R., and E. Bourne. 1984. Does the concept of the person vary cross-culturally? In *Culture theory*. Edited by R. Schweder and R. LeVine. Cambridge: Cambridge University Press.

Sivard, R. 1985. *Women: A world survey*. Washington: D.C., World Priorities.

Sperber, D. 1985. Anthropology and psychology, Toward an epidemiology of representations. *Man* 20:73–89.

Spiro, M. 1984. Some reflections on cultural determinism and relativism. In *Culture theory*. Edited by R. Shweder and R. LeVine. Cambridge: Cambridge University Press.

Thomas, D. 1978. Cooperation and competition among children in the Pacific Islands and New Zealand: The school as an agent of social change. *Journal of Research and Development in Education* 12:88–95.

White, G., and Kirkpatrick, J. eds. 1985. *Person, self and experience: Exploring Pacific ethnopsychologies*. Berkeley: University of California Press.

Whiting, B., and J. Whiting. 1975. *Children of six cultures*. Cambridge, Mass.: Harvard University Press.

Wilson, E. 1975. *Sociobiology*. Cambridge, Mass.: Harvard University Press.

World Bank. 1987. *World development report 1987*. New York: Oxford University Press.

6 Self-Perception in Infancy

GEORGE BUTTERWORTH

The starting point for this chapter on the development of self through perception is Gibson's (1966, 1979) ecological theory of direct perception. It offers some new ways of approaching fundamental issues on the development of self and raises the question whether the self-concept may have its roots in processes of sensory perception. According to Gibson's direct realist theory, perception involves detecting the nature of the relationship between the organism and the environment. His ecological approach is founded upon the premise that perception has two poles, subjective and objective, specified in sensory information itself in terms of the variant and invariant properties of sensory stimulation. Invariant properties of stimulation correspond to the unchanging aspects of the environment, while an important subset of the variants of stimulation has subjective reference since these variants are transformations of sensory stimulation that occur as a consequence of the observer's movement.

This chapter will distinguish between two aspects of self: the existential self, or "I," and the empirical self, or "me," in James' (1890) terms. The existential self is defined as the experiencer or the agent of activity, while the me is the empirical, or categorical, self—the sum total of one's constituent parts, including the body and possessions. Damon and Hart's (1988) comprehensive analysis of James' distinctions between the I and the me will be helpful here. The I is experienced through four kinds of self-awareness: an awareness of agency, from which is derived personal autonomy; an awareness of distinctness, from which is derived a sense of individuality; an awareness of continuity in time, from which is derived the stability of self; and a capacity for reflection on self, from which is derived a sense of personal meaning. These four components make up the self as the *subject* of experience. The primary constituents of the me include a hierarchy of attributes ranging from the material (bodily) self through the social (personality, roles) and cognitive characteristics of the individual. The I-me combination gives a comprehensive framework for theorizing on the self-concept—a framework which will be followed in tracing the origins of self in infancy.

For an account of the origins of self through perception, the most fundamental implication of Gibson's direct realist approach is that the initial infant-environment relation, generally described as an "adualistic confusion" in so many developmental theories (e.g., Piaget 1954), is replaced by a more appropriate stress on the complementarity of infant and environment, with no implication of fusion with the physical or social milieu. In Gibson's terminology, information that specifies the self is called propriospecific, while information that specifies objects and events in the environment is called exterospecific. He argues that self-specifying information is a general function of perceptual systems and that all the senses are both proprioceptive and exteroceptive. Proprioception can be understood as a general form of self sensitivity. Evidence will be presented in this chapter to suggest that the perceptual precursors of the self-concept are to be found in the structured sensory stimulation available to proprioceptive systems.

Mirror Self-Recognition Studies

Before turning to the main thesis of this chapter—namely, that self-knowledge originates in processes of sensory perception—it will be useful to review briefly the literature on the development of self in infancy. Most research on the development of the self-concept in babies has used the mirror self-recognition task pioneered by Gallup (1970) with primates, and this might seem the prototypical case of self-perception. Mirrors, of course, offer self-perception by turning back the reflected light onto its source. But mirror self-recognition is not a simple case of perception; it is not the prototypical case of self-awareness that a casual examination might imply. Rather, it requires cognitive development, experience with mirrors, and perhaps other conditions that will be hinted at later in this paper before self-recognition will develop. Self-knowledge as exemplified by studies using mirrors may nevertheless form a convenient point of departure because it enables a distinction between the information contained in re-reflected light that must be attributed to self and the more elementary idea that information available in sensory stimulation may allow self-perception from an early age.

Using the methods developed by Gallup (1970) on mirror recognition of self in chimpanzees and other primates, a number of studies have been published in recent years on the development of mirror recognition in babies. A technique, similar to that of the monkey studies, involving surreptitious marking of the face of the baby is often used. Additional data, particularly relevant to understanding how the contingency of the image is related to self-recognition, come from delayed video-feedback (Lewis and Brooks-Gunn 1979). The age at which babies reach to the mark on the face after it is seen in a mirror is taken as evidence for the development of self-recognition. There is no need to refer to these studies extensively here, because several good reviews already exist (see Anderson 1984; Cicchetti et al., in this volume; Damon and Hart 1982, 1988; Harter 1983; Lewis and Brooks-Gunn 1979).

There is reasonable agreement that self-recognition by distinctive features in human infants develops in the second year of life, at around fifteen months, as revealed by self-directed behavior. Evidence for a contribution of cognitive developmental processes to mirror self-recognition comes from a number of sources. Bertenthal and Fisher (1978) found that six-month-old babies would observe themselves in a mirror and detect the contingency between their own action and the reflection, as if they understood the causal relation between their own action and the contingent image. From about ten months, babies became able to adjust their actions, using information reflected in mirrors. Adjustments were initially directed to the body, such as removing a hat, but the babies could eventually grasp an object placed out of the direct field of view, on the basis of its reflection. These behaviors are said to reveal a further cognitive advance since they require the infant to distinguish between contingent movements of the self and movements of others in the mirror-image. Not until age fifteen months did infants remove rouge from the nose, the first evidence that the infant recognizes self as an object of experience, based on recognition of facial features. This sequence of mirror-directed behaviors has been correlated with cognitive development in Piaget's six sensorimotor stages of object permanence.

There is also a general suggestion that prior to self-recognition, as measured by rouge removal, infants often behave to the reflected image in a social fashion, as if viewing another child, without referring the image back to self. The social nature of the response to the mirror-image may be an important component of eventually acquired self-recognition for it may indicate that one component of self-concept development is the perception of others as social objects. In classical socially based accounts of self-concept development, such as Baldwin's (1902), the process of imitation plays a central role. He said, "My sense of myself grows by my imitation of you and my sense of yourself grows in terms of myself" (p. 185). One factor that may require further consideration, therefore, is whether processes in perception may underlie the ability to imitate and hence contribute a social dimension to the development of the self-concept.

Table 1 summarizes the main stages of infant self-recognition as revealed by mirror studies and by the contemporary technique of contingent or delayed video-recorded feedback (see table 1). Further evidence for a cognitive component in mirror self-recognition tasks comes from studies of mentally

Table 1. Summary of Main Stages in Mirror and Video Self Recognition Tasks during Infancy

Developmental Stage	Age	Characteristics
Unlearned attraction to images of others.	3–8 months	Interest in mirror reflection; approaches, touches, smiles, behaves "socially" to reflection.
Self as permanent object	8–12 months	Aware of stable categorical features of self; locates objects attached to body, using mirror image; differentiates contingent from noncontingent videotape recordings of self.
Self-other differentiation	12–15 months	Uses mirror to locate others in space; differentiates own videoimage from that of others.
Facial feature detection	Begins at about 15 months; well established by 2 years	Recognition based on self-specific features; success in "rouge removal" tasks. Correlates with Piaget's Stage VI in object concept development.

Source: Based on data reviewed in Bertenthal and Fisher (1983), Damon and Hart (1988), Harter (1983), and Lewis and Brooks-Gunn (1979).

retarded babies. These show that delays in mirror self-recognition parallel delays in cognitive development. For example, Mans, Cicchetti, and Sroufe (1978) showed that not until three to four years of age did the majority of their sample of Down syndrome children succeed in removing rouge from the nose in a mirror test (see also Cicchetti et al. in this volume).

Cross-species comparisons have also implicated cognitive developmental factors in mirror self-recognition. According to Gallup (1982), humans, chimpanzees, and orangutans are the only species to recognize themselves in mirrors on the rouge removal task (note, however, that the gorilla, another higher primate, apparently does not). Thus, it can be argued that although mirror self-recognition occurs by means of perception, it is nevertheless a process that requires a fairly high degree of cognitive development before the mirror-image will be attributed to self.

These studies therefore suggest that cognitive development, at least as measured in terms of Piaget's sensorimotor stages, contributes to the development of mirror self-awareness. However, the precise interrelationships between perception of the contingent nature of the mirror-image, self-identification by means of distinctive features, comprehension of the identity of the reflected image, attribution of the reflected image to self, developments in memory, reasoning, and the contribution of social experience have yet to be unraveled empirically. It seems reasonable to agree with Gallup (1982) that the level of self-awareness which mirrors self-recognition tasks is cognitively advanced and not explicable by recourse to sensory perception alone.

Visual Proprioception and Posture

Let us consider a more fundamental source of information for the visual perception of self than the mirror reflection. Gibson's (1966) emphasis on the intermodal properties of information available to the senses led him to coin the term *visual proprioception* to draw attention to the role of vision in providing information for movement of the self, over and above the traditionally recognized interoceptive information given by the mechanical and vestibular systems. Visual proprioception specifies self-movement by dynamic transitions of the optic array that occur when an observer moves through a stable space. As the observer moves through a textured visual environment, light reflected from the surroundings is projected as a textured flow field at the eye, outward from a stationary central point. The optic flow field is said to specify that an observer is moving in the direction given by the stationary focus of the optic flow pattern.

Under conditions of the natural ecology (where the surroundings may be considered stable), such a flow pattern can only occur when the observer is moving; hence, it (the pattern) is sufficient to specify the distinction between self and "the world." Gibson argued that the optic flow pattern is a structured form of sensory information. The developing child need only attend to the available information; there is no necessity to construct the invariants or to learn what the visual flow pattern specifies as a result of extensive experience. Gibson suggests that posture and locomotion are controlled through visual proprioception and that this control system may be innate. Until the early 1970s, little empirical information existed on the origins of visual proprioception. It seemed possible that optic flow patterns might become informative through the infant's developing mobility, and hence be learned, rather than being *inherently* informative (as Gibson maintained).

Lee and Aronson (1974) were the first to show that infants use visual information to monitor their posture. Babies who had recently learned to stand were tested standing on a rigid floor within a movable room comprising three walls and a ceiling. The infants faced the interior end wall, and the whole structure, except the floor, was moved so that the end wall slowly approached or receded. Babies compensated for a nonexistent loss of balance signaled by the optic flow pattern (generated by the movement of the surroundings) and consequently fell in the direction appropriate to the plane of instability specified. If the end wall moved away from the baby, the infant fell forward; if the wall moved toward the baby, the infant fell over backward.

Subsequent studies demonstrated that vision does not acquire its proprioceptive function as a result of motor development. Butterworth and Hicks (1977) found that infants too young to walk would nevertheless compensate for visually specified instability when seated in the moving room. The research has been extended to prelocomotor infants by Pope (1984), who showed that even before babies can crawl they are responsive to discrepant visual feedback. He investigated the role of visual proprioception in the maintenance of a stable head posture in infants as young as two months old supported in an infant chair. Babies too young to be able to sit without support and certainly not capable of independent locomotion nevertheless will make directionally appropriate compensatory movements of the head under conditions of discrepant visual feedback.

Further studies showed that information arriving in the periphery of vision is particularly important for maintaining postural stability. Pope (1984) showed that movement in the center of the visual field did not result in postural adjustment, whereas the slightest movement in the periphery of vision is sufficient to result in complete loss of stability when a posture is first acquired. Bertenthal, Dunn, and Bai (1986) replicated this finding. They showed that movement of the side walls was as disruptive as movement of the whole room in relation to infants age twelve to fifteen months who were facing the interior end wall of the room. By contrast, movement of the end wall alone had much less disruptive an effect on posture, which again suggests that the important information for postural control may fall on the periphery of vision.

Such data may be interpreted in terms of the theory of "two visual systems," whereby peripheral vision is "body centered" and maps onto a somatotopically organized representation of space (Paillard 1974; Trevarthen 1968), whereas focal vision is thought to be "object centered" and outer directed. Hence, according to this theory, postural adjustments occur under the nonecological conditions of the moving room because the material, embodied self is implicated in the normal adjustments of posture that ordinarily bring about the optic flow pattern. The obvious moving-room experiment that still needs to be published is with neonates, but there is good reason to suppose that the infant's sensitivity to the optic flow pattern will prove to be innate.[1]

The implication is that the optic flow pattern is inherently informative about movements of the infant in relation to the environment. From the earliest age, the infant seems to make use of the optic flow pattern to maintain the head under a stable posture, as if the flow field is a form of prestructured feedback

1. Francois Jouen (pers. comm. 1985), of the University of Paris, has evidence for visual-vestibular interactions among one-month-old infants, which may suggest that visual proprioceptive control of posture is an innate, intrinsic coordination. Scania de Schonen (pers. comm. 1985), of the University of Marseilles, reports that it is possible to elicit the stepping reflex in a newborn baby placed in a "moving" room.

informing the perceiver about the relation between his or her own motion and the environment. It can therefore be argued that the infant does make use of available visual information to specify a distinction between self and environment.

How can these studies be related to the problem of self? First, the moving-room studies suggest that Gibson was correct in arguing for an implicit polarity in perception. That is, these studies may be taken as evidence for a differentiated self/nonself starting point for development in which an existential basis for the I (in William James' terms) is available. The I is the experiencer, the agent—that aspect of self that acts in the world. Optic flow pattern may be considered to inform the infant of his or her own agency in the natural ecology. Of course, the moving-room studies demonstrate that the infant does not yet have objective conceptual knowledge of self, since babies lose balance when in fact they are objectively stable. The acquisition of relatively autonomous self-control over posture may nevertheless be a function of experience of proprioceptive feedback. Although the infant is limited in the ability to evaluate or reflect upon the information within the optic array that specifies a stable posture, the basis for development of reflective self-consciousness may be contained in the structure of sensory stimulation itself.

This argument can be elaborated more satisfactorily by looking at data from moving-room experiments in relation to both the infant's experience of various postures and the onset of locomotion. These show that visual proprioceptive information becomes integrated in development with higher-order forms of self-control, as demonstrated by looking at the influence of postural experience on the infant's response to discrepant visual feedback.

Pope (1984) studied the influence of discrepant visual feedback on head control in babies aged two to seven months in a moving-room task. Infants were seated with support in an infant seat, and head movements in relation to movements of the surround were measured. The slightest movement of the head in relation to the movement of the surround showed up in the video recordings. Pope found that infants made a directionally appropriate compensatory movement of the head from two months (the youngest age tested), with no significant decrement in response intensity until approximately seven months, when there was a significant decrease in the effects of discrepant visual feedback. Experience in sitting was *not* responsible for this decline; Pope was able to demonstrate that babies with equal amounts of sitting experience were differentially responsive, depending on whether they could crawl or not. That is, the onset of crawling coincides with a significant decrease in sensitivity to the moving surround, relative to the precrawling level. Babies who can crawl may be said to have acquired a new level of autonomous, or "self," control of activity that may override to some extent the misleading visual information to which they are subjected in the moving room. It is as if the infant has gained sufficient autonomous control over posture—perhaps by calibrating the initially unstable head control system against information from the visual surround—for independent movement to be possible. This model suggests that development proceeds from control by specification of self-stability to autonomous self-control.

Butterworth and Cicchetti (1978) showed that babies' length of experience with the sitting or standing posture was negatively correlated with susceptibility to misleading visual feedback. The maximum disruption by discrepant visual feedback occurred during the three-month period after each posture was acquired, and declined thereafter. Normal infants and Down syndrome babies were matched for their experience of the sitting and standing postures and tested in the standard moving-room situation. Figure 1 summarizes the data, using a weighted averaging technique of scoring. A score of 300 would indicate that an infant fell over on every trial, 200 indicates that the average intensity of response is a stagger, and 100 indicates that a slight sway occurred. Zero indicates no noticeable postural adjustment.

The data show clearly that normal babies and Down syndrome babies become increasingly able to withstand the effects of room movement. The

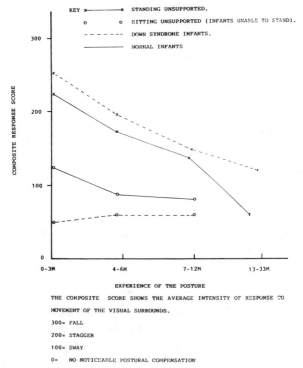

Figure 6.1. Experience of the posture.

upright, bipedal standing posture is the most unstable in the face of misleading visual feedback. During the first three months of standing upright, the infants would fall over on virtually every trial when the room moved. However, at about 15 months of age, normal infants develop sufficient reflective self-awareness to turn to see "who has made the room move" (Butterworth and Cicchetti 1978). That is, the infant does not attribute an independent cause to the discrepant visual feedback until well into the second year of life. Until then, for postural stability, he or she behaves as if dependent, to a greater or lesser degree according to the particular posture, on the information currently available to perception. Note that adults placed in a moving room in an unfamiliar posture, such as balancing on a beam, also lose their balance under conditions of discrepant visual feedback (Lee and Lishman 1975). Clearly, even though the adult is presumably in possession of a self-concept, there is still a powerful effect of visually specified instability. The data suggest that, under conditions of the normal ecology, perceptual specification of self is embedded within congruent self-knowledge. It is not a form of information for self that we outgrow.

An interesting further avenue that may be explored concerns the effects of different postures on susceptibility to the effect of discrepant visual feedback. The Down syndrome babies were significantly less responsive than normals in the seated posture and significantly more responsive than normals in the standing posture. When tested in the two postures, the same Down syndrome infants would also show extreme stability or instability in the face of discrepant visual feedback. That is, the particular posture the child was in determined the degree of sensitivity to the visual flow pattern.

It might be argued that these experiments have nothing to do with the development of self-control and that the phenomena they explore may better be described as reflexive processes, since not until relatively late in development do we observe the acquisition of mechanisms capable, at least in part, of overruling the misleading sensory input to which the infant involuntarily responds. However, to argue thus might be to ignore the fact that, under normal conditions, the optic flow pattern would occur only under circumstances where the infant has moved. Since we have suggested that the meaning of the optic flow pattern is not something that is learned, we might wish to argue that it is inherently goal directed: it serves to maintain a stable posture. The optic flow pattern is not a stimulus that gives rise to a reflex response in the traditional sense. Rather, it both provides a motive for corrective behavior (by informing about loss of postural stability) and is goal directed in that it specifies when a well-controlled posture has been achieved. It is an instinctive mechanism which, we may conjecture from our evidence, presupposes a self in motion.

The moving-room studies have been examined at length because they do seem to offer strong evidence for an existential self specified in perception from the earliest age. This is not the only evidence one can bring forward for the self as an agent of activity in infancy. Many other examples from research on early infant perception suggest that development begins from a differentiated self-object relationship for which an existential self may be reasonably postulated. Relevant studies range from research on neonates' responses to "looming," in which newborn infants make defensive responses to a visual stimulus on a collision course (Bower, Broughton, and Moore 1970), to research on auditory-visual coordination in newborns (Castillo and Butterworth 1981), which demonstrates that newborns localize a sound in visual space. Each of these examples implies a distinction between self as experiencer and the external objects of experience.

Origins of the Categorical Self

The second part of this chapter will review some evidence for the perception of the categorical self in early infancy, the me, as opposed to the I of our previous discussion. Church (1970) suggests that early evidence for self-awareness can be found in the baby's response to a cleaning tissue draped over the upper part of the face to occlude the eyes. He describes a developmental sequence from no response, to vocal fussing, to ineffectual reaching in the area of the head, to removal of the tissue by wiping it away (typically at about five months).

Response to tickling, by a movement of the body or change in facial expression to frowning or smiling, is observed between one and four months. Visual localization of the tickled part of the body is said to begin at about four months, and manual localization is said to begin at about six months. Church also comments on the baby's discovery of the body through a fairly stable sequence of self-exploratory behaviors. The hands, the feet, all form objects of intense interest to the baby in the first few months of life, and it seems reasonable to argue that these behaviors reveal awareness of a categorical self: The baby's response to sensory stimulation is self-referent; it relates to "me" from the baby's point of view. Although Church considered the newborn baby's attempts to remove the tissue from the face as reflexive, it is interesting to note that a varied sequence of behavior is observed if the infant's initial attempts are unsuccessful. The sequence includes marked head and body movements which may ensure that the airways are not restricted. Gunther (1961) also describes vigorous pushing movements of the newborn infant when there is danger of suffocation while feeding. Thus, it can be said that behaviors whose goal is self-preservation can be observed in the neonate.

Kravitz, Goldenberg, and Neyhus (1978) asked 100 mothers to keep a diary and note the order in which their babies began to explore themselves tactually by grasping themselves between two or more fingers of one hand. They found that finger-to-finger exploration occurred first (at a median age of twelve weeks), then finger to body (fifteen weeks), then finger to knee (eighteen weeks), finger to foot (nineteen weeks), and a form of tactual self-exploration that Freud would have been interested in—fingers to genitals—at twenty-three weeks. This evidence suggests that there is differentiated tactual self-awareness early in life.

A challenging and very early example of self-awareness comes from a paper by Martin and Clark (1982). They noted the well-documented tendency of newborns to cry when they hear the cries of another baby in the nursery and wondered what would be the effect on the infant of hearing his or her own cries. They tested forty-seven newborns in the first day after birth, in a counterbalanced design in which calm or crying babies heard either their own cry or the cry of another newborn baby. They measured the total amount of crying in a four-minute post-test. The results showed that infants who were calm at the start of the test and heard the cry of another baby vocalized significantly more than infants who heard their own cry. Infants who were crying at the start of the test cried less after the sound of their own cry than after the sound of another baby crying. These data, therefore, confirm the often noted phenomenon that babies cry when they hear the cries of another baby. But the research results go beyond previous findings in suggesting that the newborn infant is somehow able to recognize its own vocalizations and discriminate them from those of other babies. It is difficult to explain this phenomenon away as a simple primary circular reaction to an undifferentiated crying sound, as Piaget (1954) might have done. On the basis of further experiments, Martin and Clark suggest that infants' response to crying is both species-, peer-, and self-specific. If this is correct, then we may argue for the existence of auditory specification of self from birth, although we admittedly have little notion of how this comes about!

Kravitz et al. (1978) also studied the order of emergence of hand-to-head movements in twelve newborn babies in the first day of life and noted the order of onset of tactual exploration of the mouth, face, head, ear, nose, and eyes. They noted an emerging order of tactual self-exploration in the first few hours of life, beginning with the mouth (at a median of 167 minutes after birth), then the face (192 minutes), head (380 minutes), ear (469 minutes), nose (598 minutes), and eyes (1,491 minutes). Tactual self-exploration was observed almost exclusively in the waking state. Here, we have evidence for differentiated self-awareness in the neonate. In fact, Kravitz et al. suggest that these behaviors occur soon after birth because they are a continuation of similar movements in utero. The authors report finger-to-mouth movements as soon as seven minutes after birth, and these they believe to be the first examples of tactual self-exploration. They suggest that tactual self-exploration may be important in the elaboration of the body schema.

Further evidence for self-awareness comes from the phenomenon of neonatal hand-mouth coordination, which we (Butterworth and Hopkins 1988) have been studying in collaboration with Brian Hopkins of the University of Groningen. In this study of self-directed behavior in neonates, we filmed the spontaneous motor activity of seventeen newborn babies (mean age 79 hours), using a split-screen video system. The infants were placed on their backs and filmed for approximately five minutes. The video recordings were then analyzed by two observers acting independently, who noted the first episode in which the hand came into the region of the face and nineteen subsequent episodes. For each infant, the observers noted the posture of each hand at the beginning and end of the episode (open, intermediate, closed), of the mouth just before contact (open, intermediate, closed), of the eyes just before contact (open, closed), and of the head and body (facing left, right, at the midline).

The episodes fell into four categories: direct movement of hand to mouth (15 percent), movements stopping short of the face and resulting in no contact (22 percent), movements going to the mouth after contact with the face (20 percent), and contacts with the face that did not terminate in the mouth (43 percent). Statistical analyses revealed that the mouth was significantly more likely to be open throughout the arm movement in the case where the hand goes directly to the mouth than in the three other classes of arm movement. This suggests that the mouth "anticipates" arrival of the hand, even before the arm starts to move. Other analyses revealed that visual guidance of the hand to the mouth may not be necessary for this coordination, since the eyes are equally likely to be closed as open just prior to contact with the mouth. Once the hand touches the mouth, it is withdrawn and there is little evidence of sucking the fingers or of "self-comforting" behaviors. There was no evidence for self-stimulation of the Babkin reflex prior to these episodes, since neither hand is clenched. Finally, the active hand is invariably ipsilateral to the orientation of the head, and right- or left-handed movements to the mouth are equally probable.

The hand can also reliably find the mouth after contact with the perioral region. However, when the hand lands more distantly (e.g., on the nose or ears or eyes), it is no more likely to move toward the mouth than away from it. There is no evidence of rooting after contact, the head is invariably held still, and the hand moves immediately in the direction of the mouth. Again, the majority of movements are ipsilaterally coordinated with the head posture, and the eyes are equally likely to be open or shut. This category of movement does not appear to be reflexive either; it simply seems less "well aimed" than the former.

The mouth is clearly the goal of quite a proportion of the arm movements, and the hand can find its way to the mouth without benefit of visual guidance. Such coordination suggests an innate body schema (or schemata) which relates the hand to the mouth and which may be considered as the basis for the bodily self, or "me." The fact that the coordination is rather specifically between the hand and the oral region suggests that it is not based upon a facial schema. Other forms of neonatal sensorimotor coordination, such as eye-hand coordination (studied by Von Hofsten 1983) or auditory-visual coordination (see Butterworth 1981, for a review), may also be taken as evidence for the existence of a coordinating body schema (or schemata) which ensures that the infant behaves as an organized totality in relation to sensory stimulation. From a developmental point of view, it is also important to note that many of the coordinations present at birth drop out in early development, to reappear later in the first year. It is to these successive reorganizations of basic coordinations that we may wish to turn when offering a theory of the development of the self-concept from its already organized, innate constituents (Mounoud and Vinter 1981).

One final example will illustrate that information for a categorical self may be available by direct sensory perception. Recent evidence shows that babies four to six months of age are sensitive to biomechanical motions specified by "point light walkers" (Fox and McDaniel 1982). Point light walkers are created by placing lights or luminous tape on the head, torso, and limb joints of a person dressed in black who is then filmed in the dark while traversing a path normal to the observer's line of sight. Adults viewing the filmed dots in motion report a compelling experience of seeing a human figure walking. Infants prefer to look at a display showing this biological motion than one in which the same number of dots simply move randomly (Bertenthal et al. 1985), so we may suppose that the infant perceives the moving light display as an animate event. The interesting implications for the development of self come from a suggestion by Bower (1982) in a report of work by Stuart Aitken (a doctoral student at Edinburgh University), who found that babies of about fourteen months prefer to look at a walking point light display of an infant of the same gender as themselves rather than at a point light display of an infant of the opposite sex. Bower suggests that the dynamics in the patterns of movement may be gender typical. Perhaps sex differences in skeletal articulation may lead the infant to perceive the point light display of the same gender as "like me." Further research evidence of this kind could be taken as strong support for the specification of categorical aspects of self in sensory stimulation.

Neonatal Imitation

A final source of evidence for the specification of self through perception comes from studies of neonatal imitation. We have already mentioned that imitation is a favorite vehicle for the many theories which emphasize the contribution of social experience to the child's developing knowledge of self. There is an extensive literature on the development of imitation in babies, and I intend to touch only on recent studies that suggest that a form of imitation may be innate, to round off my argument. (See Meltzoff, in this volume, for an in-depth treatment of imitation.) The report of neonatal imitation by Maratos (1973) was replicated and extended by Meltzoff and Moore (1977), and this research has itself recently been replicated by Vinter (1984) at the University of Geneva. Thus, we have independent sources of evidence for neonatal imitation, and some agreement that imitation of tongue protrusion and mouth opening (gestures not visible to the infant) and of finger movements (visible gestures) is present at birth. Vinter suggests that these abilities drop out at about six weeks of age in the case of hand movement and by about three months for mouth and tongue movements, to reappear at seven months for manual imitation and around one year for facial imitation. The neonatal imitation literature suggests that babies can match visual information from the face or hand of another to kinesthetic information for their own tongue and mouth and that hand movements can also be imitated through visual and/or kinesthetic matching, although the developmental relationship between "early" and "late" forms of imitation remains to be unraveled.

It is possible to understand the neonatal phenomena in terms of the previous discussion of proprioception and the body schema. An innate body schema may authorize the match between visual input and motor output in imitation tasks (Mounoud and Vinter 1981). Meltzoff (1981) has suggested that the ability to imitate "invisible" gestures, such as tongue protrusion, must require an abstract ability to relate the properties of visual sensory input to motor output. This ability is similar, he argues, to that involved in detecting the equivalence of information across sensory modalities. In a series of converging studies, he showed that infants in the first month of life can relate visually perceived shapes to the same shapes perceived through oral-tactual exploration. At some abstract level of description, vision and tactual exploration yields equivalent information for shape. Thus, one way to understand how imitation—a process considered by many to be fundamental to the social elaboration of self—is possible is by reference to its basis in sensory perception and the body schema, as a fundamental prerequisite for the categorical self, or "me."

Conclusion

All of these examples of self-specification through perception can be understood in terms of Gibson's ([1964] 1982) assertion that proprioception is best understood as a general form of self sensitivity, regardless of the modality in which information arrives. In the example of hand-mouth coordination, the fact that the hand can find the mouth without visual guidance suggests that the coordination is based on kinesthetic information alone. In the case of visual proprioception, stability of the body posture clearly is specified to some degree in the optic flow pattern; so again, a postural schema may be involved in mapping visual information to motor activity. Finally, it has also been suggested that neonatal imitation can be explained if sensory information maps onto a body schema in the neonate.

The concept of the body schema is a familiar one in psychology, but it is difficult to define and indeed may be insufficient to describe the mechanisms which control posture. Nevertheless, Bairstow (1986) captures the essential characteristics admirably. He defines a body schema as a superordinate representation at the interface between sensory and motor processes that both externally and internally specify a posture. This definition unifies the various strands of research discussed above, because it provides the necessary link between sensory and motor domains that underlie both existential and categorical aspects of self.

The problem remains, however, of explaining the relationship between the specification of self in perception and the acquisition of reflective self-awareness. How is a concept of self acquired that may continue to be elaborated throughout the life span? Perceptual specification and conceptual knowledge are not at the same level of functioning. All that has been offered so far is an approach to the problem of the origins of self. The suggestion that even elementary sensory perception may be self-referent in a variety of ways allows us to progress beyond the logical impasse presented by totally constructionist (or totally socially determined) theories of self-concept development in which the problem of accounting for the experiencing organism is glossed over. As Ayer (1968) once said:

> If one speaks of the construction of objects out of the flux of experience, it is indeed natural to ask who does the construct-ing and then it would appear that whatever self is chosen for this role must stand outside the construction; it would be con-tradictory to suppose that it constructed itself. . . . To construct either the material or the spiritual self is to do no more than pick out the relations within experiences which make it possible for the concept of a self of this kind to be satisfied and these relations exist whether or not we direct our attention to them. (P. 261)

It is both logically and psychologically entailed that some form of self stands behind experience, and perhaps all that is being said here is that the self originates in the fact that we are embodied (although motivational factors such as "will" might be usefully invoked even among the youngest infants).

However, this is a long way from explaining self-recognition or the advanced forms of reflection on self of which humans are capable. Here, perhaps, one may be permitted to speculate. Mounoud and Vinter (1981) have revised the standard constructionist Piagetian stage theory of sensorimotor development to suggest that there exists a succession of processes that regulate the interaction of the infant and environment. The most basic, and the one that characterizes the initial state of coordination we have been discussing, they call the "sensory" code. This is not the same as Gibsonian terminology, but one can see a close affinity.

The approach carries with it the important assumption that the initial coordination also constitutes the program for later reorganizations of that coordination. A new level of organization, a "perceptual" code, is elaborated from about three months of age, which involves the beginning of representation. Now activity begins to be regulated not only by direct sensory information but also by stored information in memory. At around eight or nine months, a further reorganization is said to occur by an internal coordination of the relations among representations, giving rise to recall from memory, mental imagery, and the beginnings of symbolic thought at about eighteen months. This sequence may be readily mapped into the existing body of knowledge summarized in table 1.

The important theoretical question is how each new level of organization develops out of the preceding one, and this has not been solved. Nevertheless, we may speculate that the infant may store information of adaptive significance by habituating those aspects of sensory information constantly available to sensory perception, including self-specifying information, whether derived from its own activities or obtained in the course of social interaction. This will give a basis of stored information which may form the foundation for self-recognition and, in more elaborated forms, for self-conscious thought. Another developmental progression, a concept of causality, certainly seems necessary for the level of self-awareness attained by organisms who show self-recognition in mirrors. While many organisms and young infants clearly perceive the contingency between their own behavior and its outcome, it seems that only the higher primates have sufficiently elaborated concepts of causality to attribute their own mirror reflections to themselves. The question of how a concept of causality is acquired in development may return to the same basic problem that arises in explaining the origins of the self-concept. Even if causality is perceived directly, as Michotte (1963) maintained, it is still necessary to explain how the relatively advanced understanding of causal relationships arises that is necessary to attribute a perceived mirror-image to self. By the same token, only an organism that already has a concept of its own identity would seem able to identify itself in a mirror.

In conclusion, there is information for self in perception. What is required now is a theory of how successive processes of reorganization transform the product and processes of self-perception into the forms of self-conception that we typically associate with the higher primates and for which we take as evidence self-recognition in mirror tasks.

References

Anderson, J. R. 1984. The development of self recognition: A review. *Developmental Psychobiology* 17 (no. 1): 35–49.

Ayer, A. J. 1968. *The origins of pragmatism,* part 2. London: Macmillan.

Bairstow, P. 1986. Postural control. In *Motor skill development in children: Aspects of coordination and control.* Edited by H. T. A. Whiting and M. G. Wade. Dordrecht: Nijhoff.

Baldwin, J. M. 1902. *Social and ethical interpretations in mental development: A study in social psychology.* New York: Macmillan.

Bertenthal, B. I., S. Dunn, and D. Bai. 1986. Infant's sensitivity to optical flow for specifying motion. Paper presented at the Fifth International Conference on Infant Studies, Los Angeles, April 1986. Abstract in *Infant Behavior and Development* 9:35.

Bertenthal, B. I., and K. W. Fisher. 1978. Development of self recognition in the infant. *Developmental Psychology* 14:44–50.

Bertenthal, B. I., D. R. Proffitt, N. B. Spetner, and M. A. Thomas. 1985. The development of infant sensitivity to biomechanical motions. *Child Development* 56:531–43.

Bower, T. G. R. 1982. *Development in infancy.* 2d ed. San Francisco: Freeman.

Bower, T. G. R., J. Broughton, and M. K. Moore. 1970. Infant responses to approaching objects: An indicator of response to distal variables. *Perception and Psychophysics* 9:193–96.

Butterworth, G. E. 1981. The origins of auditory-visual perception and visual proprioception in human infancy. In *Intersensory perception and sensory integration.* Edited by R. D. Walk and H. L. Pick, Jr. New York: Plenum.

Butterworth, G. E., and D. Cicchetti. 1978. Visual calibration of posture in normal and motor retarded Down syndrome infants. *Perception* 7:513–25.

Butterworth, G. E., and B. Hopkins. 1988. Hand-mouth coordination in the newborn baby. *British Journal of Developmental Psychology* 6 (no. 4): 303–14.

Butterworth, G. E., and L. Hicks. 1977. Visual proprioception and postural stability in infancy: A developmental study. *Perception* 6:255–62.

Castillo, M., and G. E. Butterworth. 1981. Neonatal localisation of a sound in visual space. *Perception* 10:331–38.

Church. J. 1970. Techniques for differential study of cognition in early childhood. In *Cognitive studies,* vol. 1. Edited by J. Hellmuth. New York: Brunner/Mazel, 1–23.

Damon, W., and D. Hart. 1982. The development of self understanding from infancy through adolescence. *Child Development* 53:841–64.

_____. 1988. *Self understanding in childhood and adolescence.* Cambridge: Cambridge University Press.

Fox, R., and C. McDaniel. 1982. The perception of biological motion by human infants. *Science* 218:486–87.

Gallup, G. G. 1970. Chimpanzees: Self recognition. *Science* 167:86–87.

_____. 1982. Self awareness and the emergence of mind in primates. *American Journal of Primatology* 2:237–48.

Gibson, J. J. 1966. *The senses considered as perceptual systems.* Boston: Houghton Mifflin.

_____. 1979. *The ecological approach to visual perception.* Boston: Houghton Mifflin.

_____. [1964] 1982. The uses of proprioception and the detection of propriospecific information. Unpublished paper. Reprinted in *Reasons for realism: Selected essays of James J. Gibson.* Edited by E. Reed and R. Jones. Hillsdale, N.J.: Erlbaum.

Gunther, M. 1961. Infant behaviour at the breast. In *Determinants of infant behaviour,* vol. 1. Edited by B. M. Foss. London: Methuen.

Harter, S. 1983. Developmental perspectives on the self system. In *Handbook of child psychology,* vol. 4. Edited by M. Hetherington. New York: Wiley, 275–385.

James, W. 1890. *The principles of psychology,* vol. 1. New York: Holt.

Kravitz, H., D. Goldenberg, and A. Neyhus. 1978. Tactual exploration by normal infants. *Developmental Medicine and Child Neurology* 20:720–26.

Lee, D., and E. Aronson. 1974. Visual proprioceptive control of standing in human infants. *Perception and Psychophysics* 15:529–32.

Lee, D., and J. R. Lishman. 1975. Visual proprioceptive control of stance. *Journal of Human Movement Studies* 1:87–95.

Lewis, M., and J. Brooks-Gunn. 1979. *Social cognition and the acquisition of self.* New York: Plenum.

Mans, L., D. Cicchetti, and L. A. Sroufe. 1978. Mirror reactions of Down syndrome infants and toddlers: Cognitive underpinnings of self recognition. *Child Development* 49:1247–50.

Maratos, O. 1973. The origin and development of imitation during the first six months of life. Ph.D. thesis, University of Geneva.

Martin, G. B., and R. D. Clark. 1982. Distress crying in neonates: Species and peer specificity. *Developmental Psychology* 18:3–9.

Meltzoff, A. N. 1981. Imitation, intermodal coordination and representation in early infancy. In *Infancy and epistemology: An evaluation of Piaget's theory.* Edited by G. E. Butterworth. Brighton: Harvester.

Meltzoff, A. N., and M. K. Moore. 1977. Imitation of facial and manual gestures by human neonates. *Science* 198:75–78.

Michotte, A. 1963. *The perception of causality.* Translated by T. and E. Miles. London: Methuen.

Mounoud, P., and A. Vinter. 1981. Representation and sensori-motor development. In *Infancy and epistemology: An evaluation of Piaget's theory.* Edited by G. E. Butterworth. Brighton: Harvester.

Paillard, J. 1974. Le traitement des informations spatiales. In *De L'espace corporel a l'espace ecologique.* Edited by Bresson et al. Presses Universitaires de France, 1–63.

Piaget, J. 1954. *The construction of reality in the child.* New York: Basic.

Pope, M. J. 1984. Visual proprioception in infant postural development. Ph.D. thesis, University of Southampton.

Trevarthen, C. 1968. Two visual systems in primates. *Psychologische Forschung* 31:299–377.

Vinter, A. 1984. Imitation, representation et mouvement dans les premieres mois de la vie. Ph.D. thesis, University of Geneva.

Von Hofsten, C. 1983. Foundations for perceptual development. In *Advances in infancy research,* vol. 2. Edited by L. Lipsitt and C. K. Rovee-Collier. Norwood, N.J.: Ablex, 241–61.

7 Foundations for Developing a Concept of Self: The Role of Imitation in Relating Self to Other and the Value of Social Mirroring, Social Modeling, and Self Practice in Infancy

Andrew N. Meltzoff

Questions about the origin and early manifestations of a notion of self have intrigued developmentalists since the founding of the discipline. Tiedemann (1787) and Darwin (1877) provided the first systematic notes on infancy. Among the issues explored by both was the question of when infants could first recognize themselves in a "looking glass" and begin fashioning a self-concept. Both were convinced that by about two years of age infants could recognize themselves and had developed at least a primitive notion of self.

Although it struck Tiedemann and Darwin that infants' reactions before the mirror provided a natural experiment in the psychogenesis of the self, neither was overly concerned about exactly what behaviors should be taken to indicate self-recognition. Tiedemann used the infant's seeming "pleasure" at mirror self-regard to determine that the twenty-one-month-old recognized "that is myself; those features are my own" (quoting from Tiedemann). A modern-day experimentalist would want to check that such "pleasure" would not also be exhibited to other faces with babyish features, inasmuch as these may be pleasing gestalten in themselves (Lorenz 1943), without the recognition that the babyish features belong to oneself. Darwin was intrigued by the dual facts that his infant son turned to look at himself in the mirror when his name was called and also that he systematically exclaimed "ah" when he saw his reflection. Today, we might wonder whether the child could just as easily have been trained to look at the parent in the mirror when the child's name was called. We might also inquire whether the "ah" was a greeting to any familiar face in the mirror, without recognition that the person in the mirror was, in fact, the self.[1]

Preparation of this chapter was supported by grants from the National Institute of Child Health and Human Development (HD-22514) and the MacArthur Foundation. I thank Craig Harris for assistance on the studies, and Patricia Kuhl, Keith Moore, and Craig Harris for thoughtful discussions on the issues addressed here. I am indebted to Alison Gopnik and Patrica Kuhl for valuable comments on an earlier draft.

1. These observers, Darwin especially, did not rely solely on the mirror task to draw inferences about infants' notions of themselves; but for many generations of investigators, the mirror situation became the quintessential task to evaluate the notion of self in the preverbal period.

139

Following Darwin and Tiedemann, many observers in the first half of this century explored when an infant seemed to recognize himself or herself in a mirror, but few (if any) devised a situation that showed with certainty that the infant apprehended the identity between the virtual self in the mirror and the true self that was the origin of this reflection. A breakthrough in mirror research came when Gallup (1970), using chimpanzees, and Amsterdam (1972), using infants, devised a new procedure for operationalizing self-recognition with a mirror. In Gallup's version, the subject's forehead and ear were unobtrusively marked with an odorless red dye, and self-recognition was indexed if the chimps looked in the mirror and then reached up to touch the marks on their own heads. This behavior was rare to nonexistent in marked chimps with no mirror and thus attributable to the chimpanzees using the information in mirrors to tell them about themselves. Gallup reported that among primates the only nonhuman species capable of succeeding on this mark task were chimpanzees and orangutans; all other primates so far tested have failed (Gallup 1982; Gallup and Suarez 1986).

Numerous studies have now adapted Gallup's technique and asked about the ontogenesis of mirror self-recognition in infants. The results show that infants exhibit self-recognition, as indexed by touching the mark, at about eighteen to twenty-four months of age but not before. The findings are quite consistent across several studies from independent laboratories (Amsterdam 1972; Bertenthal and Fischer 1978; Johnson 1983; Lewis and Brooks-Gunn 1979; Schulman and Kaplowitz 1977). Moreover, mirror self-recognition has been found to be delayed in children with Down syndrome, such that it emerges at a later chronological age than in normal children but when the subjects are approximately the same mental age or level of perceptual/cognitive sophistication (Loveland 1987; Mans, Cicchetti, and Sroufe 1978). This empirical convergence is certainly striking.

Given this area of settled data, it is tempting to infer that infants first develop the rudiments of a notion of self at about eighteen to twenty-four months. Such an inference may well be incorrect, however (see Butterworth, in this volume; Meltzoff 1985b). Mirror self-recognition is only one measure, one aspect of a broader concept of self, and it is possible to imagine that an infant who has begun to form a meaningful self-concept would still fail the mark test. The argument is not that Gallup's ingenious method is not a good test. It is just that it is not the *only* test of primitive self-awareness (Bower 1989; Gallup and Suarez 1986; Kagan 1981, 1984, 1989; Meltzoff 1985b; Stern 1985); and as I will argue in this chapter, when one expands the range of measuring devices, infants under eighteen months exhibit the foundations for a notion of self and some primitive apprehension about their basic similarity to others.

I want to underscore immediately what this argument is not: it is not a claim that young infants already possess a well-formed concept of self. Clearly, a concept of self is greatly elaborated in early childhood and undergoes developmental changes for years afterwards, as described by others in this volume and elsewhere. The principal point I will try to make is that experiments can also be directed toward the initial origins of the notion of self—its foundation and earliest manifestation in the preverbal child. Recent studies of imitation and related phenomena in infancy provide new insights that complement the work that has already been done with mirror recognition. Moreover, because these newer studies involve infants younger than those used in the mirror test, they allow a glimpse of an even more embryonic notion of self than is reflected in the mirror studies. I will argue that these recent studies have uncovered aspects of the primordial notion of self from which subsequent development proceeds. By understanding the initial condition of the self during early infancy, we can better understand the subsequent critical developments that occur at eighteen to twenty-four months, when children are acquiring language and finally become able to recognize themselves in a mirror.

The new series of experiments described here used imitation as a tool for investigating infants' perception and knowledge about the self. Three different lines of experimentation were involved: they investigated "social mirroring," "social modeling," and "self practice."

In the first line of research, I adapted the traditional mirror studies but used an adult to act as a kind of social mirror to reflect the infants' behaviors back to them. This sidestepped some difficulties infants have in understanding the rather unique properties of a physical reflecting surface, and it revealed new facts about infants' apprehension of self-other similarities. In the second line of research, I investigated the capacity of infants to treat adults as social models, as sentient others whom infants can use as leverage in the early elaboration of self. Finally, in the third line of experiments, I explored how infants use imitation as a way of representing information to the self, of reenacting past events, and how this type of representation in action may affect subsequent cognitive representations of the self and the world.

My aim is to show that these three aspects of imitation—social mirroring, social modeling, and self practice—provide an important foundation for the development of self and a means by which we adults can catch a glimpse of the earliest workings of the self in the preverbal child. I will also argue that imitative interactions provide infants with a unique vehicle for elaborating the similarity between self and other and for understanding that others, like the self, are sentient beings with thoughts, intentions, and emotions. In other words, imitation may be an important, primitive building block in the nascent development of a "theory of mind" (Astington, Harris, and Olson 1988; Flavell 1985) in the child.

Adults as Social Mirrors: Seeing Oneself in the Actions of Others

When investigators use mirrors or photographs of the self to elicit self-recognition behavior, it is often the static featural information about the self that is being emphasized. A different tack is to inquire about self-recognition of actions and movement patterns.

If normal adults are allowed to watch their own hands move, they have no difficulty identifying the hand as their own. Indeed, they readily recognize the moving hand as their own even if it is featurally disguised by a glove. In contrast, when self-produced movement is eliminated and the purely static features of our own hands are captured in a photograph, it has been demonstrated that adults are surprisingly poor at recognizing their hands from among a group of other objects (Wuillemin and Richardson 1982). Evidently, to know something "like the back of one's own hand" is not a sterling achievement—at least when purely featural cues are isolated.

From a developmental perspective, this suggests that it might be useful to separate the growth of self recognition based on featural information from that of self-recognition based on spatiotemporal movement patterns. A self-recognition test using photographs addresses only the former. A typical mirror test assesses the former and possibly combines the two, for infants often sway or move while watching the image, thereby gaining both movement and featural information. To date, few tests have focused on the latter—on infant self-recognition as mediated by pure spatiotemporal movement patterns. This is unfortunate because there are good theoretical reasons for thinking that *the first, psychologically primary notion of self concerns not one's featural peculiarities but rather one's movements, body postures, and powers.*

How can we test infants' sensitivity for recognizing that human movements are "like me" in the absence of providing featural information about the self? Several approaches are possible; we chose one in which an adult experimenter acted as a kind of social mirror to the infant, reflecting back everything the baby did while, of course, not reflecting the infant's specific features. We wanted to know if infants could recognize this self-other similarity in the absence of featural identity. Because we believed this ability would develop prior to solving the mark test, which relies on physical mirrors, we tested infants at fourteen months of age.

A series of three experiments was conducted, each designed to isolate in successively greater detail the nature and basis of infants' ability to recognize when their own behavior was being reflected back to them by another. The first experiment asked at the most basic level whether or not infants showed any such recognition. Twenty-eight infants fourteen months old served as subjects. The procedure involved two experimenters sitting side by side across a table from the subject. One experimenter was assigned the task of shadowing the infant, immediately imitating everything the child did with his or her toy. When the subject banged the toy three times, the experimenter banged his three times; when the subject mouthed the toy, the experimenter did likewise. The second experimenter was the control, sitting passively and holding a toy loosely in her hands on the table top. The two experimenters and the infant were each given an identical toy at the beginning of each trial. Each trial was forty-five seconds in duration; and the experiment consisted of a series of seven such trials, each with a different toy. In short, there were three participants, each with the identical-looking toy; one experimenter continuously imitated the infant across seven trials, and the other passively held the same kind of toy as used by the other two. The experimenter who acted as imitator, the side (right/left) on which the imitator sat, and the order of test objects were counterbalanced across infants. The infants' behavior was video-recorded and subsequently scored by observers who could not see the experimenters and thus had no artifactual cues as to which experimenter was imitating the infant.

We thought that if infants could detect that their own actions were being duplicated, they would prefer to look at the imitating experimenter and also smile at him more. We also predicted that they would tend to "test" whether the adult was acting as a social mirror by investigating the self-other relation in special ways. For example, the infant might stare at the adult as the infant carefully produced a behavior; the infant then might modulate his act by going faster and faster to check if the experimenter was shadowing him, or suddenly stop to see if the experimenter stopped. In short, the infant was presented with the same situation as Harpo Marx and a variety of actors since, in which an actor facing a mirror must determine if the image is really his own: does it stroke its chin when he strokes his, shave when he shaves, and so forth? The actor typically engages in odd actions: slowly moving his hand while staring at the mirror image, then waving it, then sharply deviating from one motion to another to check if the image does the same. We thought the infant might act in a similar manner and the scorer, who was blind to which side the imitating adult was on, recorded all instances of such testing behavior from the video record.

The results show that infants looked significantly longer at the imitating adult than at the control ($p < .001$). Similarly, more smiles were directed toward the imitator than toward the control ($p < .001$), and infants directed more test behavior at the imitator than at the control ($p < .01$).

One interpretation of these results is that infants can recognize the self-other equivalence that is involved when an adult imitates them. Alternative interpretations are also possible. It is plausible, on the basis of experiment 1 alone, that infants are simply attracted to adults who actively manipulate toys. This could explain why they look longer and smile more at the imitator than at the passive control, without invoking any detection of action equivalence. Such an interpretation is more strained to account for why infants would show a tendency to test the imitating adult, but one might hypothesize such behavior is displayed to any active adult, whether or not the adult is mimicking the baby.

In experiment 2, the general procedure was identical to the first study, except that the control experimenter did not remain passive. Instead, this adult actively manipulated the toy. Furthermore, we wanted the experimenter not only to be active but to do "babylike" things with the toy, so that no preference for the imitating experimenter could be based solely on a differentiation of adult versus infantile actions. This was achieved by using a yoked control procedure. The room was arranged such that there were two TV monitors situated behind the subject and in view of the experimenters. One monitor displayed the actions of the current infant, live. The other monitor displayed the video record of the immediately preceding subject.

The effect was that both experimenters were actively imitating infant behaviors and thus were good controls for one another; but in relation to the infant, one was a "self-imitator" and the other an "other-imitator." The experimental question was whether the infant could recognize which adult was acting like he/she was. Fifty-six fourteen-month-olds served as subjects. The results showed that infants again succeeded on the task. Infants looked longer at the self-imitator ($p < .05$), smiled more often at him ($p < .001$), and, most important, engaged in more testing with the self-imitator than with the other-imitator ($p < .01$).

This experiment constrains the possible interpretations of the phenomenon. The demonstrated effects cannot be explained as simple reactions to activity versus nonactivity, for both experimenters were active. Nor can they be explained as recognizing a generic class of babylike actions, for both experimenters were copying the acts of babies. It would seem that the subjects were recognizing the relationship between the actions of the self and the actions of the imitating other.

What is the basis for detecting this relationship? Broadly speaking, two classes of information are available. The first is purely temporal contingency information. According to this alternative, the infant need only detect that when he does X, the adult does Y. The infant need not detect that X and Y are in fact equivalent, only that they are temporally linked. The second alternative is that the infant can also recognize that the actions of the self and other are structurally equivalent. How can we separate these two alternatives?[2]

In experiment 3, we tested another fifty-six normal fourteen-month-olds, using a design similar to the previous two experiments. In this study, the purely temporal aspects of the contingency were controlled by having both experimenters act at precisely the same time. This was achieved by having three predetermined pairs of "target actions." Both experimenters would sit

2. Note that these alternatives are not separated in the classical studies using mirrors, because the mirror image is both moving contingently and in the same structural manner as the self.

passively with the toy until the infant performed one of the target actions on this list. If the infant exhibited one of these target actions, both experimenters would immediately begin to act. The imitating experimenter would perform the infant's act, and the control experimenter would perform the other behavior that was paired with it from the predetermined target list.

Let me make this more concrete. The three pairs of actions were (*a*) shake = slide, (*b*) pound = poke, and (*c*) touch mouth with toy = touch nonoral region on the head, neck, or shoulders. These pairs were chosen from an extensive video review that showed that these were six common "action schemes" of infants this age and that the acts within each pair were similar. In the experiment, whenever an infant shook a toy, the imitating experimenter would also shake his toy, carefully shadowing the infant. The experimenter's behavior was thus under the complete control of the infant. However, the behavior of the other experimenter was also under complete temporal control of the infant. Whenever the infant *shook* his toy, the control experimenter would *slide* his matched toy, also carefully shadowing the infant so that he matched the temporal envelope of the subject's behavior. In sum, whenever the subject shook a toy, he saw a paired-comparison display of two adults acting: one was shaking a replica of his toy; the other was sliding the replica. As soon as the infant stopped, both experimenters stopped; and as soon as the infant started shaking again, the experimenters again started shaking and sliding, respectively. If the infant stopped shaking and began waving his toy, both experimenters stopped acting in unison, because waving was not one of the target acts to which they were programmed to respond. Note that the target pairs were fully reciprocal in that whenever the infant either shook or slid his toy he saw both shaking and sliding—it's just that the experimenter who performed these acts would reverse if the infant changed from one action to the other, because the imitating experimenter always matched the infant's behavior and the control experimenter always mismatched it. Table 1 displays the set of contingencies presented to the infant.

Table 1.   Stimulus-Response Contingencies Presented in the Social Mirroring Experiment

Infant's Behavior	Imitating Experimenter	Control Experimenter
Shake	Shake	Slide
Slide	Slide	Shake
Pound	Pound	Poke
Poke	Poke	Pound
Mouth	Mouth	Head, neck, shoulder
Head, neck, shoulder	Head, neck, shoulder	Mouth
Other	Passive	Passive

This design achieves the goal of having both the adults' actions contingent on the infant's. What differentiates the two experimenters is not the purely temporal relations with the acting subject but the structure of their actions vis-à-vis the subject. One adult consistently matches the structure of the infant's behavior; the other adult consistently mismatches it. The experimental question is whether this self-other relation is psychologically salient to the infant.

The results show that the infants looked ($p < .05$) and smiled ($p < .001$) more at the matching than at the mismatching actor. Most important, the infants directed more testing behavior to the matching actor ($p < .01$). These results show that, with temporal contingency information controlled, infants can recognize the structural equivalence between the acts they see others perform and the acts they do themselves. In that sense, they have already begun to elaborate a notion of self which, if not based strictly on a visual self-image, consists of a kind of extended "body scheme"—a system of body movements, postures, acts, and their relation to like behaviors by others. This recognition of the equivalence between self and other in infants as young as fourteen months old (prior to success on the classic mirror "mark" test) is important for theories of social development, as will be discussed later in this chapter.

Adults as Social Models

In the studies just discussed, the situation was arranged so that the adult acted as a kind of social mirror. The emphasis was on infants' ability to recognize matches *of* the self. A complementary skill is the ability to produce matches *by* the self. If the first case is one of social mirroring, the second is one of social modeling. The adult becomes the model which the infant tries to match, to imitate.

It is broadly agreed that at some stage in development the imitation of others plays a role in the growth of the self, its skills and proclivities. Children learn to speak Arabic rather than English and become enculturated to that way of life at least in part through imitation of adult models. The abilities of the self, the roles we take on, the standards to which we adhere are influenced by social models. In brief, imitation is relevant to self development because it is a process by which something of the other is taken on by the self (Baldwin 1906; Bandura 1986; Kagan 1981; Mead 1934).

From the perspective of early self development, one intriguing question is whether infants can acquire new behaviors merely from watching another act. This is a question of the imitation of novel acts. We want to know if infants are constrained to imitating only actions that are highly familiar to themselves or whether the self-other mapping is so facile that the infants can learn something about his or her own body and its possible actions simply by observing the behavior of another. Especially relevant is the imitation of novelty after a lengthy delay. If the infant is limited to immediate mimicry, imitation can play only a limited role in broadening the self's repertoire and in long-term changes in the self. For imitation to be of more value, infants must have some sort of representational capacity, allowing them to "read out" at a later time the information previously picked up from the other. The developmental literature terms this "deferred imitation."

We conducted a study in which infants were tested to see if they could imitate a range of behaviors, including at least one novel one, after quite lengthy delays were imposed (Meltzoff 1988b). The subjects were thirty-six healthy fourteen-month-old infants. The delay interval was one week. The infants were exposed to an adult who performed a series of acts on different toys during the first visit to the laboratory; then a one-week delay was imposed before infants were brought back to the laboratory and given access to the toys. The experimental question was whether they themselves would now perform those acts exhibited by the adult actor one week earlier.

Six objects were selected so that none would be overly familiar to the infants. One object was a small box with a plastic orange panel for a top surface. The novel act demonstrated by the experimenter was to lean forward from the waist and tap the panel with the top of his forehead. The second object was a dumbbell-shaped toy; it consisted of a short section of double tubing with one section inside the other and cubes attached to the ends. The action demonstrated by the adult was to pick up the object by the cubes and to pull it apart. Four other objects and the simple acts performed on them completed the set of six stimuli.

The subjects were randomly assigned to one of three test conditions: baseline control, adult-manipulation control, and imitation. The design consisted of two test sessions, one week apart. The following is a description of the procedure used in the first test session. In the imitation group, each subject was sequentially shown the six target actions. Each demonstration consisted of a twenty-second period in which the target action was repeated three times. For example, the experimenter leaned forward and touched the panel with his forehead and then straightened up, repeating this three times. The demonstrations were presented on the tabletop out of reach of the subjects, so that they could only observe the event, not touch or play with the toys.

In order to isolate true deferred imitation, two control groups were used to check whether infants would tend to produce the target actions even without any exposure to the adult model. Infants assigned to the baseline condition came to the laboratory for a first visit and sat across the table from the experimenter while he talked to the parent. This helped acclimate them to the test room, just as the infants in the imitation group had been brought into this room in session 1. These infants were then sent home and returned one week later.

Infants in the imitation condition saw the experimenter pick up and manipulate the test objects. It is possible that simply seeing the adult handle the test objects motivates infants to manipulate the objects when they are subsequently presented in the second session. Such active, exploratory manipulation might in turn lead the infants to produce the target actions by chance. The baseline control does not provide a stringent check of this type of nonimitative production of the target actions; thus, a second type of control is also desirable. In this adult-manipulation condition, the subjects were exposed to a series of six stimulus-presentation periods just as the imitation group had been. For each presentation, the experimenter reached out and manipulated the test object just as he had done for the imitation condition, save that he did not exhibit the target act. As in the imitation condition, the presentation lasted twenty seconds, and the control manipulations were performed three times in the twenty-second period. The inclusion of this control condition tests for the possibility that infants are simply induced to produce the targets for nonimitative reasons, because they see the toys handled by the experimenter. Using this design, the inference of imitation is warranted if subjects differentially produce more of the specific target acts after seeing those acts modeled than in the two controls.

Subjects in all three groups (baseline, adult-manipulation, and imitation) were treated identically on the second visit. The test objects were simply re-presented in their original test order. Each object was placed on the table in front of the infant, and a twenty-second response period was timed for each object, starting from the moment the infant first contacted the toy. The infants' behavior was video-recorded and subsequently scored by observers who remained naive as to the subjects' original test conditions.

Each subject was given six test stimuli and thus assigned a score (0–6) according to the number of target behaviors produced. The results were analyzed using a 3(condition) $\times$ 2 (sex) ANOVA. The main effect for condition was significant, F (2,30) = 12.00, $p < .001$. There was no main effect for sex and no condition $\times$ sex interaction, F's < 1. A Newman-Keuls test showed that infants in the imitation condition produced significantly more target behaviors ($M = 3.42$) than those in either the baseline ($M = 1.25$) or the adult-manipulation controls ($M = 1.67$). There was no significant difference in the number of target behaviors produced by the two controls. The strength of the imitation effect is shown in table 2, which provides a raw data matrix of the number of target acts performed as a function of experimental treatment, $\chi^2(10) = 24.46$, $p < .01$. As shown, eleven of the twelve subjects in the imitation condition duplicated three or more target behaviors, while only three of the twenty-four control subjects did so—thus providing clear evidence for the modeling effect ($p < .0001$).

Did infants imitate the novel act of touching the orange panel with their foreheads? The data indicate they did. First, the data show that head touching

Table 2.   Number of Subjects Producing Different Numbers of Target Acts as a Function of Test Condition

Test Condition	Number of Target Acts Produced						
	0	1	2	3	4	5	6
Baseline control	3	4	4	1	0	0	0
Adult-manipulation control	2	4	4	0	2	0	0
Imitation	0	1	0	6	3	2	0

Note: Maximum score = 6.

is indeed a novel act in that it simply was never performed by any of the control infants: none of the twenty-four controls leaned forward and touched the panel with their heads. Nonetheless, 67 percent of the infants who saw head touching produced this action ($p < .0001$). That infants observed this rather odd action and then "read it out" in their own actions after a one-week delay attests to the long-lasting effect of social modeling on infants. The experiment thus provided a good case of infants directly picking up a behavior from seeing it performed by another.

It is of interest for theories of cognitive development that these fourteen-month-olds exhibited deferred imitation of novelty without a period of trial-and-error groping in the second test session. For the children who successfully performed the head-touch gesture on the second session, the mean latency to produce the head touch was 3.21 seconds. The inference is that upon seeing the demonstration in the first session, infants were able to represent this new act in long-term memory even though it did not fit in with a habitual motor pattern of their own. Infants were able to accommodate their mental scheme internally, before and without any motor practice or what Piaget (1952) called "directed groping." This is relevant because this type of deferred novel imitation is often cited as a constituent of a global psychological shift at about eighteen to twenty-four months of age, the so-called "sensorimotor stage VI" (Piaget 1962). The current work does not definitively address this idea of a global "stage VI" cognitive shift, because measures of the putatively related skills (object permanence, productive language, symbolic play) were not also recorded on these same subjects. However, the results show that a robust capacity for deferred imitation is present early in the second year, a finding recently replicated with even younger (nine-month-old) infants (Meltzoff 1988c), and this is well before other developments have been typically observed. I have proposed that the ability to defer imitation of the acts of others is psychologically quite basic and does not emerge as a late achievement, contemporaneously with other aspects of the "symbolic function" (Meltzoff, 1985a, 1985b, 1988a).

From a social-developmental viewpoint, it is noteworthy that the design involved showing infants a series of acts in sequence and only then allowing them to respond. Thus, infants were confined purely to watching during the modeling period and did not have access to the toys. It is striking that so many different acts could be remembered and read out one week later ($M = 3.42$), especially in view of the fact that each demonstration lasted only twenty seconds. The results invite speculation about how such a capacity might be of service in everyday life. Consider that parents and especially other children do not always allow infants access to one toy before showing other potentially competing acts with different toys. The current findings show that even young infants can hold in mind more than one event for subsequent reproduction once they get access to the toy. This strongly suggests that imitation and social learning could be functional between infants and their peers, siblings, and other real-world models who do not allow response before proceeding to display other acts. Indeed, recent work in our lab has demonstrated imitation among fourteen-month-old peers, confirming that infant models, as well as adult models, influence infant behavior during this age period (Hanna and Meltzoff 1989, 1990).

Imitation and "Self Practice": The Value of Imitation for the Self

The previous study was intentionally designed such that infants were confined solely to observing the social model. While this embodies a rather pure case of deferred imitation, observations of parent-child interactions reveal that parents often simplify their own behavior patterns and encourage infants to attend to/imitate one constituent of a complex skill before moving on to the next component (Bruner 1973, 1975, 1983). One's curiosity is piqued as to why this is such a "natural" mode of pedagogy.

The possibility arises that giving infants a chance to imitate an act immediately after it is shown may help them to consolidate that behavior. If so, subsequent reproduction of the behavior might be especially robust if such consolidation is permitted *before* the delay is interposed. On this view, one function served by early imitation would be to incorporate an observed act solidly into one's own repertoire, to commit it to memory. This idea can be operationalized and reduced to test by comparing two groups of infants. Infants in one condition would be treated as in the previous study, in which no imitation was allowed before the lengthy delay. Infants in the other condition would be given the opportunity for immediate imitation, before the delay was imposed. The question under test would be whether or not these two treatments had an effect on infants' tendency to duplicate the target after the delay.

The subjects used to test this question were a new group of forty-eight normal fourteen-month-olds. The stimuli were two objects, an orange plastic egg that made a rattling sound when shaken and a small stuffed animal that could be dangled on the tabletop by an attached string. Infants were randomly assigned to one of the two different types of deferred conditions, each with twenty-four subjects.

The procedure entailed two visits to the laboratory. In group 1, infants were shown the two target acts but not given the opportunity for immediate imitation. The first target was demonstrated, then that object was removed and the other target act was then demonstrated with the second toy. The infants then were sent home for the twenty-four–hour delay. Infants in group 2 followed a slightly different procedure. After the first target was demonstrated, the infant was given the object for a twenty-second response period, thereby permitting immediate imitation of the adult display. The same procedure was then followed for the second object.

In the second session, infants from both groups were treated identically. The infants simply were presented with the test objects, one at a time, each for a twenty-second response period. The infant's behavior during this period was video-recorded and subsequently scored by observers who were naive to the infant's test condition.

Infants received a score of 0, 1, or 2 according to how many targets they produced. A chi-square test revealed that these scores varied as a function of test condition, with infants in group 2 producing more of the target behaviors than those in group 1; indeed, infants in group 2 were twice as likely to produce both target gestures as infants in group 1 (50 percent versus 25 percent, respectively).

The present study thus shows there is a difference in the strength of imitation after a one-day delay as a function of whether infants (*a*) were constrained solely to observing the adult's actions on day one (group 1) or (*b*) observed the adult's actions on day one and also were given access to the toys and allowed to engage in on-line immediate imitation before the delay was instituted (group 2). Something appears to be gained if infants are given the opportunity for imitation immediately after seeing the adult modeling.

My interpretation of these findings is that immediate imitation serves the function of a kind of nonverbal rehearsal for the infant, raising the possibility that imitation is not only a tool for the experimenter to assess infant memory after a delay but also a means by which infants enhance their own memory of behaviors they see. The data from previous studies amply documented that infants are influenced by the actions of others. The additional point made by this study is that infants are given a boost if they quickly incorporate an observed act into the self's system of actions—as, for example, under the group 2 procedure. As conceived here, imitation is a repetition of a perceived event by the self; it is a type of self practice and, as such, is one tool infants have for consolidating the memory of an event for themselves. It is a way nonverbal infants have of taking something of the other and making it their own.

Games Infants Play and Their Relation to Social Mirroring

One common observation about early parent-infant games is that they are often reciprocally imitative in nature. First, the infant begins with an act of banging a tabletop. The parent seizes the opportunity for making a communicative connection and bangs in return. Next, the child repeats the same, then the parent, and so on, in a kind of nonverbal-exchange game. Theorists have been struck by the *temporal patterning* of these exchanges, the conversation-like turn-taking they embody; and a variety of hypotheses about social development have emerged to incorporate them (Brazelton and Tronick 1980; Bruner 1975, 1983; Papoušek and Papoušek 1986; Stern 1985; Trevarthen and Marwick 1986).

Our recent experiments on social mirroring provide an additional perspective on thèse everyday observations. Without taking away from the temporal side of the exchange, our experiments bring to the forefront the equivalence in the *form* of the participants' behavior. The results from our social mirroring studies demonstrate that when temporal contingency information is equated, infants still can detect when the structure of their own actions is being matched. Moreover, and of more relevance to the games under consideration, the experimental results show that infants prefer to look at an adult who is matching them, and they also smile more at him or her.

On the basis of these results, I would suggest that, in addition to finding pleasure in the temporal patterning of adult exchange games, infants also may take delight in the fact that the parent is acting as a kind of social mirror. Indeed, in these everyday games, parents are performing exactly as the imitating experimenter in our social mirroring study. As our experiment shows, one easy way to attract the infant's attention and to elicit smiles is to act like the baby acts, which is just what the adult partner does in these games. Following this reasoning to another communicative channel, it is also worth considering the vocal phenomenon of "motherese," in which adults speak in a high-pitched voice while talking to infants. Recent cross-language work shows this is probably a culturally universal phenomenon (Grieser and Kuhl 1988). It would be interesting if one reason infants find the high-pitched motherese signal so captivating is that the pitch is closer to the infants' own register than is normal, adult-directed speech. Parental vocal games spoken in motherese may be providing, in the vocal channel, something akin to the social mirroring I have discussed here in terms of gestural acts. (For data and arguments regarding the acoustic salience of motherese for infants, see Fernald and Kuhl 1987; Grieser and Kuhl 1988.)

The Developmental Origins of Social Modeling Effects

In social mirroring, the adult is doing most of the productive work. The adult is busily shadowing the infant, and the infant need only recognize that his or her behavior is being matched. Because recognition runs ahead of production in many aspects of development, the possibility may be raised that social mirroring is the primordial imitative relationship. Perhaps infants first learn to imitate others by having others imitate them.

Cast in the terms of this chapter, this issue concerns the developmental priority of social mirroring versus social modeling. At a more general theoretical level, it is a question of the degree to which the "other" gives structure to an initially meaningless self. Such a question has been addressed by many writers, notably Baldwin (1906), Cooley (1902), Mahler, Pine, and Bergman (1975), Mead (1934), and Piaget (1952, 1954). I believe that our recent data also bear on it. Looking at it as a developmental issue amenable to experiment, we may ask: How much and what type of experience in interacting with an adult other is necessary for the infant to apprehend self-other equivalences? Is experience with social *mirroring* necessary for infants to respond to social *modeling*? Theories at the extreme of assuming no sense of self in early infancy and those postulating a lead role for the other in the infant's construction of self have suggested that infants first learn to imitate others by virtue of the fact that sensitive parents initially act as a kind of biological mirror and imitate the infant. The infant is thought to learn to imitate through at first being imitated. This postulate can be tested, and we have done so.

Social Modeling Effects in the First Year

In the studies previously discussed, fourteen-month-olds served as subjects; this gives parents ample opportunity for engaging in social mirroring games. We wanted to trace infant imitation to an earlier age, before such games become so popular. A further study was therefore conducted, using nine-month-old infants (Meltzoff 1988c). Sixty subjects were seen in an immediate imitation test, and sixty in a deferred imitation test using a twenty-four–hour delay. The tasks used were three simple actions with novel objects. The design used was one in which infants were not given access to the toys during the modeling episodes (a "group 1" design). Appropriate control groups, both baseline and adult-manipulation, were employed.

Infants' responses were scored from video record by observers who were blind to the subjects' test conditions. Each infant was assigned a score reflecting how many target actions he or she produced. A condition $\times$ delay ANOVA showed that the main effect for condition was significant, $F (3,112) = 10.39, p < .001$, and a planned comparison showed that infants produced significantly more of the target behaviors in the imitation condition than in the controls, t (116) = 5.22, p < .0001. There was no delay effect and no condition × delay interaction, F's < 1.

This study shows that infants as young as age nine months will imitate simple actions using novel toys both immediately and after a twenty-four hour delay. Social modeling influences infant behavior even over quite lengthy delays in children well under one year of age.

Social Modeling Effects in the First Month

So far, we have considered the imitation of object-directed behaviors. A different type of imitation is the copying of pure body movements without objects (e.g., the imitation of facial gestures). For such imitation, the subjects must translate the body transformations they see into body movements of their own with no external object beyond the movement pattern itself playing a role. Classic developmental theory predicts that the imitation of pure body movements is highly constrained in infancy, with implications for theories about the development of self. The onset of spontaneous facial imitation is predicted to occur at about one year of age (Piaget 1962). Before this age, infants are thought to be unable to match a gesture they see with one of their own that they cannot see, unless specifically shaped to perform such tasks. In 1977, we conducted two studies investigating facial imitation in two- to three-week-old infants (Meltzoff and Moore 1977).

In this work, we wanted to be careful to distinguish infants' imitative responses from global arousal responses, and controls were instituted to accomplish this. For example, suppose an experiment was designed with a baseline period in which no face was presented, and this was followed by a tongue-protrusion demonstration by an adult experimenter. Further suppose that there were significantly more infant tongue protrusions to the adult tongue display than during the baseline condition. Such results would not permit the inference of infant imitation. Infants might be aroused at the sight of a moving human face, and infant oral movements including tonguing could be part of this general arousal response.

To address this problem, we used a "cross-target" comparison (Meltzoff and Moore 1977, 1983b) in which infants were shown several gestures (targets) in a repeated-measures design and their responses across these different targets were monitored. For example, we showed an infant both a mouth-opening display and a tongue-protrusion display. If infants responded with more mouth opening to the mouth display than to the tongue display and, conversely, responded with more tongue protrusions to the tongue display than to the mouth display, this could not be due to a general arousal. Both gestures were presented by the same experimenter, at the same distance, and

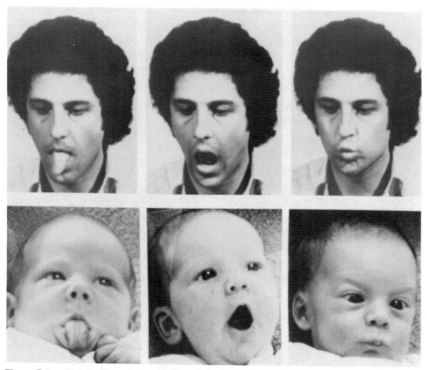

Figure 7.1. Sample photographs of two- to three-week-old infants imitating facial gestures demonstrated by an adult. From A. N. Meltzoff and M. K. Moore, Imitation of facial and manual gestures by human neonates, *Science* 198 (1977): 75–78.

at the same rate of movement. The differential matching response to both displays cannot be explained by a general arousal response.

Following this logic, we conducted two studies. Although the designs were slightly different, they both yielded evidence for facial imitation in infants less than three weeks old (figure 1). In the first study, twelve- to seventeen-day-old infants were each shown four gestures in a repeated-measures design. The four gestures were lip protrusion, mouth opening, tongue protrusion, and sequential finger movement. The infants' facial behaviors were video-recorded and subsequently scored by judges who remained uninformed as to the infants' stimulus conditions. The results showed that infants differentially imitated all four gestures.

Infants in this first study were allowed to respond while the display was presented. We next wondered whether early imitation might be constrained to some form of "motor resonance" or coaction that could easily be disrupted if a short delay was imposed between the modeling and response. To investigate this, study 2 was conducted, using a new group of sixteen- to twenty-one-day-old infants. Again a repeated-measures design was used, in which each infant served as his/her own control. The target displays were mouth opening and tongue protrusion. We developed a pacifier technique in which the presentation of the visual stimulus and the infant's response were temporally split by providing infants with a pacifier to suck on during the visual displays. For example, the mouth-opening display was demonstrated while the infant was sucking on a pacifier. After the demonstration was complete, the experimenter assumed a passive-face pose and only then removed the pacifier. A 150-second response period was then timed, during which the adult maintained a passive facial pose. Immediately thereafter, the pacifier was reinserted, and the second gesture was presented in an identical manner. Order of gesture was counterbalanced across infants.

It is noteworthy that the infants actively sucked on the pacifier during the stimulus-presentation periods. They did not tend to open their mouths and let the pacifier drop out during the mouth display; nor did they tend to push the pacifier away with their tongues during the tongue display. The sucking reflex took precedence over any imitative tendency and ensured that infants engaged in competing motor activity during the presentation of the display (Meltzoff and Moore 1977, 1983b). Even with this pacifier technique, the findings supported the hypothesis of imitation. Taken together, the two 1977 experiments showed that very young human infants can generate matching responses to certain simple body movements presented by adult models.

How can we account for this unexpected infant competence? If pressed, an advocate of the primacy-of-social-mirroring perspective might argue that infants had learned to copy these displays during the mother-infant interactions that occur in the very first postnatal weeks, often surrounding feeding (Brazelton and Tronick 1980). The goal of the next study was to test this idea.

Social Modeling Effects in the Newborn

If early infant matching behavior depends upon prior social learning, then newborn infants should fail at these tasks. To address this question, we tested forty newborns with a mean age of thirty-two hours (Meltzoff and Moore 1983a). The youngest subject was only forty-two minutes old at the time of test.

The infants were tested in a laboratory located within a newborn nursery. Following the logic of the cross-target comparison, infants acted as their own controls. Each was presented with both a mouth-opening and a tongue-protrusion gesture in a repeated-measures design, counterbalanced for order of presentation. The experiment was videotaped and subsequently scored by an observer who was blind to the modeled behavior. The results showed that the infants matched the adult behaviors. There were significantly more infant mouth openings in response to the mouth display than to the tongue display

$(z = 2.26, p < .05$, Wilcoxon matched-pairs signed-ranks test). Conversely, the frequency of infant tongue protrusions was greater to the tongue display than to the mouth display $(z = 3.31, p < .001)$. Recently, these findings have been replicated and extended in another sample of forty infants less than seventy-two hours old (Meltzoff and Moore 1989). One of the gestures used in this new study was a nonoral gesture, head movement, thus demonstrating that the newborn matching phenomenon has some generality and is not restricted to tongue protrusion and mouth opening. We can conclude that extended postnatal learning from interactions with caretakers is not a necessary condition for imitation in humans. Some primitive capacity to copy the actions of adults appears to be present from birth.

What psychological mechanism could possibly underlie this behavior? I have written at length about several alternative models, ranging from the notion that it is a mindless response, to some sort of intentional copying (Meltzoff 1985b; Meltzoff, Kuhl, and Moore, in press; Meltzoff and Moore 1977, 1983a, 1983b, 1985, 1989). While recognizing that the available data invite alternative inferences, one hypothesis we developed bears mention here. This view holds that infants can, at some level of processing, apprehend the equivalences between body transformations they see and body transformations of their own that they proprioceptively "feel" themselves make. Infants see the adult's display and incorporate it as a kind of target against which they can compare their ongoing movement patterns and body postures. This immediately raises the problem of the coding of the adult's display. It could not be a purely iconic visual image of the behavior, because then there would still be the problem of how the infant links up the visual image of the other and the motor image of the self. Thus, we have proposed that the infant may encode the spatiotemporal events that constitute human actions in some sort of *supramodal* code, a non-modality-specific description of the human act. Such a representational code would be akin to the supramodal phonetic unit postulated by Kuhl and Meltzoff (1984, 1988) to encompass both the auditory and articulatory representations of speech in the preverbal child, which was necessitated by findings of vocal imitation and lipreading phenomena in very early infancy (Kuhl and Meltzoff 1982). The empirical and theoretical work by Bower (1977, 1982, 1989) and Gibson (1966, 1979) has led them to develop and elaborate very similar notions.

The idea of a supramodal representational system means, metaphorically, that the visual, motor, and possibly auditory systems "speak the same language" right from birth. There is not a gradual stitching together of initially independent spaces—a visual space, a buccal space, an auditory space—all of which are functionally independent and coordinated with growth and experience, à la Piaget (1954). Rather, information picked up by the separate sense organs could be represented within a "common space." This idea of a perceptual system that operates on supramodal information has not been fully mined for its implications about the notion of self. It is, however, extremely relevant to the development of self, because it allows us to hypothesize that even during early infancy the "other," as picked up through one modality (such as vision), is represented in a code accessible to the self, as picked up through proprioception. Discussed next are the fuller implications of this view and a way it can be integrated with the findings from older infants, discussed previously.

Conclusions: Implications for Self, and Extensions to Understanding "Other Minds"

Three aspects of imitation—social mirroring, social modeling, and imitation as self practice—that may be particularly relevant to developing a theory of the self have been highlighted.

In the first, the adult acts as a kind of social mirror (analogous to a physical mirror) and reflects the infant's own behavior back to him/her. The infant's appreciation of social mirroring was demonstrated in a preprogrammed interaction in which an adult purposely imitated the infant. We compared the infant's reaction to this mirroring adult versus an adult whose behavior was also temporally contingent on the infant's but who consistently mismatched the infant's behavior. We found that infants preferred the adult who was actually imitating them; infants seemed able to recognize human acts that were structurally equivalent to their own. They looked and smiled more at the mirroring other. They also "tested" the adult, possibly checking where the identity between self and other broke down.

This social mirroring effect is not purely a laboratory phenomenon. The gestural dialogues between infants and their caretakers are well documented, and theorists have commented that infants seem to take pleasure in the temporal aspects of these early exchange games. The perspective added in this chapter is that infants may also take pleasure in the fact that in these episodes the adult's acts become more "like me" in their form. Social mirroring may be a primordial form of communication between adult and infant. It would be meaningful to both partners because both could recognize their common acts.

This would also help provide the infant with a growing sense of the self, because such exchanges are one natural way (in addition to physical mirrors) infants can discover what their acts look like. In these special interactions, the infants can, in a sense, see a reflection of themselves in the other (Lacan 1977; Winnicott 1967). This might enhance and solidify the infant's sense of causality and self-agency. Moreover, I would propose that social mirroring is a unique and important constituent of early enculturation, because a social mirror (unlike a physical mirror) is both *selective* and *interpretive* in its reflections. Parents, as social mirrors, provide "creative reflections" to their infants, reflections that capture aspects of the infant's activity but then go on beyond it to read in intentions and goals to that behavior. The infant may wave an object, but the parent interprets this as waving in order to shake and therefore waves intensely enough to shake the toy and produce a sound, which in turn leads the infant beyond his or her initial starting point. Likewise, selected actions, especially those that are potentially meaningful in the culture, will be reflected back more often than others (Bruner 1975, 1983). What I am calling social mirroring is one aspect, an important one I believe, of the larger issue of parental teaching strategies and what Bruner and others have called parental "scaffolding."

Imitation is used not only by caretakers but by the infants themselves to mark salient events. This raises the hypothesis of imitation as "self practice," which was a further facet of imitation highlighted in this chapter. In one study, infants were tested for deferred imitation of a target with and without an opportunity for immediate, on-line imitation during the display itself. We found that infants given the opportunity for immediate imitation were superior imitators after a twenty-four–hour delay than were those treated identically but without the initial opportunity for immediate imitation. It appears that in imitating an act themselves, infants may confer it with a privileged or enriched status. It is intriguing to think there is a link between the infants' immediate imitative reactions, which are re-presentations to themselves in action, and their consolidation of internal representations and memories. The notion of imitation as self practice deserves further study.

The social modeling effects discussed here provide a productive measure of infants' appreciation of self-other correspondences (as opposed to the recognitory measures provided by either the social or physical mirror studies). Infants are posed a problem: An adult produces a novel behavior such as touching an orange panel with his forehead, and now the infant is faced with the same panel. Even assuming some motivation for duplication, should the infant use his foot, his hand, his tongue? What behavior of the infant's corresponds to the act he observed? By age fourteen months, infants have no difficulty accurately imitating the head-touch behavior after a one-week delay. Other studies used pure body actions, without objects, including a sample of newborns, the youngest of whom was forty-two minutes old at the time of test. The data show that even newborns will generate matching responses: they will poke out their tongues when they see that display and will switch to mouth opening/closing when they see that performed. The range of actions imitated by young infants is quite broad and, in addition to oral movements, includes hand movements (Meltzoff and Moore 1977) and even head movements (Meltzoff and Moore 1989). We concluded that some primitive form of imitation is literally natural to humans from birth.

The mechanisms underlying this early behavioral matching are under investigation in our laboratory and others'. But as a working model, we have proposed that infants, even these newborns, are capable of apprehending the equivalence between body transformations they see and ones they feel themselves perform. According to this view, early matching behavior is a manifestation of an active intermodal mapping process. It may not be too much to suggest that the young infant possesses an embryonic "body scheme," including equivalences between body acts perceived and body acts performed. Of course, this body scheme develops—perhaps in part through social mirroring experiences and self practice of the type discussed earlier in this chapter. But my interpretation of the early imitation results is that some body-scheme kernel is present as a "psychological primitive" right from the earliest phases of infancy. This nascent notion of self is a foundation from which self development proceeds, not an endpoint that is reached after months or years of interactions with the social environment.

How Imitation May Contribute to the Infant's Grasp of "Other Minds" and Emotions

Interviews with parents in my laboratory suggest that they enjoy playing mutual imitative games with their infants because this accentuates for them that their infant is, like them, a sentient human being. Evidently, this is an attribution that comes easily when there is successful nonverbal communication, even for a fleeting moment, between the parent and infant. However scientifically uncontrolled and epistemologically naive these parental opinions may be, that is what the parents experience—that is what is going on in their hearts and minds. It appears to be a natural psychological attribution.

The point I will make here is that such imitative episodes may serve to raise this "sentience" issue for the naive infant as well as for the adult. In other words, just as parents base their inference of infant sentience on communicative encounters with their child, this "natural psychological attribution" may also be operative in infants and form a basis for them to make inferences about the sentience of the adults. At what point in development and by what mechanism does the infant see the adult as an "other mind" with intentions, thoughts, and emotions (Astington, et al. 1988; Perner, in press; Wellman, in press)? One hypothesis would fix the beginning of this development at the age at which children begin to use "internal state" words (e.g., happy, sad) as descriptors (e.g., Bretherton and Beeghly 1982). The data reported here, however, suggest that infants may have the tools to make some initial headway on this problem before these first verbalizations, in part through early imitation and the capacities that underlie it.

To clarify the relevance of the work on imitation to the problem of "other minds," I will focus on one example involving the earliest understanding and attribution of emotion to other human beings. Ekman's findings (Ekman 1984; Ekman, Levenson, and Friesen 1983) suggest that there is a basic connection between certain emotional states and their manifestations in facial expression. If so, infants could, in principle, come to detect the conjunction in themselves between the facial movements they feel themselves make and these underlying states. Assuming that infants detect these regularities in themselves, could this experience help them "read" the faces of others? Unfortunately, it would be of no use to young infants if there were no way for them to bridge from themselves to others. Indeed, that is the situation they are left in, according to orthodox developmental theory.

However, the new findings of early facial imitation become very relevant here. This work demonstrates precisely and quite strongly that infants can relate the gestures they see on another's face to their own unseen facial behavior. The fact that infants imitate the expressions they see suggests that they can detect similarities, *at least at a behavioral level,* between the actions of the self and the other (Meltzoff 1985b; Meltzoff and Moore 1985, 1989). This detection of the similarity could be pivotal in developing a theory of mind that includes the other as a sentient being, for it would provide infants a way of giving subjective meaning to the emotional expressions they see in others. Inasmuch as infants perceive regularities between their own expressions and emotional states (à la Ekman) and also perceive similarities between others' unseen expressions and their own (à la our work on facial imitation), they would have the information necessary to appreciate that the other has emotional states similar to their own. The line of reasoning involves the following three steps:

1. When I am in a certain emotional state, my face makes a certain behavioral expression (the facial behavior–emotional state link reported by Ekman).

2. I can recognize that the behavioral expression in another is similar to the one I make (the visual-proprioceptive link reported by Meltzoff and Moore).

3. If the other is producing the same behavior I produce when experiencing a certain emotional state, then perhaps the other is experiencing that emotion (the emotion that goes with that behavior in me).

The suggestion is that the foregoing process infuses the expressions seen in others with meaning from personal experience. The hypothesized three-step process could also be applied to recognizing "intentionality" and "desires" in the other, as well as to a host of issues related to the psychogenesis of other minds. Baldwin (1906), Mead (1934), and other psychologists and philosophers have long explored these problems. The three new empirical elements that can now be brought to bear on the problem of other minds are (*a*) Ekman's findings, (*b*) Meltzoff and Moore's data that young infants can match the behaviors of others, and (*c*) the fundamental theoretical notion that cross-modal links between the seen and the unseen (the other's face and one's own) can be apprehended very early in life. I believe these three factors contribute to the development of the notion of self and to an infant's impression of the psychologically sentient other. Imitation lies at the cross-roads of infants' elaborating a concept of self and expanding their understanding of the minds and emotions of others.

References

Amsterdam, B. 1972. Mirror self-image reactions before age two. *Developmental Psychobiology* 5:297–305.

Astington, J. W., P. L. Harris, and D. R. Olson. 1988. *Developing theories of mind.* New York: Cambridge University Press.

Baldwin, J. M. 1906. *Mental development in the child and the race.* 3d ed. New York: Kelley.

Bandura, A. 1986. *Social foundations of thought and action.* Englewood Cliffs, N.J.: Prentice-Hall.

Bertenthal, B. I., and K. W. Fischer. 1978. Development of self-recognition in the infant. *Developmental Psychology* 14:44–50.

Bower, T. G. R. 1977. *The perceptual world of the child.* Cambridge, Mass.: Harvard University Press.

―――. 1982. *Development in infancy.* 2d ed. San Francisco: Freeman.

―――. 1989. *The rational infant: Learning in infancy.* San Francisco: Freeman.

Brazelton, T. B., and E. Tronick. 1980. Preverbal communication between mothers and infants. In *The social foundations of language and thought.* Edited by D. R. Olson. New York: Norton, 299–315.

Bretherton, I., and M. Beeghly. 1982. Talking about internal states: The acquisition of an explicit theory of mind. *Developmental Psychology* 18:906–21.

Bruner, J. S. 1973. Organization of early skilled action. *Child Development* 44:1–11.

―――. 1975. From communication to language—A psychological perspective. *Cognition* 3:255–87.

―――. 1983. *Child's talk: Learning to use language.* New York: Norton.

Cooley, C. H. 1902. *Human nature and the social order.* New York: Scribner.

Darwin, C. 1877. A biographical sketch of an infant. *Mind* 2:285–94.

Ekman, P. 1984. Expression and the nature of emotion. In *Approaches to emotion.* Edited by K. Scherer and P. Ekman. Hillsdale, N.J.: Erlbaum, 319–43.

Ekman, P., R. W. Levenson, and W. V. Friesen. 1983. Autonomic nervous system activity distinguishes among emotions. *Science* 221:1208–10.

Fernald, A., and P. K. Kuhl. 1987. Acoustic determinants of infant preference for motherese speech. *Infant Behavior and Development* 10:279–93.

Flavell, J. H. 1985. *Cognitive development.* 2d ed. Englewood Cliffs, N.J.: Prentice-Hall.

Gallup, G. G. 1970. Chimpanzees: Self-recognition. *Science* 167:86–87.

―――. 1982. Self-awareness and the emergence of mind in primates. *American Journal of Primatology* 2:237–48.

Gallup, G. G., and S. D. Suarez. 1986. Self-awareness and the emergence of mind in humans and other primates. In *Psychological perspectives on the self,* vol. 3. Edited by J. Suls and A. G. Greenwald. Hillsdale, N.J.: Erlbaum, 3–26.

Gibson, J. J. 1966. *The senses considered as perceptual systems.* Boston: Houghton Mifflin.

_____. 1979. *The ecological approach to visual perception.* Boston: Houghton Mifflin.

Grieser, D., and P. K. Kuhl. 1988. Maternal speech to infants in a tonal language: Support for universal prosodic features in motherese. *Developmental Psychology* 24:14–20.

Hanna, E., and A. N. Meltzoff. 1989, April. Peer imitation in 14-month-old infants. Paper presented at the meeting of the Society for Research in Child Development, Kansas City, Mo.

_____. 1990, April. Deferred imitation of peers by 14-month-old infants. Paper presented at the meeting of the International Conference on Infant Studies, Montreal, Canada.

Johnson, D. B. 1983. Self-recognition in infants. *Infant Behavior and Development* 6:211–22.

Kagan, J. 1981. *The second year: The emergence of self-awareness.* Cambridge, Mass.: Harvard University Press.

_____. 1984. *The nature of the child.* New York: Basic.

_____. 1989. *Unstable ideas: Temperament, cognition, and self.* Cambridge, Mass.: Harvard University Press.

Kuhl, P. K., and A. N. Meltzoff. 1982. The bimodal perception of speech in infancy. *Science* 218:1138–41.

_____. 1984. The intermodal representation of speech in infants. *Infant Behavior and Development* 7:361–81.

_____. 1988. Speech as an intermodal object of perception. In *Perceptual development in infancy.* Edited by A. Yonas. *Minnesota Symposia on Child Psychology,* vol. 20. Hillsdale, N.J.: Erlbaum, 235–66.

Lacan, J. 1977. *Ecrits: A selection.* New York: Norton.

Lewis, M., and J. Brooks-Gunn. 1979. *Social cognition and the acquisition of self.* New York: Plenum.

Locke, J. 1690. *An essay concerning human understanding.* London: Bassett.

Lorenz, K. 1943. Die angeborenen Formen möglichen Vererbung. *Zeitschrift für Tierpsychologie* 5:235–409.

Loveland, K. A. 1987. Behavior of young children with Down syndrome before the mirror. *Exploration* 58:768–78.

Mahler, M. S., F. Pine, and A. Bergman. 1975. *The psychological birth of the human infant.* New York: Basic.

Mans, L., D. Cicchetti, and L. A. Sroufe. 1978. Mirror reactions of Down's syndrome infants and toddlers: Cognitive underpinnings of self-recognition. *Child Development* 49:1247–50.

Mead, G. H. 1934. *Mind, self, and society from the standpoint of a social behaviorist.* Chicago: University of Chicago Press.

Meltzoff, A. N. 1985a. Immediate and deferred imitation in fourteen- and twenty-four-month-old infants. *Child Development* 56:62–72.

_____. 1985b. The roots of social and cognitive development: Models of man's original nature. In *Social perception in infants.* Edited by T. M. Field and N. A. Fox. Norwood, N.J.: Ablex, 1–30.

————. 1988a. Imitation, objects, tools, and the rudiments of language in human ontogeny. *Human Evolution* 3:45–64.

————. 1988b. Infant imitation after a one-week delay: Long term memory for novel acts and multiple stimuli. *Developmental Psychology* 24:470–76.

————. 1988c. Infant imitation and memory: Nine-month-olds in immediate and deferred tests. *Child Development* 59:217–25.

Meltzoff, A. N., P. K. Kuhl, and M. K. Moore. In press. Perception and the control of action in newborns and young infants: Toward a new synthesis. In *Newborn attention: Biological constraints and the influence of experience.* Edited by M. J. Weiss and P. R. Zelazo. Norwood, N.J.: Ablex.

Meltzoff, A. N., and M. K. Moore. 1977. Imitation of facial and manual gestures by human neonates. *Science* 198:75–78.

————. 1983a. Newborn infants imitate adult facial gestures. *Child Development* 54:702–9.

————. 1983b. The origins of imitation in infancy: Paradigm, phenomena, and theories. In *Advances in infancy research,* vol. 2. Edited by L. P. Lipsitt. Norwood, N.J.: Ablex, 265–301.

————. 1985. Cognitive foundations and social functions of imitation and intermodal representation in infancy. In *Neonate cognition: Beyond the blooming, buzzing confusion.* Edited by J. Mehler and R. Fox. Hillsdale, N.J.: Erlbaum, 139–56.

————. 1989. Imitation in newborn infants: Exploring the range of gestures imitated and the underlying mechanisms. *Developmental Psychology* 25:954–62.

Papoušek, H., and Papoušek, M. 1986. Structure and dynamics of human communication at the beginning of life. *European Archives of Psychiatry and Neurological Sciences* 236:21–25.

Perner, J. In press. *Towards understanding representation and mind.* Cambridge, Mass.: MIT Press.

Piaget, J. 1952. *The origins of intelligence in children.* New York: International Universities Press.

————. 1954. *The construction of reality in the child.* New York: Basic.

————. 1962. *Play, dreams and imitation in childhood.* New York: Norton.

Riesen, A. H. 1947. The development of visual perception in man and chimpanzee. *Science* 106:107–8.

Schulman, A. H., and C. Kaplowitz. 1977. Mirror-image response during the first two years of life. *Developmental Psychobiology* 10:133–42.

Stern, D. N. 1985. *The interpersonal world of the infant.* New York: Basic.

Tiedemann, D. 1797. Beobachtungen über die Entwicklung der Seetenfähigkeiten bei Kindern. *Heissischen Beitrage zur Gelehrsamkeit und Kunst* 2:313–33; 3:486–502.

Trevarthen, C., and H. Marwick. 1986. Signs of motivation for speech in infants, and the nature of a mother's support for development of language. In *Precursors of early speech.* Edited by B. Lindblom and R. Zetterström. New York: Stockton, 279–308.

Wellman, H. In press. *Children's theories of mind.* Cambridge, Mass.: MIT Press.

Winnicott, D. W. 1967. Mirror-role of the mother and family in child development. In *The predicament of the family: A psycho-analytical symposium.* Edited by P. Lomas. London: Hogarth. 26–33.

Wuillemin, D., and B. Richardson. 1982. On the failure to recognize the back of one's own hand. *Perception* 11:53–55.

8 Language about Me and You: Pronominal Reference and the Emerging Concept of Self

ELIZABETH BATES

People like to talk about people. Most of all, we like to talk about ourselves (I, we) in relation to our listener (you) and a world full of family, friends, co-workers, enemies, and strangers (he, she, them). Although natural languages vary greatly in their grammatical structure, they all take this fundamental fact about human nature into account, providing systematic ways to distinguish among speaker, listener, and some third party. The formal means that have evolved to convey this person-marking function almost always include a set of personal pronouns (e.g., I, you, he, it) and may also include a variety of agreement markers on the verb and (less often) on other elements of the sentence. Because person-marking pervades the grammar at so many levels, I will argue that the acquisition of any natural language requires a preexisting theory of self—a theory of the self as distinct from other people, and a theory of the self from the point of view of one's conversational partners. This means that we can use data on the acquisition of person-marking and pronominal reference as a window to the child's emerging self-concept during the transition period from infancy to early childhood (see also Cicchetti et al., in this volume).

To illustrate this point, consider some simple contrasts in the English system of pronominal reference. Suppose that I am an eighteen-month-old girl named Kate, setting out to conquer the English language. Table 1 illustrates some of the contrasts that I will have to make in order to refer to myself appropriately and to understand just when and how other people are talking about me.

Across the top of table 1, we find the different roles that I/Kate can occupy in a conversation, roles that are captured in traditional grammars under the category of "person." "First person" refers to my role as speaker; when I am the one who is talking, I am supposed to refer to myself with one of the forms chosen from column 1 (I, me, mine, etc.) The fact that there are several speaker forms listed in column 1 is only the beginning of my problems (see below), because each and every one of those pronoun forms can refer to

Table 1. Forms of Reference in English for One Child Kate

Semantics	Speaker Role	Listener Role	Third-Person Role
Nominative			She
Singular	I	You	Kate
			The baby
Plural	We	You	They
Objective			
Singular	Me	You	Her
			Kate
			The baby
Plural	Us	You	Them
Genitive			
Singular			
Adjectival	My	Your	Her
			Kate's
			The baby's
Nominal	Mine	Yours	Hers
			Kate's
			The baby's
Plural			
Adjectival	Our	Your	Their
Nominal	Ours	Yours	Theirs
Reflexive			
Singular	Myself	Yourself	Herself
Plural	Ourselves	Yourselves	Themselves

another person entirely when he/she is the one doing the talking. That is, Mommy becomes "I/me/my" when she is the speaker, Daddy becomes "I/me/my" when he is the speaker, and so forth. The various second-person forms in column 2 are the forms that refer to me when someone else is directing a comment my way: you, your, yours, yourself. But, again, Mommy is supposed to become "you/your/yours" when people (including me) are talking to her, and Daddy is supposed to become "you/your/yours" when he is the one doing the listening. This is the problem of shifting reference, an issue that has interested linguists and philosophers of language for more than a century.

Because the referent for any person marker can shift, depending on who is doing the talking, acquisition of these forms presupposes at least a rudimentary grasp of shifting speaker/hearer roles, together with some concept of the speaker's communicative intentions. The problem is posed not only with regard to the I/you distinction but in various forms of third-person reference. Column 3 contains a set of third-person forms that are used when someone is talking about me to someone else—for example, when Mommy is telling

Grandma about something funny that I did at the grocery store yesterday. These include pronominal forms such as "she," "her," and "herself," as well as use of my full name, as in "Kate," "Katie," or "Kate's." They may also include a variety of noun phrases that refer to me in terms of my relationship to the speaker. For example, "my daughter" is something that Mommy might say when talking about me to a stranger, "the baby" is a form that Mommy still uses when she is talking about me to Daddy, and "the little girl with the blonde hair" is something that a stranger might say about me in the grocery store. In order to learn which of these many forms refers to me, I am going to have to figure out who the speaker is, to whom the speaker's comments are directed, and what kind of relationship (i.e., are they intimates or strangers?) the speaker and listener have to each other and to me.

But this is not the whole answer either. Each of the columns in table 1 is broken down further to reflect some of the semantic roles that a given referent can play in the context of a conversation. For example, let us assume that I am the speaker and that I am trying to make some point about myself to Mommy. If I am the actor and/or the experiencer of the activity or event in question, I am supposed to use the nominative pronoun "I" (as in "I want to hold that"). If I am instead the one who is affected by an action carried out by someone else, I am supposed to use the objective pronoun "me" (as in "Give that to me" or "Hug me"). There is yet another set of forms to be used if I am talking about my possessions (e.g., "Mine!" or "My truck"), but these vary further depending upon whether I believe that the goal is already in my (legal) possession ("That's mine!") or whether I want to have that object come into my possession—in which case I will eventually have to learn to use the dative form "to me," which puts me back into the world of affected objects. There are also some mysterious caselike forms called reflexives (as in "Wash myself" or "Do it myself") which, as far as I am concerned in these tender years, are used primarily to make a very strong point. These reflexive forms do some other kinds of grammatical work as well, but it is probably going to take me a few more years to figure those out. For present purposes, the point is that my theory of self will have to be reasonably well articulated if I am going to be required to choose the correct form from among the various case contrasts in column 1.

In fact, as we can see from table 1, each of the person columns has its own corresponding list of case contrasts. For example, "I" becomes "my" in the possessive adjective form, "you" becomes "your," "she" becomes "her," and so forth. Taken together, the columns and rows in table 1 form a systematic matrix, or paradigm. In order to understand language about me and to distinguish language about me from language about someone else, I am going to have to master the whole paradigm. But even with that accomplishment, I will still not be done. There are other subdivisions that run obliquely through table 1 (affecting some decisions, leaving others alone). For example, there is the issue of number. If I am talking about something that Mommy and I did together, I need to use a first-person plural form such as "we" (or us, our, ours, ourselves). This singular/plural dimension will not matter much in English for the second person, but it comes up again in the third person ("she" and "he" versus "they"; "her" and "him" versus "them").

The contrast between "him" and "her" raises the additional problem of gender marking. Gender is marked in English only for third-person singular pronouns. At the very least, this means that children have to have some primitive notion of gender in order to decode third-party conversations about themselves. So our Kate will have to learn, for example, that "she/her/hers" refer to herself, while "he/him/his" do not. To all of this add a few more confusing facts, such as the contrast between imperative and declarative sentences: If I want to tell you to do something right away, I am not supposed to refer to you with any pronoun at all (e.g., "Give me that!"); but if I am talking about some past or present fact, then I have to put the second-person pronoun back in (e.g., "You gave me candy yesterday"). All of these contrasts will have to be mastered before I become a reasonably fluent native speaker of English. And virtually all of them require me to think of myself and others from some temporal, spatial, and/or societal point of view.

It should be clear by now that the English-speaking one-year-old has a lot of work to do in order to acquire the system of personal pronouns. But in fact, he or she is very lucky when we consider the full paradigm of case contrasts required for a language such as German or Hungarian. In these languages, case is marked not only on pronouns but on every single noun phrase in the language. And the case contrasts are much more extensive than the few summarized for English in table 1. In addition to nominative, accusative, and genitive, a language may also require contrasting inflections for the dative (e.g., when I am the receiver of a transferred object), for the benefactive (e.g., when something is done expressly for me), for the locative (indicating that I am, or should be, located in a particular position relative to some object or person), and/or for the instrumental/concommitative (e.g., to talk about someone who is "with" me).

A related set of problems is posed by the verb system in a language such as Italian. For the most part, English verbs are blessedly unaffected by the shifting roles of speaker and listener. There is a contrast between the third-person singular (as in "He eats bananas") and just about every other form of the verb (as in "I/we/you/they eat bananas"). But this fact about verb conjugation, and agreement between subject and object in person and number, constitutes an exception in English that can be ignored for awhile if the child needs to concentrate on other things. In fact, many (though not all) English-speaking children have found a handy way to avoid the pronoun problem—and thus avoid the whole problem of shifting reference for many months. If the child insists on referring to himself/herself and the listener by name, the problems of noun declension and verb conjugation are temporarily solved—for example, "Kate do it!" "Mommy do it," "Give Kate!" "Give Mommy!" Parents often hit on this solution too, so it becomes a chicken-and-egg problem to figure out who initiated the baby talk and who is responsible for plunging into the pronoun system at last. At some point, this "Tarzan-Jane" stage of communication will have to be abandoned, but it provides a convenient resting place for some parents and children during the early stages of language development.

Italian children sometimes use the Tarzan-Jane strategy to avoid person-marking. But whereas the English-speaking child can still keep most communication intact with this move, the Italian child will necessarily leave a great deal more information out of his or her message by ignoring person-marking. The reason is that shifting contrasts in person have an enormous effect on the structure of the verb in Italian (i.e., on conjugation as well as declension). All of this structure is not simply embroidery placed in the language to confound small children; these verb contrasts have come to play a critical role in Italian, a role that is conveyed primarily by word order in English.

To help clarify this point, table 2 illustrates, for the common verb *mangiare* (to eat), some of the person contrasts built into the Italian verb system. For the simple present tense alone, the same verb can take six distinct forms (across eight combinations of person and number, including formal and informal second person—see below). This state of affairs is multiplied across all the different parameters of verb conjugation: tense (e.g., the contrast between *mangio* [I eat] and *mangero* [I will eat]); aspect (e.g., the contrast between *ho mangiato* [I have eaten] and *mangiavo* [I was eating]); and mood (e.g., *mangerei* [I would eat], *mangiasse* [Oh, that he would eat!]).

Clearly, a great deal of information is built into the Italian verb, information that may be crucial to message interpretation. This is true to some extent in all morphologically rich languages, but it is particularly true in so-called pro-drop languages such as Italian, where the rules of informal speech permit the speaker to omit the subject of the sentence far more often than we can in English. For example, an Italian must say "*Piove!*" ("Rains!" instead of "It rains"). And the English utterance "I'm going! I'll pick up a newspaper" would be translated as "*Vado! Prendero' un giornale*"—which literally translates back into English as "Am going! Will pick up a newspaper!" Bates (1976) reports that Italian adults tend to omit the subject of a sentence or clause about 70 percent of the time in informal speech. And because subject ellipsis is so common, Italians have to rely on verb markings much more often to figure out who did what to whom.

Table 2. Partial Conjugation for One Italian Verb

Infinitive: *mangiare* (to eat)
Present Participle: *mangiando* (eating)
Past Participle: *mangiato* (eaten)

	First Person	Second Person (Informal)	Third Person (Second-Person Formal)
Simple present			
Singular	Mangio	Mangi	Mangia
Plural	Mangiamo	Mangiate	Mangiano
Imperfect past			
Singular	Mangiavo	Mangiavi	Mangiava
Plural	Mangiavamo	Mangiavate	Mangiavano
Recent past			
Singular	Ho mangiato	Hai mangiato	Ha mangiato
Plural	Abbiamo mangiato	Avete mangiato	Hanno mangiato
Remote past			
Singular	Mangai	Mangiasti	Mangio'
Plural	Mangiammo	Mangiaste	Mangiarono
Future			
Singular	Mangero'	Mangerai	Mangera'
Plural	Mangeremo	Mangerete	Mangeranno
Imperative			
Singular	—	Mangia!	Mangi!
Plural	Mangiamo!	Mangiate!	Mangino!
Conditional			
Singular	Mangerei	Mangeresti	Mangerebbe
Plural	Mangeremmo	Mangereste	Mangerebbero
Present Subjunctive			
Singular	Mangi	Mangi	Mangi
Plural	Mangiamo	Mangiate	Mangino
Imperfect Subjunctive			
Singular	Mangiassi	Mangiassi	Mangiasse
Plural	Mangiassimo	Mangiaste	Mangiassero

The situation is complicated still further by the fact that Italian (like many other richly inflected languages) permits extensive variation of word order to emphasize or foreground information. For example, the sentence "Mary eats the spaghetti" can occur in Italian in six possible word orders. Some of these word orders are much more frequent than others, but all of them are possible with the right kind of sentence intonation and with appropriate pronominal markings:

Maria mangia gli spaghetti.	(subject-verb-object)
Maria gli spaghetti mangia.	(subject-object-verb)
Gli spaghetti li mangia Maria.	(object-verb-subject)
Gli spaghetti Maria li mangia.	(object-subject-verb)
Mangia gli spaghetti Maria.	(verb-object-subject)
Li mangia Maria gli spaghetti.	(verb-subject-object)

Italian children cannot depend on either the presence or the position of the subject of the sentence to tell them who did what to whom. They will have to plunge into the system of verb marking, as well as pronominal reference, to understand the people around them and to make themselves understood. Hence, the Tarzan-Jane stage of communication ought to be very short. And indeed, evidence suggests that productive control over subject-verb agreement is acquired very early in Italian, at least in expressive language (Bates 1976; Caselli and Taeschner 1986; Hyams 1986). Necessity is apparently one of the parents of language acquisition.

As I hinted earlier, Italian children face a still more complex problem of person marking when they acquire the contrast between formal and informal "you." As can be seen from table 2, completely different pronouns and forms of the verb are used, depending on the level of formality that holds between the speaker and the listener. This situation is roughly similar to the contrast between "Ed" and "Dr. Jones" in English; but because it is built directly onto the verb stem, the contrast is much harder to avoid. Indeed, the contrast between formal and informal second person holds throughout the entire system of verb conjugation. In English, one can avoid the embarrassment of not knowing just how formal or informal to be with the boss's wife, by using polite generic forms like "Could you pass the potatoes?" Imagine trying to find a way to get the same potatoes without using any second-person verbs at all (e.g., "Uhmm, could I possibly have some potatoes? Are those the potatoes that I see over there?"). In fact, Italians become quite adept at skirting second-person reference in an ambiguous situation, but this avoidance behavior itself is an acquired skill (the author still does not have it, after twenty years of speaking Italian).

For very small children in Italy, the informal *tu* form is universal; but by the time children start school, they are expected to have control over the formal/informal contrast when speaking to elders who are not intimate with the family. This problem may not seem as serious as the fundamental challenge of figuring out who did what to whom. But, in fact, the existence of formal address may present problems for comprehension even before the child is expected to show appropriate deference to adults. The reason is that formal "you" is identical in structure to third-person singular "she"— including both the form of the pronoun and the form of the verb (see table 2). There are historical reasons for this. The formal level of address supposedly comes from a deferential use of the third person in speaking to one's superiors, as in "Does his lordship desire dinner?" (where the Latinate base for "his lordship," *La vostra Signoria,* occurs in feminine gender). But two-year-olds cannot be expected to understand this fine historical point. The child who goes to the grocery store in the evening with mother will encounter sentences like *E Lei che cosa vorrebbe?*—which is ambiguous between "And you (formal) what would you (formal) like?" and "And she what would she like?" This adds still more confusion to an already difficult problem of shifting pronominal reference.

Assuming that the child finally figures out that this particular pronoun can mean both "she" and "you," the next step will be to acquire the social rules that govern formal or informal address. As described in some detail by Brown and Gilman (1960), the question of levels of address reflects a tension between two dimensions: power (a function of age and social status) and solidarity (a function of intimacy and/or family and group membership). In a complex society, decisions about how to classify a relationship can yield different answers, depending on which of these two dimensions we weigh more heavily. Bates and Benigni (1978) have shown that the decision to use formal or informal address in modern Italy interacts with age, social status, political affiliation, and a host of more specific local problems. The rules seem to change all the time, and adult Italians often disagree on the answer to questions such as "What form would you use with the twelve-year-old son of the president of the republic?" or "Which form should a thirty-year-old woman use when meeting the fifty-year-old parent of a young friend at a casual cocktail party?" Hence, the problem of levels of address constitutes a major challenge to child and adult alike in mastering the system of personal reference. These complications may seem irrelevant for our purposes here, as we examine the earliest stages in the development of a self-concept. But they are relevant even for very young children in languages like Japanese and Korean, which have many more levels of address than the mere two built into the grammars of most Indo-European languages. In many oriental languages, different forms are used depending on the sex of the speaker and the sex of the listener, as well as their relative age and status. Mastery of the pronoun system in a language like this requires not only a fledgling theory of self but a theory of sex roles and a theory of one's own place in society.

Stages in Pronominal Reference Acquisition

To summarize so far, the child will need a great deal of social/cognitive knowledge in order to acquire person-marking systems in any natural language. Given the magnitude of this challenge, exactly when can we say that person marking is acquired? The available data suggest three major stages in the acquisition of pronominal reference and in corresponding systems of person marking in verb conjugation: noncontrastive reference (from age nine to eighteen months), contrastive reference (lasting roughly from twenty to twenty-eight months), and a final, more adult-like stage that we will describe as paradigmatic reference (from twenty-eight months onward, with modifications occurring as long as life permits).

Noncontrastive Reference

By nine months of age, children begin to use external objects as a means of communicating with adults (Bates, Camaioni, and Volterra 1975; see Bates, O'Connell, and Shore 1987, for a review). In this way, a system of I-thou communication (which has been under way at least since birth) gradually differentiates into the essential triangle of human communication: I, thou, and an object of joint reference. This development usually begins with showing, when the child extends an arm with toy in hand and looks toward the adult for smiles and approval. Showing gradually merges into giving, to the point where a ten- to twelve-month-old may spend a happy hour piling gifts at the adult's feet. But the pivotal development is communicative pointing: index finger extended, arm outstretched, the child indicates or refers to some interesting object or event to the adult. We know that this is an intentional act of communication, because children will often repeat or vary their performance, perhaps looking back up in the adult's face, until some kind of response or acknowledgment is given (Leung and Rheingold 1981; Murphey 1978; Murphey and Messer 1977). Furthermore, although pointing is often used in requests, human children also seem to delight in pointing things out to the adult just for the sheer joy of it. In this last respect, communicative pointing really is peculiar to our species (Savage-Rumbaugh 1979), not in form (other primates do occasionally point) but in the extent to which the young child engages in this activity for no apparent reward other than "mutual contemplation of the world" (Werner and Kaplan 1963). And if one thinks about it, what better preverbal preparation could there be for a species that has such a lust for gossip and small talk?

Because this pointing activity is so striking and so pervasive in early communicative development, it is quite interesting to note that the hearing one-year-old rarely points either to himself/herself or to the addressee. Pointing is restricted almost exclusively to third-person reference at this stage. The identities of the sender and receiver of the message are implied in the fact that the child demands an answer from the adult. But the child does not refer explicitly either to herself/himself or to the receiver of the message as an "object of contemplation." Deaf children are occasionally reported to point at themselves or the listener in these very early stages of development. However, as noted by Petitto (1985), this kind of first- and second-person pointing disappears entirely in the fifteen- to twenty-month range, when (as we shall see in more detail below) children begin to refer to themselves and their listeners explicitly by name. It is as though the child now has some idea what first- and second-person references really mean, at least enough to know that the problem is very complicated and to therefore inhibit any such activity until the problem clears up. This would suggest that the earlier pointing-to-self of the deaf child was actually a rote imitation, the result of constant exposure to a gestural language where such pointing gestures play an important grammatical/lexical role that is still quite opaque to the infant.

Putting these data together, I would suggest that the first phase of pointing from age nine to at least fifteen–eighteen months consists of noncontrastive reference to the external world. The child is the subject, but not the object, of a referring activity. This noncontrastive reference is maintained from preverbal communication through the first phases of real speech. Several lines of evidence support this conclusion. First, pronouns are quite rare before eighteen months, and the few that are observed are usually restricted to a particular context and meaning—for example, the expression "Mine!" Second, the lack of person marking is also observed in the verb system, even among children who are acquiring a richly inflected language. In fact, there tend to be relatively few real verbs of any kind in the productive language of nine- to eighteen-month-old children. But when verbs are produced, they almost invariably occur in a single conjugation—usually the most frequent and/or most neutral form of the verb, typically the third-person singular (although this varies from language to language and from one verb to another). For example, in the longitudinal transcripts of one Italian child, Francesco, the verb "to want" (*volere*) first occurred only in the first-person singular (*Oio,* a baby form for *Voglio*). Other verbs, such as "to open" (*aprire*), first occurred with a sound pattern *ape,* which is somewhere in between *apre* (she/he/it opens) and *apri* (you [informal] open). This kind of pattern suggests that the first forms selected by the child are conditioned primarily by the most frequent and useful context for each verb (Bates 1976; see also Bloom, Hafitz, and Lifter 1980). This selectivity may be the precursor of person contrasts—indicating at least some implicit sensitivity on the child's part to the relationship between a particular form (first, second, third) and particular roles ("want" is especially important with reference to the child himself; "open" is an activity that is most interesting and useful when it is carried out by a competent adult). But such selectivity is still, at best, a protoform. The child does not explicitly mark a contrast of person on either a verb or a pronoun.

Contrastive Reference

Somewhere between eighteen and twenty months of age, on the average, children begin to mark a person contrast in some explicit and productive way. The most striking development for those interested in the emerging concept of self is the emergence of the child's own name—used not only in little games or routines (which can occur much earlier) but also to express semantic roles that can be taken either by the child or by another person, who is also named. For example, the child may start up a game of pretend eating from a fork and hand the fork around, saying "Mommy" when it is mommy's turn, "Kate" when it is Kate's turn, and so forth.

Around the same time, children who are acquiring a richly marked verb system may begin to use contrasting forms for the same verb. For example, the above-mentioned Italian child Francesco began to say *"Apo"* when he himself was opening something, whereas *"Api"* was used while Francesco held an object out for someone else to open. A related contrast between third-person singular and other verbs may occasionally occur this early, even in English, though most English-speaking children do not begin to mark verbs contrastively until around twenty-four months (Brown 1973).

Some children begin to make a systematic contrast between "I" and "you" as early as twenty months of age. Others avoid the pronoun system for a while, opting instead for the above-mentioned Tarzan-Jane strategy, referring to the speaker and the listener by name. In this fashion, everything is reduced to third-person reference, and the problem of shifting identities can be postponed. Still more often, we see a combination of the two, as the child vacillates between pronominal and nominal forms. A great deal of research has recently gone into this transition stage in an effort to determine why forms like "I" and "Kate" coexist in some children and why there is so much variation in noun versus pronoun use across children of approximately the same age.

The coexistence case has been used by some investigators to argue for a "competition" approach to early child language (Bates, Bretherton, and Snyder 1989; Bowerman 1985; MacWhinney 1987). The idea is that children evaluate their linguistic evidence by a kind of quantitative strategy, counting up occurrences (presumably at an unconscious level) and keeping competing forms around until one of those two forms clearly "wins." Bates et al. (1989) offer an example from one child that seems to typify the idea of vacillation and competition among forms for the same functional and formal slot. This child, at approximately twenty-four months, sat among her toys, about to carry out some action, and announced her intentions with "I do that . . . Julia do that . . . Me do that." This was followed by a long silence and a look of puzzlement (on the part of both child and mother). It is difficult to escape the inference that some kind of battle is being waged among competing ways of saying the same thing.

A somewhat different view has been presented by Budwig (1986), Clark (1978, in press) and Deutsch and Budwig (1983). These researchers stress the idea that children prefer clear-cut, one-to-one relations between form and meaning. There is no such thing as a true synonym. If a natural language seems to use two expressions for the same meaning, a close examination will show that each expression is used for a different reason. For example, the choice between "this man" or "this guy" or perhaps "this fellow" hinges on differences in formality, style, social nuance. If it is indeed true that languages only provide contrasts for a reason, then it would make sense that children come into the world equipped with a drive to find the basis for contrasting forms. In this vein, Deutsch and Budwig reanalyzed Brown's (1973) longitudinal data for two children, Adam and Eve, concentrating on a period in which both children seemed to vacillate in the use of "Adam" and "Eve" versus "my" or "me" to talk about possessions. The investigators discovered some subtle but systematic contrasts in the way these forms were used. A phrase like "My knife!" tended to occur when Adam was trying to regain or reassert his territorial rights over some object. An expression like "Adam truck" was more likely to occur when ownership was not being threatened, as a proud statement of ownership or in the context of describing some operation on a possession (e.g., "Cut Eve finger"). From this point of view, the child's apparent vacillations between forms may actually reflect a great deal of fine-grained semantic analysis. The results of this analysis appear to conflict with the Julia example cited above, an expression produced by a single child in a single situation. However, as Bowerman (1985) points out, competition and a drive for contrast can coexist as complementary forces in child language. It is likely that both positions are correct—and, perhaps, correct to a different degree for different children.

This brings us to a broader question concerning individual differences in early language development, as seen through the early acquisition of pronouns (Bates et al. 1989; Bloom, Lightbown, and Hood 1975; Nelson 1981; Peters 1983). In particular, why do some English-speaking children use person pronouns very early, while others opt instead for the Tarzan-Jane strategy? In both cases, the child seems to have "zeroed in" on the issue of contrasting reference. Interestingly, this phase coincides well with other, nonlinguistic forms of evidence on the emergence of an explicit and conscious concept of self (as attested in this volume and in several recent works on the emerging self-concept, e.g., Kagan 1981; Lewis and Brooks-Gunn 1979; see also Bretherton and Beeghly 1982; Bretherton, McNew, and Beeghly-Smith 1981; Bretherton et al. 1983). But why should children react so differently to the pronoun system if they are all approaching language acquisition with the same underlying social-conceptual base?

This question has two answers. First, the concept of self is not an all-or-none discovery. The child will have to discover and integrate many different versions of "me" from many different points of view. This series of reorganizations will affect and perhaps be affected by the kinds of linguistic paradigms that the child has to master in order to acquire a complete person-marking system. Second, language acquisition is only partially driven by conceptual discoveries like the concept of self. Language learning also involves some purely formal games—and by this, I mean quite literally "games"—as the child learns to find and manipulate patterns of sound for their own sake. These two points bring us into the third and final phase in the acquisition of pronominal reference and person marking.

Paradigmatic Reference

I have argued that a rudimentary contrast between self and other is marked explicitly in child language between eighteen and twenty months—coinciding with nonverbal evidence on the emergence of an explicit concept of self. But this does not mean that the child has worked through all the consequences of this discovery. Many "selves" are seen in the eyes of many different observers, and a competent member of society has to navigate through the expectations and responsibilities of a multidimensional "me." Language provides a window onto these social developments; however, as the child struggles with the kinds of systematic person-marking paradigms that we examined earlier, language also poses a series of formal problems.

The very first I/you distinctions are often fraught with error—errors that are quite informative from a psycholinguistic point of view. It is quite common at age twenty to twenty-four months for a child to say "carry you/hold you/help you" to mean "carry me/hold me/help me" (Bates et al. 1989). This kind of error probably derives initially from a learning situation in which the parent says, "Do you want me to carry you/hold you/help you?" The child splits off the relevant fragment of the adult utterance and incorporates it into his or her own requests without the required change in declension and conjugation. With nonverbal behavior, the child makes it clear just who is supposed to carry whom. So the confusion clearly lies at a linguistic level, as the child tries to figure out how to map underlying semantic relations onto the appropriate linguistic forms.

As Petitto (1985) has observed, the same kind of you/me confusions occur in the deaf child's acquisition of pronominal pointing. To us adults, the pointing gesture seems so transparent in its meaning that confusion ought to be impossible. Nevertheless, the deaf child that Petitto studied from age eighteen to twenty-four months avoided second-person pointing altogether at first; when second-person pointing finally reemerged, the child made quite striking errors in the production and comprehension of this seemingly transparent gestural form. Like the hearing twenty-month-old who says "carry you" to mean "carry me," the deaf toddler interpreted all shifting "you" signs as though they referred to the child herself. The pointing sign had become, at least for a while, another version of the child's own name!

Petitto interprets this finding to mean that a special language acquisition device has now taken over, changing a prelinguistic gesture (which was presumably quite transparent) into an arbitrary sign (which is not transparent at all). But I am not at all convinced that we need to invoke a special language device to explain these findings. Because first- and second-person pointing seems to be rare in hearing infants (Volterra and Caselli 1983), where the gesture presumably has no special grammatical status, I think the problem derives from the inherent difficulty of shifting reference in any form—linguistic or not. The twelve-month-old who produces any you/me pointing gestures at all probably does so in an imitative fashion, with no real grasp of the intended contrast (an interpretation that is supported by the report that pointing to self is more common in deaf infants, who are exposed to a barrage of different pointing gestures in sign language). The eighteen-month-old who produces gestures like these has a fledgling understanding of the contrast between self and other—but the grasp is still too tenuous to handle a paradigmatic shift in which the same form is applied across different referents and different forms are used for the same referent. He/she will need considerably more practice with the self-other contrast before being able to switch gracefully from one point of view to another. One way to deal with the problem is to avoid it altogether, at least for a while. Another way is to jump into the system and risk making a lot of errors.

However, I do agree with Petitto in one aspect of her very interesting analysis: the relationship between form and meaning is not a simple one, and linguistic paradigms do not fall directly out of cognitive development. Linguistic forms have to be listened to, handled, and played with for their own sake before they are truly mastered—in much the same way that the child handles and plays with objects for their own sake in the sensorimotor period. In this process, the human genius for imitation clearly plays a major role: it enables the child to reproduce a piece of language long before he/she knows quite what it is for or how it works, which in turn "buys time" for the kinds of detailed form/meaning mappings that have to be worked out. But imitation is certainly not enough; full-scale linguistic analysis is ultimately required.

From this point of view, let us return for a moment to the mysterious pattern of individual differences mentioned earlier: Why do some children dive directly into the pronoun system, while others use proper names (i.e., the Tarzan-Jane strategy) until they have things worked out? As we describe in much more detail elsewhere (Bates et al. 1989 in press), this pattern of individual differences seem to reflect a difference among children in their relative reliance on rote memory and imitation, versus a "deeper" mode of learning where the object in question is broken down into its component parts. Children who rely heavily on rote processes tend to use pronouns quite early; children who rely more on analysis and segmentation tend to avoid pronouns early on or to use them only in a restricted and ''safe'' set of contexts.

This interpretation, if correct, leads to a prediction that seems at first glance to be counterintuitive. If early pronoun use reflects a rote approach to language while reference to self by name reflects a more analytic approach, then we might expect to find that early use of pronouns is *negatively* correlated with the age at which pronouns are finally mastered. This seems to fly in the face of the commonsense belief that head starts lead to an early finish, practice makes perfect, and the early bird catches the worm. However, our recent longitudinal study did show that ''nominal style'' at twenty months is associated with more rapid mastery of pronoun and person-marking paradigms by the time the child is 2½ years old. In other words, the child who *avoided* shifting reference at the early stages did a little better in the long run. This, in turn, suggests that the first signs of pronoun use at twenty months probably reflect rote imitation of language that the child does not fully understand—a point that is underscored by the proliferation of you/me confusion errors like the ones we described above.

But lest we think that production without comprehension is a bad thing, we should point out that rote processing is absolutely essential for any child to pick up the idiosyncratic conventions that history has built into natural languages. Human children have to be very good at the analysis of ''forms for their own sake,'' a kind of distributional pattern analysis that may or may not have a conceptual base. Take the oft-cited example of German gender. How is the child supposed to figure out that the word for little girl is neuter, while the word for bottle is feminine? In languages such as German, there is very little relationship between grammatical gender and semantic gender. In order to figure out the complex set of relations that define gender in German, a certain amount of brute force memorization is unavoidable. Without it, language acquisition could never proceed. After that, the various rote-memorized forms have to be cross-classified into a paradigm through some kind of conscious or unconscious distributional analysis.

The partial autonomy of form from meaning is also illustrated in some of the errors that children make during acquisition of complex syntax. Consider the following example from my diary records for my daughter Julia in the twenty-four to twenty-eight–month period:

DADDY MAKE JULIA'S CRY

The important point about this particular sentence is the incorrect use of the genitive form (Julia's) in one of the child's first attempts to stage a complex embedded syntactic structure. I suggest that this error occurred not because of semantic confusions but because Julia was scouting around for some kind of "template" for this new complex construction. A well-established analogue was located in sentences like

DADDY TAKE JULIA'S BOOK

where the genitive construction is semantically and syntactically appropriate. Julia "borrowed" the more familiar genitive structure in order to stage an utterance with a markedly different meaning.

A similar point is made in Bates (1976), in an analysis of subject-verb agreement in the longitudinal records for one Italian child. Between twenty and thirty months of age, Francesco also vacillated between the use of a first-person pronoun (*io*) and his own name (*Checco*). Interestingly, however, he seemed to pick up the required person contrasts on the verb *before* deciding on one and only one form of reference for himself. This point is nicely illustrated by the following sample:

IO TAGLIO, BATTE CHECCO QUI

which means

I CUT, HITS FRANCESCO HERE

It was quite clear from the context that Francesco was the intended agent/subject for both verbs (that is, he was doing both the cutting and the hitting). We must therefore conclude that Francesco had learned how to match verbs with different *surface forms* and not just with different people in different roles.

It is a very good thing that children can trade off the relationship between form and meaning, or full paradigms like the ones illustrated in tables 1 and 2 would never be acquired. To acquire mastery of the pronoun system, subject-verb agreement, and a host of other problems beyond the ones discussed here, human children need an array of learning strategies: principles of competition and contrast, mechanisms for rote reproduction of elements, and mechanisms of segmentation and analysis. There is no single, right way to acquire a natural language. Individual differences reflect the *degree* to which a given child relies on one or the other of these learning tools; but in the long run, all of the tools will be needed.

Conclusion

Many students of child language prefer to focus on the unique and special properties of language as a system that develops separately from the rest of cognition and emotion (e.g., Chomsky 1981; Hyams 1986; Petitto 1985). I have argued, instead, that the apparent coincidence between pronominal reference and the development of the self-concept is no accident. However, the relationship between form and function is necessarily quite complex. This has some unfortunate consequences for the use of language as a "window" onto the developing concept of self. Like every other window seat that we are provided in the social sciences, this one provides us with a blurred view. For the moment, the important point is that full paradigms of the sort illustrated here are acquired by most normal children by three–four years of age. This gives us an upper and a lower limit on the period in which the child learns to map the concept of self (a shifting self seen in the eyes of others) onto an equally complex set of grammatical and lexical forms. The linguistic and conceptual systems undoubtedly nourish each other at every stage: language provides children with clues about their relation to their social world, while an ever increasing stock of evidence about that social world illuminates their acquisition of language.

References

Bates, E. 1976. *Language and context: The acquisition of pragmatics*. New York: Academic.

Bates, E., and L. Benigni. 1978. Rules of address in Italy: A sociological survey. *Language and Society* 4:271–88.

Bates, E., I. Bretherton, and L. Snyder. 1989. *From first words to grammar: Individual differences and dissociable mechanisms*. New York: Cambridge University Press.

Bates, E., L. Camaioni, and V. Volterra. 1975. The acquisition of performatives prior to speech. *Merrill-Palmer Quarterly* 21:205–26.

Bates, E., B. O'Connell, C. Shore. 1987. Language and communication in infancy. In *Handbook of infant development*. Edited by J. Osofsky. New York: Wiley.

Bloom, L., E. Hafitz, and K. Lifter. 1980. Schematic organization of verbs in child language and the acquisition of grammatical morphemes. *Language* 6:386–412.

Bloom, L., P. Lightbown, and L. Hood. 1975. *Structure and variation in child language*. Monographs of the Society for Research in Child Development, vol. 40, serial no. 160.

Bowerman, M. 1985. What shapes children's grammars? In *The crosslinguistic study of language acquisition*. Edited by D. I. Slobin. Vol. 2, *Theoretical issues*. Hillsdale, N.J.: Erlbaum, 1257–1320.

Bretherton, I., and M. Beeghly. 1982. Talking about internal states: The acquisition of an explicit theory of mind. *Developmental Psychology* 18:906–21.

Bretherton, I., S. McNew, and M. Beeghly-Smith. 1981. Early person knowledge as expressed in gestural and verbal communication: When do infants acquire a "theory of mind"? In *Infant social cognition*. Edited by M. E. Lamb and L. R. Sherrod. Hillsdale, N.J.: Erlbaum, 333–73.

Bretherton, I., S. McNew, L. Snyder, and E. Bates. 1983. Individual differences at 20 months: Analytic and holistic strategies in language acquisition. *Journal of Child Language* 10:293–320.

Brown, R. 1973. *A first language: The early stages*. Cambridge, Mass.: Harvard University Press.

Brown, R., and A. Gilman. 1960. The pronouns of power and solidarity. In *Style in language*. Edited by T. Sebeok. Cambridge, Mass.: MIT Press.

Budwig, N. 1986. Agentivity and control in early child language. Doctoral dissertation, University of California, Berkeley.

Caselli, C., and T. Taeschner. 1986, October. The acquisition of morphology in Italian. Paper presented to the Boston Child Language Forum, Boston.

Chomsky, N. 1981. *Lectures on government and binding: The Pisa lectures*. Dordrecht: Foris.

Clark, E. 1978. From gesture to word: On the natural history of deixis in language acquisition. In *Human growth and development: Wolfson College lectures, 1976*. Edited by J. S. Bruner and A. Garton. Oxford: Clarendon.

_____. In press. The contrast principle. In *Mechanisms of language learning*. Edited by B. MacWhinney. Hillsdale, N.J.: Erlbaum.

Deutsch, W., and N. Budwig. 1983. Form and function in the development of possessives. *Papers and Reports on Child Language Development* 22:36–42.

Hyams, N. 1986. *Language acquisition and the theory of parameters*. Dordrecht: Reidel.

Kagan, J. 1981. *The second year: The emergence of self-awareness*. Cambridge, Mass.: Harvard University Press.

Leung, E., and H. Rheingold. 1981. The development of pointing as a social gesture. *Developmental Psychology* 17:215–20.

Lewis, M., and J. Brooks-Gunn. 1979. Toward a theory of social cognition: The development of self. In *New directions in child development:* Social interaction and communication during infancy. Edited by I. Uzgiris. San Francisco: Jossey-Bass, 1–20.

MacWhinney, B., ed. 1987. *Mechanisms of language acquisition*. Hillsdale, N.J.: Erlbaum.

Murphey, C. 1978. Pointing in the context of a shared activity. *Child Development* 49:371–80.

Murphey, C., and D. Messer. 1977. Mothers, infants, and pointing: A study of gesture. *Studies in mother-infant interaction*. Edited by H. R. Schaffer. London: Academic.

Nelson, K. 1981. Individual differences in language development: Implications for development and language. *Developmental Psychology* 17:170–87.

Peters, A. 1983. *The units of language acquisition*. Cambridge: Cambridge University Press.

_____. 1985. On the use of prelinguistic gestures in hearing and deaf children: Implications for theories of language acquisition. Paper presented at the tenth annual Boston University Conference on Language Acquisition, Boston.

Savage-Rumbaugh, S. 1979. Symbolic communication—its origins and early development in the chimpanzee. In *New Directions in child development,* vol. 3. Edited by I. Uzgiris. San Francisco: Jossey-Bass.

Volterra, V., and C. Caselli. 1983. From gestures and vocalizations to signs and words. In *SLR 1983: Proceedings of the III International Symposium on Sign Language Research*. Edited by W. Stokoe and V. Volterra. Rome.

Werner, H., and B. Kaplan. 1963. *Symbol formation*. New York: Wiley.

9 Being of Several Minds: Voices and Versions of the Self in Early Childhood

Dennie Palmer Wolf

New Symbols for Selves

Our most immediate definition of self is that of a coherent and distinctive center: a bodily container, an anchor point for our sense of agency, a single source for our emotions (no matter how chaotic), or a kind of volume where the chapters of a very personal history accumulate. Experientially as well as clinically, we worry not just about the wholesale dissolution of a self into multiple personalities but about any fissure in that center: false and true selves (Kohut 1977; Winnicott 1958); frictions and border wars between id, ego, and superego (Freud 1923, 1933); or the danger that a more verbal and socialized self may dominate a more intuitive core self (Stern 1985). So deeply etched is this image of the self as a coherent whole that our everyday language is full of phrases that mark moments of distress as times when the self comes "unglued" or "falls to pieces." We describe those times with metaphors of decay and disarray, often marking the fracture of the self by making it into both subject and object: "*I* hardly knew *myself.*" or "*I* lost *my* mind."

But actually, we rarely attend to the internal voice of *the* self. Much more often, we listen to the murmur of *"voices"* in an internal dialogue. Decisions, and possibly even development in our moral lives, depend on our being able to phrase the several sides of a dilemma (Emde and Buchsbaum, in this volume; Gilligan 1982; Kohlberg 1981). Whether we design a physics experiment, play Mozart, or tune an engine, we often overhear an imagined conversation between self and mentor; self and audience; self, colleague, and critic. When we edit what seemed so wise when we wrote it or look back over old photographs, we sense what Sir Lawrence Olivier called the capacity to be "both horse and rider." As parents, we all live in the play of inner voices that takes up as we watch our children do what we once did and we hear ourselves use phrases we swore we'd never speak.

To recognize this heterogeneity of self neither as pathological nor occasional but as constitutive substantially changes the notion of self. It is to argue that what we hear when we listen in is not a single clear voice but a diversified internal dialogue (Bakhtin 1981; Dore 1989; Todorov 1981). It is to suggest that, like more observable and public forms of cognition, our most private moments of reckoning are profoundly social: they involve either the interplay of recollected voices or interchanges between several portions of our self—interchanges very similar to and perhaps even stemming from our conversations with others (Luria 1976; Vygotsky 1962). If this is the case, we may owe much to these fissures in ourselves: metacognition, moral deliberation, editing, and possibly all those moments in which we select from our experience to make versions, fictions, or lies.

Even in the first year, the experience of self is multifaceted. To totter around the edge of a table is to be someone who delights in the speed and uprightness of walking at last, the self who fears tumbling, and the self who checks to see the approving or fearful eye of a parent (Emde and Sorce 1983). During each of these moments, a baby lives in a strikingly different and behaviorally coherent envelope of experience. The tottering, delighted self smiles, concentrates on forward motion, and vocalizes in rhythm with her or his own steps; the self who seeks social connection scans the room, stands still, and calls out distantly to mother over by the window. From the distinct responses that each of these performances provokes in an observing other—smiles in the first case, reassurances in the second—we know that these envelopes of experience are observable, vivid, and differentially provocative ways of being, not merely private fluctuations in internal states.

But these distinct, communicable states of being are only the beginning of what will eventually become multiple selfhood. An infant has multiple selves only insofar as he or she enters or experiences different events. There is a rigorous match between the infant's actions, experiences, and communications to others. In effect, infant selves are limited to being experiencers (the one who feels the plunge of forward motion) or actors (the one who calls out or seeks to snag mother's visual regard). In this way, an infant may be one *situational self* after another. However, infants don't create or seem to participate in events that demand an exchange between several selves. While a ten-month-old may hesitate at the top of a forbidden flight of stairs, babies (from all that we can observe) don't suffer moral dilemmas. Just as notably, children under a year rarely edit or transform their experience or attempt to deceive others about it. Infants may be agents in different states, but they are not several selves at once (Johnson 1988; Kohut 1971, 1977).

This paper is about an early moment in the formation of such a heterogeneous self. It is a moment that builds on but substantially changes the infant's experience of the situational fluctuations in activity, intentionality, and relatedness. It is a period roughly between the ages of two and four when children begin to exhibit an *authorial self:* a self independent enough of any given situation to select which voices and what versions of experience to acknowledge. It is a new kind of self, one who can speak as object or subject, as observer or participant. This is also a self who can pretend, joke, lie, or choose among renditions.

Authorship: The Ability to Separate Self and Situation

Authorship is the ability to act independent of the impinging facts of a situation. Between the ages of two and four, two abilities appear that make this separation possible. The first is the ability to "uncouple" various lines of experience. This can take many forms: simulation and pretense (when a person transforms the actual situation through thought or fantasy), obfuscation (when a person refuses to claim or share what he/she really knows), or deceit (when a person deliberately distorts or denies what he/she feels or knows). In each of these situations, the self rearranges, edits, or changes the "facts" to align with some exogenous goal, hope, or wish. This cleavage essentially creates a new experience of self. The self becomes an author with the freedom to take up and to move among a variety of stances. For example, in looking at photographs of their own past, children can speak alternately as the subject and as a knowing outside observer. In their play with siblings and peers, they zigzag between the roles of real-world collaborators and fictional witches or doctors. While handling small figures, their speech moves between the perspectives of an all-knowing narrator, the characters in a drama, and a real-world self. Thus, a three-year-old can "be" a toy lion, the meditative observer who asks if the figure is real, *and* the person who throws the lion away because it is frightening (Scarlett and Wolf 1979; Wolf and Hicks 1989). In effect, the onset of an authorial self enables the child to move *simultaneously* among any number of possible worlds.

The second capacity articulating authorship is the emergence of explicit forms of representation to mark the nature of and movement among the stances of the self. Through the acquisition of a much richer syntax as well as a set of discourse-level understandings, children make their capacity for different stances public and articulate. First, by age three, children use different *voices* to signal the several perspectives they can take on experience. Thus, a child, telling about what happened yesterday, uses the past tense, many declaratives, and a series of temporal markers. By contrast, when the child is in the here and now of conversation, his or her talk is typically in the present indicative, full of questions and imperatives, and often lacking many temporal markers. Moreover, children begin to experiment with different *versions,* or genres, for portraying their experience. By the age of four, many children can render the "same" experience in a variety of formats. For instance, they can tell about going to bed in general, recall a particular and personal bedtime anecdote, or make up a story where the very specific emotional contours of their own nighttime rituals are projected onto someone else, in some other time and place. Often, in spontaneous talk, these forms intermingle, conveying the fluctuating point of view of a self who lives in, knows about, or is concerned with what is customary, actual, or only possible in fiction at different moments.

These new forms of talk are powerful signals. They are one of those developmental events which have the power to bring on socialization (Fischer et al. 1984; Lerner and Busch-Rossnagel 1981). They make the diversity of a child's internal world public and shareable. Once children begin to use language to compare their older and younger selves, to step back and consider their own behavior, or to express different perspectives, parents, siblings, or even casual observers see quite a different child. That child shares with them at least the beginnings of a history with different chapters, a hint of being ''horse and rider,'' and the complexity or uncertainty of being ''of two minds.'' In response, these observers draw children into just those situations and conversations that are likely to crystallize and amplify children's experience of themselves as heterogeneous selves.

To illustrate, the following is taken from a series of naturalistic observations made as a part of a larger study of early symbolic development in nine children from middle-income families (Shotwell, Wolf, and Gardner 1980; Wolf 1982; Wolf and Gardner 1981). It focuses on J., a firstborn, normally developing boy in a two-parent family. He and his parents contribute the core of examples throughout this paper. In this first extract, J. is just about to turn two. Although he is only beginning to experiment with representing and communicating experience in the diverse ways just described, his efforts are impressive and his father's response sensitive:

> In recent weeks J. has started some very simple use of number words. His parents are quite excited and one day when a visitor comes, they want him to show off his new skill. J. watches as some pennies are laid out for him to count. He is not much interested and wanders off, picking up his blanket, Ni-ni, on the way. His parents, who are looking on, try to draw him back to the pennies, asking him to count for them. J. scatters the pennies. The adults pick them up and arrange them again and ask J. to count them once more. This time, with the blanket masking his hand, J. scatters the pennies again. He quickly ''checks'' with the adults to see what their reaction is. He holds up the blanket draped over his hand and announces, ''Ni-ni did it.'' His father laughs and shakes his finger at Ni-ni. ''Try and count 'em, Ni-ni,'' says his father, joining in. ''Noooo,'' says J., very much in his own voice.

Clearly, J. is more than a situational self. He has begun to be an authorial self whose gestures and words can transform the "facts" of the actual scene. He uses both words and behavior to uncouple the identity between himself and the penny scatterer by substituting his blanket in the role of agent. He uses his language, sparse as it is, to argue for a certain selection of the facts. When he insists "Ni-ni did it," he is asking his father to pay attention to the waving, wiggling blanket and to wink at the way his own arm pokes into and animates Ni-ni. Only moments later, when J. says "Noooo," he makes public the heterogeneity or internal diversity of his self. When he speaks about Ni-ni, he is deep in the fiction, using a playful voice, alleging that *he* didn't scatter the pennies. But when he refuses to count, he speaks in his own *voice*. He can speak from inside the play or squarely from a different possible world, that of face-to-face interaction in which the conventions of truthful exchange prevail (Grice 1975).

At the same time, the shifting stances which characterize J.'s talk throughout this episode appeal to his father, getting him to exercise several potential perspectives on the situation. Even though his eyes tell him a two-year-old has willfully scattered the money, he hears and follows J.'s request to quarantine that perception. He enters the play world, carrying on as if J. were innocent and the blanket were petulant. Later, when J., with his "Nooo," refuses to count, he implicitly asks his father to shift ground and take his identity and talk as a two-year-old seriously. A kind of incipient subtext beneath the quick fluctuations in this exchange may be that people, by their very nature, have and exercise "several minds."

In order to flesh out the concept of an authorial self and to argue for its emergence during late toddlerhood, I want to turn to a combination of sources: a review of current developmental research on early cognitive and symbolic development in the early preschool years; findings from a longitudinal study of children's discourse skills (Shotwell et al. 1980; Wolf and Gardner 1981; Wolf and Grollman 1982; Wolf and Pusch 1985; Wolf, Rygh, and Altshuler 1984); and finally, the case study of J., a participant in that longitudinal study.

The Emergence of an Objective Self: Cognitive Foundations for an Authorial Self

As early as their second year, children give ample evidence of having several minds. Kagan and his colleagues report that during the second half of the second year, children "behave as if they are acquiring a new set of functions that centers on the sensitivity to standards and the ability to meet them, as well as an awareness of the self's behavioral effectiveness" (Kagan 1981, 47). What this means is that children can think about their own behavior, apart from the behavior itself, either in anticipation or reflection.

In the case of anticipation, children evidently respond to several voices "inside their heads," even within the compass of the first year. Spitz's (1957) observations of children approaching forbidden objects eagerly, while uttering the "no" they have undoubtedly heard from behind them, provide ample evidence. Later, during their second year, children exhibit signs of distress (crying, clinging, refusals, etc.) when an examiner models a complex series of actions that the child is expected to imitate. This distress in response to the model suggests that children are aware of their ability or lack of ability to meet the momentary standard (not even a long-ingrained familial or community expectation) of imitating the sequence. Here, there is a kind of bifocal vision: children can, at one and the same moment, represent to themselves a desired or requested sequence of behavior and their own likely-to-be-less-than-perfect performance. Consequently, they panic or withdraw. These findings coordinate remarkably with observations of preplanning in children's spontaneous and elicited symbolic play. For example, Nicolich (1978) found that, while object transformations and short episodes of play occur early in the second year, as children advance toward their second birthdays they are increasingly likely to gather needed objects and make arrangements prior to launching into a sequence of make-believe. Thus, across a range of paradigms and situations, children provide evidence of anticipating and even appraising sequences of actions they have not as yet performed.

At the same time, children begin to reflect back on sequences of actions just performed. Kagan's data suggest that during this same period there is an increase in mastery smiling—smiles that follow a moment when the child perceives that he or she has attained a previously generated goal after considerable effort. Kagan (1981) also reports a 1935 study by Buhler in which one- and two-year-olds were forbidden to touch a toy. The adult left the room, and many infants touched the prohibited toy. When the adult returned, more than half of the children aged 1:4 and all of the children aged 1:6 showed great embarrassment, blushed, and turned to the adult with a frightened expression. From 1:9 on, they attempted to make good on what happened by returning the toy quickly to its place. This sort of conflict may be a familiar experience, but what seems new is the sense of a standard which, once the child's behavior falls short, causes embarrassment and maybe even shame. There is, henceforth, at least an incipient sense of a willful actor and a censuring observer.

Given these findings on anticipation and reflection, it is not surprising that studies of internal state language show that, as early as in their second and third years, children acquire an interest in and the terms for describing their own and others' interior lives (Bretherton and Beeghly 1982; Cicchetti et al., in this volume; Hood and Bloom 1979; Johnson 1988; Johnson and Maratsos 1977; Johnson and Wellman 1980). While this is usually taken to signify a jump in semantic and/or emotional development, it also points out that children are eager as never before to reflect on and raise questions about the relationship between what was done by the self as agent and what was felt by the self as an experiencer. An example taken from observations made early in J.'s third year illustrates:

> J. and his father are recollecting a recent trip to a children's zoo.
> *Father:* Tell D. about the animals. . . . You fed the goats, right?
> *J:* In my hand. Like this [*holds his hand out palm up*]. Da goats' mouth on me.
> *Father:* You were a big boy, huh? Very brave.
> *J:* Scary.

J. held out his hand and fed the goats, but "inside" it was just as he says, "scary."

During this same period, as many observers have remarked, children begin to treat mirror images and photographs as representations of themselves (Amsterdam 1972; Butterworth, in this volume; Cicchetti et al., in this volume; Kaye 1982; Lewis and Brooks-Gunn 1979; Snow, in this volume). Usually, this event is taken to signify a growing coherence of self in its many manifestations. But these moments are sites for the formulation and articulation of a self that is a laminated one, as the following instance with J. indicates:

> J. and his mother have just come home from errands. One of their packages contains recently developed photos of a weekend outing when their family and another family went for a cruise on a harbor boat. J. sits beside his mother on the couch as she turns through the images. He narrates:
> *J:* K. and J. on a boat. Hafta put jackets on. Zip up. I was mad, Mommy?
> *Mother:* Yeah, you didn't want yours on.
> *J:* I cried?
> *Mother:* I told you "Everybody is going to wear a jacket. Even daddy and mommy. Even K." Then you were okay, right?

As they talk, J. can refer to himself as an objective other in the snapshot, just as he might speak about a character in a book illustration. But he just as readily shifts to a more subjective account of what happened in which he constructs the continuity between his present and his weekend experiential selves. He marks this change with his switch from proper names to "I."

Becoming the subject of your own thoughts entails a kind of multiplication of selves: you have to stand outside yourself in order to look on. As James ([1890] 1950) would have it:

> Our considering our spiritual self at all is a reflective process, it
> is the result of our abandoning our outward-looking point of
> view, and of our having become able to think of subjectivity as
> such, *to think of ourselves as thinkers* . . . in the thoughts that
> do resemble the things they are "of" (percepts, sensations),
> we can feel, alongside of the thing known, the thought of it
> going on as an all together separate act and operation in the
> mind. (P. 296–7, James' italics)

Still later, in summing up, he writes:

> Personality implies the incessant presence of two elements, an
> objective person, known by a passing subjective Thought and
> recognized as continuing in time. *Hereafter let us use the
> words ME and I for the empirical person and the judging
> Thought.* (P. 371, James' italics)

These remarks and the research just sampled show that during the second
year, even in the realm of nonverbal behavior, children give us evidence that
they know something of the me that acts and the I who anticipates, compares,
remembers, and judges. The self becomes an observable entity as well as a
subjective state (Kagan 1981; Lewis and Brooks-Gunn 1979; Stern 1985).
While this knowledge is anything but complete (as will be discussed later), it
is a significant foundation for the continued development of a healthy and
productive conversation between multiple selves.

The Appearance of Stances: The Language of Different Voices

The emergence of standards and of language which permits both the
objectification of self and reference to different aspects of experience signals
the onset of quite a different kind of multiple self than is carried in the infant's
successive states. This multiple self is capable of taking up any of a number
of different *stances* toward a situation. Thus, J. can be both the person in the
photograph and the individual who comments upon that image.

It is in the context of a sharply differentiating sense of self that children
acquire a set of linguistic markers which may either partake of or amplify their
shifting notion of self. In the months around their second birthday, children
acquire a network of terms for the self—both proper names and nominals as
well as personal pronouns and the possessive morpheme (see Bates, in this
volume). In addition, they gain mastery of the dyadic complexities of personal
pronouns which permit them to talk about "mine" and "yours," "you" and
"me" (Bates, in this volume; Brown 1973; Kagan 1981; Leopold 1939; Sully
1896). During this same period, children also learn to mark agreement

between subject and verb. This array of terms and devices makes it possible to mark sentences for point of view, even if in a primitive way. For example, children can speak about their own or someone else's experience (''I want big pants''; ''You got on big pants''; ''He has big pants''). But more important for the issue of the development of a heterogeneous self, they can also speak from the vantage point of either a subject (''I want big pants'') or an observer on their own experience (looking at self in the mirror, ''J.'s got big pants'') (Snow, in this volume). In the subsequent year, most children also learn additional morphemes which allow them to distinguish fairly reliably between the present and the past in their accounts of personal or imagined experience. For example, Brown's (1973) data indicate that the highly noticeable forms of the irregular past appear in his three subjects between ages 2:3 and 2:11, and the regular-past morpheme (-ed) comes to be used reliably between the ages of 2:2 and 4:0. The result is the emergence (or at least the crystallization) of a new kind of multivocal discourse, one in which several different strands work in combination to create a larger whole. Each of the voices, or lines, ''speaks'' for a particular stance or perspective. As pointed out earlier, these stances may have existed in behavioral terms for quite a while. Language, however, makes them unmistakable. It makes possible a juggling of several selves, which shows up in any number of forms: framing talk, memory talk, insider-outsider talk, and play talk.

Framing Talk

In their simplest forms, these voices are distinguishable in everyday conversations or narratives, when the child momentarily drops the frame of the ongoing talk, makes a comment, and then returns to the original topic (Schegloff 1971; Schriffrin 1982). Or, using the contrasts between past and present, the child may talk about different chapters or moments in her or his evolving autobiography. To return to the case of J.: At the age of 2:2, he is taking off his sweater, hat, mittens, and boots in the hallway after returning home from child care:

> *Mother:* Here, give me the mittens.
> J. holds out his hands and his mother tugs off the mittens.
> *Mother:* Those are wet. Did you play in the snow this afternoon?
> *J:* We made a snowman. A big one.
> *Mother:* Yeah? Did you give him a face?
> *J:* Rocks . . . eyes.
> *Outside the late afternoon train rolls by.*
> *J:* Train's coming. [*He listens for a minute and then looks back to his mother.*] . . . And sticks for his arms.
> *Mother:* No wonder these mittens are sopping.

J. and his mother are talking about a snowman when the train hurtles by, distracting him. For a moment, he focuses on its roar, then comes back to the snowman, signaling his return to the earlier topic with "and" and "his." Already, he can juggle the roles of the present-tense observer (the one who listens to the train) and the backward-looking reciter of an anecdote.

Memory Talk

This ability to locate the self in several distinct worlds has more complex forms as well. One is the *memory talk* between children and adults, in which the two partners move between comments made in the present tense and recollections couched as historically distant. In this talk, as children take an increasingly prominent role, they use at least two *voices* in the conversation: the person who identifies with the younger, distant person (the object of the memory) and the person who engages in recollection (the subject who currently has the memory). Here is J., at 2:6, again returning from child care at the end of the day. He talks with his mother about a drawing he has brought home with him. It becomes the occasion for comparing his younger and his current selves.

> *Mother:* Did you make that? Such a big one.
> *J:* At school. With big marker.
> *Mother:* By yourself? Or did the teachers help?
> *J:* No, J. See [*points to where an adult has written his name*].
> *Mother:* I like it. I didn't know you could make people.
> *J:* Not people. A man with gray pants. See [*he points to gray scrawl on top of what may be a tadpole-like figure*].
> *Mother:* Is it Daddy going to work in his gray pants?
> *J:* Yeah, a Daddy man. Put it on a 'frigerator. Take that one down. It's old. It's yuck.
> *Mother:* I like it. You just did it when you were little.
> *J:* I was little, yuck. Not now. Do the new one. Do the daddy-man one up there. It's a big daddy-man one now.

Even though his command of temporal markers is just beginning and his vocabulary is borrowed in part from his mother, J. draws an effective contrast between "then," when he "was little" and made "yuck" drawings, and "now" (which is cast in the present tense), when he makes "new" and "big" drawings. Even as this bigger self, he distinguishes between himself as object, as when he points to the signature and gives his proper name, and the person who is speaking, "I." In the period between 2:6 and 3:0, it is increasingly J., not just his mother or father, who constructs episodes of talk where he contrasts the past and the present versions of himself. For instance, at 2:10 he is playing in the middle of his bedroom floor, when he looks up at his father and refers to an episode of their joint play when he (J.) battered one of his trucks.

> *J:* Need to make a garage for my big dump truck . . . we need to make a big garage for this truck. Let's not crash into the garage because they still need fixing, the garage man's, ya, this is broken (examines front of the truck) this one haves a broken muffler. 'Member the other time, when a man, he crashed in, and he had a broken muffler, a broken muffler, the other day?

Insider-Outsider Talk

A similar interplay of voices also shows up in *insider-outsider talk,* in which children zigzag back and forth between what the artist Ben Shahn (1957) calls the role of the "active imaginer" and "the critic of inexorable standards." Here, as with the memory talk, children mark the different voices with remarkable clarity. Close to his third birthday, J. is drawing:

> J. takes yellow marker and draws big loose yellow oval.
> *J:* Like this . . . all round.
> J. slashes across the oval with a vertical line.
> *J:* Then this. Big one.
> J. sits back and appraises what he sees.
> *J:* Think I made an airplane.

Here, J. speaks in two voices. The first is that of an on-line sportscaster rendering a blow-by-blow account of what he is doing. The second is the more fully realized, past-tense voice of his reflective self.

This interplay of voices is not only reflective, but often quite critical. Thus, during this period, J. often steps back from his own activities to judge his own performance, saying things like "Wow" or "Dummy, that is stupid." This sort of alternation between engaged participant and reflective or skeptical outsider is not reserved for his own activities. He also uses it to examine and question much of what he encounters. Here is J., reading a picture book in the last quarter of his third year.

> J. reads a book about a naughty puppy, taking the stance of an engaged story-teller, until he becomes troubled and reflective:
> *J:* He's running down the stairs. He's opening the door.
> The next illustration shows the puppy on a stretcher, being carried off to an ambulance. Suddenly J. is confused, and then critical.
> *J:* Why I didn't see the car crash?
> J. flips back to the start of the book and goes through the pages again, this time thoroughly the critic.

J: Where's the boy's mother [*over an illustration where just a boy is scolding the dog about having run through a flower bed*]?

J: This is dumb . . . no car crash [*over the illustration of the dog on the stretcher*].

J: This is funny, dogs don't go in bed, they just go to sleep on the floor. Why he is in bed [*over the illustration of the dog, now healed, curled up in a basket, back at home*]?

Play Talk

Children's play with small objects offers some of the most elaborate examples of this interplay of voices. In play, children freely enter and exit the world of a narrative, sometimes speaking as the teller and imitating the voices of distinct characters and other times dropping out to ask for information or help in remembering, then returning to the tale never having dropped a stitch (see Cicchetti, et al., in this volume). In this kind of talk, children make use of many of the voices they have developed elsewhere: the direct discourse of the speaking subject, the voice-over of a narrator, and the outsider voice of a critic or commentator. Here, children achieve considerable *intratextuality,* juggling several lines of information within their discourse without destroying the overall coherence or cohesion of their talk. Earlier studies (Wolf, Goldfield, and Beeghly 1984) showed that many three-year-olds could move between at least three prominent voices: stage-managing, character dialogue, and narrative.

Additional studies (Wolf and Hicks 1989) have shown how children use their emerging knowledge of grammar and discourse to distinguish further between the several voices. For instance, children make differential use of pronouns in each voice: stage-managing and character dialogue are marked with first and second persons, while narrative utterances are marked with the third person. Children also employ various forms of utterance to signal the perspective from which they are speaking. Narrative segments are normally recounted through use of declarative utterances, since what is being encoded in the narrative voice is "what happened." Dialogue and stage-managing, however, reflect a more interactive stance, so that questions and commands may be used as well as declarative utterances.

Additionally, children use various aspects of the temporal system to encode various facets of the kinds of temporal perspective native to the different voices. They employ different patterns of verb inflections, verb semantic types (*aktionsart*), and sequential connectives across each of the voices. The use of verb inflections reflects the obvious distinction between past and present tense, as well as aspectual dimensions of duration or ongoing activity. The differential use of verb semantic types reflects the distinction noted in

Vendler (1967) between verbs which encode events (take, get, come), those which encode processes (play, swim, run), and those which encode physical states (have, be) and internal states (feel, think, know). The use of sequential (and-then, after, before), temporal (while), and causal (because) connectives reflects the child's awareness of order and causal connections between narrative events.

Here is J. playing with some small figures and a toy car at 2:6:

> *J:* Let's go in the car. Let's go visit.
> *Observer:* Who's he gonna go visit?
> J. holds out a little girl figure.
> *J:* This girl want go visit . . . in a car.
> J. puts the girl in a toy car and drives it quickly until the figure falls out.
> *J:* [*making loud, angry crying sounds*] I fall car.
> J. puts the girl back in the car and drives it again until the figure falls out.
> *J:* (Sh)e fall again.

In this early session, the character and narrator voices are distinguished largely in performative terms: the narrative comments are evenly delivered, while the character speech is quite animated and high-pitched. While first-person pronominals mark the character speech and third-person references denote narrator speech, few other grammatical features distinguish the voices.

However, between 2:6 and 3:0, J. developed additional voices as well as the ability to mark those voices linguistically rather than chiefly with performative contrasts. To indicate what this sounds like, here is an excerpt of J. playing out a very similar scenario just several weeks later:

> J. is playing with several figures inside a doll house.
> *J:* He has to go upstairs, Mommy.
> *J:* Watch, Mommy.
> J. releases the figure so that it rolls down the steps.
> *J:* He fell down, Mommy. He's crying, Mommy. He's a boo boo on his head.
> J. makes crying sound effects for the figure.
> *J:* Ouch, ouch, I hurt my head.

Here J. has three voices operating. In the voice of a stage manager he commands his mother's attention and explains to her how the fictional world he has created operates. That voice is one of direct address, it is in the present tense, and it takes the form of imperatives and mandates. When J. speaks as the narrator, he explains the main events of the story ("He fell down, Mommy"). It is a voice which fluctuates (at least at this early stage) between present-tense replay and past-tense encoding. It is full of action and state verbs and declarative utterances. By contrast, when J. speaks as a character, this speech is often the most richly performed: it has varied contours and sharply pitched tones. Typically, it occurs in the first and second person and the present tense, with varied sentence types.

But as J. continues to play, he comes to distinguish the separate voices in his narratives on the basis of an increasingly complex network of linguistic features within each voice. Stage-managing utterances become distinctive in that they are a forum for interactions with the experimenter about the nature of the fictional world that is being created. In this sense, these utterances represent an excursion from the story world itself, not unlike the asides or departures that adult speakers index with changes of tone, "push-pop" markers, or shifts in topic (Polanyi 1985; Schriffrin 1982). Stage-managing utterances are linguistically distinguished from narrative and dialogue by the frequent use of a collaborative second-person proform (we're, let's, etc.) and use of the future to forecast what will happen in the play ("And then he's gonna go in the tree"). The narrative strands come to be marked with the past tense and to carry clear markers for temporal sequencing (and, then, while). Dialogue strands are marked with the present tense, a high frequency of first- and second-person pronominals, deictic speech (come here, take this, etc.) and conversational conventions (hi, bye, how ya doing).

At 4:0, J. is playing with a puppet theatre and a set of small figures, including the members of a family, a cat, and a pirate. (The transcript is marked to indicate which roles J. is taking at each point when he speaks.)

> J. knocks down some of the trees in the theatre.
> *J.:* [*narrator*] And all the trees fell down.
> *J.:* [*cat character, to clown*] Put your legs down.
> *J.:* [*pirate character, stalking in, threatening voice*] I am the pirate.
> *J.:* [*speaking as himself to the observer*] See his sword? Is he really a pirate?
> *Observer:* Yeah.
> *J.:* [*speaking as himself to the observer*] Are you telling the truth?
> *Observer:* Yeah.
> *J.:* [*speaking as himself*] Not really. Just in here.
> *J.:* [*cat character, scratching pirate*] Scratch, scratch, scratch.
> *J.:* [*pirate character*] Don't you dare.
> J. has the figures continue to fight.
> *J.:* [*man character*] Don't kill me, don't kill me . . . and don't kill any of my friends either.

This episode of play lasts not more than ten or fifteen seconds. But within it, J. is by turns the organizing, framing narrator; the scrappy, aggressive characters; and a young boy candidly mapping out the reality status of a plastic pirate. Possibly, he uses the interplay among those several voices to explore the power and the limits of the pirate. First he uses the character voices to portray how mean the pirate is, then he uses his own voice (the stage-managing strand) to check on the limits of that power. Once he has established for himself just where the pirate is powerful, he resumes his aggressive play. Potentially, then, these voices are not merely a part of the conventional way to play. Possibly, they are one way of talking around a question and raising its several sides, or even a way of talking one's way toward resolution of that question.

One way of thinking about the early and elegant emergence of several voices within children's narratives is to suggest that the linguistic distinctions "piggyback" on a fundamental understanding of the different stances, or perspectives, that a person can take—or find oneself in—with respect to events. The role or voice of a narrator, with its distance on events, may encode the experience of looking on, or observing, what Britton (1982) terms a *spectator* stance. When children engage in character dialogue, however, their perspective on events is much more intimate in nature, so that this voice may be representative of what Britton terms a *participant* stance, a stance which may encode what it is like to be in the midst of an event. The role and voice of the stage manager is a kind of *executive, or explanatory,* stance; it may come from the position of someone who shepherds events towards their end without wanting to observe and without being in the midst of what is going on. It is the voice of someone who can explain the workings of the fictional world to someone else who is puzzled. Perhaps it has its earliest roots in the nudging and explanations of mothers and fathers.

Fictions and Versions: The Appearance of an Authorial Self

This capacity for adopting different perspectives is only a part of what enables the emergence of an *authorial self.* It has a complement in children's capacity for and interest in fiction, with all of its selections, transformations, and distortions. Usually, what comes under this rubric is transformation made possible by symbolic play (Nicolich 1978; Piaget 1962; Scarlett and Wolf 1979). But tea parties and fantasy alligators under the bed are only one aspect of children's (or adults') capacity for fiction. In this same period, children begin to participate in various forms of cultural shortcuts which certainly involve a kind of editing and condensation: the overregularization and compacting of experience into scripts, and the telling and creating of instances of acceptable lore from the rawer materials of familial experience (Nelson 1989; Wolf, in press). Thus, in this period, when his mother asks what happened during his day at child care, J.'s accounts typically trim out reams of detail, saving only the highly patterned events—saying he had "outside time" on a day when the rain kept children and teachers indoors.

Equally a part of this pattern are the small lies children tell in order to make themselves safe or "good" within the moral framework of the family and community (Dunn 1988). In his third year, J. doesn't just pretend in the context of playing at going camping or animating his toys, he understands the kinds of selection and editing that are part of looking like you are behaving—even when you aren't. He is quite capable of shaping his behavior or his accounts of his own actions to preserve the boy he "should be," rather than the role he is actually playing. Thus, when the birthday child at a party received a very enticing dump truck with a loader that cranked up and down, J. engaged that child in play, doing wild stunts with a quite ordinary car, so as to transform it into a very desirable object—quite possibly in order to get his hands on the dump truck.

Thus, to fictionalize is more than to pretend. An *authorial self,* as the maker of fictions, moves between possible worlds *and* shapes the contents of those worlds. In a particularly sharp example, J., at 3:0, is struggling to build some stairs out of blocks. He has tried this several times before, growing frustrated and simply scattering the blocks. When he fails on this occasion, he uses the voice of a fictional character to mock his own performance, acknowledging what he observes but displacing it.

> J. struggles to place a block so that he gets a jagged outline, but instead, he produces a rectangular, wall-like structure.
> *J:* I can't do it. I don't know how.
> J. goes on and turns the wall-like structure into a building. As he continues to play, he comes upon a bag of marbles. Taking several out, he jokes at trying to stack them up, hamming it up when they tumble and roll away.
> *J:* These stairs are too hard to make.
> J. makes a little figure hop up to the top of a stack of blocks. He makes that figure call down to another one to join him.
> *J:* [*for figure 1*] Hey, come on up here.
> J. makes the second figure struggle up (as there is only a stack with no toe-holds). When the stack topples, he makes that second figure complain.
> *J.:* [*for figure 2*] Hey you dummy, that didn't work, you make dumb stairs.

J.'s fictions are not private or relegated to the realm of play. His parents sense their place in his life. They comment on it in the diary they keep and in interviews. For example, his mother picks up on the way in which he uses the options of fictional stories to explore elements of his own life. She writes:

Also in the last month there has been a marked increase in his talking about his pretend friends, Jack and Jill. He doesn't refer to them as pretend, I do. Jack and Jill seem to do a lot of the things he is not supposed to. . . . he knows that he sleeps in his own bed—for a while we had problems with him coming into our bed at night—so last night he told me that Jill came into Jack's bed and she shouldn't.

The Development of Versions of Telling

Having learned the selections and transformations of personal and cultural fictions, young children also come to appreciate and use a variety of distinct discourse forms, or *versions*. These versions are akin to what in adult speech is often termed *register* or *genre* (Bakhtin 1981; Dore 1989; Fowler 1982). The term designates a recognizable form for making and conveying a particular kind of meaning. As compared to the more codified genres, versions can be as formal and recognizable as a fairy tale or as informal and private as the pattern of talk a particular child and parent develop during a bedtime ritual (Dore 1989). Versions are recognizable along any number of channels. Each version has its own distinctive content: consider the princes and caskets of fairy tales or the talk of sleep, waking, and tomorrow characteristic of bedtime conversations. Versions can also be picked out, based on formal linguistic markers: think about the past tenses of a fairy tale as compared to the future-oriented chat of bedtime rituals ("Tomorrow, when you wake up, we'll . . ."). We also cue listeners about which version of telling we are in through performance qualities: a tale is often given a dramatic rendition with different character voices and a lilting delivery for the voice-over narrative portions, while a bedtime sequence frequently is marked by hushed tones, which give way to whispering, singing, and cuddling.

Each of those channels is marked in quite elaborate ways. Take, for example, the case of linguistic marking. We signal, with at least three levels of features, that we are outlining the generalized script for an event, not giving a report or telling a tale. At the level of the individual clause, we use the second person and the historical present ("First, you get in the car") to signal that this is a general, not a specific, past-time narrative. At the level of rhetorical features (e.g., the texture of the telling), we tell a script very plainly. There is little detail or evaluative language. We use chiefly a narrative voice, omitting dialogue or many side comments. At the level of structure, a script moves steadily forward in time (there may be branches but no forecasts or flashbacks) and lacks any kind of high point or resolution—quite unlike what we expect of a story.

As sophisticated as these abilities may seem, considerable research in child language and discourse analysis now shows that children as young as three and four make rather clear distinctions between versions, particularly narrative ones. Thus, when telling highly scripted narratives, even three-year-olds typically mark their accounts by use of the present-tense, second-person pronominals, simple sequencing connectives in a matrix of rather spare language, and a steady, forward temporal organization (Mandler 1984; Nelson 1986; Nelson and Hudson 1986). By contrast, when engaged in storytelling, children typically mark their utterances with patterns of first- or third-person pronouns, predominance of the past tense, more specific sequential connectives, (e.g., "later," "and again"), richer language, and more complex temporal organizations (Applebee 1978; Eisenberg 1985; Peterson and McCabe 1983; Wolf, in press). When children provide running commentary on ongoing events, they may also make use of first- or third-person pronominals and sequential connectives; but in those "on-line replays," they combine these features with distinctive patterns of temporal features, such as the predominant use of the English progressive form (Gee 1986; Heath 1983, 1985).

Longitudinal data show that, by age four, children can distinguish scripts, on-line accounts, and personal anecdotes along numerous dimensions (Wolf, in press; Wolf and Hicks 1989). Moreover, once they initiate a particular form, children can sustain its features or mark an exit and change to another form of telling. However, my emphasis here, in the context of describing the emergence of a heterogeneous self, is not so much the sheerly performative or linguistic distinctions children can draw as it is the point that different genres also offer distinct ways of framing or presenting the self (Goffman 1986).

What follows are three of J.'s versions of what he knows about mythical superheros: Superman, Batman, and a fabulous giant. Even though the content of these versions is largely similar and each of them is told within a month of his fourth birthday, the various tellings frame his self in subtle but significantly different ways. In the first of these excerpts, J. is involved in an on-line narrative as he paints a picture of Superman. The focus is on his very current abilities and knowledge, his negotiation of moment-to-moment problems and obstacles. It gives a portrait of him as pragmatic problem-solver, operating in the here-and-now world:

> As he draws, J. directs himself:
> J: I am going to make a green person [*paints green area*] . . .
> His legs [*adds patches below original area*].
> J. adds a circular area above the original area, making dabbing motions within that circular area.
> *Observer:* Are those his eyes?
> J: Yup. And his arms [*he paints patches to either side of the original torso area*]. And his capes [*makes more area on*

each side of the figure]. I am making Superman *[dips into red, making a zigzag across the chest].*
J. adds two red areas at the bottom of the page.
J: I am making his boots.

Only a week later, J. talks with his father about superheros in the context of fantasy-reality distinctions and the question of whether Batman is a man like his father is a man. In this version, the emphasis is on his world knowledge, not so much on his performance. Here we get a picture of a self outside the pressing demands of an immediate task; it is a self who can step back far enough to think about the general case and who can worry through the relation between specific instances and more abstract categories. (In this light, it is interesting that his father, listening to all this, responds to J.'s final question with ''What do you *think?*'') Throughout, J. portrays himself as someone who probes:

J: To be Batman you have to put on his shirt with this *[makes gesture of an insignia on his chest].*
Father: Yeah.
J: And his boots and capes.
Father nods.
J: And then you find bad guys who are being mean. Like robbers. And then you catch them and put them in jail. And then you wait for more bad guys to come and you kill them. Until there aren't any more.
Father: Then what?
J: Then do you take the shirt and the boots off? And the cape? And then are you a man? Or Batman still?
Father: What do you think?

During these same weeks, J. also tells stories about fictional superheros, like giants. Compared to his on-line account and his script, his stories are full of evaluative and expressive language and extremes of action (e.g., chases, killing, and squashing houses). In this context, J. presents a very different side of himself: the self that knows about, or at least wants to explore, fear and anger and aggression. The following excerpt comes from a much longer episode of play in which a mean giant crunches everything in sight:

J: And now he's crunching everything.
J. picks up a tree.
J: Now he's crunching this.
J: And he's crunching all those *[more trees].*
J: And this.
J: And this *[tossing each new object away as it is crunched].*
J: Boy, he has a lot of stuff to crunch *[more crunching].*
J. sees an object under a nearby chair.
J: And along came a bomb and dropped right on him.

Again, the adults around him respond to his interest in versions. For example, his parents note in their diary the way he uses scriptlike language to state and reflect on the general case. One of them jots down a song they hear him chanting not long after he had a tantrum and slammed the door to his room: it runs, "Sometimes you get mad and you close the door real fast and you want to be alone."

They also hear how he moves between versions, presenting different sides of himself. One day, J.'s father stands in the doorway, watching J. play with an observer.

> *Observer:* [*taking a plastic dinosaur figure*] This could be a
>   dragon.
> *J:* Is he a mean one?
> *Observer:* Better talk to him [*pointing to the dinosaur*].
> *J:* Are you a mean one? [*He does not make it answer.*]
> *J:* [*turning to observer*] Would you think he's a mean one?
> *Observer:* Do you think he is mean?
> *J:* I mean, you *could* make him be mean.
> *Observer:* How shall we make him be?
> *J:* I don't think he lives here. He's gonna go in the forest—
> J. sets the dragon apart.
> *Father:* [*commenting to observer from the sidelines*] He and I
>   were playing with his adventure people the other day. Usu-
>   ally it's chaos, with people flying and jumping, and going
>   off in ambulances. But nothing happened, we kept stopping
>   to have these long discussions about whether to make the
>   diver a bad guy, and how bad, and whether people *really*
>   died or just really in the play.

Contemporary with these kinds of observations, his parents' interactions with J. come to trade on the many discourse forms he now handles and, consequently, the many ways in which he appears to be able to frame experience. For example, at this time, they develop a genre of "moral talk" that alternates between talk about a specific past-time episode and discussing rules about or scripts for the general case. In an interview at this time, J.'s mother describes what has become a kind of ritual event.

> One day D. (J.'s father) was riding the bus into the square with
> J. J. noticed a very fat man and started pointing and asking
> "Why he is fat?" D. tried to divert his attention, but J. just
> wouldn't be put off. Since then, J. comes back to it all the
> time, over and over, asking "Why Daddy didn't want me to
> talk about the fat man?" I explain to him, "Some people are
> short, some people are tall, fat, thin, and that's just the way
> they are. They don't like it when other people talk about them.
> It makes them unhappy. So that's why Daddy said no."

During this same period, J. and his parents develop a particular kind of late-afternoon talk that occurs in the time period between returning from child care and supper, when J. often plays near one of his parents who is cooking. The talk which runs through that play is, in effect, a conversation between several aspects of J.'s by now very complex self and the corresponding aspects of his parent. Here is a transcript of part of one such conversation on a day when J. was building with blocks. (The transcript is marked to suggest the several kinds of discourse in which he and his mother engage.)

> J. is building a house for a little toy figure named Bert. He lays out a red rectangular block.

On-line narrative
J: This is gonna be Bert's bed . . . and this is the gate.
J. lays a drum mallet beside it. (His own early life if full of gates, since he and his parents lived through a very contentious period when he was climbing out of bed and coming into his parent's room at night. As a result, there was a gate between the two rooms.)

Recollection
J: Mommy, where's the gate I had before I was a little baby?
Mother: The one for between you and Mommy and Daddy's room?
J: That one. Where's that one?
Mother: We still have it. But you don't need it anymore because you're staying in your bed all night.
J: Why I needed it?
Mother: Because you weren't going to bed very nicely at night. But now you do.

On-line narrative resumes
J. builds more of the house, including a bathroom with a toilet. He talks to himself, directing the arrangement of the blocks.
J: This one's gonna go here . . . need 'nother red one . . . Where's the red one like this one . . . here . . . here it goes . . . now a big long one . . . [*When he is done, he drops the Bert figure into the house.*]

Projected play narrative based on specific past-time occurrence
J: Oh look, he's turning on the hot water. He got burned like I did last night. He burned, he wants to go to bed. Better turn the cold water on, he got to turn off the hot.
J. turns the water off in imaginary gestures.
J: Now his mommy is gonna take him out.

Stage-managing
J: I go get her. [*He leaves and comes back with another fig-ure.*]

Projected narrative resumes
J: Mommy, Mommy [*speaking for the Bert figure*].

Stage-managing/actual conversation
Mother: What?
J: No, he is calling his mommy, not your mommy.

Projected narrative resumes
J. uses the Ernie to lift the Bert out of the house.
J.: [*speaking through the Ernie figure*] Okay, Bert, little Bert.

On-line narrative
J. builds a very elaborate horizontal structure.
J: That's his bed.
   As J. is running out of blocks, he comes to a series of short columns. He stops, apparently considering whether he wants to use them. At last he lines these up along the bed.
J: Lights.

Reflection
J: [*looking over at his mother*] These are *your* lights. This one the bright one, this one the not bright one, this another one. [*His mother has a series of lights by her bed which includes a bright one for lighting the room and a dimmer one for nighttime reading.*] Like in your room.
Mother: Mmm.
J. adds more blocks until he gets quite a spectacular form of many colors and shapes.
J: Hey mom, you like this house?
Mother: Yes, that's a wonderful house.
J. is working very carefully. She helps him adjust a block.
J: You be very careful, not to knock down my big house.
J. runs to get several small figures to nestle in different small niches. He and his mother hunt carefully and gently place the figures throughout the structure.

J. presents many aspects of himself in this short episode. In the on-line narratives concerned with the building of block structures, he exhibits his mastery-oriented, engineering self who lives quite squarely in the here and now. When he pauses and recollects about the gates from months ago or the hot water burn from last night or the system of lights in his mother's room, he exhibits the side of himself which gathers experience and tries to bind it into a history. It is intimate, made personal by remembered detail. When he plays out the building of the gate or the saving of "Bert, little Bert," he discloses that he recollects more than chronology—he recalls the affective tone of events. These he projects into story, changing the names to protect the innocent but going over the saved contours of those moments.

The Limits of an Authorial Self

For some, this description of J., and by implication other preschoolers, will seem too rich an interpretation, one that attributes both too much decision making and reflection to very young children and too many subtexts to family conversations. But at the most, I am positing only a very particular under-standing of a heterogeneous self on the part of children, not a systematic deductive theory about internal conversations and their consequences for be-havior and communication (Chandler 1988; di Sessa 1985). As mentioned earlier, children lack at least three aspects of a mature heterogeneous self, no matter how subtle their grasp of the several aspects may be.

To begin, there is evidence that children as young as J. may not coordinate, or simultaneously hold, multiple representations of the same information. For instance, research on family and role relations (Fischer et al. 1984) clearly shows that it is only between the ages of four and seven that children understand role intersections (e.g., that a doctor can also be a parent and a spouse) or that the same individual can be both nice and mean. Along similar lines, Flavell and his colleagues (Flavell 1986; Flavell, Green, and Flavell 1986) have demonstrated that children as old as four have tremendous difficulty holding in mind the actual and the apparent identities of objects. Thus, a four-year-old looking at a rock through a transparent blue gel can describe how it looks but not what it is.

It is equally apparent from investigations of children's theory of mind that if preschoolers understand something about the multiplicity of selves, that concept may be quite parochial—possibly even limited strictly to them-selves. As far as other people are concerned, it is not until later that children appear to grasp that human beings *in general* may hold different beliefs, thoughts, or fantasies, depending on what they happen to know at any given moment (Wellman and Estes 1986; Wimmer, Gruber, and Perner 1984; Wimmer and Perner 1983). Thus, it is improbable to think of children below school age understanding, as a matter of principle, how the several aspects of their selves are coordinated into a single, albeit multifaceted, self. Similarly, before that time, it is unlikely that children realize that the multistranded quality of their own internal experiences is a general property of human minds. Thus, J. and his peers may lack the explicit coordinations among the past and present selves and the different kinds of internal experiences which inform this seven-year-old's recollection of an evening when she found no one at home:

> I knock on . . . and no one came . . . and I thought that some-
> thing bad had happened to my parents . . . and it got me re-
> ally, really scared . . . cause I was five when this happened
> . . . and then I sat on the front porch and I started to cry . . .
> and then someone . . . some people came out and they said,
> "What's the matter?" and I said, "No one's home and I think
> they all died." (Then she narrates how her mother eventually
> came home) and I said, "It wasn't my fault Mom . . . it was
> my friend's fault because she didn't walk me all the way."
> (Wolf, unpublished data)

In all probability, J. and other children his age also are missing a clear sense that other people, like themselves, have different facets to their selfhood. This sort of a theory of self, or mind, may not appear until the school years, when it comes to infuse and organize much of children's daily experience. Here, seven-year-old M. remembers a day when her car pool did not pick her up after school. She reenacts her own internal dialogue, as well as her conversation with the people in the car pool. She portrays both her uncertain and her confronting self, and their planning and forgetting sides:

> (Imitating herself musing): Where are they . . . I just can't imag-
> ine where they went . . . I know this is the second time . . . they
> ought to remember. (Then, switching to the conversation when
> she confronted them): You left me at school again. . . . But you
> do something different every Thursday. . . . Uh-uh, *Tuesday*. . . .
> Alright, we won't forget you again . . . (whispering) At least we
> hope we won't. (Wolf, unpublished data)

Finally, no four-year-old is concerned with that which occupies adoles-
cents: the work of finding the through-lines in the moment-to-moment flux of living and thinking (Chandler 1988; Elkind 1967; Inhelder and Piaget 1958; Kohlberg 1981). Not until adolescence or adulthood do the integrative motives or the reflexive thought structures behind the search for a self in the several selves become absorbing:

> After soccer today, I went to find K., he coaches . . . um vol-
> leyball . . . He told me to go get his pushup bar . . . It goes
> like this (he traces out a kind of u-shaped bar and demonstrates
> how, if you rest your hands on the outside, upper edges, you
> can lower your body quite far down.) He says, "You're not
> getting off easy, one hundred and fifty, no stopping." So there
> we are together, doing pushups, trying to beat each other out,
> like he-men . . . and what's so funny . . . what we start joking
> about . . . is I'm this scrawny kid and he's gay and there we
> are doing our macho routine, trying to prove it to each other
> . . . and it's got nothing to do with who either one of us is
> . . . really. (Wolf, unpublished data)

While these findings certainly raise questions about the status of children's representations of their multiple selves and about the coherence among these representations, there may be a wide gap between what children exhibit in the hypothetical and highly linguistic conditions of laboratory investigations and in the affectively charged, socially meaningful scenes of real life. In moments when they bother to talk about what has happened to them or what they feel or wish at the moment, children's holds on what it is to be a multifaceted self may be, if intuitive, quite complex.

Similarly, a critic might well argue that I give much too much credit to families. But, on the part of families, I am picking out only an additional way in which the language of parents is acutely attuned to the talk of children. Others have pointed out how singing and peaked intonations are designed to catch and hold a baby's interest (Fernald and Simon 1984) or how the grammatical and semantic complexity of parents' speech increases in concert with children's language development (Snow, in this volume). To this I add the observation that parents hear and respond at the most intuitive level to the self, or selves, that children present through their talk. In this light, rather than being too rich an interpretation, to posit the essential heterogeneity of children's selves and the attunement of families to that emerging complexity seems a parsimonious way to account for the diversity and nuance which characterize parent-child interactions in the third and fourth years of life.

Conclusion

What I have suggested in this chapter is that one defining characteristic of selfhood is heterogeneity. As selves, we have to recognize, coordinate, and make good use of the many voices and versions of our internal experience. But realizing this takes two important ingredients: a mind sophisticated enough to represent the "same event" in multiple lights and also, I would argue, the means to make that diversity of perspectives public, clear, and useful. To illustrate how early this diversity of selves emerges, I have pointed out that during their second year young children are already capable of adopting a range of stances toward experiences. For example, they can be both the subject who willfully reaches out for a forbidden toy *and* the critic who only a moment later turns into a censuring or ashamed self. In the years that follow, children's language development provides the means for marking these stances with distinctive *voices,* or patterns of performance, content, and linguistic features. However, that shift, fundamental as it may be, is only a part of what happens. There is also a burst of changes which signals the onset of a whole range of editorial, fictional, and even deceitful behaviors: these show up in pretense play as well as in the white lies children tell when they are discovered breaking rules. Together, the onset of stances and their articulation in voices and versions of events result in the emergence of what I have called an *authorial self.*

Only descriptive data are presented here. With only observations, it is difficult to get at the specific anatomy of the cluster of developmental events I am suggesting. At this juncture, I can simply suggest the onset, at about the age of two, of a capacity for representing and reflecting on experience. I can only argue for the conceptual similarities between the discourse forms, voices, and versions which appear in the ensuing months, and underscore that they appear to co-occur. Without additional measures, it is difficult to guarantee a link between this apparent cognitive shift, the appearance of novel discourse forms, and a measurably different sense of self. The significance of these changes in children's language may actually lie in a somewhat different direction. To speak as subject and object, author and critic, character and narrator, may or may not crystallize a more differentiated sense of self. The significance of these new forms of discourse may be that children *appear* substantially different to others. Suddenly, they sound old enough to be drawn into discussions about what is right and wrong, recollections of the past when it brushes with the present, and talk which hinges on at least some intuitive understanding of point of view. In fact, the linguistic acquisitions may not so much create a diversified self as signal to others that a child is "old and wise enough" to become a part of just those situations which will develop the "several minds" of the self.

In all of this, I do not want to give symbolization a causal role as much as an enabling one. Without the clearly articulated language forms which appear at this time, the heterogeneity of children's minds and selves would exist submerged. Without the public face which play and talk give, parents, siblings, and teachers would be slower to realize and amplify the complexity of children's selves with invitations to joke, remember, or step back and consider. But once those varied forms of telling appear, they act as signed stimuli. Children are seen as having become heterogeneous selves, and they are welcomed into a community of similar selves. They are invited to move between fiction and tough-minded explanation, between specific occurrences and generalizations, between unfolding behavior and a thoughtful critique of that behavior. These are experiences which have tremendous power to continue and sustain the development of a profoundly dialogic self.

Writing about the origins of the self, Mead (1934) opened his essay with the paradox that what we think of as most private and unique—ourselves—owes its ontogenesis first and foremost to others. "The self is something which has a development: it is not initially there at birth but arises in the process of social experience and activity, that is, develops in the given individual as a result of his relations to that process as a whole and *to other individuals within that process* (p. 199, italics mine)." Children like J. are no exception. As his discourse changed, making the diversity of his internal worlds more articulate and more public, his family responded, mirroring and drawing out those possibilities.

References

Amsterdam, B. K. 1972. Mirror self-image reactions before age two. *Developmental Psychology* 5: 297–305.

Applebee, A. 1978. *The child's concept of story.* Chicago: University of Chicago Press.

Bakhtin, M. 1981. *The dialogic imagination: Four essays.* Austin: University of Texas Press.

Bretherton, I., and M. Beeghly. 1982. Talking about internal states: The acquisition of an explicit theory of mind. *Developmental Psychology* 18: 906–21.

Britton, J. 1982. Spectator role and the beginnings of writing. In *What writers know.* Edited by M. Nystrand. New York: Academic.

Brown, R. 1973. *A first language.* Cambridge, Mass.: Harvard University Press.

Chandler, M. 1988. Doubt and developing theories of mind. In *Developing theories of mind.* Edited by J. Astington, P. Harris, and D. Olson. New York: Cambridge University Press, 387–413.

di Sessa, A. 1985. Learning about knowing. *New Directions for Child Development* 28: 97–124.

Dore, J. 1989. How monologue re-envoices dialogue. In *Narratives from the crib.* Edited by K. Nelson. Cambridge, Mass.: Harvard University Press.

Dunn, J. 1988. *The beginnings of social understanding.* Cambridge, Mass.: Harvard University Press.

Eisenberg, A. 1985. Learning to describe past experiences in conversation. *Discourse Processes* 8: 177–204.

Elkind, D. 1967. Cognitive structure and adolescent experience. *Adolescence* 2: 427–34.

Emde, R. N., and J. E. Sorce. 1983. The rewards of infancy: Emotional availability and social referencing. In *Frontiers of infant psychiatry,* vol. 2. Edited by J. D. Call, E. Galenson, and R. Tyson. New York: Basic Books.

Fernald. A., and T. Simon. 1984. Expanded intonation contours in mothers' speech to newborns. *Developmental Psychology* 20: 104–13.

Fischer, K. W., H. Hand, M. Watson, M. Van Parys, and J. Tucker. 1984. Putting the child into socialization. In *Current topics in early childhood education,* vol. 5. Edited by L.G. Katz, P. J. Wagemaker, and K. Steiner. Norwood, N.J.: Ablex, 27–72.

Flavell, J. H. 1986. The development of children's knowledge about the appearance-reality distinction. *American Psychologist* 41: 418–25.

Flavell, J. H., F. L. Green, and E. R. Flavell. 1986. *The development of knowledge about the reality-appearance distinction.* Monographs of the Society for Research in Child Development, vol. 51, no. 1. Chicago: University of Chicago Press.

Fowler, A. 1982. Kinds of literature: An introduction to the theory of genres and modes. Cambridge, Mass.: Harvard University Press.

Freud, S. 1923. *The ego and the id.* Standard edition, vol. 19. New York: Nortan, 12–66.

———.1933. *New introductory lectures on psychoanalysis.* Standard edition, vol. 22: 5–182.

Gee, Julie. 1986. Beyond semantics: A discourse analysis of the verb inflectional system in distinct narrative-like and communicative formats in the speech of a two year-old. Paper presented at the Symposium on the Acquisition of Temporal Structures in Discourse. Chicago Linguistics Society Meetings, Chicago.

Gilligan, C. 1982. *In a different voice: Psychological theory and women's development.* Cambridge, Mass.: Harvard University Press.

Goffman, E. 1986. *Frame analysis.* Boston: Northeastern Universities Press.

Grice, H. P. 1975. Logic and conversation. In *Syntax and semantics.* Edited by P. L. Cole and J. L. Morgan. Vol. 3, *Speech acts.* New York: Academic.

Heath, S. B. 1983. *Ways with words: Language, life and work in communities and classrooms.* Cambridge: Cambridge University Press.

———. 1985. The cross-cultural study of language acquisition. Keynote address, Stanford Child Language Research Forum, Stanford, California.

Hood, L., and L. Bloom. 1979. *What, when, and how about why: A longitudinal study of early expression of causality.* Monographs of the Society for Research in Child Development, serial no. 181.

Inhelder, B., and J. Piaget. 1958. *The growth of logical thinking from childhood to adolescence.* New York: Basic Books.

James, W. [1890] 1950. *The principles of psychology.* New York: Dover.

Johnson, C. N. 1988. Theory of mind and the structure of conscious experience. In *Developing theories of mind.* Edited by J. Astington, P. Harris, and D. Olsen. New York: Cambridge University Press, 47–63.

Johnson, C. N., and M. Maratsos. 1977. Early comprehension of mental verbs: Think and know. *Child development* 48: 1743–47.

Johnson, C. N., and H. M. Wellman. 1980. Children's developing understanding of mental verbs: Remember, know, and guess. *Child development* 51: 1095–102.

Kagan, J. 1981. *The second year: The emergence of self-awareness.* Cambridge, Mass.: Harvard University Press.

Kaye, K. 1982. *The mental and social life of babies.* Chicago: University of Chicago Press.

Kohlberg, L. 1981. *The philosophy of moral development.* San Francisco: Jossey-Bass.

Kohut, H. 1971. *The analysis of the self.* New York: International Universities Press.

———. 1977. *The restoration of the self.* New York: International Universities Press.

Leopold, W. F. 1939. *Speech development of a bilingual child, vol. 1,* Evanston, Ill.: Northwestern University Press.

Lerner, R. M., and N. A. Busch-Rossnagel, eds. 1981. *Individuals as producers of their own development: A life-span perspective.* New York: Academic.

Lewis, M., and J. Brooks-Gunn. 1979. *Social cognition and the acquisition of self.* New York: Plenum.

Luria, A. R. 1976. *Cognitive development: Its cultural and social foundations.* Cambridge, Mass.: Harvard University Press.

Mandler, J. 1984. *Stories, scripts, and scenes.* Hillsdale, N.J.: Erlbaum.

Mead, G. H. 1934. *Mind, self, and society.* Chicago: University of Chicago Press.

Nelson, K. 1986. *Event knowledge: Structure and function in development.* Hillsdale, N.J.: Erlbaum.

_____. ed. 1989. *Narratives from the crib.* Cambridge, Mass.: Harvard University Press.

Nelson, K., and J. Hudson. 1986. Repeated encounters of a similar kind: Effects of familiarity on children's autobiographic memory. *Cognitive Development* 1: 253–71.

Nicolich, L. M. 1978. Beyond sensorimotor intelligence: Assessment of symbolic maturity through analysis of pretend play. *Merrill-Palmer Quarterly* 23: 89–101.

_____. 1988. On the origins of beliefs and other intentional states in children. In *Developing theories of mind.* Edited by J. Astington, P. Harris, and D. Olsen. New York: Cambridge University Press, 414–26.

Peterson, C., and A. McCabe. 1983. *Developmental psycholinguistics: Three ways of looking at a child's narrative.* New York: Plenum.

Piaget, J. 1962. *Play, dreams, and imitation.* London: Kegan-Paul.

Polanyi, L. 1985. *Telling the American story: A cultural and structural analysis of conversational story-telling.* Norwood, N.J.: Ablex.

Scarlett, W. G., and D. Wolf. 1979. When it's only make-believe: The construction of a boundary between fantasy and reality. In Early symbolization. Edited by D. Wolf. *New Directions for Child Development* 3: 29–40.

Schegloff, E. A. 1971. Notes on conversational practice formulating place. In *Language and social context.* Edited by M. Giglioli. Hammondsworth: Penguin.

Schriffrin, D. 1982. Discourse markers: Semantic resource for the construction of conversation. Doctoral thesis, University of Pennsylvania.

Shahn, B. 1957. *The shape of content.* New York: Knopf.

Shotwell, J., D. Wolf, and H. Gardner. 1980. Styles of achievement in early symbolization. In *Universals and constraints in symbol use.* Edited by M. Foster and S. Brandes. New York: Academic.

Spitz, R. 1957. *No and yes: On the genesis of human communication.* New York: International Universities Press.

Stern, D. 1985. *The psychological world of the human infant.* New York: Basic.

Sully, J. 1896. *Studies in childhood.* New York: Appleton.

Todorov, T. 1981. *Mikhail Bakhtin: The dialoguic principle.* Minneapolis: University of Minnesota Press.

Vendler, Z. 1967. *Linguistics in philosophy.* Ithaca, N.Y.: Cornell University Press.

Vygotsky, L. S. 1962. *Language and thought.* Cambridge, Mass.: Harvard University Press.

Wellman, H., and D. Estes. 1986. Early understanding of mental entities: A reexamination of childhood realism. *Child development* 57: 910–23.

Wimmer, H., S. Gruber, and J. Perner. 1984. Young children's conception of lying: Lexical realism-moral subjectivism. *Journal of Experimental Child Psychology* 37: 1–30.

Wimmer, H., and J. Perner. 1983. Beliefs about beliefs: Representation and constraining function of wrong beliefs in young children's understanding of deception. *Cognition* 13: 103–28.

Winnicott, D. W. 1958. *Collected papers*. New York: Basic.

Wolf, D. 1982. Understanding others: The origins of an independent agent concept. In *Action and thought: From sensorimotor schemes to symbol use*. Edited by G. Forman. New York: Academic.

_____. 1988. Genre and experience. A presentation to the MacArthur Study Group on the Representation of Affective Processes, New York.

_____. In press. Envelopes for meaning: The emergence of genre in young children's narratives. In *New directions in developing narrative structure*. Edited by A. McCabe. Hillsdale, N.J.: Erlbaum.

Wolf, D., and H. Gardner. 1981. On the structure of early symbolization. In *Early language: Acquisition and intervention*. Edited by R. Schiefelbusch and D. Bricker. Baltimore: University Park Press, 287–328.

Wolf, D., B. Goldfield, and M. Beeghly. 1984. "There's not enough room," the baby said. Paper presented at the Boston University Language Conference, Boston, October 10–11.

Wolf, D., and S. Grollman. 1982. Ways of playing: Individual differences in imaginative play. In *The play of children: Current theory and research*. Edited by K. Rubin and D. Pepler. New York: Karger.

Wolf, D., and D. Hicks. 1989. The voices within narratives: The development of intertextuality in young children's narratives. *Discourse Processes 12* (no. 3): 329–51.

Wolf, D., and J. Pusch. 1985. The origins of autonomous texts in play boundaries. In *Play, language, and stories: The development of children's literate behavior*. Edited by L. Galda and A. Pellegrini. Norwood, N.J.: Ablex, 63–78.

Wolf, D., J. Rygh, and J. Altshuler. 1984. Agency and experience: Actions and states in play narratives. In *Symbolic play: The development of social understanding*. Edited by I. Bretherton. Orlando, Fla.: Academic.

10 Building Memories: The Ontogeny of Autobiography

Catherine E. Snow

As they have for many other areas of development—language, cognition, affect—theories of the development of self have emphasized factors internal to the child rather than those located in the social environment. Thus, children have generally been seen as "doing the work" of differentiating self from other, or of building their internal working models, relatively autonomously. While there is undoubtedly some truth in this position, it may be as valuable for the domain of self development as for other domains to assess the contribution of adults to the changes observed in the child. While models of self development have acknowledged the role of the other in cases of pathology, deviance, and extremely poor parenting, the explicit contributions of the "good enough" parent to the development of children's notions of self have not, to my knowledge, been much explored. We know almost nothing about the nature of the interactions which constitute the locus of parental input to children's developing sense of self. I will argue that careful attention to such interactions reveals the difficulty of distinguishing between a self-constructed self and an other-constructed self (Watson, in this volume) and places the development of at least some aspects of self firmly in the interpersonal space where parent and child work together. The purposes of this chapter, then, are to consider some ways in which adults might contribute to the development of self in children, and to present examples of interactions that may constitute such contributions.

In the interactions on which we will focus, parents and their children converse about important events in the child's life, in effect producing chapters of the child's autobiography. The stories about a child's past

I would like to express my appreciation to the John D. and Catherine T. MacArthur Foundation for funding the Child Language Data Exchange System, which made the analyses reported here possible; to Jacqueline Sachs and Roger Brown for sharing their transcripts; and to the participants in the Self Conference for arousing my interest in this topic. Preparation of this chapter was also supported by the National Institute of Child Health and Human Development (HD-23388).

213

experiences which are told to children, elicited from children, or told collaboratively by parent and child to a third party may constitute not only reflections of but also contributions to the child's sense of self. The familial production of the child's autobiography in these cases reveals a number of processes: the selection of incidents considered appropriate for inclusion; the production of canonical versions of those incidents; the presentation of the incidents to participants and to nonfamily members as revealing something important about the child; the imposition of links between incidents, which enables them to form part of the larger autobiographical enterprise; and finally, the transfer of responsibility for both memory about and retelling of the incidents to the child (the transition from biography to *auto*biography). In the context of these demonstrations, the argument will be made that the "self" the development of which this book is devoted to studying is essentially a social construct; that is, its definition, development, and maintenance depend on social interaction and require interpersonal work.

The notion of self that informs this argument derives from a number of lines of thought: considerations of how the social persona is maintained by the interactant's attention to his positive face, as articulated by Goffman (1987) and elaborated by Brown and Levinson (1978); discussions of the role of narrative in human thinking, particularly with reference to socially negotiated (re)narrativization in psychotherapy (e.g., Schafer 1981; Spence 1982), in interviewing (Mishler 1986), and in autobiography (Bruner 1986; McAdams and Ochberg 1986) and to story as the locus of cultural agreement about the proper roles and actions of various members of the society (Polanyi 1985); analyses of the degree to which meanings, even the meanings firmly rooted in basic "hard fact," are negotiated in the process of being communicated (e.g., Scollon and Scollon 1981); and finally, observations of the degree to which adults forgive inadequacies in, scaffold, and support children's contributions to social and linguistic interactions (e.g., see Nelson 1986; Ninio, in press; Snow 1978).

Views of the Developing Self from the Study of Child Language and Social Interaction

If we accept, at least for the sake of discussion, the notion that an individual's self is a socially constructed and socially maintained phenomenon, we might expect that social interaction could contribute to its development in a number of different ways (see Cicchetti et al., in this volume). Parents are, for example, often telling their children they are good, or smart, or clever, or perhaps naughty and evil. Much thinking in self-concept theory derives from the assumption that children come to believe these statements as part of their self-definition. More subtly, parents express their opinions of their children's abilities and failings by their choice of questions to ask, by their decisions when to offer help, by virtue of the nature of the activities they expect children to engage in and succeed at, and in many other ways. Wylie (1984) has identified and coded many of these more subtle social influences on the nature of the self-concept children come to develop, referring to the process as "attribution."

Another context for observing children's sense of self and parental contributions to it comes from interactions centered around opportunities for child self-display. Many children in this culture are given the opportunity to learn verses, songs, and dances partly so that their skills can be displayed both to the parents and to presumably entranced grandparents and parental friends. Analyzing games such as "Teensy-Weensy Spider" played by parents with infants aged three to six months led us to suggest several years ago (Snow, Dubber, and de Blauw 1982) that one major function of such games is to enable infants who learn them to display their social achievements (at least in certain, admittedly rather limited contexts). Infants who take their turns in such games have achieved a certain level of autonomy; toddlers who seize center stage at family reunions to sing "Twinkle, Twinkle" have developed that autonomy much further. Self-display is clearly, to some extent at least, a cultural norm for children growing up in North America; nursery schools and day-care centers teach songs and routines for children to display at home, and regularly send home bags full of two-year-olds' sticker and macaroni collages or finger paintings to be admired by parents and exhibited on refrigerator doors. Well-meaning middle-class parents play their role in confirming the appropriateness of this sort of self-display on the part of the child by solemnly discussing the merits of the various pieces, selecting the best for hanging or for adding to the child's archive, and by avoiding denigrating comments about the more banal productions.[1]

1. An example, probably quite typical, of a parent-child interaction involving discussion of the child's artwork is presented here. Clearly, such discussions offer considerable potential for analysis of how parental responses shape a child's sense of competence, effectiveness, praiseworthiness, and right to adult attention (Katie is the grandmother).

Father: Katie, look at Nathaniel's pictures.
Katie: Oh, I know they're wonderful.
Nathaniel: I make the, eh, I made that, eh, I made the, ahhhh . . .
Katie: They are beautiful.
Mother: Nathaniel, you know what you should do? You should show Katie all the pictures we have, the photographs.
Katie: Oh yes. I wanted to ask you about those, but I was too tired last night.
Nathaniel: I make that picture.
Mother: You did.
Katie: You certainly did. It's very good. I like them.
Nathaniel: And I make that picture.
Katie: You have verve and style there. [*continued on next page*]

Children's use of self-reference and their production of linguistic expressions of their own autonomy constitute additional contexts for observing the social emergence of the self (see Bates, in this volume). "No," for example, can be observed early in the second year of life as an expression of resistance to others' interventions, subsequently as a marker of the intention not to comply with adult requests, later in self-prohibitions that reveal the internalization of adult norms for appropriate behavior, and later still in denial of others' propositions. Each of these developments reveals an increased degree of differentiation of the self's intentions from the social context that can control one's actions. (In Rorty's [1976] terms, they reflect the emergence of a sense of oneself as a person rather than as a figure; see below for further discussion.) Similarly, the emergence of explicit self-reference in utterances with first-person agent (e.g., "I do it" versus "do it," "me do it," or "baby do it") reveals linguistically the differentiation between action and agent and between agent and intender-to-act. Budwig (1986; in press) has analyzed the development of self-reference during the second year of life, in ways that reveal both individual and developmental differentiation of these semantic dimensions through the choice of linguistic form (I, me, my, [child's name], baby).

Observing children's reactions over time to photographs of themselves and their family members provides another source of information about their self development. For example, a twenty-one-month-old named Ali was observed, after several months of looking at photographs and correctly naming "Ali," "mommy," and "daddy" in response to the pictures, to look up excitedly from a picture of daddy one day, and point to daddy and back to the photo alternately, saying "Daddy! Daddy!" Immediately afterward, she found a picture of herself, labeled it, then pointed to herself and the picture alternately, saying "Ali," as if she had just related the identity of the pictured child to her own persona. Photographs often are taken in order to provide an artifact of events (birthdays, holidays, trips, visits of family members) considered important by the family; thus, within any particular family, the photograph album can provide a context for discussion of locally significant events and an opportunity to observe the emergence of the child's understanding of those events and her own place in them.[2] Engel (1986) used discussions of photographs as one technique for eliciting past-event narratives from mothers and children.

Nathaniel: An I make that picture, and I make that picture.
Katie: It looks like prehistoric animals.
Nathaniel: Oh, I make that picture. Ohhhh, I make that picture.
Mother: What's that a picture of?
Nathaniel: Oh, I make that picture.

2. One interesting aspect of talk about photographs is the possibility for "fictionalization" of the child character (see Scollon and Scollon 1981, for a discussion of fictionalization of self). The

Just as photographs constitute physical reminders of important events in children's lives, so do the child's possessions. The mere fact that, in Western society, children from birth are considered to have their own possessions (their own rooms, furniture, toys, books, clothes, and piggy banks—all

---

following excerpt from a long discussion of a photo album between Nathaniel (at age 3:0.20) and his parents and grandmother (Katie) shows him and all the other participants consistently using third-person reference to self.

Father: Who are those kids?
Nathaniel: At the playground.
Mother: Yes.
Katie: And this is?
Father: Probably doesn't know who it is.
Katie: Mommy, I think.
Father: Is it?
Nathaniel: And Rene?
Nathaniel: Uh, uh, uh, na, and eh, and eh, eh, and they're playing yellow truck.
Katie: Yes, you and Rene working with the trucks.
Nathaniel: And Rene and Nathaniel and Daddy.
Katie: Yeah. Is that Nathaniel? Is that, eh, Rene? Oh yeah, that's Rene.
Nathaniel: De-de-they're in the water.
Katie: Nathaniel way out in the water. My goodness, he's a brave boy, way up to his knees.
Nathaniel: And, and Michael.
Mother: That's Michael. That's right.
Katie: Who's that little girl?
Nathaniel: That, eh, . . . Jessica?
Mother: No, . . . look carefully.
Nathaniel: Is it . . . it Nathaniel?
Katie: There you have . . .
Mother: It's Nathaniel and . . .
Nathaniel: Eh, dere. Who's dat?
Mother: Who's that? It was taken in Montreal.
Nathaniel: Was taken in Montreal. Taken in Montreal.
Mother: Come on, don't you remember her name?
Nathaniel: Yeah.
Father: What is it?
Nathaniel: What is it?
Father: Emma.
Nathaniel: Emma. Is dat Emma?
Mother: Yes.
Katie: She looks like that's Emma.
Mother: That's Emma.
Nathaniel: Dis . . . eh, dat's Emma again. De-de-de-dere's Nathaniel riding his, eh, de, eh, de-de-de-de, eh, de-de-de-ridin', ridin', ridin' de-dat bike dere.
Katie: Whose bike?
Mother: That bike.
Katie: That bike? Whose is it? It's a big one. It's a big one, isn't it?
Father: Mm-hm.
Nathaniel: He's ridin' it.
Katie: Yes, he's doing a good job of riding that bike.

frequently marked with the child's name and typically replicated for siblings) reflects a cultural agreement about the autonomous status of children. In many families, it is considered important to keep track of the source of the child's possessions—who gave each object, and for what occasion—and considerable effort goes into catechisms designed to transfer that knowledge to the child. Such discussions of gifts can be seen as a way of making concrete for the child important social relations with sometimes distant or unfamiliar individuals. As such, these discussions can be seen as contributing to the child's sense of self-in-society, as confirmation of the child's worthiness to be treated well by people of importance outside the immediate family.

Any of these various sources of data on language and social interaction might provide useful avenues along which to explore the contexts for the development of self in young children. However, in this chapter, I will concentrate on yet another source of information about the social construction of self: the stories that are told within families.

Personal-Event Narratives

Considerable work has now been reported about the development of narrative ability in young children, much of it focused on the class of narratives known as "personal event" narratives, which are those that recount an event the child has personally experienced (e.g., Eisenberg 1985; Eisenberg 1983; Nelson 1986; Peterson and McCabe 1983). In light of the research on autobiographical memory, which converges on the conclusion that adult recollections of childhood do not precede age three (e.g., Kihlstrom 1982), it is perhaps surprising how much talk about personally experienced past events occurs between children younger than three and their mothers. Engel (1986) found an average of seven past-event discussions in a half hour of interaction at age seventeen months and thirteen at twenty-four months.

Most of the narratives young children tell are at least partly personal-event narratives, although some fantasy elements may enter into the retellings. It is crucial to realize that personal-event narratives are *true* narratives, constrained by the same factors that govern fantasy narratives and that differentiate narratives from simpler descriptions. Narratives center around some problem, instantiate a theme, and have a point. Perhaps the clearest way to differentiate narratives from descriptions is by noting what is omitted; in good narratives, the details included are relevant to the problem and its solution or to characterization and atmosphere. There is no demand for completeness or even total veracity if omission or distortion of detail produces a "better" story. Narratives produced in conversational contexts may also be shaped by additional, nonnarrative constraints (e.g., taking into account shared background knowledge with the audience, emphasizing details or relationships of particular interest to the audience, allowing for audience participation). Nonetheless, such narratives retain their ''rhetorical shape'' as true narratives, with points and themes that can be analyzed as revealing deeply shared cultural values and expectations (Polanyi 1985).

Very young children are not competent to produce such narratives by themselves, though they can and very early do collaborate with adults to produce them. Engel (1986) found that mothers took more responsibility for providing information in discussions of the past than in discussions of the here and now but that children's contributions of information to past-event discussions increased from age seventeen to thirty months. The collaboration between parents and children to produce narratives takes a variety of forms; parents may ask a series of questions designed to elicit crucial information bits from the child or may even supply most of the information and wait for the child to repeat it. For example (Nathaniel is age 2:6.0):

Mother: Well, we're gonna get you a second pair of glasses so you have two pairs.
Nathaniel: Two pairs.
Mother: In case you lose one.
Nathaniel: Lose one.
Mother: Or break one.
Nathaniel: Break one.
Mother: Like, remember we lost your lens the other day?
Nathaniel: Lens the other day?
Mother: Remember losing your lens?
Nathaniel: Losing the lens.
Mother: And that would have been terrible if we hadn't had another . . . if we hadn't found it.
Nathaniel: Found it.
Mother: So we think you should have two pairs of glasses.
Nathaniel: Two pairs of glasses.

Alternately, parents may ask questions to initiate the story but leave room for the child to add information, as in this example of a twenty-four-month-old quoted from Engel (1986b):

Mother: Did you tell Susan about your party?
Child: Party.
Mother: Did you have a party?
Child: Yeah.
Mother: What song did they sing for you?
Child: ''Happy Birthday.''
Mother: Yeah, how old were you at your party?
Child: Mm . . .

Mother: How old?
Child: Two.
Mother: Two?
Child: Yeah.
Mother: Were your friends there?
Child: Yeah.
Mother: Who was at your party?
Child: Pat.
Mother: Who? Pat? Who else?
Child: Lea.
Mother: Lea. Who else?
Child: Bobby.
Mother: Bobby and who else?
Child: Lea.
Mother: Lea and who else?
Child: Pat.

Somewhat older children may start the story themselves but rely on parental collaboration for clarification and suppletion, as in the following example from another of Engel's (1986b) twenty-four-month-old subjects:

Child: [*looks at observer*] Uncle Gary—restaurant.
Mother: He's talking about his Uncle Gary.
Child: Uncle Gary.
Mother: We went with him to a restaurant.
Child: Uncle Gary restaurant.
Mother: Yes, he took us to a restaurant. What did we eat in the restaurant?
Child: Noodles.
Mother: Noodles! That was the name of the restaurant too, yeah, that's very interesting. That was a nice restaurant, wasn't it? And Uncle Gary was there and you had all kinds of noodles. That's all they have on the menu is noodles, and it was a busy restaurant. Did you talk to people? Did you say hi to everybody in the restaurant? Do you remember that?
Child: Remember that.
Mother: It's a while ago. We went to the restaurant a couple of weeks ago, but it was really nice. And Gary was there with a friend. Uncle Gary.
Child: Uncle Gary, restaurant.
Mother: We pass a lot of restaurants in this neighborhood and he always says "Uncle Gary restaurant." That was a really nice evening. You were funny at the restaurant.
Child: I funny.
Mother: Yeah, you were funny. You were talking to people at all the tables, and you said hello and then you told—

Child: Hi there!

Mother: Yes you said that, and then you started talking and you said that you had made a peepee.

Child: Potty.

Mother: Yes, because you had just gone to the bathroom. That was really something. They all laughed.

It has frequently been commented upon in the child language literature that the shared knowledge of parent and child is crucial to the success of these early narrative endeavors. Attempts by relative strangers to elicit narratives flounder on the stranger's ignorance about which questions to ask or how to supplement the information offered by the child (see, for example, Snow 1978), though children as young as twenty-nine to thirty-five months can respond with some success to relative strangers' questions about past events (Fivush, Gray, and Fromhoff 1987). Even school-age children often have difficulty fully displaying their comprehension of narratives they have read, without the scaffolding offered by the questions of teachers familiar with the text (MacNamee 1980).

In collaborating with their children to tell and retell stories about personally experienced events, parents are building up a system of narrative memories that elaborate upon (if they do not replace entirely) the memories of the events as originally experienced. These narrative memories, in fact, need to be kept distinct from the more automatically laid down event memory, which is a generalized event representation that omits details identified as specific to any particular instantiation of the relevant event class (Hudson and Nelson 1986; Nelson 1986). Generalized event representations, or scripts, do not constitute good narratives, though they often define the "normal" course of events from which good stories represent a deviation. Children as young as $2\frac{1}{2}$ or 3 years tend to provide script reports, not specific personally experienced event descriptions, when asked about birthday parties or visits to McDonald's. Thus, personal narratives with details that constitute deviations from or elaborations of children's generalized event representations must be differentiated from scripts in memory. In fact, discussions of past events between mothers and their two-year-olds tend to focus on idiosyncratic, specific events, not on events which can be entirely subsumed under scripts (Lucariello and Nelson 1982).

Narratives told by parents and children could be analyzed in a number of ways to reveal their contribution to the child's development of self:

a. The relative contribution of parent and child can be assessed longitudinally to determine to what extent the parental version of the story is adopted by the child.

b. The narrative could be compared to the original event itself to see what distortions are introduced by the process of narrativization.

c. A reduction of the stories to the "cultural primitives" they reveal could be carried out, using methods elaborated by Polanyi (1985) and applied by her to adult stories.

d. The roles played by the child in the stories could be identified in order to cast light on the socially constructed concept of child as actor.

e. The roles played by the child could be contrasted to the roles played by other characters in the story, in order to see how the child's self emerges in contrast to others.

The goal of the analyses presented in this chapter is considerably more modest: to confirm that participation in jointly constructed renditions of autobiographical stories develops as children get older, that responsibility for the retellings of the stories shifts from parents to children, and that the stories have the potential to constitute a contribution to children's continuity of memory about self and a factor in the specific nature of their developing self-representations.

"Remembering" across Families: Naomi

In a first attempt to consider conversational sources of information to children about their selves and their roles within the family, I chose to search through three corpora of parent-child language transcripts available through the Child Language Data Exchange System (MacWhinney and Snow 1985). The first, collected by Jacqueline Sachs (1983), consists of recordings of her daughter Naomi between the ages of 1:6 and 4:9 in interaction with her parents. The recordings were more frequent during the first two years. They were typically made in the evenings as the family was preparing dinner or engaged in various leisure and child-care activities after dinner. The corpus has the advantage of including relatively long stretches of parent-child talk, of having been collected in the course of quite normal activities, and of having been collected with an interest in the child speech, not the parent speech. Naomi's discussions of past events have been previously analyzed from a slightly different perspective (Sachs 1979; 1983).

The analysis I conducted was quite simple; it involved using automatic search procedures to locate in the entire corpus all the occasions when either parent or child used the verb *remember*. This verb was chosen on the assumption that it would be a frequent (though not prerequisite) marker of discussion of autobiographical episodes. Of course, as one would expect and as the analysis confirmed, remember is not limited to autobiographical discussion. The word marked many other activities as well. Occurrences of the word *remember* in either parent or child speech are tabulated in table 1, along with an estimate of the size of the total corpus available at each of the age ranges indicated.

Table 1. Uses of the Word *Remember* by Naomi's Parents

| Sessions | Naomi's age | Total bytes | Purpose of "remember" discussions (percent of total) | | | |
			Tutorial questions	Behavior control	Past event	Autobiographical
1–66	1:2.29–2:6.5	489,997	23.5%	41.2%	29.4%	5.9%
67–80	2:6.5–2:11.24	143,065	45.5	9.1	36.4	9.1
81–90	3:2.10–3.8.19*	119,860	11.1	22.2	11.1	33.3
91–93	4:7.28–4:9.3	66,111	0.0	60.0	20.0	20.0

*During this period, Naomi started to use the word *remember* herself. Some adult uses were unclassifiable.

Talk about remembering gets more frequent as Naomi gets older. More significant, though, the kinds of items remembered change markedly with age. The early uses of remember almost all fell into one of only three categories:

a. Tutorial questions about words or other information from frequently read books the parent thought Naomi should know. For example:

Mother: Windy.
Naomi: Windy.
Mother: Do you remember what wind is?
Naomi: [*Makes sound of wind blowing.*]

b. Reminders about appropriate behavior and injunctions to be patient, such as:

Naomi: [*Crying because she want toast.*]
Mother: Nomi, remember it's toasting, Nomi. We're making it hot. We're making the toast out of the bread.

c. Discussions of past events in which Naomi was not a major actor. For example:

Mother: Nomi, what were the names of the dogs in xxx? Do you remember? What were the names of Grandma and Grandpa's dogs?
Naomi: xxx friendly dogs.
Mother: No. They were friendly dogs, too, but not those dogs. Do you remember the other dogs in Chicago?
Naomi: xxx doggies, xxx, xxx, xxx, monkey chased the weasel, all around the mulberry bush. . . .

One could make the case that all these types of language interactions could contribute to the child's development of self: the first by attributing to the child competence with material that has been "taught" previously, the second by invoking the child's past experiences as a basis for current action, and the third by making claims about the child's typical behaviors and reactions. None of these early discussions is truly autobiographical; but as early as 1:11, Naomi participated (minimally) in discussions that came close to autobiography:

Naomi: De bib bib. De bib.
Father: Nomi, do you remember how you used to hate to have the bib put on?
Naomi: Put it on. Dirty bib.

When Naomi was 2:3, her mother used remember in a discussion of a *future* autobiographical entry, namely, Naomi's attendance at a birthday party. This is a significant discussion because it reveals how parents help shape children's experiences of significant events in their lives by predicting what will happen and by referring repeatedly to the prediction in preevent discussions as well as by discussing ex post facto what has already happened.

Mother: Where are we going today?
Naomi: Where are we going today. Where are we going today.
Mother: Do you remember?
Naomi: Julia.
Mother: Yes, to Julia's. What are we going to do at Julia's house, Nomi?
Naomi: What are we going to do at Julia's house? I want breakfast.
Mother: Do you want some of this roll, Nomi? With butter and jelly on it?
Naomi: No.
Mother: Nomi, what are we going to do at Julia's house? What are we going to do?
Naomi: What are we going to do at Julia house. What are we going to do at Julia house.
Mother: Do you remember? We're going to have a birthday party.

When Naomi was 2:11.8, both recorded uses of remember invoked true, though fairly brief and trivial, autobiographical memories:

Mother: Remember what you said once? Where did you think we were going?
Naomi: Movies.
Mother: Oh yeah? Nomi said earlier, "I thought we were going to another store." Remember that?
Naomi: We thought we're going home.
Mother: Oh. We thought we were going home?

*****

Father: They're going to stay asleep [*referring to dolls that had been put to sleep*]?

Mother: Now you have a bunk bed. Remember? Like over at the party the other day? When you were up on the top of the bunk bed?

Naomi: Yeah.

These discussions show characteristics that are quite general in children's personal-event narratives in the third and perhaps fourth years of life. Although children evidence some access to and interest in the incidents recalled, the full-blown memory of the event and the responsibility for narrating most of the event lies with the parent (Engel 1986). Discussions such as the two quoted above can be seen to have two functions in children's development:

1. Biography to autobiography transition. The discussions serve to transfer the details of the relevant memories, and thus the responsibility for narrating the incidents, to the child.

2. Identification of reportability. Perhaps more important, such discussions mark for the child the incidents that should qualify as memorable and thus as narratable.

In the conversations presented above, and indeed in all but three of the total cases where remember occurred, it was a parent who used the word. Naomi's first recorded use of remember occurred when she was 3:3.27, in the following excerpt from a session where she is "reading" a book to her mother:

Naomi: One two three four five six seven eight nine ten eleven twelve. Thirteen. Sixteen. Eighteen. Nineteen. See these little things. These little things. I don't think you remember these little things. I don't think you remember these little tiny things. Wanna see something else?

By 4:9.3, Naomi was using remember very effectively during role play to fulfill the same functions as her parents' uses two years earlier, controlling the behavior of a sick doll:

Naomi: [*to "sick" doll who has just received a shot*] Don't cry. It's all right. I'm a good doctor. I'm a fine . . . doctor. My name is Katherine. Remember I use to baby . . . sit for you? Remember? And tonight I'm going to babysit for you too. . . . Remember I used to babysit . . . for you? And tonight I am, yes. She . . . [*turns to mother*] when I babysitted for her she really liked it, cause I tickled her so much.

It would be naive to think that the technique of selecting conversations with the word *remember* in them successfully captures all the cases of autobiographical (re)construction in the Naomi corpus. In Naomi's family, however, remember did mark true autobiographical retellings increasingly as Naomi got older (see table 1). When she was 3:2.10, the following conversation occurred:

Naomi: And where's the pampers? I want pampers on.

Mother: You didn't want pampers last night, remember? Remember when you were so sleepy when we came home and we wanted to put a pamper on you and you had a fit! And you said "No pamper!"

This anecdote recalls adult anecdotes analyzed by Polanyi (1985), in the degree to which it reveals cultural themes, such as the appropriate role of the child versus parent (here violated by the child's assumption of a contrary position and therefore worthy of narration). The anecdote also endorses Naomi's autonomy and thus might provide one bit of evidence (among many available) to this middle-class American child that autonomy, independence, and a strong will are acceptable, even desirable traits. Two weeks later, the following discussion took place, revealing some of the same themes (acceptance of child's right to express negative affect, but invocation of some standards of reasonableness for emotional display):

Mother: Hey, sweetheart, tell me what you did at nursery school this morning when you got there. Remember you were unhappy when I left you at nursery school this morning. Why were you unhappy then? Do you remember?

Naomi: Because you didn't do the blinking light.

Mother: Oh, I apologized for that though.

Family Styles in Remembering: Sarah

Repeating the search analysis used on the Naomi transcripts with transcripts from other children reveals family "styles" in the use of the term *remember.* Naomi's parents used remember most often in book reading and to invoke general rules about emotional display for purposes of behavior control, and we saw that Naomi first used remember herself in very similar ways. The parents of Brown's (1973) subject, Sarah, on the other hand, most often used remember to invoke cognitive content from previous teaching episodes (e.g., Do you remember how to spell Sarah? Do you remember how to count? Do you remember what 2 + 2 make?). Sarah's family thus looks more like the group Engel (1986) descries as "practical rememberers" than like the discursive "reminiscers." Some of the teaching episodes marked with the word *remember* dealt with fairly general cultural knowledge (literacy, numeracy, nursery rhymes, what happens on Halloween), whereas others rehearsed knowledge about family members, their residences, their habits, and important incidents in their lives. These exercises in family history paralleled the ways in which Sarah's mother used the word *remembering* in developing Sarah's autobiographical episodes. Autobiographical episodes in conversations with Sarah focused on events such as her visit to the circus, a birthday party, the beach, the zoo, and the animal farm and her experiences at Christmas (here object source discussions shade into autobiography). Some examples of Sarah's autobiographical conversations are presented in the Appendix to this chapter, where it can be seen that the focus is on factual recounting (rather than emotions experienced, as in the Naomi transcripts).

Sarah's earliest recorded use of remember, at age 3:8, mimics her parents' nonbiographical, tutorial uses: she challenges the interlocutor to recall specific facts. For example:

Mother: Who's Arthur?
Sarah: My cousin. Don't you remember?

Very soon afterward, though, at 3:11, she initiates both recounts and accounts of her own activities marked by remember, such as:

Mother: We left it over at the dance recital. And I don't know if she's got it.
Sarah: How you left it over to the . . .
Mother: Because I forgot all about it, honey.
Sarah: You left it there this morning, remember? Joanne came in . . . you come . . . take the bath . . .
Mother: Oh yes, in the tub downstairs. . . . It's broken, and Joanne had to come here and take her bath. Yeah.
Sarah: And she had to go dancing school yesterday, remember? In the car.

Sources of Memories: Nathaniel

The incidents of true autobiographical remembering selected from the various sets of transcripts searched seem to fall into two categories: memories located in the parental mind, which are transferred to the child but not actually shared by the child before transferral, and memories which children have some personal access to, though they are undeniably enriched and structured by parental intervention. A clear example of the first type, parental stories about the child, is cited above, when Naomi's father reminds her how she hated bibs as an infant. Another such example, drawn from transcripts of Nathaniel (Snow 1981; Snow and Goldfield 1983), concerned a discussion when he was 2:5 of an event that had occurred when he was 1:10:

Nathaniel: That's broken (referring to juice cup).
Mother: That's broken, that's right.
Father: Mmmm.
Nathaniel: That's broken that.
Father: Yeah.
Nathaniel: That's broken that.

Father: Hm-mmm.
Nathaniel: That's . . .
Father: Broken handle.
Nathaniel: Broken handle. Fix it.
Father: No.
Mother: Do you know how that got broken, Nathaniel?
Nathaniel: Got broken.
Mother: It got broken on the terrace.
Nathaniel: Terrace.
Mother: In Pleasant Street.
Nathaniel: Pleasant Street, outside.
Mother: Outside, that's right, where you threw it.
Nathaniel: Da pleasant street.
Mother: On Pleasant Street.
Nathaniel: In the car.
Mother: What about the car?
Father: Used to park in the basement in the garage, remember?
Nathaniel: The garage.
Mother: Remember the garage in the basement?
Nathaniel: The base . . . the basement?
Mother: Had to go with the elevator?
Nathaniel: Elevator.
Mother: Remember that?
Nathaniel: Remember that? Go inside?

Whereas Nathaniel obviously did have some memory of his previous residence in which this incident took place, memory of the incident itself (a tantrum that led to the cup-throwing) comes entirely from his mother.

More recent autobiographical events were recounted with considerable participation and contribution from Nathaniel; in the following two discussions (separated by two days) of the same visit to the optometrist, Nathaniel (age 2:5.17 and 2:5.19) both initiated the remembrance and contributed considerable information about it:

Nathaniel: Eh de glasses on.
Mother: Put your glasses back on? Okay. They're kind of tight, aren't they?
Nathaniel: Tight eh de fixit.
Mother: We got them fixed.
Nathaniel: Fixed . . . clean them off . . . right there.
Mother: Cleaned them up right there, yeah, and then what did we do after we got them fixed?
Nathaniel: Fixed.
Mother: What did we do yesterday after we got your glasses fixed?

Nathaniel: Glasses fixed yesterday.
Mother: Remember what we did?
Nathaniel: Did eh had eh had eh ice cream.
Mother: We had the ice cream, that's right. . . . We went to Bailey's for ice cream.
Nathaniel: Bailey's eh ice cream.

*****

Nathaniel: Hashes . . . de de hashes . . . de glasses fixed right there.
Mother: We got your glasses fixed, didn't we?
Nathaniel: Right there.
Mother: Yeah, now they're tight.
Nathaniel: Tight . . . oof [*tight noise*].
Mother: Do they feel good now?
Nathaniel: This uh this.
Mother: What else did we do after we got your glasses fixed?
Nathaniel: Glasses de clean them off.
Mother: She cleaned them up, that's right. And then what?
Nathaniel: Put the glasses on.
Mother: You put your glasses on. And then what?
Nathaniel: Ha comin home de trol . . . de trolley de de . . .
Mother: We came home on the trolley.
Nathaniel: De coat.
Mother: The boat. . . . Did we see a boat?
Nathaniel: De de buy a ?? . . . De de get the boots.
Mother: We put your boots on and went ice-skating, didn't we?
Nathaniel: De de nathaniel's shoes too tight.
Mother: Nathaniel's shoes were too tight, so we put on his boots.
Nathaniel: Boots.
Mother: We went in the car.
Nathaniel: Car.
Mother: And we got out your ice skates.
Nathaniel: Ice skates.
Mother: We put your ice skates on.
Nathaniel: Ice skates on.
Mother: And we went ice-skating.
Nathaniel: Ice-skating.
Mother: 'Member going ice-skating?
Nathaniel: 'Member going ice-skating?
Mother: Was it fun to go ice-skating?
Nathaniel: Fun . . . slip.
Mother: You slipped, yes.
Nathaniel: Fell down.

Mother: You fell down and bumped you head.
Nathaniel: Head hurt.
Mother: It hurt, didn't it? But you were very brave.
Nathaniel: Brave.
Mother: You didn't cry very long.
Nathaniel: Cry very long.
Mother: Nooo.
Nathaniel: Noo.
Mother: Didn't cry very long.
Nathaniel: Cry.
Mother: And then we came home in the car.
Nathaniel: Came home the car.
Mother: And then what did we do?
Nathaniel: Do go in the house.
Mother: Yeah, we went in the house, that's right. And then what?
Nathaniel: What?
Mother: Then what did we do?
Nathaniel: Do?
Mother: We ate lunch.
Nathaniel: Ate lunch.

The ice-skating discussion at 2:5.19 was reinstituted about an hour later while Nathaniel and his mother were looking at a picture of children ice-skating:

Mother: What's she doing? . . . Look, what's he got on his feet?
Nathaniel: Feet?
Mother: What he got on his feet?
Nathaniel: Feet?
Mother: He's got skates on.
Nathaniel: Skates on.
Father: What's he doing then?
Nathaniel: Ice . . . ice-skating.
Father and Mother: Ice-skating, right.
Nathaniel: More ice-skating.
Mother: Yes, that's ice. . . . They're all ice-skating.
Nathaniel: Ice, ice, ice, ice, ice [*making skating movements*].
Mother: That's right.
Mother: That's how you do it.
Nathaniel: Nathaniel fell down.
Mother: Oh, Nathaniel fell down.
Father: Bump his head.
Mother: You want to go ice-skating again?
Nathaniel: Go ice sk . . . the coats on.
Father: Put coats on.

Mother: Put coats on, yeah.
Nathaniel: Boots on.
Father: Next time, we're gonna put your helmet on too.
Nathaniel: Not shoes, boots.
Mother: That's right, no shoes, boots.

These excerpts exemplify many of the interactive processes that I have claimed are relevant to the development of self through collaborative autobiography: relating remembered to future events, differentiating report-able from routine events, and identifying the affect appropriate to the unusual events.

A few weeks later, Nathaniel's mother initiated recall of an apple-picking expedition that had occurred the previous fall (five months earlier). The discussion was triggered by a picture of an apple orchard in a book:

Nathaniel: Apple tree.
Mother: Apple tree, yeah, all the apples fallin' off.
Nathaniel: Falling off the tree.
Mother: Nathaniel . . .
Nathaniel: Bus.
Mother: That's a bus.
Nathaniel: Bus.
Mother: Do you remember picking apples with Lizzie?
Nathaniel: De bus.
Mother: There's another bus. . . . Do you remember picking apples?
Nathaniel: Picking apples e de picking apples e de trees?
Mother: From the trees, in the orchard?
Nathaniel: E Liz.
Mother: With Liz and John and Carol.
Nathaniel: More apples.

The next day, reading the same book, Nathaniel turned again to the picture of the apple orchard and started a very labored and disfluent retelling of the incident (one that was sufficiently unclear that his mother never did get the whole story straight):

Nathaniel: Tree.
Mother: What kind of a . . .
Nathaniel: Tree apples . . . under the tree . . . [*very excitedly*] picked up these ??? in these.
Mother: What?
Nathaniel: Pick up these, put in these ? . . .
Mother: What's in the trees?
Nathaniel: Who's this there.
Mother: Who's this where?

Nathaniel: [*with great effort*] da da da pick up apples da like Nathaniel like Liz.

Mother: Pick up apples like Nathaniel and Liz . . . did under the trees, that's right long time ago, that was.

Nathaniel: Dit dit out to eat apples and . . . and . . . anne anne anne jam

Mother: You eat apples in . . . school?

Nathaniel: School?

Mother: In where?

Nathaniel: Inne / 'pam

Mother: In the pum? You eat apples in the pum?

These two excerpts show how an adult's identification of an incident as significant enough to be remembered and narrativized can structure children's later memories of the same incident. In this case, it was clear that Nathaniel remembered the apple-picking—he even remembered something about it his mother was unable to reconstruct. Without the first reminiscence from his mother, however, it seems unlikely that the incident would have emerged as significant enough for Nathaniel to refer to again. This particular incident became a permanent part of Nathaniel's childhood memories, remained eight years later the only memory associated with "Liz" (who moved away), and was the theme of one of his early literate accomplishments (see figure 1).

Autonomous Remembrances

Ultimately, children become the authors of their own autobiographies and the repository of their own memories. A marker of their emerging autonomy is the occurrence of disagreements between mothers and children on the details of remembered events. Such disagreements have been noted as early as age twenty-four months but are much more frequent by thirty months (Engel 1986). Another step in children's emergence as "first authors" is their provision to parents of reports about activities of which the parents had no first-hand knowledge. Heath (1986) has referred to such reports as "accounts" to distinguish them from "recounts," or reports such as those presented above in which the parent shared the experience and thus can help the child to retell it. Accounts emerged in Sarah's transcripts when she was three years, eleven months old, and in the Nathaniel transcripts just after his third birthday. Comparison of a recount and an account from the same recording session (when Nathaniel was 3:0.21) shows how much more complex the information is that children convey in recounts. In the account, Nathaniel produced only five informative utterances, whereas in the recount he produced seven. The "full story" in the account never emerged, whereas the coparticipation in the event recounted made a more complete retelling possible. First, the account:

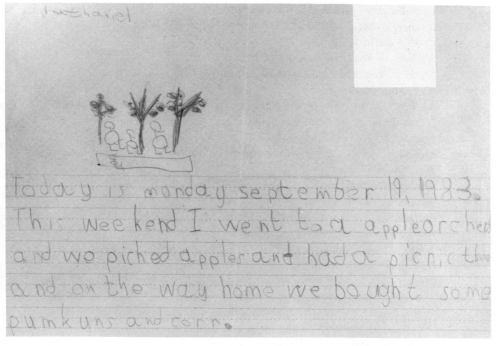

Nathaniel

Today is monday september 19, 1983. This weekend I went to a appleorcher and we piched apples and had a picnic the and on the way home we bought some pumkuns and corn.

Figure 10.1.   Nathaniel's composition based on remembered apple-picking expedition.

Mother: Who'd you play with at school today?

Nathaniel: Greg . . . and Scott.

Mother: Greg and Scott. What did you play with Greg and Scott? Did you play fire engines?

Nathaniel: I helped Greg and Scott get the ladder down.

Mother: Get the ladder down.

Nathaniel: Yeah, for . . . for, for Scott.

Mother: What did he need the ladder for?

Nathaniel: He needed the ladder down.

Mother: What did he need it down for?

Nathaniel: He goes like that [*moving hand from above head to waist height*].

Mother: He went down it?

Nathaniel: Yeah.

Mother: Is that, is that what that means when you move your hand down, that you're going down something?

Nathaniel: Yeah, the hook and ladder goes down.

The recount was elicited for the benefit of Nathaniel's grandmother; who initiated the conversation:

Grandmother: Did you like Washington?

Mother: What'd you do in Washington, Nathaniel? What did we do when we were in Washington?

Nathaniel: Read books with daddy.

Mother: You read books with daddy, did you?

Nathaniel: Yeah.

Mother: On the train, on the plane going, you read books. What, what did you do when we were there? 'Member?

Nathaniel: Yep.

Mother: 'Member going on the underground?

Nathaniel: Yep.

Mother: On the metro.

Nathaniel: Yeah.

Mother: Where'd we go visit?

Nathaniel: Where go visit . . . Where go visit.

Mother: Don't you remember?

Nathaniel: Uncle John and and Carolyn.

Mother: Uncle John and Carolyn, yeah, that's who we went to visit. We went to visit some museums. Remember all the airplanes in the air and space museum, remember going inside the airplanes in the air and space and seeing them? All hung up in that building.

Nathaniel: And, and eh we go in the airplane.

Mother: We, you went in an airplane, that's right.
    What kind of an airplane did you go in?

Nathaniel: A eh a, up a upstairs airplane.

Mother: An upstairs airplane?

Nathaniel: Yeah . . . a old-fashioned upstairs airplane.

Mother: An old-fashioned upstairs airplane. That's the kind you flew in?

Nathaniel: Eh eh and you saw helicopter.

Mother: And we saw helicopters, that's right.

Nathaniel: Eh and, and one, and one turned around.

Mother: That's right, that's exactly right. And we saw movies of airplanes, remember?

Nathaniel: Where de movies where de movies of airplanes?

Mother: We saw it in the museum.

Nathaniel: Why?

Mother: Well, 'cause that was what they were showing.

It is worth noting here that the account requested dealt with a fairly unmemorable event, whereas the recount dealt with a trip, an associated family visit, and sightseeing—experiences much closer to the real stuff of autobiography.

One exchange during this recount focused on making clear to Nathaniel which parts of the trip—the museum visit, not the activities engaged in to pass time on the airplane—were meant to be included in the story. The transfer, to children, of adult notions about the reportability of events is a source of cultural and subcultural differences in the construction of self. The vast majority of personally experienced events are not reportable, because they instantiate no theme that is recognized by the participants. Obviously, there are individual and familial as well as cultural differences in selection of reportable content. These differences will have their cumulative effects on the autobiographies ultimately composed. Miller (1987), in an analysis of personal-experience narratives told by working-class mothers and their children, found a preponderance of negative and personal-injury themes; most strikingly, the stories initiated by the children focused on these themes even more than the stories the mothers initiated, indicating that the children had learned very early what constituted a possible story within their families.

Self as Agent

One can see parallels between the child's construction of self and the literary construction of the "individual." In the emergence of the modern novel from Greek drama, Rorty (1976) has identified four stages in the development of the main actor: First, narratives center around the actions of a "character," who acts as he does because of the force of circumstances. In a second stage, we see the emergence of the "figure," who acts in a certain way because of traits that govern the actions. In nineteenth-century novels, we see "persons," who constitute thoughtful and responsible actors in conflict with other persons in society. Only in the modern novel do we see "selves" and "individuals" who possess their traits rather than being defined by them, who are susceptible to identity crises and internal conflicts, whose actions are determined by their subjective experiences, and whose being is located centrally in their consciousness.

Similarly, I believe, one can see that the stories told to children about their earliest experiences portray them as characters in family stories and subsequently as figures with traits (love of ice cream, dislike of bibs, tendency to tantrums, unwillingness to go to sleep, etc.). But the stories about themselves that children participate in telling and retelling emphasize their motives for action, their emotional responses to events, their expectations and—most centrally perhaps— their own memories. The attribution to children of memory for the significant events of their lives (even in the face of considerable evidence that such memories are partial and inaccurate, as many of the early recounts cited above confirm) constitutes a recognition of their role as agents, as individuals with intentions, whose subjective experiences are relevant to the narrative.

The semiliterary analysis offered here of children's autobiographies-in-the-making conflicts with dominant conceptions of the "life story" as an intrin-sically oral form (Linde 1987). Clearly, the autobiographies that emerge in interaction between parent and child are subject both to updating and to revision in the process of retelling, characteristics of oral rather than derived-literate forms. As they are retold, incidents must be modified to enhance their coherence with incidents already well established in the larger story. The adult's life story, like the child's, is formed in the telling; it is the intrinsically social nature of this process that this chapter has attempted to display.

Continuity of memory is a major factor in the subjective sense of self. The centrality of memories of one's own past as a locus of self-identity was first pointed out by Locke (cited in Butler 1900) and has been criticized as too narrow in omitting one's plans for the future as a source of self-identity Butler 1900). We have seen that mother-child discussions elaborate both past and future experiences as part of the child's life story. A careful look at the memories for the past, and conceptions of future plans, available to children age two and three makes clear that their subjective experiences, unlike adults', are not private and personal but intrinsically social. The selection of memories, their formation into "good" narratives, and their consolidation into a larger picture of who the child is and what her or his life has been like rely deeply on parental collaboration.

It may be, of course, that the internal and autonomous notion of self that we assume is the endpoint of the kind of collaboration displayed in this chapter is itself somewhat anomalous. Geertz (1984) has commented on the peculiarly asocial concept of self that is typical of American culture, and Rosaldo (1984) and Shweder and Bourne (1982) have documented cultural conceptions of the individual much more firmly rooted in the social context than is the North American notion. There is a tendency in psychology to distinguish between the "autonomous self" and the "self in relationship" (see Connell, in this volume), or the "self-constructed self" and the "other-constructed self" (Watson, in this volume). One possibility opened up by a deeper study of the social construction of self is that these dichotomies make empty distinctions—that the autonomous self is made possible only by social processes of development and maintenance. The processes of social construction that we have seen here at work in developing a sense of self for Naomi, Sarah, and Nathaniel may be more richly exploited in other cultural contexts to modify and maintain the self throughout the life span and may be more important in the self construction of North American adults than is commonly acknowledged.

References

Brown, P., and S. Levinson. 1978 Universals in language usage: Politeness phenomena. In *Questions and politeness: Strategies in social interaction*. Edited by E. Goody. Cambridge: Cambridge University Press.

Brown, R. 1973. *A first language: The early stages*. Cambridge, Mass.: Harvard University Press.

Bruner, J. 1986. *Actual minds, possible worlds*. Cambridge, Mass.: Harvard University Press.

Budwig, N. 1986. Agentivity and control in early child language. Doctoral dissertation, University of California, Berkeley.

————. In press. Self and joint categories in early child grammar. In *Children's language*, vol. 7. Edited by G. Conti-Ramsden and C. E. Snow. Hillsdale, N.J.: Erlbaum.

Butler, T. 1900. Of personal identity. In *The works of Bishop Butler*, vol 2. Edited by J. H. Bernard. London.

Eisenberg, A. 1985. Learning to describe past experiences in conversation. *Discourse Processes* 8:177–204.

Eisenberg, N. 1983. *Early descriptions of past experiences. Scripts as structure*. Princeton, N.J.: Educational Testing Service.

Engel, S. 1986a. Learning to reminisce: A developmental study of how young children talk about the past. Ph.D. thesis, City University of New York.

————. 1986b, May. Remembering together. Paper presented to the New York Child Language Group, Teachers College, New York.

Fivush, R., J. Gray, and F. Fromhoff. 1987. Two-year-olds talk about the past. *Cognitive Development* 2:393–409.

Geertz, C. 1984. "From the native's point of view": On the nature of anthropological understanding. In *Culture theory: Essays on mind, self and emotion*. Edited by R. Shweder and R. LeVine. New York: Cambridge University Press.

Goffman, E. 1987. *Forms of talk*. Philadelphia: University of Pennsylvania Press.

Heath, S. B. 1976. Separating "things of the imagination" from life: Learning to read and write. In *Emerging literacy*. Edited by W. Teale and E. Sulzby. Norwood, N.J.: Ablex.

Hudson, J., and K. Nelson. 1986. Repeated encounters of a similar kind: Effects of familiarity on children's autobiographic memory. *Cognitive Development* 1:253–71.

Kihlstrom, J. 1982. On personality and memory. In *Personality, cognition and social interaction*. Edited by N. Cantos and J. Kihlstrom. Hillsdale, N.J.: Erlbaum.

Linde, C. 1987. Explanatory systems in oral life stories. In *Cultural models in language and thought*. Edited by D. Holland and N. Quinn. Cambridge: Cambridge University Press.

Lucariello, J., and K. Nelson. 1982. Situational variation in mother-child interaction. Paper presented at the International Congress of Infant Studies, Austin, Texas.

MacNamee, G. D. 1980. The social origins of narrative skills. Doctoral dissertation, Northwestern University, Evanston, Il.

MacWhinney, B., and C. E. Snow. 1985. The child language data exchange system. *Journal of Child Language* 12:271–75.

McAdams, D. P., and R. L. Ochberg, eds. 1986. Psychobiography and life narratives. *Journal of Personality* 56 (no. 1).

Miller, P., and L. Sperry. 1987, April. The early acquisition of stories of personal experience. Paper presented at the meeting of the Society for Research in Child Development, Baltimore, Md.

Mishler, E. 1986. *Research interviewing.* Cambridge, Mass.: Harvard University Press.

Nelson, K. 1986. *Event knowledge: Structure and function in development.* Hillsdale, N.J.: Erlbaum.

Ninio, A. In press. The roots of narrative: Discussing recent events with very young children. *Language Sciences.*

Peterson, C., and A. McCabe. 1983. Developmental Psycholinguistics. New York: Plenum.

Polanyi, L. 1985. *Telling the American story: A structural and cultural analysis of conversational story-telling.* Norwood, N.J.: Ablex.

Rorty, A. 1976. A literary postscript: Characters, persons, selves, individuals. In *The identities of persons.* Edited by A. D. Rorty. Berkeley, Calif.: University of California Press.

Rosaldo, M. 1984. Toward an anthropology of self and feeling. In *Culture theory: Essays on mind, self and emotion.* Edited by R. Shweder and R. LeVine. New York: Cambridge University Press.

Sachs, J. 1979. Topic selection in parent-child discourse. *Discourse Processes* 2:145–53.
_____. 1983. Talking about the there and then: The emergence of displaced reference in parent-child discourse. In *Children's language,* vol. 4. Edited by K. E. Nelson. Hillsdale, N.J.: Erlbaum.

Schafer, R. 1981. *Narrative actions in psychoanalysis.* Worcester, Mass.: Clark University Press.

Scollon, R., and S. Scollon. 1981. *Narrative, literacy and face in inter-ethnic communication.* Norwood, N.J.: Ablex.

Shweder, R., and E. Bourne. 1982. Does the concept of the person vary cross-culturally? In *Cultural conceptions of mental health and therapy.* Edited by A. J. Marsella and G. M. White. Dordrecht: Reidel.

Snow, C. E. 1978. The conversational context of language acquisition. In *Recent advances in the psychology of language,* vol. 2. Edited by R. Campbell and P. Smith. New York: Plenum.
_____. 1981. The uses of imitation. *Journal of Child Language* 8:205–12.

Snow, C. E., C. Dubber, and A. De Blauw. 1982. Routines in parent-child interaction. In *The language of children reared in poverty.* Edited by L. Feagans and D. Farran. New York: Academic.

Snow, C. E. and B. Goldfield. 1983. Turn the page please: Situation-specific language acquisition. *Journal of Child Language* 10:551–69.

Spence, D. 1982. *Narrative truth and historical truth: Meaning and interpretation in psychoanalysis.* New York: Norton.

Wylie, R. 1984. Mothers' attributions to their young children. Paper presented at the Symposium on Self, Cardiff, Wales.

Appendix: Examples of Sarah's Autobiographical Discussions

Age: 2:5
Situation: Sarah is playing with a toy merry-go-around.

> *Sarah:* xxx. xxx go fast.
> *Mother:* It goes too fast, don't you like the merry-go-round? Huh? And the horses? And you go on the cars when you go to the beach. What else? Do you remember? 'Member going to the beach? And the water and everything. Hmm?
> *Sarah:* [*Nods.*]

Age: 2:9
Situation: Start of tape.

> *Mother:* How about telling me about the circus? What did you see over at the circus?
> *Sarah:* Unh.
> *Mother:* Who did you go with? Who took you to the circus?
> *Sarah:* Daddy!
> *Mother:* Daddy, of course, and who else?
> *Sarah:* Uhh, Mummy!
> *Mother:* And Mummy, yeah. And what did you see over there?
> *Sarah:* xxx. Su wu ga.
> *Mother:* The what?
> *Sarah:* The circus.
> *Mother:* The circus, yeah, and you saw Bozo? Uh-uh, yes, and what else?
> *Sarah:* Uh.
> *Mother:* Oh, now you remember.
> *Sarah:* Lions.
> *Mother:* The lions, yeah, yes. And do they have long tails? Huh, what, and big mouths? Uh-uh, yes, and you saw what else?
> *Sarah:* Uh.
> *Mother:* The elephant.
> *Sarah:* Elephant.
> *Mother:* Elephants, yeah, yes, you saw the elephants.
> *Sarah:* Yeah, yes!
> *Mother:* And they had a big long what?
> *Sarah:* Nose.
> *Mother:* Big long nose? They did? Was it longer than your nose? It was? I see.
> *Sarah:* Is a big circus in is.
> *Mother:* It was a great big circus? I'll bet it was. What else did you see?
> *Sarah:* Uh, sh, quiet, uh, uh.
> *Mother:* What're you thinking about? Don't you remember? I think you're tired. Are you tired right now?

Age: 2:11
Situation: Sarah picks up a hat.

Father: What hat is that?

Sarah: My hat.

Father: Yeah, but when do you wear this? When you go to a what?

Sarah: Go party.

Father: When you go to a party. And you went to a party last week?

Sarah: [*Nods.*]

Father: Whose party? Remember?

Sarah: xxx party.

Father: No, Annie's party. And you cried because you had to blow out the candles, huh? Yeah. When's your party?

Sarah: Where's my party.

Father: When's your party?

Sarah: xxx

Father: Next month? And how old will you be?

Sarah: Two.

Sarah: Two.

Father: No, you're two now. What comes after two?

Sarah: Two? Three.

Father: Three, you'll be three.

Sarah: Yeah!

Father: Yeah. You'll be big.

Sarah: Yeah, biggy big. See? I xxx me. See? I xxx me. I big big be big me.

Father: You'll be a big girl. Some day you'll be as big as Mummy.

Sarah: As big as you too.

Father: I hope you're not as big as me.

Age: 3:0
Situation: Beginning of tape.

Mother: Tell Courtney all about Provincetown. What'd you do?

Sarah: I want a Provincetown.

Mother: More about all the sand, and the sand dunes, and the jeep. Remember the jeep?

Sarah: xxx

Mother: The jeep.

Mother: What happened in the jeep?

Sarah: xxxx dere.

Mother: xxx saw all the water.

Sarah: Yes.

Age: 3:1

Situation: Sarah's mother discussing Santa Claus.

Mother: What do you want him to bring you?
Sarah: Umh, two bugs. Two bugs.
Mother: Oh, two bugs.
Sarah: I xxx poodle me right there.
Mother: Remember, what'd Santa Claus bring you last year? Do you remember? What?
Sarah: Um, two lady bugs.
Mother: Yeah, two lady bugs.
Father: Two lady bugs?
Mother: All the things under the tree and you remember two lady bugs!
Sarah: Two lady bugs.
Father: Do you remember what he brought you? . . .
Sarah: What?
Father: Didn't he bring you Little Chatty?
Sarah: Baby.
Father: Baby brother and Little Chatty baby sister?

Age: 3:10

Situation: Melissa and Sarah looking at animal book.

Melissa: Sarah, have you ever seen an elephant?
Sarah: [*Nods yes.*]
Melissa: Where? In . . .
Sarah: In my book.
Melissa: In a book.
Mother: xxx
Sarah: A funny book.
Mother: Did you ever see a real one?
Melissa: Did you ever see a real one? In a circus or a zoo?
Mother: Seen two.
Sarah: Yep.
Mother: She saw one at the circus, and you saw them at the zoo. xxx.
Sarah: I didn't go to the zoo yet.
Mother: You went to the zoo last year. But you don't remember.
Sarah: That last Thursday?
Mother: No, not last Thursday. Last summer.
Sarah: Last summer?
Mother: Yeah.
Sarah: Oh. I go last summer.

Age 4:1

Situation: Melissa and Sarah's mother discussing Sarah's father's homing pigeons.

Melissa: Where are they kept?

Mother: There, on the roof.

Melissa: Over across the street?

Mother: Yeah, on that big house there, up on the roof. There's a great big pigeon coop. You can't see it from here.

Sarah: Last night, remember?

Mother: Last?

Sarah: We went to woosky.

Mother: To where?

Sarah: To Woosky.

Mother: Woosky's?

Sarah: Woosky's. With the pigeons. With Daddy. xxx. With the xxx. Remember? I go with my Daddy. And you didn't come, and Donna was here.

Mother: No, I don't.

Sarah: I remember.

Mother: And the pigeons went home?

Sarah: Yeah. The pigeons were home. Remember? Remember that? What I just said and you didn't come and Donna was here. Remember? I remember.

Mother: Uh-uh.

Age: 4:5

Situation: Mother and Sarah discussing the picture on the can of Bumble Bee tuna.

Mother: You got stung by a bee.

Sarah: Huh?

Mother: Remember when . . . the bee got you down at the beach? You had to go to the hospital?

Sarah: Where'd he bite me?

Mother: In the belly.

Sarah: Oh. Right here?

Mother: Yeah. Don't you remember?

Sarah: No. I remember the bee bite me in the belly, though, but don't remember I don't had to go to the doctor's. I'll make today a cat, awright? Want me to make a cat? See?

11 Sensorimotor and Representational Internal Working Models of Self, Other, and Relationship: Mechanisms of Connection and Separation

SANDRA PIPP

The infant's emerging sense of self has historically been hypothesized to be inextricably bound to and embedded in relationships with significant caregivers, according to developmental psychologists (Bretherton 1987; Harter 1983; Main, Kaplan, and Cassidy 1985; Sroufe, in this volume; Sroufe and Fleeson 1985) and psychoanalytic theorists (Emde 1983; Emde and Buchsbaum, in this volume; Kernberg 1976; Kohut 1984; Mahler, Pine, and Bergman 1975; Stechler, in this volume; Stern 1985). Yet, confusion arises in specifying the domains in which the sense of self and the sense of other overlap and the ways they are different in the mind of the infant.

Traditional psychoanalytic thought presupposes that the sense of self *is* the sense of the other at birth: Newborns must struggle out of an undifferentiated matrix of self/mother confusion. By postulating that the newborn's initial state is one of intrapsychic connection or inability to differentiate self from other, the key developmental issue becomes the infants' developing ability to differentiate self from other. For example, Mahler et al. (1975) suggested that the key developmental task in infancy is that of "separation-individuation," defined as how the infant individuates, or constructs the sense of self, by separating from the representation that confuses self and mother.

The focus on separation—to the exclusion of an equal role for processes of connection—unnecessarily restricts an account of the development of how infants relate senses of self, others, and relationships (Gilligan 1987; Kegan 1982). The structure of our species fosters both connection and separation. Connection is fostered by the prolonged immaturity of our species, which results in dependency upon an interwoven system of others (Bronfenbrenner 1979; Sameroff and Chandler 1975; Silvern 1984). Separateness is fostered by living in a body that provides different sensorimotor and biological codings of

Warm thanks to Dante Cicchetti, Cliff Siegel, and Louise Silvern for helpful comments on previous versions of this manuscript and to Arthur Huntley, Lyz Jaeger, Bill Overton and Marsha Weinraub for discussions on the topics covered in this chapter.

self and other and that forces different perspectives on the self than on the other (Pipp, Easterbrooks, and Harmon 1989; Pipp, Fischer, and Jennings 1987).

The metaphor of connection and separation will be used to explore the development of the relation between infants' developing senses of self, other, and relationship. My thesis is that if these concepts are differentiated, more precise statements about the developing sense of self may be obtained by comparing domains in which the sense of self arises in the context of the other and domains in which the sense of self arises in the context of the relationship. Additionally, particular attention will be paid to parameters of infants' sensorimotor and representational internal working models (Bowlby 1973; Bretherton 1985; Main et al. 1985) in order to show how the development of structures of thought influences infants' and preschoolers' differentiation of self, other, and relationship.

Sensorimotor and Representational Internal Working Models

In both object relations and attachment views, the infant's sense of self is said to derive from relationships with significant others. The relationship, however, is embedded in one's interactions with the significant other, and there has been little conceptual distinction between sense of relationship and sense of other. One exception is the work of Bretherton (1985), who suggested that infants' models of self and others are closely intertwined because they are constructed out of dyadic experiences. Initially, infants may construct models of relationships, not self or other. It is not until later that senses of self and other are differentiated from the relationship. In large part, the purpose of this chapter is to explore the boundary conditions of this important statement.

Attachment theorists suggest that an infant's behavior in a relationship is guided by an internal working model, defined as dynamic internalized representations of the relationship (Bowlby 1973; Bretherton 1985, 1987; Cicchetti et al., in this volume; Main et al. 1985). The construct of internal working models was initially designed to account for infants responding differently when separated from and reunited with primary attachment figures: a securely attached infant has a different internal working model than does an insecurely attached one.

One unresolved question, however, is whether the differences observed in infants' behaviors are due to differences in concrete, behavioral interactions between infants and mothers or to differences in infants' internal working models of relationships (Main 1987). Internal working models have been hypothesized to guide infants' behaviors as early as four months (Main et al. 1985). This statement stands in clear contrast to both Bowlby and Piaget. Bowlby (1982, 365) pointed out that "during the first year or two the stability of attachment pattern . . . is a property more of the couple in which the child is a partner than the behavioral organization within the child itself.'' After the first year or two of life, a child's attachment pattern becomes increasingly more internally organized. And, according to Piaget ([1936] 1952), internal working models should not be able to guide young infants' behavior, because sensorimotor infants are incapable of representational thought. How then can we account for younger infants' responses to separation from the caregiver?

One way to resolve the dilemma is to differentiate between symbolic representation in a strict, Piagetian sense and "enactive representation" (Bruner, Olver, and Greenfield 1966). Piagetian representation refers to the ability to call forth and manipulate symbols. Representation in this sense refers to the ability to "evoke by a sign or a symbolic image an absent object or an action not yet carried out" (Piaget [1936] 1952, 243). This is in contrast to Bruner and associates' use of enactive, or "sensorimotor," representation. Sensorimotor infants' behaviors are guided by action, not symbolic thought; and while infants are unable to evoke or manipulate symbols, they are quite capable of relating actions together in order to act appropriately in a given situation.[1]

Sensorimotor internal working models, therefore, should have different characteristics than representational internal working models. Sensorimotor infants' behavior should be guided more by the actual ongoing interaction, while representational infants' behavior should be guided more by symbolic thought. Each will be treated in turn.

Sensorimotor Internal Working Models

Interactions with caregivers are based on real-time interactive sequences in which each behavior serves as a cue for a response, which in turn serves as a cue for the partner's response. Sensorimotor internal working models may inform infants interactions with their caregivers at the level of generalized event structures. In contrast, the onset of representational thought provides a symbolic structure which serves to guide older infants' and toddlers' behavioral sequences in any ongoing interaction. Thus, sensorimotor internal working models, *because they are composed of temporally based, interactive sequences,* should be more sensitive to parameters of the ongoing interactive sequences within a relationship than are representational models that symbolically guide interactions.

1. Mandler (1983) correctly points out that there is little substantive difference between Bruner and associates' definitions of enactive representation and Piaget's definitions of sensorimotor thought. Bruner and associates' use of the term *representation,* however, does underline the point that sensorimotor infants are capable of internalized schemata that are a form of representation.

Enactive representation may be coded in the form of scripts (Bretherton 1985, 1987; Main 1987). At the sensorimotor level, a script may be defined as temporally ordered sequences of actions, or generalized event structures (Fivush 1987; Nelson 1986; Nelson and Gruendel 1981). For example, the infant's script for eating includes climbing up on the high chair, having a bib put on, seeing the food placed on a high-chair tray, and so on. Note, however, that the cognitive ability to string actions together to form an expected script is different than the cognitive ability to form and manipulate symbolic structures of these actions. It is somewhat later before a child can symbolically manipulate the actions required for eating—for example, by making a substitute actor such as a doll perform the above actions—and even later still before the child can describe the scenario of "baby eating" (Fivush 1987; Pipp et al. 1987; Watson and Fischer 1977).

All descriptions of the stages of sensorimotor thought provide graded sequences of greater separation between the object and the infant's actions upon it: as one consolidates more actions around an object, the object becomes an entity in its own right, independent of any one particular action. Analogously, the very first separation between the actual interaction and the mental representation comes when the infant combines actual instances of similar interactions to form generalized schemata. By being able to represent an action sequence (for example, the bedtime ritual), the script has coherence independent of the particular action sequences that constitute the script. The onset of representational skills allows again more advanced forms of separation between action-based reality and the internal representation. The infant can call up rituals or event sequences independent of environmental suggestion. That is, the infant can think about the bedtime ritual when there is nothing in the environment which suggests bedtime. The mental representation exists independent of the space and time in which it is normally carried out.

In the domain of interactions, the development of sensorimotor thought can be analogously construed as increasing generalizations of particular action sequences. For example, Stern (1985) suggested that infants form "representations of interactions that have been generalized" (RIGs). The first separation between the actual interaction and the mental representation must come when the infant combines actual instances of similar interactions to form generalized event structures. According to Stern, RIGs are the components of the internal working models of relationships.

One would expect that the generality of the RIGs would increase during the sensorimotor period. Unfortunately, there is very little work on sensorimotor scripts in young infants, in the sense of examining the types of behaviors infants must understand to appropriately direct their behavior in an interaction, or on the affective meaning an infant may take from a given interaction. Instead, script-based research has focused on how infants are able to link together objects in categories (Fivush 1987). Based on neo-Piagetian theories

(Case 1985; Fischer 1980), however, three shifts in sensorimotor internal working models would be expected: at three to four months, at seven to eight months, and at around twelve months of age. The generality, scope, and complexity of the scripts that the infant can enter into should increase because the number of components that infants can coordinate increases. These theories suggest that internal working models of relationships should show developmental progressions as infants coordinate understandings about relationships. At around three months of age, infants enter into social interactions in a responsive manner (Kaye 1982). At around eight months, infants become distressed when presented with a stranger, and it has been hypothesized that this behavior signals specific attachment to the caregiver (Emde, Gaensbauer, and Harmon 1976). Later, at twelve months, many infants protest separation from the primary attachment figure, as shown by numerous studies deriving from the "Strange Situation" (Ainsworth et al. 1978). In all situations, infants evidence behaviors that indicate that they feel secure with the attachment figure (Bretherton 1985), yet the specific behaviors differ.

Three lines of evidence converge to support the notion that behavioral interactions between mother and child guide younger infants' behavior in the attachment situation. First, separation and reunion behaviors are not reliable indicators of attachment past twenty-four months of age. Once the mother is internalized through representational means, simple separation and reunion should not provide an adequate means of testing the attachment relationship, because the child no longer must rely solely on the sensorimotor interactional cues between mother and child. According to this view, separation and reunion episodes provide a means of testing infants' and mothers' adaptations to each other in terms of event representations of the interactive sequences characteristic of the relationship. In contrast, infants whose behavior is guided by representational internal working models contain the internalized image of the mother; therefore, simple separation and reunion episodes cannot provide a test of the structure of older infants' internal working models.

Additional evidence for the ongoing behavioral interaction's importance in attachment behavior comes from the data on infants' responses to separation and reunion with each parent. Bowlby (1958; 1982) initially suggested that the internal working model of relationship followed the principle of monotropy: the infant is biased to become attached to one principal attachment figure (typically, the biological mother), and all other attachments or relationships (e.g., with father) are subsidiary and should follow the model of the primary attachment relationship. Data are equivocal in support this hypothesis. Whether judged by security of attachment classifications (Ainsworth et al. 1978) or by principal component analysis (Connell 1985), attachment behavior to one parent does not reliably predict attachment to the other (Bridges, Connell, and Belsky 1988; Grossman et al. 1981; Lamb 1978). (But, see Easterbrooks 1989.) Bridges and colleagues argued explicitly that the specificity of attachment with mother and father is due to the differences in behavioral interactions that infants encounter with each parent.[2]

Finally, when coding the behavior of the mother as well as that of the infant, Aber and Slade (1987) reported differences in maternal behaviors in mothers' separation from and reunion with securely attached versus insecurely attached infants. If reliable behavioral differences are observed in maternal behavior, differences in infant behavior cannot be unambiguously attributed to internal working models. If there is a difference between sensorimotor internal working models and representational ones, one might expect relatively greater reliance on the behavioral cues of the mother earlier rather than later in development.

From Sensorimotor to Representational Thought

The onset of representational thought enables the infant to symbolically internalize features of self, other, and relationships. Piaget ([1936] 1952) believed that representational thought provided more veridical relations with the external world because, for the first time, infants think about objects independent of their actions on those objects: objects have a "necessary existence" outside of action. Representational thought has been said to presage a Copernican revolution because infants are now able to decenter from their actions. In the framework of interactions, one could say that the infant now has "interactional permanence" (analogous to object permanence). The infant can mentally represent characteristics of a person or a relationship independent of being embedded in the ongoing dynamics of that person or relationship.

The flip side of object or interactional permanence is that infants now are capable of coding any event at two levels: the actual sensorimotor level and the level of representations. The information about each interaction must be contained at the sensorimotor level (e.g., gestural and/or verbal acts that specify the interactional sequence). At the same time that representational infants are coding—or decoding—this information, they are also accessing stored representations of interactions that are similar to the one being enacted. The important and obvious point is that the representational infant must continue to code sensorimotor components of interactions while accessing, creating, or storing the representational form of the interaction. The infant now becomes a dual processor.

2. An interesting question is whether individuals consolidate internal working models of various relationships into one meta-internal working model later in development. By college, students often talk about "the parents" as if they were one psychological unit, yet differences are evident in their portrayal of their understanding of relationships with each parent (Pipp et al. 1985). Additionally, infant attachment classifications relate more strongly to six-year-olds' conceptions of attachment with mother than with father (Main 1987; Main et al. 1985).

The onset of representational ability also contains a double-edged sword: represented interactions will paradoxically result in both greater fidelity to the sensorimotor reality and greater distortion of it. Greater fidelity is obtained because objects do exist outside of one's interactions with them. Analogously, the self exists independent of specific actions or interactions. The child forms self-concepts that transcend particular instantiations from which the self-concept is developed, and the self begins to have symbolic forms that exist independent of the relationships within which it was derived. For example, toddlers show evidence of forming a concept of their own facial features, begin to refer to themselves and others by name, and can identify their own and others' sex (Lewis and Brooks-Gunn 1979). Most of the research on the development of self focuses on the development of children's representational self-concepts. (See Harter 1983, for a review of the developmental literature.)

Greater distortion, however, is also obtained by the onset of representational ability. Representational thought does not necessarily produce a "better" match to reality. Sensorimotor knowers are embedded in real time and real space. They are "confined to reflect the impress of reality" (Stern 1985, 182). Representational thought, in contrast, enables the infant to create another perspective on the reality of living in one's body and, in some sense, to transcend real time and real space. The student attending a lecture, for example, has the option to concentrate on the lecture (and maintain attention to the ongoing interaction sequence that exists in the present time and space) or to daydream (and remove the self from the ongoing interaction to mentally inhabit a different time and space). While representational toddlers cannot use the sophisticated cognitive mechanisms of the college student to mentally absent themselves, the nascent ability to remove the self from the ongoing press of reality comes with representational skills. Representational skills, then, bring the ability to distort reality, because one has the capacity to be removed from reality.

Another cause of distortion is the toddler's relative inexperience at manipulating and coordinating representations (Fischer 1980). Initial attempts at coordinating representations are often a matter of trial and error. One may have a beginning representation of "good" (or, at the level of a two-year-old, "good guys"), for instance, without the ability to coordinate that representation to the concept of "bad" (Fischer and Pipp 1984a). To an adult, it is a curious state of affairs to contemplate the nature of good without reference to the concept of bad; yet the ability to coordinate representations of good and bad requires another structural developmental level (Fischer 1980).

Implicit in this view is the notion that higher forms of thought are not necessarily more accurate forms of thought. Higher forms of thought are not "better" or "healthier," simply more complex (Fischer and Pipp 1984a). Structural developmental advance is defined by increases in complexity, not by health or adaptation. People are capable of constructing complex, developmentally advanced forms of pathological behavior (Mahlerstein and Ahern 1982; Silvern 1984), as evidenced by psychopaths showing higher stages of moral judgment than normal adults (Link, Scherer, and Byrne 1977).

These two aspects of preoperational thought—freeing representations from their sensorimotor anchor and the toddlers' difficulties in coordinating representations in the same way adults do—enables the structure of complexive thinking (Vygotsky 1978). The structure of this type of thought often resembles primary process thinking (Fischer and Pipp 1984a; Gill 1967; Holt 1967; Piaget 1962). The "logic of the illogical" follows the structures of condensation, displacement, and wish fulfillment, three basic characteristics of primary process thought. Representations are combined in ways that, while appearing bizarre to the logical structures of the adult, are applied following lawful—but not logical—rules.

Additionally, interactive scripts are no longer bounded by situational determinants, so pretend play becomes rich and imaginative: the bedtime script can be applied to the family dog, not just the self. With the onset of the ability to relate representations together, toddlers also play out both sides of an interaction (self *and* other), whereas earlier they simply were part of the ongoing interaction. This new ability has embarrassed more than one parent as the preschooler acts out the disciplining parent! (See Fischer et al. 1984, for a description of the development of pretend-play capabilities during the preschool period.)

Self, Other, and Relationship

The difference in characteristics of sensorimotor and representational internal working models will influence the relation between infants' understandings of self, other, and relationship. The bodily self and the bodily other are sources of actions that together form the action sequences that make up features of the relationship. How can the infant distinguish between self, other, and relationship? And what sources contribute to a lack of differentiation between self, other, and relationship? One approach to these questions is to determine how individuals code objects differently from interactions. An object has form, color, taste, and so forth. How do we categorize or code the content of an interaction? Except poetically, it is difficult to characterize interactions on the same dimensions as objects. In brief, I will suggest that those capabilities of the infant or features of the world that enhance the perception of a person as an object serve to aid differentiation between self, other, and relationship.

Sources of Differentiation between Self and Other

Following Baldwin (1899), a number of researchers have suggested that as the self is known, so is the other known (Bretherton 1985; Lewis and Brooks-

Gunn 1979; Sroufe, in this volume; Sroufe and Fleeson 1985; Stern 1985). Hart and Damon (1985), in contrast, pointed out that Baldwin's imitative theory was focused only on understanding the self in relation to others. When self-understanding is considered as having functions other than connection with others, differences between self and other emerge. In particular, dissimilarities between self and other emerge when each is to be known as a bodily or conceptual object.

From birth, the infant's core sense of self is distinguished from the core sense of other. These differences are obtained because the self lives in a different body than the other and because self-organizing properties exist. At the simplest, biological level, healthy neonates breathe for themselves and digest their food. While these represent autonomic nervous system functioning, these behaviors provide structure that serves to organize the biological self.

For the sensorimotor infant, the body of self and other serves as an object to be acted upon and explored and an object from which to act. Results of this exploration will result in different body maps for self and other because the architecture of the body forces different perspectives on one than on the other, both as a physical object and as an actor or recipient of action (Pipp et al. 1989; Pipp et al. 1987). Since the architecture of the body predisposes attention to some actions but not others, a differential between self and other is built into the system of knowing self and other. For example, the architecture of the body is such that the eyes turn outward, so sensorimotor featural recognition should bias infants to have a visual knowledge of the mother's face before acquiring visual knowledge of their own face. And, in fact, visual featural recognition studies support this assumption (Cicchetti et al., in this volume; Lewis and Brooks-Gunn 1979; Pipp et al. 1989; 1987). The tactile sense should also introduce differences in sensorimotor codings of self and other. As Sullivan (1953) pointed out, touching one's own hands is different than touching another's hands. When touching the self, the infant codes sensorimotor feedback of being touched as well as the actions of touching: when touching the other, the infant codes only the sensorimotor actions of touching the other.

With the onset of representation, the infant has the psychological means by which to transcend the architecture of the body. To be able to think about something without actually doing it means that the mind can take either self or other as an object to be mentally manipulated independent of the actions required for acting on either self or other. One can imagine the visual characteristics of one's own face without recourse to the mirror and can imagine the back of the other when gazing at the face. Additionally, the contents of self- and other-concepts differ. As an obvious example, adults who define themselves as psychologists do not then indiscriminately apply this label to others, just as toddlers who label themselves as a "big boy" or "big girl" do not apply that label to all others. Representations of self and other are different because the content is dissimilar. For both sensorimotor and representational knowers, then, differences can exist in the content of self and other knowledge.[3]

In contrast, the same processes may underlie how representational information for self and other is acquired and stored. Differences in time of onset between self and other featural recognition knowledge, for example, disappeared for tasks which required representational skills (Pipp et al. 1987). While infants detected rouge on their mother's nose before rouge on their own, there was no difference in time of onset to answer questions such as "Who is that?" when the correct response was either self (me) or other (Mommy).

Sensorimotor and representational infants' processes of acquiring information in general, however, differ because sensorimotor knowers are constrained by the bodily architecture and by the sensorimotor nature of knowledge acquisition. What to an adult would seem to be structurally equivalent (e.g., forming visual schemata of self's and others' faces) is not to a sensorimotor infant, because the skills needed to acquire both types of schemata are different. The different content between self and other forces differences in acquisition strategy (e.g., the need for a mirror in order to form a schema for the self's face, while no mirror is needed for the other's face). Representational structures, in contrast, allow for greater similarity in the process of acquisition. While the content may be different (e.g., the name for self is different than for mother), the process of acquiring and applying this representational label is similar because it is less sensorimotor and so less dependent on differences in bodily architecture.

The distinction between process and content of self-knowledge is reminiscent of James' (1890) differentiation between the "I" and the "me." The I referred to the self-as-knower, or that aspect of the self that processes information, while the me referred to the actual qualities of the self, or self-concept. In the context of self-other knowledge, this framework can be extended to include the "you," or concept of the other. I have argued that differences exist in the content of the you and the me for both sensorimotor and representational infants. With development, sensorimotor senses of self and other as bodily objects enlarge to include self- and other-representations

---

3. The difference in perspective of self and other maintains itself in psychological form in adulthood. For example, the actor/observer effect detailed by social psychologists (Jones and Nisbett 1971) shows that one's perspective forces different attributions for the self's actions than for other's actions: Others act because of stable traits, while the self acts because of situational determinants. For example, the other is late due to being disorganized and insensitive, while the self is late because of crosstown traffic. While the actor/observer effect may be due to differential access to knowledge about self and other, as suggested by researchers who investigate self schemata (Klein and Kihlstrom 1986), it is obvious that, whatever the explanation, an individual has a different knowledge base about the self than about the other.

of verbal labels and psychological states (Cicchetti et al., in this volume; Lewis and Brooks-Gunn 1979; Pipp et al. 1987).

The I, or self-as-knower, changes with development. The type of understanding that can be brought to bear on self and other changes with development, because changes in the structure of thought influence how people process information (Case 1985; Fischer and Pipp 1984b) and so should also influence how people are able to process information about the self. These cognitive structures serve as filters or upper limits on processing capabilities (Fischer and Pipp 1984b). The I, me, and you are interwoven in the sense that the I determines the cognitive structure of the contents about self and other. A sensorimotor I forces differences in both process and content about how infants know self and other as bodily objects, while a representational I forces differences only in the content of representations of self and other.

Sources of Confusion between Self and Other

Lack of differentiation between self, other, and relationship is aided by confusions engendered by interpersonal features. Let us first distinguish self and other from relationships. How is the sense of self (the "me") and other (the "you") distinguished from relationships (the "we")? For adults, the sense of self and other can be differentiated from the sense of relationship by assuming that self and other subsume understandings of the various relationships in which individuals are involved. The sense of the relationship will be defined as the behavioral and psychological dynamics of interactions between two or more people. While the sense of the relationship must necessarily include a self and an other, a description of a relationship represents a subset of a complete description of either self or other. For example, a more complete understanding of one's father (the other) includes an understanding of the interactions between self and father, but it also includes understandings of how he relates to others (e.g., mother, grandparents, siblings, friends, and colleagues) as well as a description of physical and psychological characteristics.

For the young infant, the relation between self, other, and relationship is more ambiguous. As suggested previously, self and other are distinguishable as separate bodily objects characterized by different contents. Confusion, or lack of differentiation, arises due to at least three factors: biological regulation, joint agency within an interaction, and affect.

Biological Regulation

After sharing the biological systems of the mother, the newborn infant must adapt to new forms of regulation. To take an obvious example, infants must learn to suck to obtain nutrients, where as fetuses they were supplied through the umbilical cord. The change in the form of regulation that occurs at birth does not imply that the organism is no longer connected biologically to others. Sander (1975), for example, suggested that the initial mother-infant interactions are based on negotiating the issue of biological regulation. Good-enough mothering in the neonate period may be defined as the dyad's skill in homeostatic regulation in the initial phases of infancy (Pipp and Harmon 1987). From the view of processing structures of the infant, homeostatic regulation would come to be expected after physiological disturbance in competent dyads. Investigating physiological responses in mammals, Hofer (1987) found that homeostatic regulation of the newborn is delegated to the interaction. Attachment, according to this view, serves to allow the mother to regulate the internal homeostasis of her infant, as well as allowing the infant to regulate the maternal functions (Field 1985; Hofer 1987; Reite et al. 1981). These regulating functions are observed in neurochemical, immunologic, metabolic, cardiovascular, endocrine, and sleep-wake cycles.

That the self exists in a body with the particular characteristics of our species leads to factors which contribute to both differentiation and confusion between self and other. Differentiation is caused by the fact that self and other reside in different bodies: confusion is created by the permeability of physiological regulation between infant and mother.

Confusion due to physiological regulation should change as a function of development. Obviously, the physiological upset felt when one-year-old human infants are separated from their mothers for a short time is different than in four-year-olds: the ability to cognitively understand that the mother will be right back is different between the two ages, and this cognition mediates physiological responses. However, the effects of long-term separation may not be that different between infants and either children or adults. In an intriguing article, Hofer (1984) suggested that biological regulation serves similar functions in adulthood as in infancy. Physiological changes in adults after bereavement bear striking resemblance to those observed in infants separated from their mothers in cardiovascular, endocrine, immunologic, and sleep-wake cycles. Intimate relationships, then, serve continuing regulating functions. At the most basic level, the biological one, we are connected and embedded in each others' biological rhythms throughout the life span. With development, however, our coping abilities and strategies may serve to mediate physiologically based connectedness.

Joint Agency

Both differentiation and confusion between self and other are also obtained in the domain of agency. Differentiation is fostered by dissimilarities in self- and other-directed behavior. Infants appear to be constructed so that certain self-directed behaviors have precedence over other-directed behaviors. Infants have a predisposition, for example, to put hand to the self's mouth, not the other. In those studies which focus simply on self- or other-directed behavior, infants and children produced actions concerning the self before applying them to others, whether they be action words (Huttenlocher, Smiley, and Charney 1983), emotion words (Bretherton et al. 1986, table 1), or the ability to act on self and on mother (Pipp et al. 1989; Pipp et al. 1987). For agency, it appears as if *decalage,* or difference in onset between self and other knowledge, is independent of whether the knowledge is sensorimotor or representational, since these differences appear throughout infancy and the preschool period. Differentiation is fostered, then, by the difference in onset of self- and other-directed behavior.

Confusion between self and other may occur because the other is known primarily through interactions. The sense of the I as an actor on the other is implicated in the we of the interaction. Infants' conceptions of the other are embedded in action sequences generated from the self. The other is known through the self's actions (either sensory or motor), so enactive representations of the other are coded in reference to self's actions. For the sensorimotor infant, then, the other's actions are "confused" with the self in the sense that codings of other are inextricably bound to codings of self.

Infants apply actions to others, of course, usually in interactive sequences. The puzzle is how these interactive sequences come together to form internalized notions of relationships. An individual represents a relationship with another by abstracting commonalities between interactions with that person. For infants, the interpersonal sense of self should also result from stereotypical action sequences, such as tickle games, change-the-diaper routines, and feeding routines. Interactional sequences that exhibit commonalities between one episode and the next will develop into sensorimotor internal working models of relationships, or Stern's (1985) RIGs, and eventually into representational internal working models. The important distinction here is that not all interactions with others are stereotyped to such a degree that generalities can or should be abstracted. It is in this sense of commonalities between instances, or games between self and other, that an interactional I derives from the we of the relationship. That is, the sense of self as an interpersonal agent is created in the matrix of shared meaning between the caregiver and the infant.

In sum, confusion between self and other results because infants know others through actions on them, while differentiation is engendered because of infants' predisposition to act on self before acting on others. With development, self and other become increasingly differentiated because higher-order representations of categories of action are formed for self and other. The self is constructed by the actions unique to the self, while the understanding of each individual other is constructed by those unique constellations of actions that characterize each of the others.

Affect

Another source of confusion between self and other is the affect generated in the interaction. The most primitive form of confusion is affect contagion, or the automatic induction of one's own affect from another's. Infants cry more, for example, when hearing another's or the self's taped cries (Sagi and Hoffman 1976; Simner 1971; Wolff 1969). While our species remains permeable to others' affect even in adulthood (e.g., adults' physiological responses to an immediate and sharp cry of distress from the other), the infant has been hypothesized to be particularly unable to affectively differentiate self from other.

Theoretical approaches which describe infants' lack of differentiation between self and other are traditionally psychoanalytically oriented. According to object relations theorists, all infants experience interactions with caregivers which are more or less satisfying to their felt needs. Infants initially separate experiences which are need satisfying and need denying (Kernberg 1976; Mahler et al. 1975; Melitto 1983). Two affectively separate "self/others" are coded: The infant's internalized images of the "good self/mother" who is reliable and comforting and the "bad self/mother" who is unreliable and frustrating.[4] (Note the parallel with data showing that adult cognitions appear to be stored as a function of the affective valence induced at the time of storage [Bower and Cohen 1982; Isen and Daubman 1984].) According to Kernberg (1976), the infant differentiates the self and mother representations within the affective valence in which they were initially coded, so that four representations obtain: good self, good mother, bad self, and bad mother. Not until the onset of representation will the child be able to coordinate need-satisfying components of the relationship into a "good mother" representation, while need-denying components are coordinated into a "bad mother" representation. (And, of course, representational ability will also enable the child to develop "good self" and "bad self" representations.) Later development enables coordination of the good and bad mother into a coherent representation of mother through the ability to coordinate the two mother representations. Likewise, an integrated affective self representation is constructed from the coordination of the good and bad self (Case et al., in press; Fischer and Pipp 1984a; Kernberg 1976). This should begin to occur between

4. "Good-enough mothers" (Winnicott 1965) still enable their infants to affectively experience the "bad mother" inadvertently. This occurs because all infants experience normal biological discomfort and because mothers cannot possibly meet all the needs of their infants at the immediate moment when the infant feels a need for her. This scheme is relevant for all infant development, therefore, not just abnormal development.

3 1/2 and 5 years of age, when children are capable of coordinating two or more representational structures. This age period is approximately the same as that identified as the beginning of object constancy (Mahler et al. 1975).

According to this theoretical approach to affective development, the relation between self, other, and relationship should shift as a function of the capabilities of the infant. For the sensorimotor infant, little differentiation should occur between the affective components of self, other, and relationship. The immediate interactions between self and other should result in access to self/other representations of the particular affective valence of that interaction. The attainment of object constancy in representational preschoolers allows for differentiation between self, other, and relationship. Integration between the good and bad aspects of significant others enables children to access the internalized need-satisfying mother when faced with frustration. Because the representations are not integrated, the infant who has not attained the beginnings of object constancy cannot access the comforting mother when the current interaction is frustrating.

The above framework can be used to explain the two-year-old's behavior when separated from attachment figures for lengthy times. After a number of days of separation, children become stressed although the substitute caregiving is more than adequate (Robertson and Robertson 1971). While two-year-olds are capable of representing the good and bad mother separately, they are still unable to coordinate these representations. Continued contact with the mother sustains the internalized representation of the good mother. After a long enough period of separation, the internal working model of the bad mother, the one who frustrates and does not meet one's needs, becomes activated because it is not yet integrated with the internal working model of the good mother.

This theoretical scheme provides an explanation of individual differences in attachment. Infants who are assessed as "insecurely attached" in the Strange Situation (Ainsworth et al. 1975) are infants who do not interact with their mothers in a way that suggests that the mother is perceived as a person who will meet their need for a feeling of security; or insecurely attached infants interact with the mother as if she is a bad mother. In light of my previous arguments about the difference between sensorimotor and representational infants' reactions in the Strange Situation, sensorimotor infants may appear to be insecurely attached for two reasons. These infants may be involved in an immediately frustrating interacton with their mothers. Because there is little differentiation between self, other, and relationship for sensorimotor infants, it is unclear whether the behavior that is judged as reflecting an insecure attachment represents the ongoing interaction or more stable, long-term difficulties between infant and mother. Likewise, it is unclear whether sensorimotor infants who are judged as securely attached are involved in a stable or a more immediate positive interaction with mother. Not until the onset of representational ability can inferences be more reliably made about whether the observed behavior is a function of short- or long-term aspects of the relationship. This is because representational skills enable more enduring, "traitlike" internal working models of relationships.

At the affective level, then, sensorimotor infants should confuse self, other, and relationships. The onset of object constancy or the integration of the other as a coherent person independent of the affective tone of the immediate interactions should enable differentiation between affective representations of self/other and the immediate interactions. Additionally, a determination of whether a particular behavior between infant and mother is due to the immediate interaction or to more stable characteristics of the relationships can be best assessed for infants who are capable of representational thought.

Mechanisms of Connection and Separation

Winnicott (1965) stated that there is no such thing as an infant. While this statement is wrong in an obvious sense (Surely, the mother is holding *something* after delivery!), it is correct in the sense that both biologically and psychologically the infant survives only in the "holding environment" provided by being in a relationship with caregiving others. How does the importance of caregiving others for the infant's survival influence infants' confusions between self and others? In the sense that Winnicott is incorrect, how does the fact that the infant exists separate from the mother—in order to be held by the mother—influence infants' understanding of separation?

To answer these questions, an exploration of what is meant by connection and separation is necessary. Traditionally, psychoanalytic theorists have assumed that connection between infant and mother is due to the infant's lack of differentiation between self and mother. With development, infants differentiate between the two. The end point of healthy development is autonomy and individuation, with internalization of the functions provided by important caregivers. In contrast, in an attempt to integrate psychoanalytic theory and findings from developmental psychology, Stern (1985) suggested that infants must develop a core sense of self and other before affective connectedness can be obtained. That is, self-regulating properties and rhythms must be consolidated before the infant can enter into the state of "intersubjectivity," the ability to share the affective state of the other through fusion of self/other boundaries or mergerlike experiences.

In part, this difference in opinion is due to a lack of clarity of the concepts. "Lack of differentiation," "confusion," "shared states," "merger," and "connection" are often used interchangably. But does merger necessarily imply lack of differentiation or confusion between self and other? A person can be connected to another and yet maintain differentiation between self and other. One can share another's affect without losing one's self boundaries, just as a relationship need not be severed in order to maintain autonomy. It is unlikely, therefore, that the radical statements of either Stern or Mahler and colleagues are correct. My thesis is that both stances are partially true. Two developmental lines—one of connectedness and one of separation—characterize an individual's development of knowledge of self and other. The developmental lines of separation and connection are present at birth and undergo changes in form throughout development. Differentiation between self and other is aided by the process of constructing sensorimotor understandings of self and other, because the locus of the self is constructed in a separate body from the other. Connection with others is enhanced by the permeability of biological regulation, joint agency within interactions, and affect sharing between self and others. The onset of representational structures of thought enables infants to construct more stable understandings of self, other, and relationship that are relatively independent of immediate interactions.

The transition from sensorimotor to representational intelligence marks the *addition* of a new level of thought, not the replacement of an old level of thought. Interactions which make up components of relationships occur in the present time. Additionally, sensorimotor components of self and other are the bases out of which interactions and understandings of self and other are built. We do not "develop out of bodies," and so we remain embedded in our biology and the present time. This anchor to reality means that we are continual dual processors: representations of the interactions occur within the context of sensorimotor interactions. This continuing duality is represented in both Freudian and Piagetian theories. As adults, our dreams still remain primary process in nature (Freud [1911] 1958), and it would be impossible to ride a bicycle without recourse to sensorimotor actions. (Piaget [1936] 1952). Mechanisms for separation and connection with others likewise exist throughout the life span.

Representational internal working models are maps of the interpersonal environment which provide individuals with predictions to understand themselves and others. The accuracy of these models depends on how well they fit the sensorimotor interactions from which they are derived. Because they are at a different level than the sensorimotor reality, distortion can arise. Verbally stored material (a result, for example, of a family narrative of what the mother's role is in the family) and material coded at the sensorimotor level (how the mother actually treats her children) may conflict (Bowlby 1980). Mothers who abuse their children, for example, may weave into the family narrative how good and caring they are as mothers. The child is left with the conscious model (e.g., "Mommy is good and caring") and the sensorimotor version (e.g., "It hurts when she hits me"). The representational internal working model is accessed consciously, while the sensorimotor internal working model is unconsciously coded. Both models can be internalized, yet an individual may be unaware of the conflict because they are coded on different levels.

The nature of being human, our evolutionary design, serves functions that enable both separation and connection throughout the life span. With development, we may change the structure of our affective and cognitive perspectives on self, other, and relationship. Yet, the twin themes of separation and connection, the reality of living in a separate body from others and yet in a community with others, are adevelopmental in nature. Winnicott's statement, "There is no infant," could be rephrased, "There is no person," in the sense that we are connected and dependent upon others for our functioning throughout the life span. Instead, we are a community. The converse of the above statements, "There is an infant/person," is also true, in the sense that we are separate entities with individual patterns of action, thought, and emotion.

References

Aber, J. L., and A. Slade. 1987. Parental detachment as a defense against separation anxiety: Behavior and representation. Paper presented at the meeting of the Society for Research in Child Development, Baltimore.

Ainsworth, M. D. S., M. C. Blehar, E. Waters, and S. Wall. 1978. *Patterns of attachment.* Hillsdale, N.J.: Erlbaum.

Baldwin, J. M. 1899. *Social and ethical interpretations in mental development.* New York: Macmillan.

Bower, G. H., and P. R. Cohen. 1982. Emotional influences in memory and thinking: Data and theory. In *Affect and cognition: The seventeenth annual Carnegie Symposium on Cognition.* Edited by M. S. Clark and S. T. Fiske. Hillsdale, N.J.: Erlbaum, 291–331.

Bowlby, J. 1958. The nature of the child's tie to his mother. *International Journal of Psycho-Analysis* 39:350–73.

———. 1973. *Attachment and loss.* Vol. 2, *Separation.* New York: Basic.

———. 1980. *Attachment and loss.* Vol. 3, *Loss.* New York: Basic.

———. 1982. *Attachment and loss.* Vol. 1, *Attachment.* 2d ed. New York: Basic.

Bretherton, I. 1985. Attachment theory: Retrospect and prospect. In *Growing points in attachment theory and research.* Edited by I. Bretherton and E. Waters. Monographs of the Society for Research in Child Development. vol. 50, nos. 1–2, serial no. 209.

———. 1987. New perspectives on attachment relations: Security, communication and internal working models. In *Handbook of infant psychology.* Edited by J. Osofsky. New York: Wiley.

Bretherton, I., and M. Beeghley. 1982. Talking about internal states: The acquisition of an explicit theory of mind. *Developmental Psychology* 18:906–21.

Bretherton, I., J. Fritz, C. Zahn-Waxler, and D. Ridgeway. 1986. Learning to talk about emotions: A functionalist perspective. *Child Development* 57:529–48.

Bridges, L. J., J. P. Connell, and J. Belsky. 1988. Similarities and differences in infant-mother and infant-father interaction in the Strange Situation: A component process analysis. *Developmental Psychology* 24:92–100.

Bronfenbrenner, U. 1979. *The ecology of human development: Experiments by nature and design.* Cambridge, Mass.: Harvard University Press.

Bruner, J. S., R. R. Olver, and P. M. Greenfield. 1966. *Studies in cognitive growth.* New York: Wiley.

Case, R. 1985. *Intellectual development: Birth to adulthood.* New York: Academic.

Case, R., S. Hayward, M. Lewis, and P. Hurst. In press. Toward a neo-Piagetian theory of cognitive and emotional development. *Developmental Review.*

Connell, J. P. 1985. A component process approach to the study of individual differences and development change in attachment system functioning. In *Patterns of attachment reassessed.* Edited by M. E. Lamb, R. A. Thompson, W. Gardner, and E. Charnov. Hillsdale, N.J.: Erlbaum.

Easterbrooks, M. A. 1989. Quality of attachment to mother and father: Effects of perinatal risk status. *Child Development* 60:825–30.

Emde, R. N. 1983. The pre-representational self and its affective core. *Psychoanalytic Study of the Child* 38:165–92.

Emde, R. N., T. Gaensbauer, and R. J. Harmon. 1976. Emotional expression in infancy: A biobehavioral study. *Psychological Issues,* vol. 10, monograph 37.

Field, T. 1985. Attachment as biological attunement: Being on the same wavelength. In *The psychology of attachment and separation.* Edited by M. Reite and T. Field. New York: Academic.

Fischer, K. W. 1980. A theory of cognitive development: The control and construction of hierarchies of skills. *Psychological Review* 87:477–531.

Fischer, K. W., H. H. Hand, M. W. Watson, M. M. Van Parys, and J. L. Tucker. 1984. In *Current topics in early childhood education,* vol. 5. Edited by L. Katz. 27–72.

Fischer, K. W., and S. Pipp. 1984a. Development of the structures of unconscious thought. In *The unconscious reconsidered.* Edited by K. Bowers and D. Meichenbaum. New York: Wiley, 88–148.

———. 1984b. Processes of cognitive development: Optimal level and skill acquisition. In *Mechanisms of cognitive development.* Edited by R. J. Sternberg. San Francisco: Freeman.

Fivush, R. 1987. Scripts and categories: Interrelationships in development. In *Concepts and conceptual development: Ecological and intellectual factors in categorization.* Edited by U. Neisser. Cambridge: Cambridge University Press.

Freud, S. [1911] 1958. *Formulation on the two principles of mental functioning.* Standard edition, vol. 12. London: Hogarth.

Gill, M. M. 1967. The primary process. In *Motives and thought: Psychoanalytic essays in honor of David Rapaport.* Edited by R. R. Holt. *Psychological Issues,* vol. 5, nos. 2–3, serial nos. 18–19. New York: International Universities Press.

Gilligan, C. 1987. Adolescent development reconsidered. In *Adolescent social behavior and health.* Edited by C. E. Irwin. San Francisco: Jossey-Bass.

Grossman, K. E., K. Grossman, F. Huber, and U. Wartner. 1981. German children's behavior towards their mothers at 12 months and their fathers at 18 months in the Ainsworth Strange Situation. *International Journal of Behavior Development* 4:157–62.

Hart, D., and W. Damon. 1985. Contrasts between understanding self and understanding others. In *The development of self.* Edited by R. L. Leary. New York: Academic.

Harter, S. 1983. Developmental perspectives on the self system. In *Handbook of child psychology.* Edited by P. H. Mussen. Vol. 4, *Socialization, personality, and social development.* New York: Wiley, 275–385.

Hofer, M. A. 1984. Relationships as regulators: A psychobiologic perspective on bereavement. *Psychosomatic Medicine* 46:183–97.

————. 1987. Early social relationships: A psychobiologist's view. *Child Development* 58:633–47.

Holt, R. R. 1967. The development of the primary process: A structural view. In *Motives and thought: Psychoanalytic essays in honor of David Rapaport,* Edited by R. R. Holt. *Psychological Issues,* vol. 5, nos. 2–3, serial nos. 18–19. New York: International Universities Press.

Huttenlocher, J., P. Smiley, and R. Charney. 1983. Emergence of action categories in the child: Evidence from verb meanings. *Psychological Review* 90:72–93.

Isen, A. M., and K. A. Daubman. 1984. The influence of affect on categorization. *Journal of Personality and Social Psychology* 47:1206–17.

James, W. 1890. *Psychology.* New York: Holt.

Jones, E. E., and R. E. Nisbett. 1971. *The actor and the observer: Divergent perceptions of causes of behavior.* Morristown, N.J.: General Learning.

Kaye, K. 1982. *The mental and social life of babies.* Chicago: University of Chicago Press.

Kegan, R. 1982. *The evolving self.* Cambridge, Mass.: Harvard University Press.

Kernberg, O. 1976. *Object relations theory and clinical psychoanalysis.* New York: Aronson.

Klein, S. B., and J. F. Kihlstrom. 1986. Elaboration, organization and the self-reference effect in memory. *Journal of Experimental Psychology* 115:26–38.

Kohut, H. 1984. *How does analysis cure?* Chicago: University of Chicago Press.

Lamb, M. E. 1978. Qualitative aspects of mother-infant and father-infant attachments. *Infant Behavior and Development* 1:265–75.

Lewis, M., and J. Brooks-Gunn. 1979. *Social cognition and the acquisition of self.* New York: Plenum.

Link, N. F., S. E. Scherer, and P. N. Byrne. 1977. Moral judgment and moral conduct in the psychopath. *Canadian Psychiatric Association Journal* 22:341–46.

Mahler, M., F. Pine, and A. Bergman. 1975. *The psychological birth of the human infant.* New York: Basic.

Mahlerstein, A. J., and M. Ahern. 1982. *A Piagetian model of character structure.* New York: Human Sciences.

Main, M. 1987. Cognitive aspects of the attachment relationship. Paper presented at the seventeenth annual symposium of the Jean Piaget Society, Philadelphia.

Main, M., K. Kaplan, and J. Cassidy. 1985. Security in infancy, childhood and adulthood: A move to the level of representation. In *Growing points of attachment theory and research.* Edited by I. Bretherton and E. Waters. Monographs of the Society for Research in Child Development, vol. 50, nos. 1–2, serial no. 209.

Mandler, J. 1983. Representation. In *Handbook of child psychology.* 4th ed. Edited by J. H. Flavell and E. M. Markman. New York: Wiley, 420–94.

Melitto, R. 1983. Cognitive aspects of splitting and libidinal object constancy. *Journal of the American Psychoanalytic Association* 31:515–34.

Nelson, K. 1986. *Event knowledge: Structure and function in development.* Hillsdale, N.J.: Erlbaum.

Nelson, K., and J. Gruendel. 1981. Generalized event representations: Basic building blocks of cognitive development. In *Advances in developmental psychology,* vol. 1. Edited by M. E. Lamb and A. L. Brown. New York: Academic, 131–58.

Piaget, J. [1936] 1952. *The origins of intelligence in children.* Translated by M. Cook. New York: International Universities Press.

———. 1962. *Plays, dreams and imitation in childhood.* Translated by C. Gateegno and F. M. Hodgson. New York: Norton.

Pipp, S., M. A. Easterbrooks, and R. J. Harmon. 1989. Infants' senses of self and other in relationships. Paper presented at the meeting of the Society for Research in Child Development, Kansas City.

Pipp, S., K. W. Fischer, and S. Jennings. 1987. Acquisition of self and mother knowledge in infancy. *Developmental Psychology* 23:86–96.

Pipp, S., and R. J. Harmon. 1987. Attachment as regulation: A commentary. *Child Development* 58:648–52.

Pipp, S., P. Shaver, S. Jennings, S. Lamborn, and K. W. Fischer. 1985. Adolescents' theories about the development of their relationships with parents. *Journal of Personality and Social Psychology* 48:991–1001.

Reite, M., R. Short, C. Seiler, and J. D. Pauley. 1981. Attachment, loss and depression. *Journal of Child Psychology and Psychiatry* 22:141–69.

Robertson, J., and J. Robertson. 1971. Young children in brief separation: A fresh look. *Psychoanalytic Study of the Child* 26:264–315.

Sagi, A., and M. L. Hoffman. 1976. Empathic distress in the newborn. *Developmental Psychology* 12:175–76.

Sameroff, A. J., and M. G. Chandler. 1975. Reproductive risk and the continuum of caretaking casuality. In *Review of child development research,* vol. 4. Edited by F. D. Horowitz. Chicago: University of Chicago Press.

Sander, L. W. 1975. Infant and caretaking environment: Investigation and conceptualization of adaptive behavior in systems of increasing complexity. In *Explorations in child psychiatry.* Edited by E. J. Anthony. New York: Plenum.

Silvern, L. 1984. Traditional descriptions of childhood emotional-behavioral disorders and an alternative: Disorder as a function of system functions. In *Developmental plasticity.* Edited by G. Gollin. New York: Academic.

Simner, M. 1971. Newborns' response to the cry of another infant. *Developmental Psychology* 5:136–50.

Sroufe, L. A., and J. Fleeson. 1985. Attachment and the construction of relationships. In *Relationships and development.* Edited by W. Hartup and Z. Rubin. Hillsdale, N.J.: Erlbaum.

Stern, D. N. 1985. *The interpersonal world of the infant.* New York: Basic.

Sullivan, H. S. 1953. *The interpersonal theory of psychiatry.* New York: Norton.

Vygotsky, L. 1978. *Mind in society.* Cambridge, Mass.: Harvard University Press.

Watson, M. W., and K. W. Fischer. 1977. A developmental sequence of agent use in later infancy. *Child Development* 48:828–36.

Winnicott, D. 1965. The theory of the parent-infant relationship. In *The maturational processes and the facilitating environment*. Edited by D. Winnicott. New York: International Universities Press.

Wolff, P. H. 1969. The natural history of crying and other vocalizations in infancy. In *Determinants of infant behavior*, vol. 4. Edited by B. M. Foss. London: Methuen.

12 Aspects of Self Development as Reflected in Children's Role Playing

MALCOLM W. WATSON

With oedipal undertones, a four-year-old was saying good night to his mother. When his mother told him that she loved him, he answered, "I love you too, and that is why I can't ever get married." His mother asked him why that was, and he said, "Because I can't be married to someone else; then you wouldn't take care of me." Within this one incident is contained evidence of several components that a child must understand and control in order to take a place in the world as a separate individual, yet remain connected to those around him/her. At a minimum, this boy had to understand himself as a separate person from his mother. Yet, he was confused by the relationships his loving someone allowed and expected and by growing, at the same time, to an adulthood in which, for him, loving someone implied marrying them. He was certainly dealing with the fact that many of his feelings and the things that he desired were tied to his role relationships to other people. If he loves someone, he should marry them. He loves his mother, but a child can't marry his mother. If he marries someone else, he will lose his relationship with his mother and will not have her around to take care of him. The confusions shown by this child are not rare; they seem to be common in preschoolers who show evidence of thinking about role relations and defining their own qualities and limits in terms of the roles they occupy, yet who do not fully understand the intersection of roles, in which one person can occupy several roles simultaneously. In some ways, this confusion seems to reflect a lack of understanding of the conservation of relationships (Sigel, Saltz, and Roskind 1967). Children often behave as if an old relationship is perforce destroyed when a new relationship is acquired.

How do these confusions seen in older preschoolers relate to the child's developing notion of self, especially as personality theorists have defined the development of self? I contend that an understanding of independent agency,

Preparation of this paper was supported by the John D. and Catherine T. MacArthur Foundation Network for the Study of Transitions in Early Childhood.

265

marking the transition from infancy to early childhood, is a major factor that propels children to a focus on role relations and, that, subsequently, a mature understanding of role relations helps children define the self in relation to others. This chapter is an attempt to explain how a notion of independent agency leads to role understanding, which leads to self understanding. Self understanding is here defined as the child's delineation of the self in terms of, first, what one can affect and the limits of one's agency and, second, what attributes one has in relation to others.

For many years, theorists attempting to describe the development of a notion of self in children have returned to the differentiation originally made by James ([1890]/1963) between the subjective "I" and the objective "me" aspects of the self. Lewis and Brooks-Gunn (1979), for example, explained how the infant's first task in developing a sense of self is to realize that it exists separate from others (i.e., the I aspect). In effect, in order to have a subjective sense of self, the child must first learn that she/he is an agent or independent cause of actions and that others are also agents who cause things to happen independent of her/his own desires and actions (Wolf 1982). The second task is to develop categories of self (i.e., the me aspect). In other words, the child, after acquiring a sense of agency and separation from others, can focus on various skills and attributes to categorize objectively the self (e.g., I am a girl with black hair who is smart, a fast runner, and a daughter to my parents).

Harter (1983) proposed a three-component process, similar to the above two tasks, in which the child must gain knowledge about the self, differentiate the self from others, and gain knowledge about others. Although these three components probably occur simultaneously to some extent, there may be a sequential order to the development of a sense of self in young children that involves differentiating the I from the me and the self from others.

The processes noted above and the differentiation of I and me and of self and other can be combined to describe a two-tier process. Seemingly, children must first learn that they are independent agents (i.e., the I, or executive, aspect of the self), and they seem to accomplish this understanding by differentiating themselves from other agents. For example, a child will fail to bring about all actions that he/she desires, such as moving a large object or causing someone to return simply by crying. At the same time, other people can make things happen against the child's wishes or without the child's actions. Therefore, the child learns to see himself or herself as whatever he/she can effect and see others as whatever they can effect. Objects that do not show causal agency would not be a part of any agent. (Incidently, this may be the reason young children personify the wind or trees, as they misperceive moving objects as necessarily being causal agents of actions.) Second, this conception of self as an agent independent of other agents, who are in turn independent of the self, would then allow and indeed encourage children to look for categories and attributes that differentially apply to themselves and to others—categories which will accentuate the differences between self and others and determine the placement of the self in comparison to other agents (i.e., the me, or objective, aspect of the self). Part of the objective categorization of the self is determining what others can do and what the self can do and how two agents are different (e.g., I am a boy, she is a girl; I am taller than my friend). Because the second step, as well as the first, depends in large part on the child observing other agents in action, the child seems to accomplish it by developing an understanding of role relationships—how one role is determined by its relation to another role through integrating the two roles. For example, in the initial observation of the son who determined that he could not marry anyone because he loved his mother, he needed to compare the two roles of mother and son in terms of the gender of each person in each role and the size, age, and power differences. Yet, after making these differentiations, he also needed to integrate the two roles such that one role depended on the other (e.g., to be a mother, a person must have a child).

One set of terms (first I and then me) describes the parts of the self that seem to develop in this two-tier process. A second set of metaphors (differentiation and integration) describes the actual process of this two-tier development. It is proposed that, first, children differentiate the self from other in the development of a notion of independent agents (the I); second, children integrate social roles in the development of a notion of social role concepts, which provides the child with many of the objective categories (the me). Harter (1986) has noted that, even though we invoke explanations based on differentiation and integration, there is a lack of sufficient attention to the actual processes. The sequences presented below focus on the two-processes—differentiation in the first tier and integration in the second tier.

We attempted to assess this two-tier development by observing children's pretend play (cf. Watson 1984). Like adults, children occupy several roles, but they often pretend to occupy additional roles in order to try out various behaviors and relations. A child who already occupies the social roles of daughter, sister, playmate, and student in dance school can also try out the roles of mother, father, teacher, and Wonderwoman. Because symbolic play seems to provide a chance for children to practice tasks and roles of concern to them and thus to provide a window onto these tasks (Rubin, Fein, and Vandenberg 1983), children's developmental level of independent agency and role understanding also should be reflected in the behaviors and comments made during their role playing.

Skill Theory

We predicted two sequences of steps in children's development across the two tiers of the differentiation of independent agents and the integration of social roles. The basis for these predictions was a theory of skill development proposed by Fischer (1980). Certain important assumptions form the foundation of Fischer's skill theory. First, development is not all or none but occurs in a series of increasingly complex levels. Second, development of skills (whether physical, social, or cognitive) occurs in an additive manner in which new skill levels are acquired by combining previous skills rather than by simple deletion of previous skills (Coombs and Smith 1973; Flavell 1972; Watson and Jackowitz 1984). Third, each level of development can be described in terms of a skill structure that is reflected in the child's way of organizing actions or representations.

Fischer hypothesized various transformation rules that would allow the child to reorganize skills at the next higher level. One such rule is that of compounding, in which one component is combined with another but the child functions essentially at the same level. For example, two actions, such as cooking and eating, can be combined with a new action, such as cleaning, to define a parent role in terms of domestic behaviors. Another rule is that of intercoordination, in which one skill is mapped onto another skill to form a new level whereby both previous skills can be used more or less simultaneously. For example, two role relations, such as mother to child and wife to husband, can be acted out or described such that both can apply simultaneously to the same person. We used these transformation rules to predict how children would represent agency and role relations and how these representations would be transformed through a series of steps. In general, in our sequences, the transformations alternate between compounding to create a transition step and intercoordination to create a major new level.

Developmental Sequence

First Tier: Differentiation of Independent Agents

Step 1: Other as Instrument of the Self.

This is a preliminary step in which the child shows no representation of agency. Some time around twelve months of age, children will begin using other people to accomplish things that they cannot do themselves (Wolf 1982). For example, a child will grab the hand of another person to make that person reach an object or perform an action. Although such activities suggest that the child sees the other person as a source of action, there is no clear evidence that the child differentiates the other person from the child's own desires or actions. Rather, the other person is treated as an instrument of the self (and then only in real life and not in pretense involving symbolic representations). However, these behaviors in children do indicate the beginning development of a notion of independent agency. Although children do not represent others as independent in play, they realize that they cannot perform all actions alone or always simply will actions to occur. They are dependent on others, and this realization may be the breakthrough that pushes children eventually to represent others as independent of themselves.

Step 2: Self as Agent

Children coordinate various actions, such as holding a cup and bringing it to the mouth. The coordination of such simple actions allows the simplest of pretense skills. Typically, at around fourteen months of age, children will pretend to eat food, wash themselves with a wash cloth, comb their hair, and perform other simple actions on themselves. When children begin demonstrating truly symbolic play, this first pretending uses exclusively the self as an agent, using only themselves as the represented agents of action (Fenson and Ramsay 1980; Lowe 1975; Watson and Fischer 1977). These pretend behaviors indicate that children still think only of themselves as agents, even though in real-life actions they have already used others to perform actions they cannot accomplish.

Step 3: Passive-Other Agent

Children then compound actions they previously performed on themselves with actions they can perform on a doll. Typically, a few months after the beginning of pretending (at around sixteen to eighteen months), a child will pretend to give a doll a drink or wash a doll's face or feed it pretend food. Children begin including other people or dolls as recipients of their actions— that is, as passive-other agents (Corrigan 1982; Watson and Fischer 1977). The child acts as though she/he is still the only active, independent agent of action but will represent another person or doll as a partaker in the action. This development seems to be a transition step toward a sense of full independence of different agents.

Step 4: Active-Other Agent

At this point, a system for manipulating a doll is coordinated with a system for some other behavior, such as walking, to allow skill use at what Fischer (1980) calls the representational tier of development. For example, by about twenty months of age, children begin demonstrating several new behaviors in pretend play: they will pretend to confer autonomous actions onto another person or doll (e.g., representing the doll as walking by itself or picking up food and feeding itself); they will talk for another agent or doll, as if it were talking for itself; they will act as if they confer internal states onto another agent (e.g., asking a doll why it is hungry or sad); and they will act as if they confer an independent line of action from their own actions onto another agent or doll. Wolf (1982) has suggested some sequential development in these various behaviors; but whether these components of a sense of an active-other agent form a sequence or not, they all indicate that the child has differentiated the self from other agents to the extent that the child can now represent others as having desires of their own, often opposite to the child's own desires. Children now differentiate one agent from another as the causes and controllers of actions (Bretherton 1984; Watson and Fischer 1977, 1980).

Thus, in addition to developing a sense of causality, one of the major developmental milestones in the transition from infancy to early childhood is children's ability to represent themselves as agents of action differentiated from other agents of action. This differentiation process leaves the child with a subjective (I) sense of self, a self who can accomplish many things and understand that others do not necessarily follow his or her desires. This first tier of development makes possible the subsequent rounding out of a sense of self through objective categorization (i.e., learning about the me aspect).

Second Tier: Integration of Social Roles

In the first tier of development in this hypothesized sequence, children essentially separate individuals from each other. Then, children must put them back together again in order to learn about the self by discovering what others' expectations are. This integration seems to be accomplished largely by developing skills in role relations and role intersections, which is not completed until well after the transition to early childhood.

Why is a sense of independent agency a necessary prerequisite for role understanding? Logically, there can be no need or possibility for social roles until a child first has separated herself/himself from other people. No other role could exist when the child understands only herself or himself as an agent. In one of our observations, a two-year-old was apparently using a chair as a washing machine and pretending to wash clothes. When asked if she were pretending to be a mother, she looked utterly confused by the question and said, "No, I'm washing clothes." When questioned further, she indicated no concern for playing at another role. She simply pretended to perform actions she had seen someone else perform.

However, with the understanding and control of independent agency, children are free to compare their behaviors and desires to those of others in the context of pretending—not just to perform other behaviors but to be other people. For example, a child no longer will simply pretend to wash clothes but will pretend to be her mother. From this point on in development, the child is, in a sense, putting the self and the other back together. Although both differentiation and integration certainly occur, integration seems to be the focus of their tier of development.

In general, psychologists think of role playing as any attempt by a person to pretend to be someone else. But in this chapter, I am defining a social role in the more restricted sense in which it has been used in role theory (Sarbin and Allen 1968). A social role is defined as a cluster of prescribed and expected behaviors that pertains to a particular category of people. The cluster of behaviors for one role is determined by the relationship of that role to complementary roles. Roles are complementary when they are normally associated and the functions of one cannot be described without reference to the other (e.g., one cannot define a husband without reference to a wife). People in complementary roles interact to determine the expected behaviors of each in terms of the other. For example, a medical doctor behaves according to a prescribed social role that requires, among other things, displaying to a person in the complementary role of patient certain medical skills, coordination, dignity, standard of dress, and obligations of trying to help the patient. Likewise, the person in the patient role is expected by the physician to treat the physician with respect, cooperate in the treatment, and pay for the services. Thus, the doctor and patient roles form a social role relation.

The major concern of role theorists has been to determine how people who occupied several roles learned to deal with the sometimes conflicting expectations from the various complementary roles that role intersections would elicit. For example, a person can be simultaneously both a husband to his wife and a physician to his patients or a father to his children and a grandfather to his grandchildren. Most adults can handle the multiple expectations in these role intersections, but how are these conflicts handled by a child who does not even understand that social relations define roles, let alone that roles can intersect? Part of the problem for the son who did not want to get married because he loved his mother was that he could not understand how he could carry out more than one relationship simultaneously or how the people in complementary roles (e.g., his mother and his future wife) could both relate to him without one role relation disrupting the other. Thus, all that a person is expands as the person is able to adapt to multiple role relations.

In order to assess children's changing competencies in handling role relations, we completed a series of studies in which we tested a second developmental sequence, which was again based on Fischer's (1980) skill theory (Watson 1984; Watson and Amgott-Kwan 1983, 1984; Watson and Fischer 1980).

Step 1: Behavioral Role

One three-year-old defined mothers as people who "buy you presents, write letters, talk on the telephone, and make you better." Other children we observed pretended to be physicians by having a doctor doll give shots and take temperatures, but they did not have the doctor doll interact with the patient doll or treat the patient on the basis of the patient's complaint. This first step of role understanding is called a behavioral role because, after they develop an understanding of independent agency and thus have the ability to pretend to be other people, children start attending to the way certain persons can be categorized together based on looks and behaviors, and they label these role categories, (as in the example just mentioned of the girl defining what a mother is).

Through the transformation of compounding, the representations of independent agents can be expanded to include several agents performing several behaviors that all fit a common category. With this step in understanding, children shift from pretending to be people they know, such as their mother, to pretending to be a prototypical person in a role, such as a normative mother. However, although they are focusing on the similarities between agents, children do not coordinate two relationships as part of the role definitions; that higher level of role integration awaits the next step of development. In children's role playing as well, there is no indication that they are aware of complementary relations. Children enact roles based on the dress and prototypical behaviors that they have observed in particular category of people, as in the case of the children pretending to be physicians.

Step 2: Social Role

At around four years of age, children in role playing focus on the relation between two complementary roles. A doctor doll, for example, is made to react to the patient's specific complaint, and a mother is defined as someone who has children and must take care of her children, regardless of the variations in looks or behaviors of different mothers. This step of understanding requires children to combine two or more behavioral roles such that each role is primarily determined by complementary expectations and relations, not simply by looks and behaviors. The actions of one category of agents (or one behavioral role) are coordinated with the actions of another category of agents (or behavioral role). In their role playing, children include both roles in the play scenario and seem to focus on the relation between two complementary roles. A person or doll in one role responds to the person or doll in the complementary role, because the level of integration is beyond simple similarities between people in the same category and is now based on the ties between categories.

Step 3: Shifting Social Role

One five-year-old said, "When my dad goes away on a trip, he isn't a father. He's a doctor, but he is a father when he is at home with me." This boy understood that his father could shift roles but did not understand that someone could occupy both roles simultaneously. Another child, obviously concerned with the conflicts in role intersections, asked her mother, "How can you be a teacher and my mother?" And in one last example, one boy announced, during doll play, "A father can become a grandpa, but then he won't be a father." This step does involve an increased awareness that social role relations can be integrated further and indeed *must* be to account for the observed real-life changes in role behaviors (e.g., changing from father to doctor or from father to grandfather); but when the second role is acquired, the first role is not conserved (see Jordan 1980). In effect, this step is a transition to the child's full understanding of role intersections. The child can compound roles across several complementary relationships (e.g., one agent is both father to his complementary son and physician to his complementary patient). However, the roles are not seen as existing simultaneously. When one role relation is added, another is dropped, often to reappear when the second role is dropped. In other words, one role relation is not fully coordinated with another.

Step 4: Role Intersection

One six-year-old concerned with his relationship to family members had asked his father, "Why do you call Grandpa dad? How can he be your dad and be my grandpa?" A few weeks later, he answered his own question, "When I grow up and get married and have children, you will be their grandpa, but you will still be my father, just like Grandpa is still your father." Also, in role playing, children can quickly shift between role relations for the same character, acting as if the character occupied both roles simultaneously. For example, some children pretended to have a doctor doll be a physician to a patient doll and also be the patient doll's father. Other children pretended to have one doll be a father to a daughter doll and a grandfather to another doll. Two separate, agent-complement role relations are coordinated so that one agent is in two role relationships simultaneously. Thus, Fischer (1980) calls this level of skill development a representational system. For example, the child is able to integrate two or more separate social role relations, such as father-daughter with grandfather-granddaughter. This level of representational system is the second major transition for the child in developing a sense of self. The child integrates the self and the other by considering his or her own multiple and simultaneous role relations and the characteristics associated with each role relation. Achievement of this level of understanding opens up a new degree of flexibility for a person to define oneself and to deal with others.

Step 5: Role Network

At this step, the child compounds several role intersections and can think about the combination of family roles—mother, father, children, grandparents, grandchildren—that form what most of us think of as a traditional family in which some roles intersect across generations. For example, spousal relations combine with parent-child relations and with grandparent-grandchild relations. A child can act out an entire scenario involving many family roles and relations or, as another example, an entire medical scenario involving many roles and activities (e.g., doctors, patients, nurses, ambulance drivers). The level of integration of roles again increases from that of the previous step. Children can combine at least two role intersections to form an entire network (e.g., an extended family).

Step 6: Network Relation

During preadolescence and early adolescence, children typically reach a level of integration in which they can map one role network onto another to understand what Fischer calls an abstract mapping. For example, some children that we observed could now discuss how traditional, two-parent families had both spousal relations and parent-child role relations and how single-parent families had parent-child role relations but not spousal relations. Many children could also understand how family relations and work relations may influence each other so that a parent must balance the expectations from a work role with those from a family role. Thus, more than one role network could be integrated.

In summary, we predicted that children would develop through these steps, which began with a differentiation of agents at the end of infancy and progressed from roles based on concrete behaviors (comparing similarities and differences between agents) to roles based on social relations and eventually on networks of relations in preadolescence. Each step is a further integration of the roles as understood and enacted at the previous step.

Assessment of the Sequence

According to skill theory, assessment of children's level of development in a predicted sequence must be accomplished by stripping down the tasks to those components that leave only the skills of interest to be tested, unencumbered by unrelated challenges and complexities. This approach allows a child to perform at or close to the child's highest level of performance. It is also important that the tasks be related to the specific domain in which one is testing skill development.

In order to determine whether the predicted sequences across both tiers of development did indeed follow the order of steps that we predicted, we attempted to assess the highest level of role play and role understanding available to children at different ages. By simply observing spontaneous free play, one cannot be certain that the child is performing at the highest level or simply at some lower level. So we used, in effect, the idea of the zone of proximal development (Wertsch 1984; Wertsch and Rogoff 1984) as a basis for our procedure. We assumed that the children would spontaneously show some level of role playing but that, with some scaffolding or elicitation, we could raise that level to the highest available to the child (i.e., the upper end of the child's zone of proximal development). We used modeling and imitation technique, in which an adult model demonstrated role playing at each predicted step in the sequence (based on the descriptions and examples presented above). We then asked the child to take a turn at role playing (Watson and Fischer 1977, 1980).

Each child was scored as having a pass or a fail for each step, based on his or her imitative play, and each play episode was scored for the highest step that the chid demonstrated. Thus, each child had the chance to demonstrate all or any number of the steps in the sequence. By having an independent assessment of each step, we could complete a scalogram analysis to determine if the steps formed at Guttman scale across all children and to what extent individuals varied from a perfect Guttman scale (Green 1956). For example, on the first three steps of agency use, a given child could show no steps, only step 1, steps 1 and 2, or all three steps or she could skip steps and show only steps 2 and 3, steps 1 and 3, or just step 3. When the child skipped steps in the sequence, we knew that the child did not demonstrate a perfectly scalable sequence. The fact that children did not randomly imitate the steps but demonstrated a developmental order, regardless of the order in which the steps were presented, showed that this technique is effective in assessing sequences and that children do not blindly copy everything but choose what they understand (Fenson and Ramsay 1981; Watson and Fischer 1977). Harter (1986) also used Fischer's (1980) skill theory to explain a developmental sequence of children's understanding of the simultaneity of two emotions, which in some ways parallels the development of role concepts.

We carried out several studies, using different samples to test both sequences and to compare results across different examples of roles—using a medical scenario and a family scenario (Watson 1984; Watson and Amgott-Kwan 1983, 1984; Watson and Fischer 1977, 1980). A total of 258 children, ranging in age from one to thirteen years, were assessed. Not only was there a strong positive relation between the age of the children and the highest step of understanding that each demonstrated, most children (91 percent) also showed the steps in the exact order predicted. The sequences were highly scalable in that rarely was any higher step shown by a child unless the child had also shown all previous steps. Green's (1956) index of consistency, a more conservative measure of sequence scalability than a reproducibility index, ranged from .58 to .89 for the different studies and was generally above .85. We concluded that both sequences were hierarchical and developmental, with each step requiring development at the previous level.

On the first tier (independent agency), typically fourteen-month-olds showed pretend play using self only as agent (step 2), eighteen-month-olds showed passive-other agent use (step 3), and twenty- to twenty-four-month-olds showed active-other agent use (step 4).

On the second tier (role integration), typically, three-year-olds demonstrated an understanding of behavioral roles (step 1) in their role playing but no steps beyond that; four-year-olds demonstrated an understanding of social roles (step 2); five- to six-year-olds demonstrated an understanding of shifting social roles (step 3); six-to seven-year-olds demonstrated an understanding of role intersections (step 4); nine-year-olds demonstrated an understanding of role networks (step 5); and by thirteen years of age, many children demonstrated an understanding of network relations (step 6).

Development of a Sense of Self

In summary, at the transition from infancy to early childhood, when able to differentiate one agent from another and represent them as independent sources of action, children should see themselves as less powerful in their ability to bring others to act as they would desire, yet at the same time also more powerful because of their independence of others' desires for them to act in a particular way. If children do not see themselves as independent of others, there is no need for them to compare themselves to others or to try to determine which characteristics differentiate them from others. Thus, the objective (me) self would never develop. The earlier ability to differentiate agents also allows children, during the subsequent preschool years, to integrate role relations in order to find how agents are still related in spite of their independence.

This comparison of agents in various roles also helps children categorize their own attributes. Although more empirical work in this area is needed, I would hypothesize that the knowledge children gain about other roles can be related back to themselves by considering their own roles and the roles that are potentially open to them. This is the crux of the relationship between the development of role understanding and the development of a sense of self. The more complex their role understanding, the more flexibility and the greater range children should have in categorizing their own attributes.

The second important transition is the understanding of role intersections. With this understanding, six- to seven-year-old children can go beyond an awareness that people are independent of each other in their desire for and cause of various actions. Such children can comprehend that people are also independent of the various specific roles they occupy, that are free to occupy several role relations and change their behaviors according to changing expectations. In this sense, understanding role intersections completes a child's understanding of independent agency. Role playing at this level also allows children to place themselves in various relationships to determine more extensively what others will expect of them and what their range of control of others can be. With an understanding of role intersections, children seem to be more likely to appreciate how a person or even the self may be quite predictable even though behaviors and relations may change drastically.

Why does it take so long for children to understand role intersections when so much recent research indicates that children are highly competent at younger ages (Gelman 1979)? Indeed, it is not difficult to find examples of early preschoolers shifting focus and comparing ideas and shifting roles. The simple fact that an early preschooler can easily shift from playing one character to playing another or shift in and out of pretense would suggest that perhaps our sequence did not assess children's true abilities at the younger ages. However, roles are not the only domain in which children do not understand intersections. When presented with two versions or categories for one item or idea, preschoolers seem to act as if any thing or person can only be categorized one way at a time (Flavell, Green, and Flavell 1987; Markman 1984). Flavell and associates have discussed this inability in preschoolers as a lack of a capability to use dual coding of objects and ideas in which two mutually incompatible identities must be considered at the same time. Some time between five and seven years of age, children seem to develop this ability to comprehend the intersecting nature of many objects and concepts, as well as the intersecting nature of role relations and also self-identities. Selman (1980) also discusses the issues children must face in ambivalent situations, in which opposing or conflicting attributes can be applied to the self or to others.

As with so many domains of development, children demonstrate some understanding of social relations and of various types of intersections at younger ages than six or seven years (see Bretherton 1984). And at an earlier age than twenty months, children are treated by parents and others as if they are independent agents in their intentions and desires. The early experiences that children have with agency and with normative roles must influence their developing understanding. Yet, when children are challenged with the organized structure of roles and the dual coding requirements of role intersections, as was done in our studies, they seem to show that they must construct their own understanding over time regardless of the help they get from parents and others. The sequences of development described above suggest that children's sense of self is gradually self-constructed even when they use others as a source of information and comparison about their own characteristics. The two sides of a sense of self—the subjective I and the objective me—come together only when children have seen their independence and then have seen how people are related and can be compared, and that level of development is not achieved until sometime in middle childhood.

Identity

Until now, I have not mentioned the development of an identity, often discussed in terms of later adolescent development (e.g., Erikson 1963). However, these earlier role concepts may determine the normal development of identity through identification with others in adolescence. If, for example, a girl identifies with her mother, which of her mother's various roles will she use, since many of the various role relations involve different expectations, attitudes, and behaviors? Will she identify with the mother in the mother-father role relation, the mother-daughter role relation, the mother-neighbor relation, or the administrator-employee role relation? This process is complicated further because the girl probably identifies with her father, her brother, her sister, and her teacher, as well as with her mother. Only a child who understands roles in terms of complementary relations and is able to intersect roles will be able to comprehend why people behave as they do and why behavior may change in different situations. Particularly with development to the last steps of role networks and network relations, the child can handle the multiple roles and identities that Gergen and Morse (1970) claimed that normal adults handle. As children develop a concept of role networks, they can form many-faceted identities and notions of self based on several role relations and yet still be able to coordinate these facets because they understand the "rules," so to speak, of role relations. Therefore, the development of a mature role understanding helps the child develop a sense of self by, first, providing the range and repertoire of attributes and behaviors open to the child and, second, providing the rules for variation in behaviors and for finding consistency amid multifaceted identities.

Affect

I have not taken into account the role of affect in children's understanding of social role relations. The relative importance and closeness of a given role to the child's own situation must surely facilitate or inhibit her or his development in this domain. For example, one six-year-old we tested, whose parents had recently divorced, seemed to understand role intersections. Yet, when he told about his parents getting a divorce and not being married, he looked worried and said, "My father doesn't live with us anymore, but he is still my father. So if he is still my father, then my mom and dad are still married. They just live in two houses." In the emotional context of determining his seemingly tenuous relation to his parents following their divorce, he seemed to confuse the husband-wife role relation with the father-son role relation and threw an understanding of role intersections out the window as a way of explaining the confusion. Because he could not see the two relations as independent yet integrated, he resorted to restoring, in his own mind, the spousal relation in order to salvage the parent-child relation. As a final caveat, then, emotional and personal experiences will sometimes override children's level of social understanding in determining how they place themselves in relation to others. Nevertheless, level of understanding—first, independent agents in late infancy and, later, role relations—should provide a foundation for many of the subjective and objective aspects of a child's sense of self.

References

Bretherton, I. 1984. Representing the social world in symbolic play: Reality and fantasy. In *Symbolic play: The development of social understanding*. Edited by I. Bretherton. Orlando, Fla. Academic, 3–41.

Coombs, C. H., and J. E. K. Smith. 1973. On the detection of structure in attitudes and developmental processes. *Psychological Review* 80:337–51.

Corrigan, R. 1982. The control of animate and inanimate components in pretend play and language. *Child Development* 53:1343–53.

Erikson, E. H. 1963. *Childhood and Society*. New York: Norton.

Fenson, L., and D. S. Ramsay. 1980. Decentration and integration of the child's play in the second year. *Child Development* 51:171–178.

———. 1981. Effects of modeling action sequences on the play of twelve-, fifteen-, and nineteen-month-old children. *Child Development* 52:1028–36.

Fischer, K. W. 1980. A theory of cognitive development: The control and construction of hierarchies of skills. *Psychological Review* 87:477–531.

Flavell, J. H. 1972. *An analysis of cognitive-developmental sequences*. Genetic Psychology Monographs, vol. 86:279–350.

Flavell, J. H., F. L. Green, and E. R. Flavell. 1986. *Development of knowledge about the appearance-reality distinction*. Monographs of the Society for Research in Child Development 51, serial no. 212.

Gelman, R. 1979. Preschool thought. *American Psychologist* 34:900–905.

Gergen, K. J., and S. J. Morse. 1970. Social comparison, self-consistency, and the concept of self. *Journal of Personality and Social Psychology 16:148–156*.

Green, B. F. 1956. A method of scalogram analysis using summary statistics. *Psychometrika* 1:79–88.

Harter, S. 1983. Developmental perspectives on the self-system. In *Handbook of child psychology*. 4th ed. Edited by P. H. Mussen. Vol. 4, *Socialization, personality, and social development*. Edited by E. M. Hetherington. New York: Wiley, 275–385.

———. 1986. Cognitive-developmental processes in the integration of concepts about emotions and the self. *Social Cognition* 4:119–151.

James, W. [1890] 1963. *Psychology*. New York: Fawcett.

Jordan, V. B. 1980. Conserving kinship concepts: A developmental study in social cognition. *Child Development* 51:146–155.

Lewis, M., and J. Brooks-Gunn. 1979. *Social cognition and the acquisition of self*. New York: Plenum.

Lowe, M. 1975. Trends in the development of representational play in infants from one to three years: An observational study. *Journal of Child Psychology and Psychiatry* 16:33–47.

Markman, E. M. 1984. The acquisition and hierarchical organization of categories by children. In *Origins of cognitive skills*. Edited by C. Sophian. Hillsdale, N.J.: Erlbaum, 371–406.

Rubin, K. H., G. G. Fein, and B. Vandenberg. 1983. Play. In *Handbook of child psychology*. *4th ed.* Edited by P. H. Mussen. *Vol. 4, Socialization, personality, and social development*. Edited by E. M. Hetherington. New York: Wiley, 693–774.

Sarbin, T. R., and V. L. Allen. 1968. Role theory. In *Handbook of social psychology*, vol. 1. Edited by G. Lindzey and E. Aronson. Reading, Mass.: Addison-Wesley, 488–567.

Selman, R. 1980. *The growth of interpersonal understanding*. New York: Academic.

Sigel, I. E., E. Saltz, and W. Roskind. 1967. Variables determining concept conservation in children. *Journal of Experimental Psychology* 74: 471–75.

Watson, M. W. 1984. Development of social role understanding. *Developmental Review* 4:192–213.

Watson, M. W., and T. Amgott-Kwan. 1983. Transitions in children's understanding of parental roles. *Developmental Psychology* 19:659–66.

————. 1984. Development of family-role concepts in school-age children. *Developmental Psychology* 20:953–59.

Watson, M. W., and K. W. Fischer. 1977. A developmental sequence of agent use in late infancy. *Child Development* 48:828–36.

————. 1980. Development of social roles in elicited and spontaneous behavior during the preschool years. *Developmental Psychology* 16:483–94.

Watson, M. W., and E. R. Jackowitz. Agents and recipient objects in the development of early symbolic play. *Child Development* 55:1091–97.

Wertsch, J. V. 1984. The zone of proximal development: Some conceptual issues. *New Directions for Child Development*, series 23: 7–18.

Wertsch, J. V., and B. Rogoff. 1984. Editors notes. *New Directions for Child Development*, series 23: 1–6.

Wolf, D. 1982. Understanding others: A longitudinal case study of the concept of independent agency. In *Action and thought: From sensorimotor schemes to symbolic operations*. Edited by G. Forman. New York: Academic, 297–327.

13 An Organizational Perspective on the Self

L. ALAN SROUFE

> The organization or synthetic function is not just another thing the ego does, it is what the ego is.
>
> Loevinger, *Ego Development*

This chapter addresses three central problems: (1) how to conceptualize self (in contrast to just actions or thoughts of a person), (2) how to account for the emergence of self, and (3) how to understand the significance of variations in self. These three problems will be approached from an "organizational" perspective, in which it is assumed that meaningful analysis is at the level of patterns, relationships, and meaning rather than particular manifest behaviors. In brief, it will be argued that the self should be conceived as an inner *organization* of attitudes, feelings, expectations, and meanings, which arises itself from an *organized* caregiving matrix (a dyadic organization that exists prior to the emergence of the self) and which has *organizational* significance for ongoing adaptation and experience. The self is organization. It arises from organization. It influences ongoing organization of experience.

An Organizational Perspective

The organizational perspective previously proposed (e.g., Sroufe 1979a, 1979b; Sroufe and Waters 1977) may be thought of as an extension of Werner's (1957) organismic theory toward fully embracing individual differences and toward a more central role for affect. It also has ties to behavioral systems notions emphasized by some ethologically oriented theorists (e.g., Ainsworth 1973; Bowlby 1969) and others (Sameroff 1983) and to neoanalytic views of the person as actively structuring experience (e.g., Breger 1974; Kohut 1977; Loevinger 1976).

In brief, within this perspective, the organized nature of both behavior and development is central (Cicchetti et al., in this volume; Santostefano 1978). The meaning of any behavior depends upon its organization with other behaviors and the total psychological context (holism). Different behaviors can have similar meanings, and the same behavior may mean different things, depending on the organization within which it is embedded. Likewise, given the rule of transformations in development, continuity can be only at the level of organization and meaning. Similar meanings are expressed through new behaviors which, while changed and elaborated, maintain basic relational or pattern characteristics of the earlier (prototypic) form. Several decades ago, Neilon (1948, 175) suggested, for example, that "the same (toddler) who cries a great deal might be subject to severe temper tantrums at preschool age, and have an inclination to impulsiveness and emotionality in adulthood." Continuity lies not at the level of particular behaviors but at the level of meaning.

Development itself is organized and is characterized in terms of increasing organization. Even in the newborn period, there are built-in biases and thresholds such that certain kinds of stimulation more likely receive responses than others; and with development, children increasingly select and structure (create) their own experience. Moreover, development is characterized by hierarchical integration, in which earlier behavior is organized with other behavior into more complex forms (thereby changing the meaning of the earlier behavior). Development is directed toward increasing organization, and individuals also typically develop toward increasing flexibility and increasing organization. "The availability of multiple means and alternative ends frees the individual from the demands of the immediate situation, enabling him to express behavior in more delayed, planned, indirect, organized, stage-appropriate terms and to search for detours that acknowledge opportunities and limitations of the environment while permitting successful adaptation" (Santostefano 1978, 23).

An organizational viewpoint may be illustrated by the behavior of a twelve-month-old infant playing with a variety of toys on the floor of a laboratory playroom. The infant's mother sits a short distance away, watching the child play with various objects in front of her. A large puzzle piece (a brightly colored carrot) captures the infant's attention. She picks up the carrot with widened eyes. Then, in a smooth motion, she turns and extends it toward the mother, smiling broadly and vocalizing. Her mother returns her smile and comments about the carrot. Much is lost from such a sequence of behavior when it is simply coded as "show toy to M." Indeed, its significance is not merely in showing the toy. This would be as commonly done with strangers as with mothers at this age (Rheingold and Eckerman 1973). It is the total organization of the behavior that is significant. First, the *integration* of the toy show with the other behaviors is most striking; showing of a toy accompanied by both smiling and vocalizing rarely is directed toward strangers by twelve-month-olds. Second, the behavior is organized *sequentially.* The child recognizes the object and then directly, virtually automatically, shares her delight with the mother. The meaning of this organized pattern of behavior (affective sharing) is fundamentally different from the meaning of toy shows to a stranger (affiliative gestures), which are not organized in the same way with respect to exploration and mastery of the object world. In some five hundred cases, we have never seen an infant in the course of intensive exploration turn and affectively share a discovery with a stranger.

The behavior pattern also reveals the *hierarchically organized* nature of development. Earlier attentional and object manipulation skills, prelinguistic communication skills, and early attachment behavior (looking, vocalizing, proximity maintaining) are incorporated into intentional social behavior, all mediated by affect.

Further, the pattern represents a *transformation* to earlier caregiver-infant physical contact, and later face-to-face engagement, to "psychological contact at a distance." (This evolves still further when the preschooler presents, with beaming face, "the pitcher that I drawed" and the college freshman makes the collect phone call home.) Though manifest in profoundly different ways, the affective meaning remains similar (Sroufe 1977): caregiver and child remain emotionally connected. And in evolving the more mature, more complexly organized pattern, the twelve-month-old has increasing flexibility to engage the world while yet retaining an affectively mediated sense of connection with the significant partner. When a smile at a distance replaces physical contact, exploration and mastery of the surrounding world are fostered.

The Self as Arising from the Organized Caregiving Matrix

The emergence of the self presents a basic developmental problem. As an inner organization of attitudes, expectations, and feelings, a self cannot be conceived in the newborn, whose cortex shows little dendritic elaboration and little interconnection with midbrain emotional structures. But if the self is seen as simply emerging at some later period (something arising from nothing), this would be a nondevelopmental solution. Sander (e.g., 1975) and others have suggested a developmental approach to this problem. Sander postulates that organization exists from the outset, an organization which resides in the infant-caregiver *dyadic system*. His developmental account traces the origins of the inner organization (self) from the dyadic organization—from dyadic behavioral regulation to self-regulation. The caregiver constructs an organized matrix around infant behavior and state changes. Within this matrix, there are organized patterns of behavior which make room for increasing participation of the infant. With continued participation in this system and with advances in cognitive development, the infant in time comes to a "dim recognition" of "his own role in determining action," and the "stage is set" for "the 'disjoin' of the self-regulatory core" (Sander 1975, 141).

Noted philosophers have viewed the self as a social product. Baldwin (1905) suggested that the self "is a pole or terminus at one end of an opposition in the sense of personality generally, and that the other pole or terminus is . . . the other person'' (p. 15) and, further, that the child is "at every stage . . . really in part someone else'' (p. 30). Mead (1934, 164) wrote:

> Selves can only exist in definite relationships to other selves. No hard-and-fast line can be drawn between our own selves and the selves of others, since our own selves exist and enter as such into our experience only in so far as the selves of others exist and enter as such into our experience also. . . .
> The process out of which the self arises is a social process which implies interaction of individuals.

Neoanalytic theorists, such as Ainsworth (1973), Kohut (1977), and Winnicott (1965), also embrace the idea of the social origins of self. Winnicott's famous statement, "There is no such thing as an infant," was meant to capture the basic embeddedness of the infant in the caregiving context. Mahler, Pine, and Bergman (1975) describe a "symbiotic phase," a period of infant-caregiver interconnection which serves as a way station on route to individuation (see Stechler, in this volume). Ainsworth and Bell (1974), in complete accord with Sander, suggest that an infant can only be competent to the extent that there is a caregiving environment that is alert and responsive to the newborn's reflexive "signals." By responding to the young infant's primitive signals and state changes, the caregiver imbues them with meaning and makes them part of an organized behavioral system. There is an organized relationship between organism and surround in the newborn period (and, in that weak sense, an incipient self), but it can be described only in the context of a responsive, caregiving environment. Thus, in the early months of life, self as organization can only be conceived within the caregiving system.

The Developmental Process

Following Sander (1975), a series of phases in the evolution of the dyadic organization toward the inner organization of self may be outlined. These phases are not tasks to be completed; rather, they represent ascending issues which then are ongoing (see table 1). When this developmental process approach is embraced, the self is viewed as emerging rather than as emergent at any given age.

Phase 1: Basic Regulation (Zero–Three Months)

Establishing "phase synchrony between mother and infant in regard to the periodicities of relative activity and quiescence" (Sander 1975, 137) is the primary issue in the first months. Infant state and caregiver intervention become coordinated. Such dyadic physiological regulation may be viewed as the

Table 1.   Phases in the Early Development of the Self

Age (in months)	Issue
0–3	Basic regulation
3–6	Coordinated interaction
6–9	The initiatory infant
9–12	Dyadic emotional regulation
12–24	Inner aims, autonomous action
18–36	Self-constancy

Source: Adapted from Sander (1975); Sroufe (1979b).

prototype for later dyadic psychological regulation, which is characterized by coordinated sequences of behavioral interactions. Such coordination, a hallmark of phase 2, will mark the beginnings of inner organization of experience.

Phase 2: Coordinated Interaction Sequences (Four–Six Months)

A dominant feature in the second three months of life is the emergence of chained interaction sequences. The infant is awake and alert more, and basic state regulation is achieved. Smiling and cooing are common, and the infant actively participates in social interaction. Many investigators (e.g., Brazelton, Kowslowski, and Main 1974; Stern 1974) have described the coordinated, give-and-take, dancelike quality of caregiver-infant interactions during this period. Such coordination, or "reciprocity," is in part illusory. The appearance of give and take, with each responding to the other, is primarily a function of the caregiver's responsiveness to the infant. Detailed study has shown a dramatic asynchrony in the conditional probabilities of responsiveness. The caregiver makes adjustments to fit the infant's action, but infants at this age have little capacity to adjust their behavior to fit changes in caregiver behavior (Hayes 1984). Sequences do exist in which infant and caregiver behavior are interdigitated (infant does A, caregiver does B, infant does C, caregiver does D). Within such an established sequence, the infant does respond to the caregiver's behavior. C occurs commonly only following B. But the infant cannot readily follow a new lead of the caregiver, whereas the caregiver commonly follows new leads of the infant (e.g., A-B-E-F).

Sensitive, engaged caregivers craft and coordinate an organized system of behavioral sequences around the infant. Infants cannot achieve such organization independently or by design; but during this phase, they can participate in such a highly organized system. The organization is not yet "represented," or internalized schematically. The infant does not intentionally initiate such a sequence and cannot fill in parts missing from the sequence. However, the infant does have action schemes and so can follow through on an interactive sequence started and kept on track by the caregiver.

Although this chained behavior is not authored by the infant, it nonetheless is critical for development of the self. Repetition of such highly organized sequences of interaction lays the groundwork for a more initiatory role in the next phase. Moreover, these sequences commonly culminate in exchanges of mutual delight (Sander 1975; Stern 1974). As Sander puts it, "The affect of joy or delight becomes established as the criterion for precision in the matching of interpersonal reciprocations" (p. 145). When the infant consolidates a scheme of the caregiver in the second half-year, such shared affect represents a reservoir of positive feelings that will be coordinated within the infant's representation.

Phase 3: The Initiatory Infant (Seven–Nine Months)

There is a surge in intentionality and goal directedness in the third quarter of life. Infants can now coordinate, initiate, and direct activities. Some of these activities are designed to elicit caregiver responses, and some even are designed to elicit caregiver prohibitions. Infants now play a more active and creative role in maintaining and continuing coordinated exchanges. They may lead in a new direction or embellish the caregiver's lead—for example, smiling and reaching to the caregiver's face when the caregiver smiles (Greenspan 1981).

In this phase, dramatic changes occur in the organization of infant behavior and, we suspect, in the infant's internal world as well. Not only does the infant initiate interactions and anticipate caregiver behavior, which indicates a coordination of present action with past experiences and with expected future events, but it is now also clear that the infant's representations of people and events are affectively toned. For example, it is during this phase that integrated greeting reactions emerge (Vaughn 1977). Upon seeing the caregiver, the infant immediately smiles, vocalizes, bounces, and raises both arms. That such a response is exclusive to caregivers suggests that by this age the visual image of the caregiver is connected with a reservoir of positive affective experiences in most cases. This also is the age at which there is a dramatic rise in negative reactions to strangers (Sroufe 1977) and in specific affects such as anger (Stenberg, Campos, and Emde 1983) and surprise and fear (Hiatt, Campos, and Emde 1979; Vaughn and Sroufe 1979). These developments also point to a coordination of affect and cognition (the emergence of affectively toned schemes), a coordination which marks the beginnings of an inner organization of experience (Sroufe 1979b).

There does appear to be a qualitative change in the caregiver-infant system during this phase. In a sense, a relationship exists where once there was organized interaction. This is nicely illustrated by important research on the effects of hospitalization (Schaffer and Callender 1959), which showed that only for infants older than seven months was there a classic picture of protest to the period of hospitalization. That picture was described as "protest during the initial hospitalization, negativism to the staff, intervals of subdued behavior and withdrawal, and a period of readjustment after return home, during which (there was) a great deal of insecurity centering around mother's presence" (p. 537).

A similar pattern has been described by Heinicke and Westheimer (1966). Infants younger than seven months showed none of these reactions. "The reactions of the older group indicate clearly that it is the break in the relationship with the mother that formed the core of the disturbance" (p. 537). We would argue that these older infants had begun internalizing the organized caregiving context. With their level of intentionality and goal directedness (toward maintaining the known organization), substitute patterns of care will not do. With younger infants, hospital staff may substitute for the caregiver by providing stimulation for the infant, general experiences with chained interactions, and shared affect; transfer back to the mother's care likewise may be readily accomplished. But by the later phase of development, the specific system is being internalized. The organized caregiving matrix has begun to become part of a core of emerging inner organization. A particular relationship and a self are emerging.

Phase 4: Specific Attachment—Dyadic Emotional Regulation (Ten–Twelve Months)

Changes in cognitive and motor capacities allow infants to organize behavior around the caregiver even more actively in the final months of the first year. They center ("focalize" [Sander 1975]) there expanding exploratory activities around the "home base" (Mahler et al. 1975) or "secure base" (Ainsworth 1973) represented by the caregiver. The infant ranges away from the caregiver, drawn by curiosity concerning novel aspects of the environment; but when the infant is fatigued, threatened, or otherwise unduly challenged and aroused, a retreat to the caregiver or a directed signal brings assistance, reassurance, comforting, and a return to organized exploration. When, at other times, positive affect arises in the course of exploration, this too is routinely shared with the caregiver. Affect, cognition, and social behavior are smoothly coordinated and organized with respect to the caregiver. Goal-directed behavior with respect to the caregiver becomes prominent, and both goals and expectations become more specific. From a repertoire of capacities, infants choose those signals or behaviors calling for the response they intend their caregiver to make (e.g., arms raised to signal a desire to be picked up). Should one initiation fail, an alternative is selected. The infant persists toward the goal. Organized, goal-directed behavior of this complexity suggests advances in inner organization as well.

Bowlby (1973) describes the emergence of "working models" during periods 3 and 4. By twelve months of age, infants have clear expectations concerning the caregiver's availability, which includes the child's expectation that the caregiver will be both accessible (present) in times of need and responsive. Such models are rooted in the history of interactions over the course of the first year. From a history of coordinated interaction—first orchestrated by the caregiver but ultimately including the intentional signals of need and desire by the infant—the infant learns that when the caregiver is available, organized behavior may be maintained, or re-achieved if lost. The presence of working models is revealed in the quality and organization of attachment behavior with respect to the caregiver by the end of the first year. Infants that expect caregivers to be responsive will explore confidently in their presence, signal needs intentionally, and respond quickly to caregiver interventions (expecting that they will be effective). Infants respond to new situations in terms of their past history and purposefully select behaviors with respect to goals. Signals to the caregiver and expectations of the caregiver's response have a prominent role in infants' regulation of affective state.

These developmental changes mark clear advances in the emergence of self. Still, the working model of the infant at this time may be better described as a model of the relationship than of the self (Bowlby 1973; Main, Kaplan, and Cassidy 1985; Sroufe and Fleeson 1986). That is, infants' major expectations concerning their own actions have to do with likely responses of the caregiver (and, to a varying degree, others). Moreover, infants under stress have great difficulty maintaining organized behavior without caregiver assistance. Only later will children firmly recognize (be aware of) their own potency as an independent center of action and be able to deal with stress and frustration more on their own.

Still, the core of what will become self is by now apparent. The quality of the attachment relationship spawns the particular organization of the individual (Ainsworth 1973; Bowlby 1973; Erikson 1963; Greenspan 1981; Mahler et al. 1975; Sroufe and Waters 1977). In Bowlby's terms:

> In the working model of the world that anyone builds, a key feature is his notion of who his attachment figures are . . . and how they may be expected to respond. Similarly, in the working model of the self that anyone builds a key feature is how acceptable or unacceptable he himself is in the eyes of his attachment figures. . . . (T)he model of the attachment figure and the model of the self are likely to develop so as to be complementary and mutually confirming. Thus an unwanted child is likely not only to feel unwanted by his parents but to believe that he is essentially unwantable. (1973, 203–4)

Phase 5: Inner Aims, Autonomous Action
(Twelve–Twenty Months)

In subsequent phases, toddlers more actively pursue their own goals and plans, even when these at times are explicitly counter to the wishes of the caregiver. "(G)uidance of behavior on the basis of the pleasure of realizing *inner aims* can take precedence at times over the more familiar (pleasurable) reinforcement of finding a coordination with the parental caretaker" (Sander 1975, 141). Children now initiate separations both physically and psychologically. They operate more autonomously. They explore away from the caregiver (Mahler's "practicing"), inevitably engaging objects more on their own. Such moves away are balanced by continued bids for reciprocation with the caregiver.

According to Sander, Mahler, and others, this balance may be maintained if proper foundations have been laid in earlier phases of the relationship. Securely attached infants are able to function more autonomously as toddlers, while still drawing upon the caregiver when challenges exceed their capacities (Londerville and Main 1981; Matas, Arend, and Sroufe 1978; Sroufe and Rosenberg 1980). In Ainsworth's "Strange Situation" procedure (Ainsworth et al. 1978; also see Cicchetti et al., in this volume) eighteen-month-old infants explore more away from the caregiver, rely more on interaction across a distance for sharing and reassurance, are less distressed by the brief separations, settle themselves more readily, and require less contact for settling when self-settling fails than do twelve-month-olds. Normal infants who fail to make these developmental advances generally would be viewed as anxiously attached.

This period marks a critical transition toward the emergence of self-awareness and inner organization, which includes a concept of self as actor. Through independent action and through the pursuit of inner plans comes the beginning sense of being an independent actor.

Phase 6: Awareness and Self-Constancy
(Eighteen to Thirty-Six Months)

With the rise of symbolic capacity, toddlers can move to a new level of awareness. Behaving autonomously fosters a dim recognition of self as actor, but recognizing that the caregiver is aware of a plan and is, for example, in opposition to it (which is greatly assisted by language) brings the "realization that another can be aware of what one is aware of within oneself, i.e., a shared awareness" (Sander 1975, 142). Sander believes this is the beginning of awareness of a self-organizing core within—"actually a core that from the outset has been operative in the service of regulation at the more biological level but is now in a position to be accorded a new priority in the guidance of behavior" (p. 142). Such awareness would allow one to describe a self at a new level.

This new level of awareness enables the infant to move toward what Sander has described as "self-constancy." Using Piaget's concepts of object constancy and "operations," Sander describes a process wherein the child "perturbs" the dyadic harmony and re-achieves it through purposeful actions and the caregiver's continued cooperativeness. Acting contrary to his or her understood perception of the caregiver's intention and yet being reassured that the relationship can be reinstated and remains intact ("reversibility") promotes the child's sense of constancy of the self-organizing core:

> The intentional disruption of previously reinforcing and facilitating exchanges with the caretaker disrupts the toddler's newly consolidating self and body representational framework. Reexperiencing his own coherence, again at his own initiative or by out reach from the caretaker, provides a situation from which self constancy as an inner structure can be established. . . .
> Self as active initiator or as active organizer is thus "conserved." (Sander 1975, 143)

One also sees the emergence of mirror self-recognition (Amsterdam 1972; Lewis and Brooks-Gunn 1978; Mans, Cicchetti, and Sroufe 1978) and "I do it" and "do it myself" assertions early in this phase (Breger 1974) and the emotions of shame, pride, and guilt as the phase proceeds (Sroufe 1979b). Early perspective taking and the roots of empathic response also emerge (Flavell 1977; Hoffman 1979; Radke-Yarrow, Zahn-Waxler, and Chapman 1983) as the child moves toward what Bowlby (1969) calls a "goal-corrected partnership." Children can recognize the caregiver's intentions as separate from their own and can coordinate their behavior in terms of these goals of the other. The coordination here is the coordination of two autonomous beings, each recognizing the other.

Self as Inner Organization

Stating the precise age at which a self has emerged is partly a semantic problem. From a developmental/organizational viewpoint, the emerging of the inner organization which we will call self is properly viewed as an ongoing process. There is some rudimentary representation and some regularity in experience, and therefore "self," even in the first half-year. However, if one requires intentionality and plans, self-recognition, self-monitoring, an understanding of different components of the self, or self-reflection, the self would be viewed as emerging at various later developmental periods (see table 2).

In the first half-year, probably due to memory limitations, there is limited evidence to suggest that experiences are carried forward. In this sense, the concept of self as an ongoing, organized core seems difficult to justify. On the

Table 2.   Stages of the Emerging Self

Age	Developmental Level
0–6 months	Preintentional self
6–12 months	Intentional self
12–24 months	Separate (aware) self
24–60 months	Self-monitoring self
Middle childhood	Consolidated self
Adolescence	Self-reflective self

other hand, there is sufficient regularity in the dyadic organization to ensure basic patterns of repeated experience—sequences of motor behavior, tension regulation, and affect—for most infants. These regularities commonly *are* carried forward to the next phase when the infant plays a more active role in the regulatory process. That is, aspects of the organized *system* are stable and carried forward well before the system is internalized by the infant.

The organization of the infant's behavior is remarkably complex by the end of the first year. Infants appraise both external and internal parameters. Immediate and past experiences, as well as ongoing affective state, provide the context for behavior (Sroufe, Waters, and Matas 1974). There is beginning recognition of the role of the "other" in maintaining constancy in affective experience and behavioral organization. Consequently, the infant purposefully acts to utilize that other. By many definitions, this marks the emergence of the self. However, there still is a lack of awareness of self (including absence of indications of self-recognition), and there is rather total dependence of organized behavior on availability of another. Continuity of experience is present, but the infant is not yet aware of this continuity. In time, the sense of inner organization that is clearly self will come from the infant's active efforts to maintain inner regulation (though centered on another).

The Core of Self

Within a process view at the core of self are the regularities in experience—cycles of environmental (or state) variation, behavioral disruption, efforts to reinstate organization, and experienced affect (Stern 1985). At first, such regulation is highly dependent on the responsiveness of the caregiver. When the caregiver is available and sensitively responsive, periods of disequilibrium are brief. Reorganization and positive affect routinely follow environmental challenge or negative state change. Repeated experiences of affective regulation (or dyssynchrony) are the rudimentary core of what will become the self.

As infants come to play a more active role in this regulatory process and to recognize the other as part of the regulation, they move toward ownership of the inner experience. Infants become aware of the capacity to elicit regulatory assistance from the other and, in time, to perturb and re-achieve the inner regulation on their own.

> The importance of a stable basic regulation has to do with a context in which the child can begin dimly to recognize his own role in determining action. . . . The emergence of autonomy as here proposed is based on the further differentiation of awareness—especially that of inner perception, which sets the stage for the "disjoin" of the self-regulatory core. (Sander 1975, 141)

The emerging self, then, is an abstracted history of experiences with behavioral/state regulation and their affective products. Recognition of others as part of that regulation, recognition of one's actions as effective or ineffective in eliciting care, and, finally, recognition of the self as the origin of experience are all part of the self system. At their core, the complementary working models of self and world have to do with expectations concerning the maintenance of basic regulation and positive affect even in the face of environmental challenge. The core of self lies in patterns of behavioral/affective regulation, which give continuity to experience despite development and environmental change. Kohut (1977) summarizes this in the following way:

> It may well be . . . that the sense of the continuity of the self, the sense of our being the same person throughout life—despite the changes in our body and mind, in our personality make-up . . . does not emanate solely from the abiding content of the constituents of the nuclear self and from the activities that are established . . . but also from the abiding specific relationship in which the constituents of the self stand to each other. (Pp. 179–80)

Empirical Implications of the Organizational Perspective on the Self

If this organizational/process view of the self has validity, two implications follow. First, the particular nature of an emerging self system should be qualitatively reminiscent of the dyadic organization (relationship) that gave rise to it. A dyadic system characterized by smooth regulation of affect and maintenance of behavioral organization in the face of stress should lead to a similarly effective self system. Second, as an active organization, the emerging self system should influence later adaptation of the child, especially with regard to social orientation, expectations concerning others, and self in relation to others. Continuity of the self system, despite developmental change, is virtually assured because of the active way in which the child engages, selects, and interprets the environment. What began as an environment/organism organization becomes a self/environment organization. It should be pointed out that these two empirical implications are very similar to Bowlby's (1969) two hypotheses: that the quality of early care will be related to the quality of the attachment relationship, and that the quality of attachment will be related to later personality organization.

Responsive Care and the Emergence of Individual Selves

The quality of affect regulation within the attachment relationship is based on the early history of affect regulation orchestrated by the caregiver. In the first two phases of development (zero–six months), most infants have repeated experiences of negative-state alleviation in the context of the caregiver, and reciprocal interaction and shared positive affect with the caregiver. This is because caregivers are routinely responsive to their infants. In the third phase, again because the caregiver is responsive and now because of infants' budding intentionality, they may begin to experience affective regulation at their own initiation.

By the end of the first year, according to Bowlby (1973), interactive experiences have become abstracted into particular models of caregiver availability and responsiveness and complementary models of self (which have little definition outside of this context). Feeling states give rise to behavioral tendencies which are expressed in accord with expectations of likely responses by the caregiver and their consequences. If the infant is threatened, the directed signal to the caregiver derives from the expectation that the caregiver will provide comforting. Where various particular actions routinely have particular consequences for ongoing regulation, a particular pattern of inner organization (self) emerges. Should these actions lead to consequences which promote smooth regulation of affect and ongoing commerce with the environment, a well-defined, functional self core is the result.

Does the quality of the early dyadic organization, orchestrated by the caregiver, predict the quality of later dyadic regulation wherein the infant plays an active role (and the self is emerging)? Ainsworth (Ainsworth 1973; Ainsworth et al. 1978) showed in her pioneering studies, that ratings of caregiver responsivity at various points in the first year predicted later quality of infant attachment behavior in both home and laboratory. When caregivers were observed to respond to signals promptly and effectively, their infants later cried less at home, explored more actively, and showed fewer negative behaviors than infants with a history of insensitive care. In Ainsworth's laboratory assessment procedure, the Strange Situation, these infants were assessed as "securely attached." They used the caregiver as a base for exploration, being reassured by the caregiver's mere presence. If distressed by a brief separation, they actively initiated interaction or contact upon reunion. Upon achieving contact, they were readily comforted (returning again to active exploration). In sum, infants who experienced a history of responsive care by the end of the first year are active, effective participants in well-regulated dyadic systems. A positive core of self emerges by virtue of participating in such a well-regulated system (Sroufe and Fleeson 1986).

In contrast, infants with a history of insensitive care either were unduly wary in the novel setting, impoverished in their exploration, and unable to be settled ("anxious/resistant") or avoided contact with the caregiver upon reunion, even when markedly distressed ("anxious/avoidant"). Both groups of anxiously attached infants were unable to return to active exploration following reunion with the mother.

Ainsworth's core finding—namely, the relationship between quality of attachment in her laboratory assessment and sensitivity of care based on home observation earlier in the first year—has been replicated by several different teams of researchers (Bates, Maslin, and Frankel 1985; Belsky and Isabella 1987; Egeland and Farber 1984; Grossman et al. 1985). In each of these studies, independent coders assessed caregiver responsiveness and later attachment, and neither set had knowledge of the other data.

The Developmental Course of Anxious Attachment

Little research has specifically related Ainsworth's two major forms of anxious attachment to the developmental sequence of self emergence outlined above, in part because from an organizational perspective little premium is placed on age of occurrence of phenomena. Thus, it is not that anxious patterns of attachment emerge later; rather, it is the anomalous organization of attachment behaviors that are of interest. Similarly, the focus on caregiving origins of anxious attachment has been not on ages that caregivers do one thing or another but on the insensitivity of care across the first year.

These findings present certain developmental features, however. First, insensitivity is referenced differently at different ages, because the infant's signals (to which the caregiver responds sensitively or insensitively) change from period to period. Second, one key difference between caregivers of infants who later show the avoidant pattern and those who show the resistant pattern is that the former rebuff their infants when the *infants* indicate a desire for physical contact. Rebuffing the infant's initiation of contact can only occur when the infant has the capacity to signal this desire. While care may have a rejecting or disinterested quality earlier, it may only be after the middle of the first year that the infant may learn the negative contingency between seeking contact and being rebuffed.

There also is some suggestion that, in the case of anxious/resistance relationships, obvious difficulties may be apparent in the dyadic interaction earlier. In one study, a subset of these cases at twelve months was predicted by a seven-day (but not a ten-day) Brazelton neonatal exam (Waters, Vaughn, and Egeland 1980). Whether this reflected an early dyadic state regulation issue or some inherent nonoptimal functioning of these newborns, it nonetheless reflected a problem of regulation which persisted through the first year and beyond. No such early state regulation problems were apparent in those dyads later classified as having an avoidant attachment relationship.

Problems can be seen in the behavior of future avoidant infants by age six months but not so readily before. For example, for one group of caregivers designated as "psychologically unavailable" ($N = 19$), most infants showed the avoidant pattern by age twelve months, virtually all by eighteen months (Egeland and Sroufe 1981). Analysis of prospectively gathered data revealed that even as late as age three months, the infants still appeared robust and well oriented despite marked insensitivity (in the form of affectlessness and nonresponsiveness) shown by their mothers. By six months, problems were apparent in the infants as well, with reduced engagement and increased lethargy. Thus, with a failure of chained, reciprocal behavior orchestrated by the caregiver, the infant fails to move toward the initiatory role.

Internal Working Models of Secure and Anxious Infants

Internal working models refer to the inner organization of emotions and states, actions, and expectable caregiver responses (When I am upset and I signal my caregiver, my caregiver will respond). Twelve-month-olds are influenced by situational context, and they do make some sort of "probability estimates" concerning caregiver responsiveness. Clearly, cognitive factors are important. However, the process is mediated by affect and is in the service of affect regulation, and it certainly is not conscious: the infant is not aware of the internal working model. As an organizing framework, it is not normally accessible to awareness, even later in development. But infants do monitor the availability and responsiveness of the caregiver, based on circumstances (Sorce and Emde 1981) and developmental history (Ainsworth et al. 1978). Their freedom to engage novelty and their thresholds for threat are mightily influenced by these assessments, all without their awareness that such calculations are being made.

When we say that infants with avoidant attachment relationships have internal working models of caregiver as unavailable and self as unable to achieve (and unworthy of) care, we do not mean to imply that these are considered conclusions on the part of the infant. They are generalizations from experience in affect regulation, not assessments of caregiver character. Repeatedly, when infants experience strong affect, they try to exercise the ingrained tendency to seek contact with the attachment figure. Being turned away is painful, and this negative experience of emotional regulation failure is associated with the caregiver. Likewise, positive affect is not routinely shared. Such experience does not eradicate the infants' desire for contact or eagerness to explore, but it does lead to distortions in normal regulatory processes. These infants rarely achieve peaks of excitement, and they learn to cut themselves off from emotionally threatening experience. The infant's affective experience is blunted, and with this comes an impoverished view of others as vital to affective richness and dynamic regulation.

In the anxious/resistant attachment case, Bowlby (1988) would describe the infant as having a model of the caregiver as inconsistently unavailable and of self as ineffective (weak) in terms of eliciting care. This need not be taken to mean that the infant thinks, "My caregiver has been inconsistent in the past, therefore I will be uncertain." Rather, because of the history of inconsistent care wherein even modest threats and challenges led to disorganized behavior, this infant finds modest threats arousing now and, despite the normal activation of attachment behavior, is unable to be reassured by caregiver presence or contact. My interpretation of the working model in infancy is as a metaphor, literally characterizing the working relationship among arousal (whether based on external or internal information), social behavior, and expectations concerning caregiver responsiveness. The concept is highly related to the origins of the self because, in time, dyadic tension regulation leads to individual patterns of self-regulation and children do form more abstracted, cognitive ideas about the availability of others and their own self-worth.

The Emerging Self as Organizer of Later Experience

Bowlby's concept of the working model of the self has certain advantages, even while having the unfortunate connotation of a concretized brain structure and perhaps overemphasizing the cognitive component of a complex process. It implies an abstraction from experience (rather than a literal copy), and in particular the term *working* implies an ongoing, constructive process. Another meaning I have taken from the term is the idea of an organizing framework, *a model within which one works*. As such, it has implications for the ongoing structuring of experience. The child moves toward or away from certain experiences, engages environmental challenges and opportunities in certain ways, and interprets experiences, all guided by working models of self and other. These ongoing encounters with the environment, in turn, feed back on the self as the inner organization is consolidated and undergoes continued modification.

Some tendency for continuity in the inner organizing core will be seen, because there is an active structuring of later experience by the self, and early prototypes of inner organization are not readily accessible to conscious awareness. Bowlby's (1973) sophisticated sensitive-period hypothesis is that the self-organizing core shows some resistance to modification even by the end of infancy, becomes rather firmly established by the end of early childhood, and becomes quite difficult to modify after adolescence. It is not rigidly fixed in the early years; neither is it simply subject to the whims of circumstance.

Substantial support now exists for the predictive power (and, by implication, the organizing significance) of early working models of self and other for development in the preschool and middle-childhood years. Groups of children, assessed using Ainsworth's Strange Situation procedure in infancy, have been followed for various periods of time through childhood. Comparisons between those Ainsworth calls secure in their attachment and those who show avoidant attachment are of particular interest. The maladaptation of the latter is apparent only in the organization of their behavior. They are not notably upset by separation; they engage both toys and strangers readily. In fact, some interpret them as merely precociously independent (Clarke-Stewart and Fein 1983) or temperamentally easy (Kagan 1982). But the failure to seek contact when distressed is interpreted here as a major breakdown in the dyadic regulation of affect. The prediction, drawn both from Bowlby's explicit statements and from organizational theory, is that these infants later will be *less* self-reliant, less able to achieve social closeness, and in general unable to deal effectively with affective arousal, leading to isolation and other socially distancing behavior. Prospective, longitudinal data now are available pertinent to each of these aspects of functioning.

Self-Reliance, Ego Strength, and Agency

Children who have experienced responsive care evolve a complementary model of self as potent. At both 2 and 3 1/2 years of age, children who had been assessed in infancy as securely attached have been found to be more confident, enthusiastic, and affectively positive in solving problems (Arend 1984; Matas et al. 1978; Sroufe and Rosenberg 1980) than children with histories of avoidant attachment. In other studies, children with histories of secure attachment were found at age 3 1/2 to be "self directed," "forceful in pursuing goals," and generally higher on ego strength (Waters, Wippman, and Sroufe 1979). They also, at age four–five years, are more curious and more "ego resilient"—that is, more confident and flexible in managing impulses, feelings, and desires (Arend, Gove, and Sroufe 1979; Sroufe 1983). These basic findings concerning self-confidence and ego resiliency have recently been reaffirmed in children age ten–eleven in a summer day camp situation.

Perhaps the most dramatic outcome data on individual adaptation concern the construct of self-reliance or emotional dependency. Preschool teachers (blind to attachment history) judged those with secure histories to be dramatically more independent and resourceful, based on Q-sorts, rankings, and ratings, with virtually no overlap between those with avoidant and those with secure histories (Sroufe, Fox, and Pancake 1983). Six years later, camp counselors (also without knowledge of individual history) provided congruent data (Elicker, Egeland, and Sroufe, in press). These teacher and counselor judgments were confirmed by observational data. For example, in circle time, those with secure histories less often sat by teachers or counselors; nor did they seek attention through negative behaviors. As preschoolers, they were noted to actively greet teachers and use teachers skillfully as resources, and actually were rated higher on "seeks attention in positive ways" (Sroufe et al. 1983).

Thus, young children with histories of secure attachment are seen to be independent, resourceful, curious, and confident in their approach to the environment. Those with avoidant histories, in spite of a seeming precocious independence (or rather, because of a pronounced absence of dyadic affect regulation), later are lacking in self-reliance and in fact are viewed by judges as highly emotionally dependent.

Self-Esteem

When the caregiver is chronically unavailable, the infant comes to feel unworthy of care. While an elusive concept, self-esteem can be accessed in various ways. One approach we have taken (Arend 1984) was to rate the child's ability at age 3 1/2 to maintain a positive orientation in the face of a virtually impossible task (the barrier box). The rating centered on the child's confidence, ability to maintain flexible organization, and capacity to keep "expecting well." Other opportunities were provided by the preschool and summer day camp settings mentioned above. In this case, composite Q-sorts on each child (made by several counselors or teachers) were compared to a criterion high-self-esteem Q-sort compiled by Waters (Waters et al. 1985). At both ages, children with a history of secure attachment were significantly higher on self-esteem than children with histories of anxious attachment. (In the preschool, there was virtually no overlap in the distribution of scores of those with secure and avoidant histories [Sroufe 1983].)

In both the preschool and the summer camps, we saw countless behavioral examples that illustrated these differences in self-esteem. These showed up in differences in engaging challenging situations, trying hard and persisting in tasks, and reacting to implicit rejections in social situations. For example, two secure boys succeeded in building a two-story wooden building, while those with avoidant histories had difficulty even engaging in such a task. Those with avoidant histories were sensitive to the slightest rebuff, whereas those with secure histories interpreted such behavior in more positive ways. For example, in the nursery school one day, several children were dancing to recorded music, a lively and inviting scene. Other children arrived. One child (RA) approached another and asked to dance. The child said no, and RA withdrew to a corner and sulked. Another child (RT) entered, approached a potential partner, and also was turned down. RT, however, skipped on to another child and was successful in soliciting a partner the second time. RT, who had a history of secure attachment, showed no evidence of being "rejected," and her persistent stance led her ultimately to receive further confirmation of her expectation that others are responsive and that she is worthy. RA, on the other hand, experienced intense rejection and cut himself off from further opportunities to disconfirm his model of himself as unworthy.

Self and Others

Children with secure histories, while not handicapped by emotional dependency, do effectively use counselors and teachers as resources. After first trying to solve a problem or settle a dispute on their own, preschool children with secure histories turn to their teachers for support. When a construction project was beyond their abilities, ten- to eleven-year-old campers with secure histories sought the expert advice of counselors. When injured or ill, such children also expect support and help from adults. Their expectations clearly are that adults are valuable resources who will be supportive and caring when sought out. Such reactions (and such expectations) were not at all typical of preschoolers or campers with histories of avoidant attachment.

Teachers and counselors, in turn, have different expectations for the children. Coders rating the behavior of preschool teachers toward individual children with secure histories found the teachers were on average warm, uncontrolling, positive, and age appropriate in their demands (Motti 1986; Sroufe and Fleeson 1988). For those with avoidant histories, teachers were significantly higher on control, negative expectations for compliance, and anger, quite reminiscent of what these children had experienced with their caregivers. For those with anxious/resistant histories, teachers were unduly nurturant and tolerant of rule violations but again controlling and with low expectations. These reactions are in remarkable accord with patterns of adaptation shown by the children and therefore confirmed the children's internal working models of self.

Preschoolers and preadolescents with histories of secure attachment also are more engaged and more affectively positive with peers. They convey their positive expectations to others. They more frequently initiate interactions with positive affect and more frequently respond to bids by others with positive affect (Sroufe et al. 1984). Across the childhood years, they are more socially competent, form friendships more readily, and have "deeper" relationships

(Elicker et al. in press; LaFreniere and Sroufe 1985; Sroufe 1983). Interestingly, we also found in our summer camp study that friendships formed along attachment history lines. When secure children choose as friends other children with secure histories, they will again tend to receive input supporting of their models of others as available.

Secure children also have been found to be more empathic with other children, being rated higher on "shows a recognition of others' feelings (empathic)," "shows concern for moral issues (reciprocity, fairness)," and "is considerate of other children (does not try to take advantage of other children)" (Sroufe 1983). Overall, children with histories of secure attachment were judged by teachers to be significantly higher on empathy than those with histories of avoidance. The empathy items were, on average, "characteristic" for the secure group, "uncharacteristic" for the avoidant group. These differences have now been confirmed in behavioral observations (Kestenbaum, Farber, and Sroufe 1989). Securely attached children, having experienced a history of empathic responsiveness, internalize the capacity for empathy and the disposition to be empathic; those with avoidant histories, having experienced emotional unavailability or rejection, do not. What was characteristic of their early relationships became part of the core self.

The Roots of Hostility and Alienation

Children with histories of avoidant attachment have profound difficulty getting emotionally close to others, including other children. Having experienced rejection and at times explicit hostility, those children, not surprisingly, often are hostile and aggressive toward other children. We have now documented this in both the preschool and elementary school (LaFreniere and Sroufe 1985; Pancake 1988; Renkin et al. 1989; Sroufe 1983). Moreover, when one or both partners of a preschool play pair had a history of avoidance, these pairs were rated significantly lower on "commitment" than were pairs without such a child. (This prediction derived from the notion that if one partner is disposed to be distant or hostile, such a characteristic will pervade the relationship; it takes two to be intimately and positively engaged.)

Without closeness, such relationships often take on an exploitative quality, where one child verbally or physically subjugates the partner in an ongoing way (Troy and Sroufe 1987). In all five cases of exploitation observed, the exploiter had a history of avoidance; the partner also had been anxiously attached (either avoidant or Ainsworth's resistant pattern). Children with secure histories neither were victimized nor were they observed to be exploitive of other children. When two children with histories of avoidance were paired, the weakest or less bright child would be victimized. Having internalized a rejecting relationship, children with histories of avoidant attachment could assume either role in their peer relationships. The active role of the victim in these relationships was illustrated repeatedly. In one case, where the exploitation routinely took the form of teasing and verbal abuse, the exploited child became upset when his partner ignored him. "Aren't you going to tease me today, RJ?" he asked plaintively. In all cases, internal working models of self, other, and relationships were apparent.

Internal working models of self and other also are revealed in the fantasy play of children with histories of avoidance. Despite IQs equivalent to children with secure histories, the play of these children lacks complexity and elaboration (Rosenberg 1984). Moreover, there is an almost complete lack of fantasy play concerning people. Social fantasies dominate the play of most preschool children and were well represented in the play of those in our sample with secure histories. The inner world of those with secure histories is richly peopled; the inner world of these with avoidant histories is not. There also are striking differences in the tendency for conflicts to come to successful resolution in fantasy ("He broke his leg, take him to the hospital!" "They fixed it."); successful resolutions were not common in the play of children with histories of avoidant attachment.

In summary, children with histories of avoidant attachment carry forward feelings of low self-worth, isolation, and angry rejection (which they sometimes turn outward). Ratings by preschool teachers and camp counselors placed them low on emotional health/self-esteem and confidence. Moreover, they were found to be more depressed, based on Q-sort data composited across three preschool teachers. Even specific items (e.g., "appears to feel unworthy; thinks of self as bad") were seen as characteristic for those with avoidant histories and uncharacteristic for those having secure relationships in infancy (Garber et al. 1985).

Conclusion

The hypothesis that individual personalities have their origins in early family experiences is not new. Numerous clinicians have posited that core deficiencies in self derive from an early lack of nurturance and esteem within caregiving relationships (Erikson 1963; Kohut 1977; Sullivan 1953). In the past, however, such a hypothesis has proved difficult to test empirically. Quality of early care, the impact of care on the emergence of the self, and personality organization all posed formidable challenges to assessment. Moreover, conceptualizing exactly how early experience influenced later adaptation proved difficult. Classic psychoanalytic accounts were vague, and simple modeling or other early social learning accounts were inadequate. For example, how would caregiver emotional unavailability lead to bullying of other children and emotional dependence on teachers and counselors?

Guided by an organizational perspective on development and drawing upon Bowlby's and Ainsworth's conceptions and procedures for assessing attachment, it has now been possible both to provide strong empirical support for the link between early care and later adaptation and to move toward an adequate explanation of such a connection. The self is viewed as an inner organization of attitudes, expectations, and feelings, which has its origins in the dyadic organization that preceded it and which will provide a framework for subsequent engagement of the environment. Simply by participating in a relationship, the child acquires an understanding of self and others in relational terms. Not just a role but an entire set of if-then propositions about relationships is learned (Sroufe and Fleeson 1986, 1988). In relationships when one is vulnerable, another nurtures (or exploits); when one approaches in a friendly manner, others respond in kind (or are disinterested); when one seeks emotional closeness, the other reciprocates; and so on. Internalization of relationships explains why the secure preschooler seeks a teacher's help when a partner complains of a stomachache, while a child with an avoidant history punches the child in the very place that hurts. Neither child likely experienced these actual reactions within his or her primary attachment relationships, but each had countless experiences with responses to vulnerability in relationships.

The organization of feelings and expectations is carried forward into new contexts, influencing not only the child's behavior but, in turn, the reactions of others. Some children expect rejection, as in the child who dreamed her teacher hurled her against a wall. When told of the dream, the teacher explained that she would never do that, whereupon the girl, astoundingly, made her explain further why she would not. Expecting rejection, such children often behave in ways that elicit anger and rejection from adults. This is not because they want rejection but because it is understandable and familiar. Some interpret behavior as rejecting even when it is not. (A child already occupied declines to play, in response to an overture from a second child. The latter goes off and sulks the rest of the morning.) Some children simply won't try to engage others or will engage them inappropriately, perhaps with aggression.

Thus, differentially guided by different inner organizations, children elicit feedback from the environment which often is congruent with their prior expectations. It is this interactive process, and not early scarring or unchanging environments, which likely is the dominant influence underlying the predictability of adaptation and its continuity over time. (Sroufe, Egeland, and Kreutzer, in press).

The data obtained in this project, linking aspects of personality and adaptation as late as age eleven to individual differences assessed as the self was emerging in the context of the early caregiving relationship, are unprecedented. Some especially strong results concern aspects of adaptation tapping most closely the organization of feelings and expectations concerning self and other. Most notable are data on the capacity to form close friendships and the persistence of emotional dependency on adults. Those children whose earliest dyadic organization was characterized by an absence of emotional responsiveness later have marked difficulties with interpersonal closeness and remain strongly dependent on adults, with score distributions showing almost no overlap with those children having histories of secure attachment.

This strong data on the continuity of adaptation over time should not lead to pessimism concerning change. The organizational perspective also is useful for conceptualizing intervention and change. The inner organization of self is a derivative of organized vital relationships and, as such, most likely will undergo change in the context of other significant relationships. Confirmation of this comes from our recent study of exceptions in the intergenerational transmission of abuse: a group of mothers who, while abused as children, were providing adequate, nonabusive care for their own children (Egeland, Jacobvitz, and Sroufe 1988). Three factors distinguished these mothers from those who perpetuated abuse: (1) an alternative available and responsive caregiving figure in childhood, (2) extensive therapeutic intervention (more than six months), and (3) a supportive partner currently. Within relationships with significant others who do not respond in ways supporting the child's past models, change in inner organization remains possible. The self was forged within vital relationships; within such relationships, it continues to evolve.

References

Ainsworth, M. D. S. 1973. The development of infant-mother attachment. In *Review of child development research*, vol. 3. Edited by B. Caldwell and H. Ricciuti. Chicago: University of Chicago Press.

Ainsworth, M. D. S., and S. Bell. 1974. Mother-infant interaction and the development of competence. In *The growth of competence*. Edited by K. Connelly and J. Bruner. New York: Academic.

Ainsworth, M. D. S., M. Blehar, E. Waters, and S. Wall. 1978. *Patterns of attachment*. Hillsdale, N.J.: Erlbaum.

Amsterdam, B. 1972. Mirror self-image reactions before age two. *Developmental Psychobiology* 5:297–305.

Arend, R. 1984. *Preschoolers' competence in a barrier situation: Patterns of adaptation and their precursors in infancy*. Doctoral dissertation, University of Minnesota.

Arend, R., F. Gove, L. A. Sroufe. 1979. Continuity of individual adaptation from infancy to kindergarten: A predictive study of ego-resiliency and curiosity in preschoolers. *Child Development* 50: 950–59.

Baldwin, J. M. 1897. *Social and ethical interpretations in mental development*. New York: Macmillan.

Bates, J., C. Maslin, K. Frankel. 1985. Attachment security, mother-child interaction, and temperament as predictors of behavior problem ratings at age three years. In *Growing points in attachment research.* Edited by I. Bretherton and E. Waters. Monographs of the Society for Research in Child Development vol. 50, series no. 209: 167–93.

Belsky, J. and R. Isabella. 1987. Maternal, infant, and social-contextual determinants of attachment security: A process analysis. In *Clinical implications of attachment.* Edited by J. Belsky and T. Nezworski. Hillsdale, N.J.: Erlbaum.

Bowlby, J. 1969. *Attachment and loss.* Vol. 1, *Attachment.* New York: Basic.

_____. 1973. *Attachment and loss.* Vol. 2, *Separation.* New York: Basic.

_____. 1988. *A secure base.* New York: Basic, chap. 7.

Brazelton, T. B., B. Kowslowski, and M. Main. 1974. The origins of mother-infant interaction. In *The effect of the infant on its caregiver.* Edited by M. Lewis and L. Rosenblum. New York: Wiley.

Breger, L. 1974. *From instinct to identity.* Englewood Cliffs, N.J.: Prentice-Hall.

Clarke-Stewart, K. A., and G. Fein. 1983. Early childhood programs. In *Handbook of child psychology.* 4th ed. Edited by P. H. Mussen. *Infancy and developmental psychology.* Edited by M. Haith and J. Campos. New York: Wiley.

Egeland, B., and E. Farber. 1984. Infant-mother attachment: Factors related to its development and changes over time. *Child Development* 55:753–71.

Egeland, B. D. Jacobvitz, and L. A. Sroufe. 1988. Breaking the cycle of abuse: Relationship predictors. *Child Development* 59:1080–88.

Egeland, B., and L. A. Sroufe. 1981. Developmental sequelae of maltreatment in infancy. In *Developmental perspectives in child maltreatment.* Edited by R. Rizley and D. Cicchetti. San Francisco: Jossey-Bass.

Elicker, J., M. Egeland, and L. A. Sroufe. In press. Predicting peer competence and peer relationships in childhood from early parent-child relationships. In *Family-peer relationships: Modes of linkage.* Edited by R. Parke and G. Ladd. Hillsdale, N.J.: Erlbaum.

Erikson, E. 1963. *Childhood and society.* New York: Norton.

Flavell, J. H. 1977. *Cognitive development.* Englewood Cliffs, N.J.: Prentice-Hall.

Garber, J., E. Cohen, P. Bacon, E. Egeland, and L. A. Sroufe. 1985, April. Depression in preschoolers: Reliability and validity of a behavioral observation measure. Paper presented at meeting of the Society for Research in Child Development, Toronto.

Greenspan, S. 1981. *Psychopathology and adaptation in infancy and early childhood.* New York: International Universities Press.

Grossman, K., K. E. Grossman, G. Spangler, G. Suess, and L. Unzner. 1985. Maternal sensitivity and newborn's orienting responses as related to quality of attachment in northern Germany. In *Growing points in attachment research.* Edited by I. Bretherton and E. Waters. Monographs of the Society for Research in Child Development, vol. 50, Series no. 209:233–56.

Hayes, A. 1984. Interaction, engagement, and the origins of communication: Some constructive concerns. In *The origins and growth of communication.* Edited by L. Feagans, C. Garvey, and R. Golinkoff. Norwood, N.J.: Ablex.

Heinicke, C., and I. Westheimer. 1966. *Brief separations.* New York: International Universities Press.

Hiatt, S., J. Campos, R. Emde. 1979. Facial patterning and infant emotional expression: Happiness, surprise and fear. *Child Development* 50:1020–35.

Hoffman, M. 1979. Development of moral thought, feeling, and behavior. *American Psychologist* 34:958–66.

Kagan, J. 1982. *Psychological research on the human infant: An evaluative summary.* New York: Grant Foundation.

Kestenbaum, R., E. Farber, and L. A. Sroufe. 1989. Individual differences in empathy among preschoolers: Concurrent and predictive validity. In *New directions for child development.* Edited by N. Eisenberg. San Francisco: Jossey-Bass, 51–56.

Kohut, H. 1977. *The restoration of the self.* New York: International Universities Press.

LaFreniere, P., and L. A. Sroufe. 1985. Profiles of peer competence in the preschool: Interrelation between measures, influence of social ecology, and relation to attachment history. *Developmental Psychology* 21:56–68.

Lewis, M., and J. Brooks-Gunn. 1978. Self-knowledge and emotional development. In *The development of affect.* Edited by M. Lewis and L. Rosenblum. New York: Plenum.

Loevinger, J. 1976. *Ego development.* San Francisco: Jossey-Bass.

Londerville, S., and M. Main. 1981. Security of attachment, compliance, and maternal training methods in the second year of life. *Developmental Psychology* 17:289–99.

Mahler, M., F. Pine, and A. Bergman. 1975. *The psychological birth of the human infant.* New York: Basic.

Main, M., N. Kaplan, and J. Cassidy. 1985. Security in infancy, childhood and adulthood: A move to the level of representation. In *Growing points in attachment research.* Edited by I. Bretherton and E. Waters. Monographs of the Society for Research in Child Development, vol. 50, series no. 209:66–106.

Mans, L., D. Cicchetti, and L. A. Sroufe. 1978. Mirror reactions of Down's syndrome infants and toddlers: Cognitive underpinnings of self-recognition. *Child Development* 49:1247–50.

Matas, L., R. Arend, and L. A. Sroufe. 1978. Continuity of adaptation in the second year: The relationship between quality of attachment and later competent functioning. *Child Development* 49:547–56.

Mead, G. H. 1934. *Mind, self and society.* Chicago: University of Chicago Press.

Motti, F. 1986. *Relationships of preschool teachers with children of varying developmental histories.* Doctoral dissertation, University of Minnesota.

Neilon, P. 1948. Shirley's babies after 15 years: A personality study. *Journal of Genetic Psychology* 73:175–186.

Pancake, V. 1988. *Quality of attachment in infancy as a predictor of hostility and emotional distance in preschool peer relationships.* Doctoral dissertation, University of Minnesota.

Radke-Yarrow, M., C. Zahn-Waxler, and M. Chapman. 1983. Children's prosocial dispositions and behavior. In *Carmichael's manual of child psychology.* 4th ed. vol. 4. Edited by P. Mussen. New York: Wiley.

Renkin, B., B. Egeland, D. Marvinney, S. Mangelsdorf, and L. A. Sroufe. 1989. Early childhood antecedents of aggression and passive-withdrawal in early elementary school. *Journal of Personality* 57:257–82.

Rheingold, H., and C. Eckerman. 1973. Fear of the strangers: A critical examination. In *Advances in child development and behavior, vol. 8. Edited by H. Reese. New York: Academic.*

Rosenberg, D. 1984. *The quality and content of preschool fantasy play: Correlates in concurrent social/personality function and early mother-child attachment relationships.* Doctoral dissertation, University of Minnesota.

Sameroff, A. 1983. Developmental systems: Contexts and evolution. In *Handbook of child psychology.* 3d ed. Edited by P. Mussen. Vol. 1, *History, theory and methods.* New York: Wiley.

Sander, L. 1975. Infant and caretaking environment. In *Explorations in child psychiatry.* Edited by E. J. Anthony. New York: Plenum.

Santostefano, S. 1978. *A biodevelopmental approach to clinical child psychology.* New York: Wiley.

Schaffer, H., and M. Callender. 1959. Psychologic effects of hospitalization in infancy. *Pediatrics* 21:528–39.

Sorce, J., and R. Emde. 1981. Mother's presence is not enough: The effect of emotional availability on infant exploration and play. *Developmental Psychology* 17:737–45.

Sroufe, L. A. 1977. *Knowing and enjoying your baby.* New York: Spectrum.

———. 1979a. The coherence of individual development. *American Psychologist* 34:834–41.

———. 1979b. Socioemotional development. In *Handbook of infant development.* Edited by J. Osofsky. New York: Wiley.

———. 1983. Infant-caregiver attachment and adaptation in the preschool: The roots of competence and maladaptation. In *Minnesota Symposia in Child Psychology,* vol. 16. Edited by M. Perlmutter. Hillsdale, N.J.: Erlbaum.

Sroufe, L. A., B. Egeland, and T. Kreutzer. In press. The fate of early experience following developmental change. *Child Development.*

Sroufe, L. A., and J. Fleeson. 1986. Attachment and the construction of relationships. In *Relationships and development.* Edited by W. Hartup and Z. Rubin. Hillsdale, N.J.: Erlbaum.

———. 1988. The coherence of family relationships. In *Relationships within families.* Edited by R. Hinde and J. Stevenson-Hinde. London: Oxford.

Sroufe, L. A., N. Fox, and V. Pancake. 1983. Attachment and dependency in developmental perspective. *Child Development* 54:1615–27.

Sroufe, L. A., and D. Rosenberg. 1980, March. Coherence of individual adaptation in lower SES infants and toddlers. Paper presented at the International Conference on Infant Studies, Providence, R.I.

Sroufe, L. A., E. Schork, F. Motti, N. Lawroski, and P. LaFreniere. 1984. The role of affect in social competence. In *Emotions cognition and behavior.* Edited by C. Izard, J. Kagan, and R. Zajonc. New York: Cambridge University Press.

———. 1977. Attachment as an organizational construct. *Child Development* 48:1184–99.

Sroufe, L. A., E. Waters, and L. Matas. 1974. Contextual determinants of infant affective responses. In *The origins of fear.* Edited by M. Lewis and L. Rosenblum. New York: Wiley.

Stenberg, C., J. Campos, and R. Emde. 1983. The facial expression of anger in seven-month-old infants. *Child Development* 54:178–84.

Stern, D. 1974. The goal structure of mother-infant play. *Journal of the American Academy of Child Psychiatry* 13:402–21.

———. 1985. *The interpersonal world of the infant.* New York: Basic.

Sullivan, H. S. 1953. *The interpersonal theory of psychiatry.* New York: Norton.

Troy, M., and L. A. Sroufe. 1987. Victimization among preschoolers: The role of attachment relationship history. *Journal of the American Academy of Child Psychiatry* 26:166–72.

Vaughn, B. 1977. *An ethological study of greeting behaviors in infants from six to nine months of age.* Doctoral dissertation, University of Minnesota.

Vaughn, B., and L. A. Sroufe. 1979. The temporal relationship between infant heart rate acceleration and crying in an aversive situation. *Child Development* 50:565–67.

Waters, E., D. Noyes, B. Vaughn, and M. Ricks. 1985. Q-sort definitions of social competence and self-esteem: Discriminant validity of related constructs in theory and data. *Developmental Psychology* 21:508–22.

Waters, E., B. Vaughn, and B. Egeland. 1980. Individual differences in infant-mother attachment: Antecedents in neonatal behavior in an urban economically disadvantaged sample. *Child Development* 51:208–16.

Waters, E., J. Wippman, L. A. Sroufe. 1979. Attachment, positive affect, and competence in the peer group: Two studies in construct validation. *Child Development* 50:821–29.

Werner, H. 1957. The concept of development from a comparative and organismic point of view. In *The concept of development.* Edited by D. Harris. Minneapolis: University of Minnesota Press.

Winnicott, D. 1965. *The maturational processes and the facilitating environment.* New York: International Universities Press.

14 The Emergence of the Self in Atypical Populations

Dante Cicchetti, Marjorie Beeghly, Vicki Carlson, and Sheree Toth

After a comprehensive review of the theoretical and empirical literature, Harter (1983) concluded that there was relatively little empirical evidence pertaining to how the self is constructed or how, from a cognitive-developmental perspective, it changes in content and structure. While progress has been made on some aspects of the ontogenesis of the self system (see, for example, Damon and Hart's [1982, 1988] work on self-understanding), several factors have conspired to inhibit research on the self from a developmental perspective. Clearly, difficulties exist in the operationalization of the term *self* (Kagan, in this volume). Additionally, dissatisfaction with the metapsychological constructs employed by psychoanalysis has been accompanied by a focus on observable behaviors and a decreased attention to intrapsychic phenomena. Furthermore, the predominance of cognition, especially the Piagetian paradigm, brought about a concomitant reduction in the study of emotional phenomena (Cicchetti and Hesse 1983). The absence of research on emotion that characterized the field of developmental psychology for approximately forty years (Cicchetti and Pogge-Hesse 1981) made it difficult to examine affective aspects of the self and to investigate the organization of self-system processes (Cicchetti 1990; Connell, in this volume; Emde 1985; Sroufe, in this volume).

Research described in this chapter was supported by grants from the John D. and Catherine T. MacArthur Foundation Network on Early Childhood, the March of Dimes (12-127), the National Center on Child Abuse and Neglect (90-C-1929), the National Institute of Mental Health (RO1-MH37960-01), the Smith Richardson Foundation, Inc., the Spencer Foundation, and the Spunk Fund, Inc. We wish to acknowledge our collaborators for their invaluable help on the projects described herein. In particular, J. Lawrence Aber, Joseph Allen, Douglas Barnett, Karen Braunwald, Cindy Carter, Wendy Coster, Jody Ganiban, Michelle Gersten, Joan Kaufman, Amber Keshishian, Carol Kottmeier, Michael Lynch, Linda Mans-Wagener, Carolyn Rieder, Karen Schneider-Rosen, Susan Shonk, Alan Sroufe, Kathryn Staggs, Joan Vondra, Bedonna Weiss-Perry, and Jennifer White deserve special recognition. Finally, we wish to thank Douglas Barnett for his valuable comments, Candace Cicchetti for her insights, and Victoria Gill for typing this manuscript.

310   Dante Cicchetti et al.

Over the course of the past decade, interest has grown in the developmental continuities and transformations underlying self-system processes during the transition from infancy to early childhood. Given the historical paucity of such work in the area of normal development, it is not surprising that there has been so little empirical research conducted on the development of the self in clinical populations of children (Cicchetti and Beeghly, in this volume). One major reason for this state of affairs involves a pitfall common to all research on childhood disorders and risk conditions. After an initial focus on normal ontogenetic processes, the emphasis shifts to the study of adult psychopathological conditions. Unfortunately, much of the research on adult psychopathology is explicitly adevelopmental in nature (Cicchetti 1984).

Despite the minimal amount of empirical research on the development of the self in atypical childhood populations, many authors have theorized about the organization of the self in such conditions. The main thrust of this conceptual work has been the elucidation of the processes whereby aberrations in the ontogenesis of the self contribute to and/or "cause" child and adult psychopathology (Adler and Buie 1979; Arieti 1967; Baker and Baker 1987; Erikson 1950; Freud 1965; Kegan 1982; Kernberg 1976; Kohut 1977; Mahler, Pine, and Bergman 1975; Pine 1974).

However, several contemporary researchers have examined empirically the self system of disordered children. Cohen (1980) describes his multidisciplinary, multidomain research on both early childhood autism and Tourette's syndrome. Each of these groups of children manifests pathological disturbances of the self. Autistic children have both semantic and pragmatic abnormalities in communication which reveal their difficulties in creating stable internal representations of themselves and of others (Baron-Cohen 1989; Caparulo and Cohen 1977; Kanner 1943; Menyuk 1978; Paul 1987; Rutter 1983; Tager-Flusberg 1981), in ordering and analyzing symbolic representations, and in keeping word and object clearly defined and appropriately separated (Hermelin and O'Connor 1970; Rutter and Garmezy 1983; Sigman and Mundy 1987). Furthermore, autistic children manifest a marked lack of awareness of other people's feelings and a profound difficulty initiating or sustaining conversations with others despite adequate speech (American Psychiatric Association 1987).

Children with Tourette's disease (the syndrome of chronic multiple tics) also exhibit problems in their self-system functioning. They provide an experiment of nature whereby we can witness the splitting of the self between good and bad, impulse driven and impulse ridden, and doing and undoing (Cohen 1980). While Cohen conceptualizes the self pathology of autism as a failure of development which may lead to a sense of selflessness and inner emptiness, he views the self disturbances in Tourette's syndrome as due to a failure of inhibition and self-regulation.

Spiker and Ricks (1984) likewise have investigated one aspect of self-knowledge in autistic children, that of visual self-recognition. They found that 69 percent of their sample of autistic children evinced mirror self-recognition (see also Dawson and McKissick 1984; Ferrari and Matthews 1983; Neuman and Hill 1978). Severity of language disturbance played a major role in differentiating the children with autism who did and did not manifest self-recognition: autistic children who were mute or lacking in communicative speech were far less likely to demonstrate the capacity of mirror self-recognition. Of equal interest was the report that 80 percent of the autistic children, regardless of whether they had acquired visual self-recognition, showed completely neutral affect upon inspecting their self-images throughout the mirror and rouge procedure. This affect finding is especially relevant, as it suggests that these children may have negative and/or shameful feelings about themselves (cf. Erikson 1950).

Goals of This Chapter

Despite the dearth of experimental investigations of the development of the self during the transition from infancy to childhood in childhood disorders and risk conditions, much of the existing work has focused on the organization and integration of multiple domains of functioning upon the emergence and consolidation of self-system processes. For the past decade, guided by the organizational perspective (Cicchetti and Sroufe 1978; Sroufe, in this volume), we have investigated the development and coherence of the self system in two groups of high-risk conditions, children with Down syndrome and maltreated children. In this chapter, we present the results of these experiments in order to expand, challenge, and affirm existing theories of the development of the self during the transition from infancy to childhood and to enhance our understanding of the developmental organization of these two "experiments of nature" (Bronfenbrenner 1979). These conditions were chosen because they vary in the relative significance that child-specific (biological) versus parent-specific (environmental) influences play in the ontogenesis of the self. Together, Down syndrome and child maltreatment define a continuum in terms of the hypothesized relative contribution that reproductive (genetic and constitutional) and caretaking (parental and environmental) casualty factors make to maladaptation (Sameroff and Chandler 1975). Finally, we provide suggestions for how our knowledge of the organization of the self system in these atypical populations of children can inform the design and timely provision of intervention services (see Cicchetti and Toth 1987; Cicchetti, Toth, and Bush 1988).

The Organizational Perspective

The organizational perspective defines development as a series of qualitative reorganizations, among and within behavioral and biological systems, which take place by means of differentiation and hierarchical integration (Atlan 1981; Cicchetti 1990; Pattee 1973; Simon 1962; Sroufe, in this volume; Varela 1981). This "orthogenetic" principle (Werner 1948) may be viewed as a solution to the problem of the individual's continuous adaptation to the environment and to the question of how integrity of function may be preserved in the face of change (Dell 1982; Guidano 1987; Varela 1976a, 1976b). Continuity in functioning can be maintained via hierarchical integration, despite rapid constitutional changes and biobehavioral shifts (Block and Block 1980; Sackett et al. 1981; Sroufe 1979b). Variables at many levels of analysis—including genetic, constitutional, neurobiological, biochemical, behavioral, psychological, environmental, and sociological—determine the nature of these reorganizations. Moreover, these variables are conceived as exerting reciprocal influences upon one another.

Normal development is defined in terms of a series of interlocking socioemotional, cognitive, social-cognitive, and representational competencies. Competence at one period of development tends to make the individual broadly adjusted to his or her environment and increases the likelihood that future competence will occur (Sroufe, in this volume; Sroufe and Rutter 1984). Moreover, normal development is marked by the integration of earlier competencies into later modes of functioning. It follows then that early adaptation tends to promote later adaptation and integration.

Pathological development, in contrast, may be seen either as a lack of integration of the socioemotional, cognitive, social-cognitive, and representational competencies that are important to the achievement of adaptation at a particular developmental level, or as an integration of pathological structures (Cicchetti and Schneider-Rosen 1986; Kaplan 1966). In keeping with the organizational perspective, it follows that an early perturbation in functioning may result in the emergence of much larger future disturbances.

This organizational model also holds when issues are explored that relate directly to the development of the self. Specifically, if competencies which are preliminary to the emergence of the self are negotiated successfully, the child is more likely to move through the self transitions adaptively. Conversely, difficulties in self development are likely to emerge if earlier developmental challenges have been failed. In this chapter, we will explore this organizational perspective on the self as it relates to the transition from infancy to childhood in children with Down syndrome and in children who have been maltreated.

The Organization of Development in
Children with Down Syndrome

A basic regulative principle of the organizational perspective on development is that the ontogenetic process occurs through the reorganization and restructuring of abilities into new behavioral or biological structures (Cicchetti and Schneider-Rosen 1986; Sroufe 1979a; Sroufe, in this volume; Werner 1948; Werner and Kaplan 1963). Such restructuring is considered to be guided by the principle of orthogenesis, which depicts the developmental process as unfolding from simple, undifferentiated forms to highly articulated structures and systems (Werner 1957).

In most cases, the organizational perspective appears to be a useful framework for conceptualizing the development of self abilities and characteristics of infants and children with Down syndrome during the transition period (Cicchetti and Beeghly, 1990; Cicchetti and Pogge-Hesse 1982). Within the various behavioral domains (socioemotional, cognitive, linguistic, and representational) examined to date, development appears to be guided by the orthogenetic principle. Although the pace of development in children with Down syndrome is much slower than in nonhandicapped, normally developing individuals, children with Down syndrome display increasingly more complex behaviors and thought structures as they mature and continue to interact with the animate and inanimate world. Their responses to the world change as their representation of the world becomes more differentiated and abstract. Similar to normally developing persons, individuals with Down syndrome become less stimulus bound and more active in shaping and determining their interactions with the world.

Additionally, the development of infants and young children with Down syndrome across a variety of domains follows a developmental course similar to that of nonhandicapped, normally developing persons. Furthermore, when developmental level is taken into consideration, children with Down syndrome generally appear to progress through the same sequences and stages of development as normally developing children. Development occurs in an orderly fashion, with children from both populations acquiring increasingly more complex skills (Cicchetti and Beeghly, 1990).

Finally, in terms of the structuring and integration of abilities, infants and children with Down syndrome demonstrate a coherence in their development which in most cases parallels that of normally developing, nonhandicapped individuals. The underlying changes in the child's ability to evaluate and mentally represent the world are concomitantly reflected in socioemotional, cognitive, linguistic, and representational systems. Such relationships suggest that their development is highly organized and coherent (Beeghly and Cicchetti

1987a; Cicchetti 1990; Cicchetti and Beeghly, 1990; Cicchetti and Pogge-Hesse 1982; Cicchetti and Sroufe 1976, 1978).

However, despite the presence of these similarities, several differences also are apparent across different domains. For example, the intensity of reactions emitted by the child with Down syndrome is weaker than that of normally developing children of the same chronological age or developmental level. Although the organization of affect and cognitive systems is similar for both populations of children, qualitative differences still persist. These differences have been tied to more fundamental differences at the level of the central nervous system (Ganiban, Wagner, and Cicchetti, 1990). Additional differences have been noted in the organization of linguistic skills, pragmatics, and cognitive development. In these cases, syntactic and vocabulary skills develop at a slower pace than pragmatic and cognitive skills (Beeghly and Cicchetti 1987a; Mundy et al. 1988). Thus, when children with Down syndrome are matched with nonhandicapped, normally developing children on the basis of developmental level, their syntax and vocabulary are significantly poorer than those of their normally developing peers.

Clearly then, while commonalities in the organization of behavioral systems exist between nonhandicapped children and those with Down syndrome, differences also have emerged. As we direct our attention toward the development of the self system in children with Down syndrome, we expect a similar scenario. That is, while certain organizational principles such as coherence of development and hierarchical integration of competencies will hold, we also anticipate qualitative differences in self-system development.

The Development of the Self System

The organizational perspective, with its emphasis on the study of interacting behavioral and biological systems and on uncovering the relation between normal and atypical forms of development, provides an excellent theoretical framework for conceptualizing research on the ontogenesis of the self system during the transition period from infancy to childhood in youngsters with Down syndrome. The toddler's emerging acquisition of a sense of self, seen as encompassing both cognitive and emotional dimensions, is a major developmental task (Lewis and Brooks-Gunn 1979; Stern 1985). The evolution of this ability enables the toddler to comprehend environmental occurrences more fully. Moreover, a well-differentiated sense of self provides the toddler with increased understanding of personal functioning as a separate and independent being. Issues of body management emerge from the context of the mother-infant relationship into the realm of autonomous function (Sroufe, in this volume). The infant becomes increasingly invested in self-managing due to the emergence of new cognitive and motor competencies, as well as to more sophisticated notions about self and other. Empathic acts also begin to emerge at this time, again a manifestation of the realization that the self can have an impact on others (Zahn-Waxler and Radke-Yarrow 1982). Caretaker sensitivity and ability to tolerate the toddler's strivings for autonomy, as well as the capacity to set age-appropriate limits, are integral to the successful resolution of this issue (Sroufe 1979b, in this volume). In contrast, intolerance for infant initiative may hinder the development of autonomy. Caretakers who tend to feel rejected by the infants' increasing independence and/or overwhelmed by their infant's actively initiated demands may inhibit the development of the child's age-appropriate independence (Mahler et al. 1975).

Visual Self-Recognition

In normal infants at approximately eighteen to twenty-four months of age, visual self-recognition and the development of shame have been found to coincide with the emergence of autonomy and positive valuation of the self (Lewis and Brooks-Gunn 1979; see also Erikson 1950). When inspecting their rouge-marked noses in a mirror, most normal infants evidence their self-knowledge by touching their own noses while examining their reflections in the mirror. The emergence of self-directed behaviors is first observed at fifteen to eighteen months of age and is common by twenty-one to twenty-four months (see Butterworth, in this volume).

Mans, Cicchetti, and Sroufe (1978) found that when infants with Down syndrome achieved the appropriate cognitive developmental level, they too showed the emergence of self-recognition. For example, prior to twenty-three months of age, only those infants with Down syndrome having a nearly normal level of cognitive functioning displayed evidence of visual self-recognition by touching their rouge-marked noses when observing themselves in a mirror. Not until age thirty-four months and beyond did virtually all toddlers with Down syndrome show self-recognition. Similarly, the affective reactions of these infants to their rouge-marked reflections paralleled those shown by normal infants. The predominant affective reaction of the younger infants was a change from positive affect before the application of the rouge, to one of being sober or puzzled afterwards. Older toddlers showed surprise reactions or increased positive affect after the rouge. Thus, their affective reactions (such as nose touching) reflected their differential understanding of this event. Moreover, the positive affect accompanying their visual self-recognition suggests that children with Down syndrome feel positively about themselves.

In a related study, Hill and Tomlin (1981) observed the responses of two groups of preverbal retarded toddlers to watching marked or unmarked television images of themselves. One group comprised toddlers with Down syndrome; the other was a multihandicapped group, including toddlers with anoxia, rubella, and seizure disorders. Hill and Tomlin found that the twelve toddlers with Down syndrome all showed the curiosity and self-conscious behaviors that characterize nonhandicapped babies during the second year of life. Moreover, eleven of the twelve toddlers recognized their television images. In contrast, fewer than half of the multiply handicapped toddlers evinced visual self-recognition, and their affective reactions were like those of normal one-year-olds. In both groups of toddlers, Hill and Tomlin reported that those who could recognize themselves had all attained mental ages comparable to normal toddlers who manifested that aspect of self-knowledge.

Similarly, Loveland (1987) found that young children with Down syndrome learned to find things, including themselves, in a mirror in a manner that strikingly paralleled that of normally developing children of comparable developmental levels. Loveland observed many similarities between the normal and Down syndrome groups, including the use of "incorrect strategies," behavioral reactions to the mirror, and pattern of task solution. In addition, Loveland concluded that the child with Down syndrome may not proceed along this developmental pathway in the same fashion as a normal youngster. She proffered this suggestion because the two groups employed different means, strategies, or exploratory tendencies in front of the mirror.

Further Self-Other Differentiation

Play and language are two mediums which normal children use to represent their early conceptions of relationships and to reflect their growing awareness of self and other (Bretherton 1984b). This developmental change typically occurs and becomes more differentiated during the transition from infancy to toddlerhood. During this developmental shift, children become increasingly knowledgeable about themselves as agents and recipients of actions (Fenson 1984; Kagan 1981).

Nonlinguistic Representations of the Self: Findings from Symbolic Play Studies

Several investigations conducted on the development of play in children with Down syndrome have documented that these youngsters progress through sequences of symbolic play that are similar to those of nonhandicapped children (Hill and McCune-Nicolich 1981; Motti, Cicchetti, and Sroufe 1983). Unfortunately, the symbolic-play scale employed in these studies has ceiling limitations for children who have entered into preoperational thought (Piaget 1962). In efforts to address this problem, several investigators have constructed and validated a variety of more advanced play scales, which tap separate aspects of symbolic-play maturity (e.g., agent use, role representation, object representation, complexity of action schemes). These scales have been utilized in studies of normal children (e.g., Belsky and Most 1981;

Bretherton 1984a; Elder and Pederson 1978; Fein and Apfel 1979; Fenson and Ramsay 1980; Overton and Jackson 1973; Rubin and Wolf 1979; Wolf 1982). (For reviews, see also Bretherton 1984b; Rubin, Fein, and Vandenberg 1983.) However, these more complex sequences of symbolic play have yet to be examined concurrently in the same investigation.

Beeghly, Weiss-Perry, and Cicchetti (1990; see also Beeghly and Cicchetti 1987a) examined the ontogenesis of these multiple aspects of symbolic play simultaneously in a cross-sectional sample of children with Down syndrome (all diagnosed by chromosome count) and two comparison groups of nonhandicapped children matched for mental-age (MA) and chronological age (CA). The children were split into two groups based on MA equivalents for purposes of statistical analyses. In the younger cohort, fifteen children with Down syndrome (eight boys and seven girls), average CA = forty-one months, range = twenty-seven to fifty-six months) were matched individually to fifteen nonretarded children (average CA = twenty-two months, range = seventeen to twenty-six months) for sex and MA as derived from the Bayley mental scales (Bayley 1969). MA matches were within a one-month range. Average MA for both groups was twenty-three months (range = seventeen to thirty months). These children with Down syndrome also were matched individually for sex and CA to a second set of nonhandicapped children. In the older cohort, an additional fifteen children with Down syndrome (eight boys and seven girls, average CA = seventy-four months, range = sixty-eight to ninety-three months) were matched individually to fifteen nonhandicapped children (average CA = thirty-eight months, range = twenty-eight to fifty months) for sex and MA (average MA = forty-eight months, range = thirty-four to sixty-one months). As in the younger cohort, these children were matched within one month of their MA.

Weiss, Beeghly, and Cicchetti (1985) developed a coding system that combined four different measures of symbolic play which have been used independently in the literature. Comparisons of children with Down syndrome's relative competencies and problems on multiple dimensions of play, including both structural dimensions (such as scheme complexity and decontextualization of object use [e.g., object substitutions]) and more socially relevant aspects of play (such as independent agency and social role representations), were of particular interest to us. These dimensions were conceived as being analogous to the structural and social aspects of early communicative development (e.g., mean length of utterance (MLU), pragmatics), respectively.

Children's play was coded from transcripts of mother-child free-play behavior. Average reliability (intercoder agreement)) for the transcripts was 93 percent for play and language content (range = 89 percent to 100 percent). Each episode of symbolic play was then scored for level of symbolic maturity on four separate play scales, which were derived from empirical data reported in the literature. The first scale assessed the increasing complexity and integration of action schemes, ranging from single schemes to scheme combinations of hierarchically integrated, multischemed play. Two scales were concerned with role representation, one focusing on social roles depicted in play with small figures (replica play) and the other focusing on play with human partners (sociodramatic play). Both of these scales ranged from self-related pretend play to the integration of roles of several actors. The fourth scale focused on the tendency of the child to utilize objects in a decontextualized fashion (object substitution). This fourth scale ranged from the use of objects in a prototypical manner (i.e., using a cup as a cup), to simple object substitutions, and finally to gestural miming and verbal ideation. For purposes of comparison, we also included Nicolich's (1977) play scheme as a fifth play scale.

Two scores were derived for each play scale: the highest level of spontaneous symbolic play observed at least twice and the average level of play (as indexed by the weighted mean of the summed spontaneous play scores). In addition, the density (number of connected symbolic play schemes per play bout) and the complexity (number of different connected symbolic schemes per play bout) were measured.

The play behavior of the children with Down syndrome was compared to the MA- and CA-matched cohorts. Correlations of play behavior with MA, CA, and MLU also were assessed within each child group. Age-related differences in symbolic play behavior between the younger and older cohorts also were examined.

Between-Group Comparisons

Table 1 contains a description of the sample characteristics and the mean levels of symbolic play performance for both groups of children.

YOUNGER COHORT.   When compared to their CA-matched controls, the children with Down syndrome exhibited play that was significantly less complex, dense, and mature on each of the play scales. In contrast, they did *not* differ significantly from their cognitively comparable (i.e., MA-matched) controls on any aspect of symbolic play assessed.

OLDER COHORT.   Slightly different findings emerged for the older sample of children. As with their younger counterparts, older children with Down syndrome did not differ significantly from their MA matches on the highest level of play emitted for either the action complexity, agent use, or role enactment play scales. They also did not differ from their comparisons on most measures of play density and complexity. The only exception to this was the total number of symbolic schemes produced, where they generated

Table 14.1 Nonlinguistic Representations of Self and Other during Symbolic Play by Children with Down Syndrome (DS) and Nonhandicapped (NH) Children (expressed as mean)

	Younger Cohort[a]				Older Cohort[b]		
	Children with DS	NH MLU[c] Matches	NH MA[c] Matches	NH CA[c] Matches	Children with DS	NH MLU Matches	NH MA Matches
Child characteristics							
MLU (in morphemes)	1.15	1.14	2.50***	4.88***	1.84	1.87	3.80***
MA (in months)	27.0	20.6**	26.0	56.2***	44.2	27.9***	43.9
CA (in months)	48.5	19.5***	21.0***	47.5	75.0	24.0***	33.4***
Symbolic-play performance							
Portrayal of pretend roles during replica play							
High play level	4.4	3.1**	4.0	6.6***	6.0	5.1**	5.9
Average play level	2.8	2.2*	2.9	3.5***	3.5	2.7**	3.1
Portrayal of pretend roles during sociodramatic play							
High play level	4.6	3.4**	4.6	7.3***	6.5	5.4**	6.0
Average play level	3.2	2.9*	3.1	4.1***	3.8	2.6**	3.4

Note: Children with DS in each cohort were compared to each set of matched NH children, using pairwise *t*-tests.

[a]Younger cohort = Children with DS in early stage I of syntactic development (MLU-1.01–1.49).

[b]Older cohort = Children with DS in late stage I of syntactic development (MLU-1.50–1.99).

[c]CA = Chronological age; MA = Mental age; MLU = Mean level of utterance.

*$p < .05$; **$p < .01$; ***$p < .001$.

significantly more schemes overall than did their nonhandicapped controls, although the groups did not differ in the total number of *different* schemes emitted. Older children with Down syndrome also were significantly *less* advanced than their MA-matched comparisons on all play scales in terms of their *average* (but not highest) scores and on the object substitution scale for all scores (average and highest). Results from the between-group comparisons for each cohort also are presented graphically in figures 1 through 4.

WITHIN-GROUP COMPARISONS.   Correlations between play variables and indices of child development (i.e., MA, CA, and MLU) also were examined within child groups. For each group of children in both cohorts, symbolic-play variables were correlated significantly with both MA and MLU but less strongly with CA.

Somewhat different patterns of correlations were revealed in the older cohort. As in the younger group, both the children with Down syndrome and their MA-matched controls had more significant correlations of play with MA controls than with CA (seven versus two and nine versus six, respectively, out of sixteen). However, different patterns were observed with respect to MLU. The MA-comparable controls in the older cohort had eleven out of sixteen play variables correlated significantly with MLU, whereas the children with Down syndrome had only four out of sixteen. These differences may be due

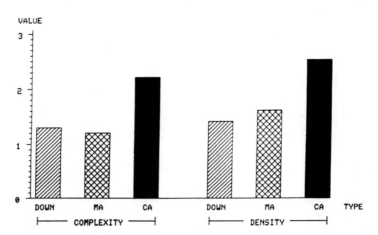

Figure 14.1. Symbolic-play density and complexity: Younger cohort. CA = Chronological-age matched comparisons; DOWN = Down syndrome; MA = Mental age matched comparisons.

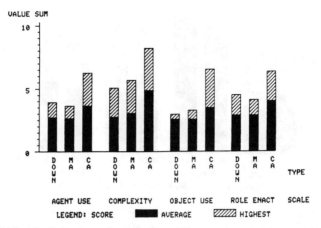

Figure 14.2. Symbolic-play scale performance: Younger cohort. CA = Chronological-age matched comparisons; DOWN = Down syndrome; MA = Mental-age matched comparisons.

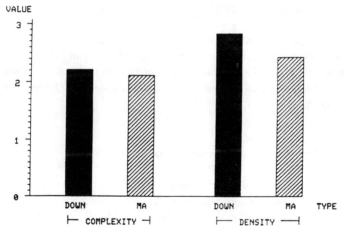

Figure 14.3. Symbolic-play density and complexity: Older cohort. CA = Chronological-age matched comparisons; DOWN = Down syndrome; MA = Mental-age matched comparisons.

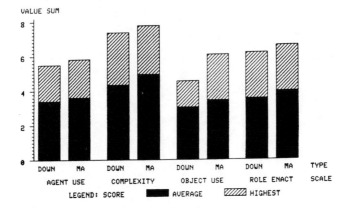

Figure 14.4.   Symbolic-play scale performance: Older cohort. CA = Chronological-age matched comparisons; DOWN = Down syndrome; MA = Mental-age matched comparisons.

to the fact that the MLUs of the older children with Down syndrome were considerably more restricted in range than those of the nonhandicapped children. These findings attest to the increasing dissociation of syntactic development and other forms of symbolic development (play, communicative skills) with advancing age in children with Down syndrome.

AGE-RELATED CHANGES IN SYMBOLIC PLAY.   Age-related changes in play also were examined by comparing the younger and older subsamples of children within each child group. Results indicated that children in the older cohort had significantly higher means on all play variables than did children in the younger cohort.

Early Linguistic Representations of the Self

In addition to symbolic play as an index of the emerging sense of self in children with Down syndrome, language also provides an important measure of self-representation (in this volume, see also Bates; Radke-Yarrow et al.; Snow; Wolf). Self-related utterances occur most commonly when children provide verbal descriptions of their ongoing activities (Bates, in this volume; Kagan 1981). Moreover, the use of self-descriptive language becomes increasingly decontextualized, with children first talking primarily about themselves in the here and now and then discussing the behavior and internal states of other, nonpresent individuals or of hypothetical situations.

Children also become increasingly facile at labeling the emotional states, intentions, and cognitions of both themselves and others (Bretherton and Beeghly 1982; Bretherton et al. 1986) and begin to use their own name and personal pronouns appropriately (see Bates, in this volume).

In a further investigation of the ontogenesis of early social understanding, Beeghly and associates (1990) assessed in children with Down syndrome the linguistic representations of self and other during two early stages of language development: early and late stage I (MLU = 1.01–1.49; 1.50–1.99, respectively). The communicative behaviors of the children were observed during a free-play session and a picture book session. The functioning of the children with Down syndrome was compared to three groups of nonhandicapped children: one matched for MLU, one for MA, and one for CA.

Language measures were derived from detailed transcripts of mother-child language and included indices of general linguistic maturity (e.g., vocabulary diversity, MLU, frequency of utterances) and measures of self-related language (e.g., proportion of statements describing actions and internal states of self and others; number of different internal state labels and personal pronouns; degree of contextualization of use of internal state language). The ability of children to use an internal state word for both self and other also was scored. Intercoder reliability was high, ranging from .84 to 1.00 for the various measures.

The results indicated that children with Down syndrome exhibited similar but delayed sequences of self-related language, compared to the nonhandicapped children. Initially, children represented themselves symbolically; with increasing age and cognitive maturity, their language became more decentered, decontextualized, and integrated. Only the most cognitively advanced children used language to represent self and other in hypothetical or nonpresent situations. Table 2 contains the means of all language variables as well as the sample characteristics for each group of children studied.

Within-Group Comparisons

As evidenced in table 2, comparisons of the linguistic performance of children in early versus late stage I revealed that both the children with Down syndrome and their MLU controls in late stage I produced significantly more frequent, complex, differentiated, and decontextualized self language than did children in early stage I. The proportion of statements describing self actions and the internal states of self and other increased significantly from early to late stage I. The quantity of different internal state words and personal pronouns also increased, as did more general indices of children's language production. Children in late stage I also were more able to utilize internal state words for both self and other and to employ internal state language in a more decontextualized fashion. In addition, use of self-related language was

Table 14.2 Early Language about Self and Other Produced by Children with Down syndrome (DS) and Nonhandicapped (NH) Children (expressed as mean)

	Younger Cohort[a]				Older Cohort[b]		
	Children with DS	NH MLU[c] Matches	NH MA[c] Matches	NH CA[c] Matches	Children with DS	NH MLU Matches	NH MA Matches
Child characteristics							
MLU (in morphemes)	1.15	1.14	2.50****	4.88****	1.84	1.87	3.80****
MA (in months)	27.0	20.6***	26.8	56.2****	44.2	27.9****	43.9
CA (in months)	48.5	19.5****	21.0****	47.5	75.0	24.0****	33.4****
Language variables							
Total utterances	156.2	75.0***	138.7	304.6****	309.7	181.0****	245.9***
Number of different words produced	30.0	21.6	74.0****	216.9****	131.7	94.9**	179.7**
Number of different personal pronouns	1.3	1.3	3.5***	9.3****	5.6	4.3	7.5*
Number of different internal state labels	3.0	3.5	7.0**	18.0****	8.0	6.0	13.5**
Percent descriptions about actions of self	8.0	5.0	15.0**	25.0****	12.0	15.0	20.0**
Percent descriptions about others' actions	23.0	3.0**	25.0	23.0	22.0	14.0**	25.0
Percent utterances about internal states	4.0	9.0	18.0***	21.0****	8.0	11.0	18.0**
Self-other attribution flexibility score	3.0	3.0	9.0***	23.9****	9.0	8.2	16.6****
Decontextualization of use of internal state language	0.4	0.5	2.0**	10.0****	2.4	3.2	6.0***

Note: Children with DS in each cohort were compared to each set of matched NH children, using pairwise *t*-tests.

[a]Younger cohort = Children with DS in early stage I of syntactic development (MLU-1.01–1.49).

[b]Older cohort = Children with DS in late stage I of syntactic development (MLU-1.50–1.99).

[c]CA = Chronological age; MA = Mental age; MLU = Mean level of utterance.

*$p < .10$; **$p < .05$; ***$p < .01$; ****$p < .001$.

correlated significantly with both MA and MLU in children with Down syndrome and in the nonhandicapped MLU controls.

Between-Group Comparisons

For the majority of the language variables, the children with Down syndrome performed at a level similar to their MLU controls at both linguistic substages (see table 2). Although the use of self-related language was correlated significantly with MA for all children, the children with Down syndrome produced significantly less mature self language than did their nonhandicapped, MA-matched comparisons. The one exception to this pattern was that children with Down syndrome described the actions of others (but not self) proportionately more often than did their MLU controls. Thus, the ability to talk about the actions and internal states of self and other is more delayed for children with Down syndrome than one might expect based on their level of cognitive development.

In a related investigation, Beeghly, Bretherton, and Mervis (1986) found that mothers of prelinguistic children with Down syndrome employed proportionately fewer internal state utterances and fewer different internal state words than did mothers of MLU-, MA-, and CA-matched comparison children. Moreover, when they did use internal state language, they attributed internal states significantly less often to social agents other than the child than did the mothers in the comparison groups. In addition, they referred to the cognitive states of their children significantly less frequently than did the mothers in any control group.

A possible explanation for these group differences is that mothers of prelinguistic children with Down syndrome may have thought that their children needed more direction. By providing such additional direction, the mothers would necessarily utilize less internal state language with their children. Bell and Harper's (1977) suggestion that an overly directive interactive style is a control strategy commonly used by parents of underactive children to bring them closer to cultural norms for children's behavior supports this conceptualization. Cross, Nienhuys, and Kirkman (1984) also reported that directiveness often accompanies the linguistic styles of mothers of handicapped children.

Interestingly, Beeghly, Bretherton, and Mervis (1986) found that the mothers of the children with Down syndrome also were unique in that they used significantly more internal state words referring to their children's physiological states than did the mothers of the MLU- and MA-matched controls. There was a tendency for these mothers to use more physiological words than even the mothers of the CA-comparable control children. A content analysis of these utterances revealed that the mothers of the children with Down syndrome employed physiological words primarily to refer to their children's state of arousal (e.g., "You're not very alert today"). In contrast, the mothers of the control children almost never referred to this particular type of physiological state but used physiological terms more often to refer to toys during pretend play (e.g., "Is dolly sleepy?"). In view of the frequently noted arousal difficulties in children with Down syndrome (Cicchetti, Ganiban, and Barnett, in press; Cicchetti and Sroufe 1976, 1978; Ganiban et al., 1990; Thompson et al. 1985), these results are not at all surprising. Moreover, because of these arousal modulation problems, caregivers of infants and children with Down syndrome may need to take an increasingly active role in promoting affectively effective stimulation (Cicchetti and Sroufe 1978; Cicchetti et al. 1988).

Now that self-system development has been explored in children with Down syndrome, we turn to the study of the acquisition of self in a very different group, children who have experienced some form of maltreatment. We believe that because of the contrast this group provides, it is an important population for enhancing our understanding of the mechanisms operative in self development. Whereas children with Down syndrome struggle primarily with factors related to reproductive casualty, children who have been maltreated illustrate the role of caregiving casualty.

The Development of the Self System in Maltreated Children

Bowlby ([1969] 1982) argued that working models (internal representations) of the self, related to self-esteem and self-concept, develop in parallel with working models of attachment figures: children with sensitive caregivers come to view themselves as worthy of care, whereas children with unresponsive caregivers learn to see themselves as unlovable. The research on patterns of interaction between maltreating parents and their children provides ample evidence of chronic insensitivity on the part of these parents (Aragona and Eyberg 1981; Crittenden 1981; Lyons-Ruth et al. 1987; Trickett and Susman 1988). Similarly, several investigators have demonstrated that the vast majority of maltreated children form insecure attachment relationships with their primary caregivers (Crittenden and Ainsworth 1989; Schneider-Rosen et al. 1985). Furthermore, a high percentage of these insecure relationships are disorganized/disoriented (type D) (Carlson et al. 1989; Crittenden 1988), a recently discovered type of attachment characterized by the child's inner conflict between approaching and avoiding the caregiver, who evolutionarily speaking represents a source of security but in the case of maltreatment represents a source of danger. (See Main and

Solomon, 1990, for a detailed description of the disorganized/disoriented category.) Just as research has found maltreated children to be at great risk for forming insecure attachments, the data support that they also have correspondingly impaired self-images (as would be predicted by the organizational perspective). In essence, because the attachment relationship has been adversely affected due to negative and unpredictable parent-child interactions, maltreated children lack a solid foundation upon which to begin to build their sense of self.

During the past decade, we have investigated several domains of self development in maltreated children. In all of our studies, the maltreated children were legally documented as being maltreated, with most children experiencing two or more of the following maltreatment subtypes: physical abuse, emotional abuse, physical neglect, and sexual abuse (Cicchetti and Rizley 1981). In fact, research has found that more than one subtype is present in most cases of maltreatment (Cicchetti and Carlson 1989). Comparison children, demographically matched with the maltreated children for sex, socioeconomic background, and age, had never appeared on any child abuse registry. In the following sections, we discuss the results of our work on the ontogenesis of the self system in maltreated children during the transition from infancy to childhood.

Visual Self-Recognition

Schneider-Rosen and Cicchetti (1984) assessed the capacity of a sample of nineteen-month-old maltreated and demographically matched nonmaltreated toddlers to develop visual self-recognition. The standardized mirror and rouge paradigm was utilized to assess the presence of visual self-recognition (Lewis and Brooks-Gunn 1979). Schneider-Rosen and Cicchetti found differences between these groups of toddlers in the organization of the relationship between attachment and visual self-recognition. In the comparison group, the quality of attachment and the capacity for visual self-recognition were related strongly; specifically, 90 percent of the securely attached nonmaltreated youngsters recognized their rouge-altered mirror-images. Conversely, in the group of maltreated youngsters, a relationship between current attachment quality and the presence of self-recognition did not emerge. In addition, the maltreated children were more likely to display either neutral or negative affect upon viewing their rouge-marked images in the mirror. The comparison children, however, tended to express a positive affective reaction (such as smiling) upon recognizing themselves in the mirror. While it is somewhat speculative, the exhibition of negative affect by maltreated toddlers might be an early precursor of a generalized low sense of self-worth.

Further Self-Other Differentiation

In a related vein, Gersten et al. (1986) found that attachment security in both maltreated and nonmaltreated twenty-five-month-olds was significantly related to variations in language performance. Not only did securely attached toddlers consistently manifest more elaborate vocabularies but they also employed syntactically more complex language than did insecurely attached youngsters. Most relevant for our purposes, a significantly greater proportion of the utterances of securely attached toddlers was directed toward describing the ongoing activities and feelings of themselves and of other persons.

In a further extension of this work, Beeghly and Cicchetti (1987b) examined the effect of early child maltreatment and quality of mother-child attachment on the emergence of internal state language in children from lower-socioeconomic status (SES) groups. The communicative abilities of the maltreated and nonmaltreated children were assessed longitudinally at three age periods: twenty-four, thirty, and thirty-six months. During a thirty-minute free-play sequence, the complexity, diversity, content, and attributional focus of children's utterances about internal states were coded from videotapes of mother-child interaction. Measures of general linguistic maturity also were examined, and the quality of mother-child attachment was coded from "Strange Situation" behavior filmed when children were twenty-four months of age (see Schneider-Rosen et al. 1985).

Results indicated that insecurely attached children at all age periods and maltreated children at thirty and thirty-six months produced less mature internal state language than did their nonmaltreated, securely attached counterparts. At each age, securely attached children talked more about internal states, had a more elaborate internal state vocabulary, were more likely to discuss the internal states of self and other, and were less context bound in their language use than the insecurely attached children, whether maltreated or not. Additionally, securely attached toddlers mentioned emotions and affective behavior more frequently and talked more about ability and obligation but less about sensory perception than did their insecurely attached counterparts. Beeghly and Cicchetti (1987b) also reported several main effects of child maltreatment history on language production. For example, maltreated children used proportionately fewer internal state words, attributed internal states to fewer social agents, and were more context bound than were their nonmaltreated peers.

Beeghly, Carlson, and Cicchetti (1986) investigated the internal state language of a group of forty thirty-month-old maltreated and nonmaltreated children. The diversity, content, and attributional focus of children's internal state words were coded from videotapes of mother-child and stranger-child interaction in four contexts. Maternal reports of children's internal state language and indices of general linguistic maturity also were assessed.

Beeghly and her colleagues found that the content and attributional focus of low-SES nonmaltreated children's internal state language were largely similar to that reported for comparably aged middle-SES children. Maltreated toddlers, however, utilized fewer different internal state words, attributed internal states to fewer social agents, and were more context bound than their lower-SES nonmaltreated peers.

Analyses of the maternal interview data generated similar patterns of results. Maltreating mothers reported that their children produced fewer internal state words and attributed internal states to fewer social agents, as compared to reports by mothers who had not maltreated their children. These results provided added support for the observational findings.

The results of the maternal-language interview revealed that, with very few exceptions, maltreated toddlers produced less internal state words than did middle-SES maltreated youngsters of the same age (see Bretherton and Beeghly 1982). In contrast, the percentages of lower-SES nonmaltreated children reported by their mothers to use different categories of internal state language were markedly similar to those reported for middle-SES children. In support of the validity of the maternal interview data for use with low-SES mothers, reported child internal state language was correlated significantly with observed child internal state language production (average $R = .50$).

Coster and associates (1989) investigated the communicative behavior of thirty-one-month-old maltreated toddlers and their mothers in both a semi-structured and an unstructured free-play setting. Maltreated and demographically matched nonmaltreated comparison toddlers (N = twenty) were assessed on mean length of utterance, receptive vocabulary, functional communication, and conversational relatedness. The mothers' language also was examined on functional communication, contingency, efforts to elicit response, and types of questions asked.

The data revealed that maltreated toddlers had shorter MLUs, used less descriptive speech (particularly about their own activities and feelings), and offered fewer utterances that were relevant to the ongoing mother-child dialogue. Moreover, maltreated toddlers engaged in shorter episodes of sustained dialogue. Allen and Wasserman (1985) contend that the origins of these language delays and impairments stem from patterns of maternal unavailability and ignoring. Coster and her collaborators (1989) found that the language of the mothers did not differ in the two groups. In the maltreated group, however, these was a positive relationship between the mother's talk about internal states and the child's self-related speech.

The confluence of these findings on the use of internal state and emotion language, as well as on the use of self-related language more generally, suggests that maltreated toddlers evidence difficulties in self development during the transition period from infancy to early childhood. In contrast, closely matched nonmaltreated toddlers display organization in their self development. The coherence manifested in the self system of the lower-SES comparisons emphasizes that the negative effects which maltreatment exerts upon self development are independent of those risk factors commonly associated with lower-SES membership.

Perceived Competence in School-Age Maltreated Children

Vondra, Barnett, and Cicchetti (1989) examined the impact of child maltreatment and grade level on perceptions of competence. First- through third-graders (N = seventy-six) and fourth- through sixth-graders (N = twenty-eight), primarily from low-SES families, served as the subjects of their investigation. Approximately 56 percent of the children in each group (forty-four younger, fourteen older) were from families indicated by state records as receiving social services due to documented child abuse and/or neglect. The other half of the children came from welfare families for whom there was no documented evidence of child maltreatment. Comparison of the two groups revealed that the children were matched evenly on a number of family demographic variables, including maternal education, welfare dependency, and presence or absence of a spouse or partner in the home.

Children in first through third grades were administered the *Pictorial Scale of Perceived Competence and Social Acceptance for Young Children* (Harter and Pike 1984). This self-report instrument assesses four domains of children's functioning: cognitive competence, physical competence, peer acceptance, and maternal acceptance. For each item, the child is presented with a pair of pictured children, one of whom is described as a child who is able to perform the pictured task competently (e.g., "good at climbing," "knows lots of things at school") or has the socially desired attributes (e.g., "has lots of friends to play with"). The other pictured child is described as lacking in the particular competency. After children select the pictured child "most like them," they are asked to further specify their choice by deciding between "always" or "usually." Hence, scores for individual items range from one to four, with high scores indicating greater perceived competence.

Children in fourth through sixth grade completed the comparable *Self-Perception Profile for Children* (Harter 1985). Items on this scale were read aloud by the experimenter, but children marked their own responses. Six-item subscales assessed five distinct domains of functioning: scholastic competence, social acceptance, athletic competence, physical appearance, and behavioral conduct. A sixth subscale, global self worth, also was included. Item format paralleled that of the younger-age version, and internal consistency of the subscales ranged from 0.71 (on the behavioral conduct subscale) to 0.86 (on the athletic competence subscale) (Harter 1985). Subscales from these two measures have been found to correlate with theoretically meaningful external criteria, including preference for cognitive challenge (Harter and Pike 1984), attachment status (Cassidy 1988), and academic functioning (Connell and Ilardi 1987).

Vondra and her colleagues (1989) found that, in general, younger maltreated children (first–third grade) presented themselves as being even more competent/accepted than same-age, low-income comparison children and also as more competent than they actually were (based on teacher ratings). This was especially true with regard to physical competence ratings. Whether this finding resulted from developmentally related inaccuracy of perception or from defensive posturing on the part of these children remains unclear.

Because the differences between ratings of maltreated and comparison children remained significant even when verbal intelligence and special-educational status were controlled statistically, they were presumably not due to global cognitive deficits on the part of maltreated children. Rather, it appears likely that socioemotional factors may have been involved, a possibility proposed by Zimet and Farley (1986) to account for inflated self-perceptions among children entering psychiatric treatment. One may hypothesize, for example, that these abused and neglected children needed to feel physical competence and control in a chaotic, uncontrollable home setting where physical needs may not have been met and physical punishment was frequent and severe. Describing oneself as physically competent and powerful and making unrealistic claims about one's physical prowess might be important strategies to develop a sense of personal control that is, in reality, very much lacking.

Also relevant to this rationale is the fact that the smallest mean difference between scores of maltreated and comparison children was in their ratings of maternal acceptance, the subscale on which the *largest* differences would be hypothesized. In fact, Harter and Pike (1984) reported the results of a small, unpublished study demonstrating that preschoolers maltreated by their fathers rated *father* acceptance significantly lower than did nonmaltreated classroom comparisons. On the other hand, young maltreated children may be especially prone to idealize qualities of themselves and of their *primary* attachment relationship. This has been found to be true among some adults with a history of child maltreatment (Hunter and Kihlstrom 1979; Main and Goldwyn 1984; Main, Kaplan, and Cassidy 1985). It therefore seems reasonable to hypothesize that young children may need to defend against rejecting behavior on the part of their primary attachment figure (see also Cassidy 1988; Cassidy and Kobak 1988); fewer defenses may be required when describing the behavior/ orientation of other attachment figures. Regardless, the failure to detect differences in ratings of maternal acceptance in the present study suggests that the maltreated children may have been denying disturbing aspects and/or exaggerating positive qualities of the mother-child relationship, in much the same way that they overstated their competencies.

Cassidy's (1988) study of attachment and the self system in six-year-olds reveals data consistent with this interpretation. "Perfection" in self-descriptions was found to be more characteristic of children evidencing an avoidant attachment relationship than of those with secure relationships. In her middle-SES sample, however, Cassidy found that subscales of the Harter measure correlated *positively* with behavioral ratings of security during reunion with mothers. Differences between Cassidy's sample and the present one in SES, pathology of relationships, and developmental level of the children may account for this notable discrepancy in results.

Hypotheses about the need for younger maltreated children to exaggerate their competencies are consistent with research conducted by Stipek (1981, 1984), indicating that young children tend to confuse real and ideal selves in their descriptions, and by Katz and Zigler (1967; see also Plummer and Graziano 1987), indicating that the discrepancy between real and ideal selves increases across the elementary and middle school years. In fact, it has been hypothesized that differences relating to maltreatment status are due to the fact that maltreated children lag behind in their socioemotional development and/or—perhaps as a consequence—are qualitatively different in their functioning (Aber and Allen 1987). Thus, we would expect to find that younger maltreated children would exhibit greater overlap between their real and ideal selves, whether from developmental or from pathological causes.

Findings from another study conducted in our laboratory and employing younger children suggest this may be the case. Aber and Allen (1987) examined data collected during two laboratory visits of ninety-three maltreated, sixty-seven low-income, and thirty middle-SES control children age four through eight years. They found a significant group effect on their empirically derived "secure readiness to learn" factor, defined as greater dependency, less novelty seeking, and lower cognitive competence. Maltreated children scored lower than low-income comparisons, who in turn scored lower than middle-income comparisons on factor scores based on measures of pictorial curiosity, variability seeking, verbal intelligence, and time spent on a simple, repetitive task in the company of a reinforcing adult.

These findings suggest that young maltreated children prefer the familiar over the novel, and what is readily solvable over what is challenging. Relations between behaviors of this kind and inflated perceived-competence scores in the current study suggest that young children who describe themselves as more competent/accepted than they are actually score *lower* on competence motivation. Interestingly, maltreated children appear to fall in this category more often than do low-income matched comparisons.

Vondra and her colleagues (1989), however, found that, by the time they reached fourth-sixth grade, maltreated children described themselves as *less* competent and accepted than did their lower-SES peers. The significant-age–maltreatment-status interaction effectively illustrated this noteworthy reversal in results. Since their teachers also rated the older maltreated children as less competent and accepted than their peers and since child scores did correlate with teacher ratings in late elementary school, these self-ratings appeared to be more accurate appraisals than those offered by younger maltreated children. As long as maltreated children are developmentally incapable of making effective social comparisons, an inflated self-image or a greater readiness to merge real and ideal views of the self may serve as useful defense mechanisms (Cassidy and Kobak 1988). By the time these children reach later elementary school, however, social comparisons may undermine such earlier efforts to preserve a positive sense of self. It is interesting, therefore, that the subscale with the greatest relation to older children's feelings of general self-worth was that of social acceptance. Perceiving themselves as accepted by peers may be a critical determinant of self-esteem once maltreated children develop certain capacities of social cognition, including aspects of social comparison.

Conclusion and Future Perspectives

In this chapter, we have presented data on the development of the self system during the transition from infancy to childhood in children with Down syndrome and in maltreated children. Our studies have examined many components of the self system, focusing on multiple developmental domains. In keeping with the organizational perspective, research on both of these high-risk groups of children highlights the importance of biological and relational factors in the development of a healthy self system.

Specifically, we found that children with Down syndrome continue to develop in a manner similar (although at a slower pace) to nonhandicapped children with respect to nonlinguistic representations of the self as assessed through studies of symbolic play during the transitional period. Overall, they did not differ significantly from their MA-matched counterparts on most symbolic play measures. Moreover, similar patterns of correlations were observed among play, language, and cognitive variables for both the children with Down syndrome and their nonhandicapped comparisons.

As has been found for communicative measures (Beeghly and Cicchetti 1987a; Mundy et al. 1988), children with Down syndrome also had strengths and weaknesses among different aspects of symbolic play. A particular strength in the area of nonlinguistic representations of the self emerged in the more socially related aspects of symbolic play that involved independent agency and social role representations. An area of deficit involved the ability to use objects in a decontextualized fashion (object substitution scale). One explanation for this deficit may be the alleged difficulty which children with Down syndrome have with abstractions (Gibson 1978). An alternative explanation for these differences might be the expressive language differences observed between children with Down syndrome and their MA-matched controls (Fowler, 1990). Recall that the higher levels of the object play substitution scale required verbal transformations or verbal ideation. In support of this, MLU was correlated highly with the object use scale for both groups of children. On the other hand, the relative linguistic deficits of the children with Down syndrome did not preclude them from engaging in long, connected bouts of play that were as complex and hierarchically integrated as that of their nonhandicapped peers.

In addition, older children with Down syndrome produced more overall symbolic schemes than did their controls, yet their play did not differ in complexity. They also had lower average scores for all play scales. This finding suggests that children with Down syndrome were more persevering in play, repeating schemes more often than did their controls, a finding also noted by Kopp, Krakow, and Vaughn (1983) and Riguet and associates (1981). Perhaps these differences reflect their slower information-processing abilities (Lincoln et al. 1985). Because the highest levels of their play did not differ from that of their controls, these play differences did not interfere greatly with their ultimate play achievements.

To summarize, during play, children with Down syndrome manifested similar but delayed sequences in their conceptions of self and other development, compared to those observed in nonhandicapped children. While children with Down syndrome first represented *themselves* symbolically, their play became more decentered, integrated, and decontextualized with increasing age and cognitive maturity. Only the most cognitively mature children utilized play to represent self and other in hypothetical situations.

These findings on nonlinguistic representations of the self and other attest to the coherence of symbolic development in children with Down syndrome. However, nonlinguistic representations of self and other in children with Down syndrome were significantly more advanced than linguistic representations. Despite this apparent asynchrony (see also Mundy et al. 1988), the finding that both linguistic and nonlinguistic variables were correlated significantly with mental age attests to the coherence of self development in children with Down syndrome.

In contrast, maltreated children manifest poor-quality internal working models, both in relationships with attachment figures and with regard to the self. Accordingly, it is not at all surprising that most maltreated children experience problems with peer relationships (Kaufman and Cicchetti 1989; Mueller and Silverman 1989). In addition, maltreated children reveal deviations in self-system processes (Connell, in this volume; Harter 1983) across a variety of ontogenetic domains during the transition period, including visual self-recognition, linguistic representations of self and other, and perceived competence. Even though they have far fewer reproductive complications than do children with Down syndrome, maltreated children demonstrate problems in the development and organization of the self system. Furthermore, these findings underscore the vicissitudes of parenting for conveying a positive internalization of the self.

Aberrations in the development of the self have been implicated in the ontogenesis of various forms of adult psychopathology, including narcissistic and borderline personality disorders and depression (Adler 1985; Adler and Buie 1979; Cummings and Cicchetti, 1990). Interestingly, a high incidence of disorders of the self system have been observed in maltreated children (Bemporad et al. 1982). Many of these disorders assume the form of borderline psychopathology. A similar relationship between maltreatment and depression, yet another disorder which is affected by and affects self-esteem, also has been documented (Kazdin et al. 1985). Conceivably, one of the pathways whereby maltreated children may later develop behavior problems and psychopathology may be through dysfunctional representational models of attachment figures and of the self in relation to others.

In view of the role of self disorders in psychopathology, interventions designed to modify these maladaptations are critical. When dealing with the needs of infants and toddlers, prevention and early intervention is indicated. Therefore, parent-child interaction and environmental modification are important areas of focus. In this regard, efforts to facilitate the development of secure attachment relationships and, subsequently, positive internal working models of attachment figures and of the self in relation to others are important. According to attachment theorists, caregiver responsiveness promotes the development of a secure attachment relationship and a positive internal working model of self, other, and relationships (Bowlby [1969] 1982; Bretherton 1985, 1987; Sroufe and Fleeson 1986). Because a secure attachment relationship promotes an internalized sense of self as worthy of love, care, and attention and of others as available and constant, it plays a central role in long-term adjustment. When intervening with maltreating parents or other high-risk populations, therapies directed at improving parental representational models of relationships are a strategy worthy of pursuit (Guidano and Liotti 1983). Individual psychotherapy, in conjunction with attention to minimizing any environmental stressors, is necessary in order to accomplish this goal. Often, it is only after parents have reworked their own negative relationship histories that they are able to respond empathically to their children (Egeland, Jacobvitz, and Sroufe 1988). In this regard, timely attention to parents may prevent extensive damage to their children's emerging self system.

In the exploration of potentially useful dyadic interventions, symbolic representation is an important area upon which to focus during the transition period. Because it has been demonstrated that dyadic discourse is an avenue through which information on the self is conveyed to the child (Radke-Yarrow et al., in this volume), controlling the nature of the communication may be necessary if self maladaptations are to be prevented. Specifically, parents need to be sensitized to the role their communications play for their children. In instances of severe parental psychopathology, where altering parental behavior can be a long-term process, it may be necessary to broaden the experience base of the toddler so that the parent is not the primary source of communication relevant to the emerging self.

As the self system becomes increasingly developed and integrated, interventions directed more specifically to the individual child may be required. In this regard, individual psychotherapy designed to promote autonomy, mastery, and improved self-esteem is indicated. Regardless of the orientation employed to attain these goals, the relationship between the therapist and the child is likely to be a critical change variable. Because children with self disorders most often experience an inadequate relationship early in life, helping them to modify these negative working models is likely to be a prerequisite to facilitating any enduring change.

In addition to the provision of individual therapy, utilization of peers may be a rich area for intervention. Because children who experience self-system difficulties are likely to exhibit deficits in their interactions with peers (Kaufman and Cicchetti 1989), the use of therapeutically guided peer interactions can provide opportunities for learning to develop more positive relationships with others. This, in turn, can enhance feelings of social self-efficacy and promote a more positive sense of self. While these can serve as suggestions for intervention with self disorders in atypical populations, research into the efficacy of various intervention approaches is necessary.

Now that the study of the self system in atypical children is gaining ascendancy, future research must adopt an organizational perspective on self development in other high-risk groups. In particular, we believe that investigations of the offspring of unipolar and bipolar mood-disordered parents (see Cicchetti and Aber 1986; Cicchetti and Schneider-Rosen 1986; Radke-Yarrow et al., in this volume), of the offspring of parents with borderline personality disorder (Bemporad et al. 1982; Cicchetti and Olsen, 1990; Pine 1974) and of the offspring of parents with antisocial personality disorder will make important contributions to the understanding of both normal and abnormal self-system processes.

References

Aber, J. L., and J. P. Allen. 1987. The effects of maltreatment on young children's socio-emotional development: An attachment theory perspective. *Developmental Psychology* 23:406–14.

Adler, G. 1985. *Borderline psychopathology and its treatment*. New York: Aronson.

Adler, G., and D. H. Buie. 1979. Aloneness and borderline psychopathology: The possible relevance of child development issues. *International Journal of Psycho-Analysis* 60:83–96.

Allen, R., and G. Wasserman. 1985. Origins of language delay in abused infants. *Child Abuse and Neglect* 9:335–40.

American Psychiatric Association Committee on Nomenclature. 1987. *Diagnostic and statistical manual of mental disorders, III (Revised).* Washington, D.C.: American Psychiatric Association.

Aragona, J. A., and S. M. Eyberg. 1981. Neglected children: Mothers' report of child behavior problems and observed verbal behaviors. *Child Development* 52:596–602.

Arieti, S. 1967. *The intrapsychic self.* New York: Basic.

Atlan, H. 1981. Hierarchical self-organization in living systems. In *Autopoiesis: A theory of living organization.* Edited by M. Zeleny. New York: North Holland.

Baker, H., and M. Baker. 1987. Heinz Kohut's self psychology: An overview. *American Journal of Psychiatry* 144:1–9.

Baron-Cohen, S. 1989. The autistic child's theory of mind: A case of specific development delay. *Journal of Child Psychology and Psychiatry* 30:285–97.

Bayley, N. 1969. *The Bayley scales of infant development.* New York: Psychological.

Beeghly, M., I. Bretherton, and C. B. Mervis. 1986. Mothers' internal state labelling to toddlers. *British Journal of Developmental Psychology* 4:247–61.

Beeghly, M., V. Carlson, and D. Cicchetti. 1986, April. *Child maltreatment and the self: The emergence of internal state language in low-SES 30-month-olds.* Paper presented at the International Conference on Infant Studies, Beverly Hills, Calif.

Beeghly, M., and D. Cicchetti. 1987a. An organizational approach to symbolic development in children with Down syndrome. *New Directions for Child Development* 36:5–29.

————. 1987b, April. *Child maltreatment, attachment, and the self system: The emergence of internal state language in low-SES children.* Paper presented at the biennial meeting of the Society for Research in Child Development, Baltimore, Md.

Beeghly, M., B. Weiss-Perry, and D. Cicchetti. 1990. Beyond sensorimotor functioning: Early communicative and play development of children with Down syndrome. In *Children with Down syndrome: A developmental perspective.* Edited by D. Cicchetti and M. Beeghly. New York: Cambridge University Press.

Bell, R. Q., and L. V. Harper. 1977. *Child effects on adults.* Hillsdale, N.J.: Erlbaum.

Belsky, J., and R. Most. 1981. From exploration to play: A cross-sectional study of infant free play behavior. *Developmental Psychology* 17:630–39.

Bemporad, J., H. Smith, C. Hanson, and D. Cicchetti. 1982. Borderline syndromes in childhood: Criteria for diagnosis. *American Journal of Psychiatry* 139:596–602.

Block, J. H., and J. Block. 1980. The role of ego-control and ego resiliency in the organization of behavior. In *Minnesota Symposia on Child Psychology,* vol. 13. Edited by W. A. Collins. Hillsdale, N.J.: Erlbaum.

Bowlby, J. [1969] 1982. *Attachment and loss,* vol. 1. New York: Basic Books.

Bretherton, I. 1984a. Representing the social world in symbolic play: Reality and fantasy. In *Symbolic play: The development of social understanding.* Edited by I. Bretherton. Orlando, Fla.: Academic.

――――, ed. 1984b. *Symbolic play: The development of social understanding.* Orlando, Fla.: Academic.

――――. 1985. Attachment theory: Retrospect and prospect. In *Growing points of attachment theory and research.* Edited by I. Bretherton and E. Waters. Monographs of the Society for Research in Child Development, vol. 50, nos. 1–2, serial no. 209.

――――. 1987. New perspectives on attachment relations. In *Handbook of infancy.* 2d ed. Edited by J. Osofsky. New York: Wiley, 1061–100.

Bretherton, I., and M. Beeghly. 1982. Talking about internal states: The acquisition of an explicit theory of mind. *Developmental Psychology* 18:906–21.

Bretherton, I., J. Fritz, C. Zahn-Waxler, and D. Ridgeway. 1986. Learning to talk about emotion: A functionalist perspective. *Child Development* 57:530–48.

Bronfenbrenner, U. 1979. *The ecology of human development: Experiments by nature and design.* Cambridge, Mass.: Harvard University Press.

Caparulo, B., and D. Cohen. 1977. Cognitive structures, language, and emerging social competence in autistic and aphasic children. *Journal of the American Academy of Child Psychiatry* 16:620–45.

Carlson, V., D. Cicchetti, D. Barnett, and K. Braunwald. 1989. Disorganized/disoriented attachment relationships in maltreated infants. *Developmental Psychology* 25:525–31.

Cassidy, J. 1988. Child-mother attachment and the self in six-year olds. *Child Development* 59:121–34.

Cassidy, J., and R. Kobak. 1988. Avoidance and its relation to other defensive processes. In *Clinical implications of attachment.* Edited by J. Belsky and T. Nezworski. Hillsdale, N.J.: Erlbaum.

Cicchetti, D. 1984. The emergence of developmental psychopathology. *Child Development* 55:1–7.

――――. 1990. The organization and coherence of socioemotional, cognitive, and representational development: Illustrations through a developmental psychopathology perspective on Down syndrome and child maltreatment. In *Nebraska Symposium on Motivation.* Edited by R. Thompson. Vol. 36, *Socioemotional development.* (pp. 275–382). Lincoln: University of Nebraska Press.

Cicchetti, D., and J. L. Aber. 1986. Early precursors to later depression: An organizational perspective. In *Advances in infancy,* vol. 4. Edited by L. Lipsitt and C. Rovee-Collier. Norwood, N.J.: Ablex.

Cicchetti, D., and M. Beeghly, eds. 1990. *Children with Down syndrome: A developmental perspective.* New York: Cambridge University Press.

Cicchetti, D., and V. Carlson, eds. 1989. *Child maltreatment: Theory and research on the causes and consequences of child abuse and neglect.* New York: Cambridge University Press.

Cicchetti, D., J. Ganiban, and D. Barnett. In press. Contributions from the study of high risk populations to understanding the development of emotion regulation. In *The development of emotion regulation.* Edited by K. Dodge and J. Garber. New York: Cambridge.

Cicchetti, D., and P. Hesse. 1983. Affect and intellect: Piaget's contributions to the study of infant emotional development. In *Emotion: Theory, research and experience*, vol. 2. Edited by R. Plutchik and H. Kellerman. New York: Academic.

Cicchetti, D., and K. Olsen. 1990. Borderline disorders in childhood. In *Handbook of developmental psychopathology*. Edited by M. Lewis and S. Miller. New York: Plenum.

Cicchetti, D., and P. Pogge-Hesse. 1981. The relation between emotion and cognition in infant development: Past, present and future perspectives. In *Infant social cognition*. Edited by M. Lamb and L. Sherrod. Hillsdale, N.J.: Erlbaum.

————. 1982. Possible contributions of the study of organically retarded persons to developmental theory. In *Mental retardation: The developmental-difference controversy*. Edited by E. Zigler and D. Balla. Hillsdale, N.J.: Erlbaum.

Cicchetti, D., and R. Rizley. 1981. Developmental perspectives on the etiology, intergenerational transmission and sequelae of child maltreatment. *New Directions for Child Development* 11:32–59.

Cicchetti, D., and K. Schneider-Rosen. 1986. An organizational approach to childhood depression. In *Depression in young people: Clinical and developmental perspectives*. Edited by M. Rutter, C. Izard, and P. Read. (pp. 71–134). New York: Guilford.

Cicchetti, D., and L. A. Sroufe. 1976. The relationship between affective and cognitive development in Down syndrome infants. *Child Development* 47:920–29.

————. 1978. An organizational view of affect: Illustration from the study of Down syndrome infants. In *The development of affect*. Edited by M. Lewis and L. Rosenblum. New York: Plenum, 309–50.

Cicchetti, D., and S. Toth. 1987. The application of a transactional risk model to intervention with multi-risk maltreating families. *Zero to Three* 7:1–8.

Cicchetti, D., S. Toth, and M. Bush. 1988. Developmental psychopathology and incompetence in childhood: Suggestions for intervention. In *Advances in clinical child psychology*. Edited by B. Lahey and A. Kazdin. New York: Plenum, 1–71.

Cicchetti, D., S. Toth, M. Bush, and J. F. Gillespie. 1988. Stage-salient issues: A transactional model of intervention. *New Directions for Child Development* 39:123–45.

Cohen, D. 1980. The pathology of the self in primary childhood autism and Gilles de la Tourette syndrome. *Pediatric Clinics of North America* 3:383–402.

Connell, J. P., and B. C. Ilardi. 1987. Self-system concomitants of discrepancies between children's and teachers' evaluations of academic competence. *Child Development* 58:1297–1307.

Coster, W. J., M. S. Gersten, M. Beeghly, and D. Cicchetti. 1989. Communicative functioning in maltreated toddlers. *Developmental Psychology* 25:1020–29.

Crittenden, P. M. 1981. Abusing, neglecting, problematic, and adequate dyads: Differentiating by patterns of interaction. *Merrill-Palmer Quarterly* 27:201–8.

————. 1988. Relationships at risk. In *Clinical implications of attachment*. Edited by J. Belsky and T. Nezworski. Hillsdale, N.J.: Erlbaum.

Crittenden, P. M., and M. Ainsworth. 1989. Attachment and child abuse. In *Child maltreatment: Theory and research on the causes and consequences of child abuse and neglect*. Edited by D. Cicchetti and V. Carlson. New York: Cambridge University Press.

Cross, T., T. Nienhuys, and M. Kirkman. 1984. Parent-child interaction with receptively disabled children: Some determinants of maternal speech style. In *Children's language,* vol. 5. Edited by K. Nelson. Hillsdale, N.J.: Erlbaum.

Cummings, E. M., and D. Cicchetti. 1990. Attachment, depression, and the transmission of depression. In *Attachment during the preschool years.* Edited by M. T. Greenberg, D. Cicchetti, and E. M. Cummings. Chicago: University of Chicago Press.

Damon, W., and D. Hart. 1982. The development of self-understanding from infancy through adolescence. *Child Development* 53:841–64.

———. 1988. *Self-understanding in childhood and adolescence.* New York: Cambridge University Press.

Dawson, G., and F. McKissick. 1984. Self-recognition in autistic children. *Journal of Autism and Developmental Disorders* 14:383–94.

Dell, B. F. 1982. Beyond homeostasis: Toward a concept of coherence. *Family Process* 21:21–41.

Egeland, B., D. Jacobvitz, and L. A. Sroufe. 1988. Breaking the cycle of abuse. *Child Development* 59:1080–88.

Emde, R. N. 1985. The affective self: Continuities and transformations from infancy. In *Frontiers in infant psychiatry,* vol. 2. Edited by J. Call, E. Galenson, and R. Tyson. New York: Basic.

Erikson, E. 1950. *Childhood and society.* New York: Norton.

Fein, G., and N. Apfel. 1979. Some preliminary observations on knowing and pretending. In *Symbolic functioning in childhood.* Edited by M. Smith and M. Franklin. Hillsdale, N.J.: Erlbaum.

Fenson, L. 1984. Developmental trends for action and speech in pretend play. In *Symbolic play.* Edited by I. Bretherton. New York: Academic.

Fenson, L., and D. Ramsay. 1980. Decentration and integration of the child's play in the second year. *Child Development* 51:171–78.

Ferrari, M., and W. S. Matthews. 1983. Self-recognition deficits in autism: Syndrome specific or general developmental delay? *Journal of Autism and Developmental Disorders* 13:317–24.

Fowler, A. 1990. Language abilities in children with Down syndrome: Evidence for a specific syntactic delay. In *Children with Down syndrome: A developmental perspective.* Edited by D. Cicchetti and M. Beeghly. New York: Cambridge University Press.

Freud, A. 1965. *Normality and pathology in childhood: Assessments of development.* New York: International Universities Press.

Ganiban, J., S. Wagner, and D. Cicchetti. 1990. Temperament and Down syndrome. In *Children with Down syndrome: A developmental perspective.* Edited by D. Cicchetti and M. Beeghly. New York: Cambridge University Press.

Gersten, M., W. Coster, K. Schneider-Rosen, V. Carlson, and D. Cicchetti. 1986. The socio-emotional bases of communicative functioning: Quality of attachment, language development, and early maltreatment. In *Advances in developmental psychology,* vol. 4. Edited by M. E. Lamb, A. L. Brown and B. Rogoff. Hillsdale, N.J.: Erlbaum.

Gibson, D. 1978. *Down syndrome: The psychology of mongolism.* London: Cambridge University Press.

Guidano, V. 1987. *Complexity of the self: A developmental approach to psychopathology and therapy.* New York: Guilford.

Guidano, V., and G. Liotti. 1983. *Cognitive processes and emotional disorders: A structural approach to psychotherapy.* New York: Guilford.

Harter, S. 1983. Developmental perspectives on the self system. In *Handbook of child psychology.* Edited by E. M. Hetherington. New York: Wiley.

——. 1985. *The self-perception profile for children: Revision of the perceived competence scale for children.* Manual, University of Denver.

Harter, S., and R. Pike. 1984. The pictorial scale of perceived competence and social acceptance for young children. *Child Development* 55:1969–82.

Hermelin, B., and M. O'Connor. 1970. *Psychological experiments with autistic children.* Oxford: Pergamon.

Hill, P., and L. McCune-Nicolich. 1981. Pretend play and patterns of cognition in Down syndrome infants. *Child Development* 23:43–60.

Hill, S., and C. Tomlin. 1981. Self recognition in retarded children. *Child Development* 52:145–50.

Hunter, R. S., and N. Kihlstrom. 1979. Breaking the cycle in abusive families. *American Journal of Psychiatry* 136:1320–22.

Kagan, J. 1981. *The second year: The emergence of self-awareness.* Cambridge, Mass.: Harvard University Press.

Kanner, L. 1943. Autistic disturbances of affective contact. *Nervous Child* 2:217–50.

Kaplan, B. 1966. The study of language in psychiatry: The comparative developmental approach and its application to symbolization and language in psychopathology. In *American handbook of psychiatry.* Edited by S. Arieti. New York: Basic.

Katz, P., and E. Zigler. 1967. Self-image disparity: A developmental approach. *Journal of Personality and Social Psychology* 5:186–95.

Kaufman, J., and D. Cicchetti. 1989. The effects of maltreatment on school-aged children's socioemotional development: Assessments in a day camp setting. *Developmental Psychology* 25:516–24.

Kazdin, A., D. Colbus, J. Moser, and R. Bell. 1985. Depressive symptoms among physically abused and psychiatrically disturbed children. *Journal of Abnormal Psychology* 94:298–307.

Kegan, R. 1982. *The evolving self.* Cambridge, Mass.: Harvard University Press.

Kernberg, O. 1976. *Object relations theory and clinical psychoanalysis.* New York: Aronson.

Kohut, H. 1977. *The restoration of the self.* New York: International Universities Press.

Kopp, C. B., J. Krakow, and B. Vaughn. 1983. Patterns of self-control in young handicapped children. *Minnesota Symposia on Child Psychology.* Vol. 16, *Development and policy concerning children with special needs.* Edited by M. Perlmutter. Hillsdale, N.J.: Erlbaum.

Lewis, M., and J. Brooks-Gunn. 1979. *Social cognition and the acquisition of self.* New York: Plenum.

Lincoln, A., E. Courchesne, B. Kilman, and R. Galambos. 1985. Neurophysiological correlates of information processing by children with Down syndrome. *American Journal of Mental Deficiency* 89:403–14.

Loveland, K. 1987. Behavior of young children with Down syndrome before the mirror: Finding things reflected. *Child Development* 58:923–36.

Lyons-Ruth, K., D. Connell, D. Zoll, and J. Stahl. 1987. Infants at social risk: Relationships among infant maltreatment, maternal behavior, and infant attachment behavior. *Developmental Psychology* 23 (no. 2):223–32.

Mahler, M., F. Pine, and A. Bergman. 1975. *The psychological birth of the human infant.* New York: Basic.

Main, M., and R. Goldwyn. 1984. Predicting rejecting of her infant from mother's representation of her own experience: Implications for the abused-abusing intergenerational cycle. *Child Abuse and Neglect* 8:203–17.

Main, M., N. Kaplan, and J. C. Cassidy. 1985. Security in infancy, childhood and adulthood: A move to the level of representation. In *Growing points of attachment theory and research.* Edited by I. Bretherton and E. Waters. Monographs of the Society for Research in Child Development, vol. 50, nos. 1–2, serial no. 209:66–104.

Main, M., and J. Solomon. 1990. Procedures for identifying infants as disorganized/disoriented during the Ainsworth Strange Situation. In *Attachment during the preschool years.* Edited by M. Greenberg, D. Cicchetti, and M. Cummings. Chicago: University of Chicago Press.

Mans, L., D. Cicchetti, and L. A. Sroufe. 1978. Mirror reactions of Down syndrome infants and toddlers: Cognitive underpinnings of self-recognition. *Child Development* 49:1247–50.

Menyuk, P. 1978. Language: What's wrong and why. In *Autism: A reappraisal of concepts and treatment.* Edited by M. Rutter and E. Schopler. New York: Plenum, 105–116.

Motti, F., D. Cicchetti, and L. A. Sroufe. 1983. From infant affect expression to symbolic play: The coherence of development in Down syndrome children. *Child Development* 54:1168–75.

Mueller, N., and N. Silverman. 1989. Peer relations in maltreated children. In *Child maltreatment: Theory and research on the causes and consequences of child abuse and neglect.* Edited by D. Cicchetti and V. Carlson. New York: Cambridge University Press, 529–78.

Mundy, P., M. Sigman, C. Kasari, and N. Yirmiya. 1988. Nonverbal communication skills in Down syndrome children. *Child Development* 59:235–49.

Neuman, C., and S. Hill. 1978. Self-recognition and stimulus preference in autistic children. *Developmental Psychobiology* 11:571–78.

Nicolich, L. 1977. Beyond sensorimotor intelligence: Assessment of symbolic maturity through analysis of pretend play. *Merrill-Palmer Quarterly* 23:89–99.

Overton, W., and J. Jackson. 1973. The representation of imagined objects in action sequences: A developmental study. *Merrill-Palmer Quarterly* 23:89–99.

Pattee, H., ed. 1973. *Hierarchy theory: The challenge of complex systems.* New York: Braiziller.

Paul, R. 1987. Communication. In *Handbook of autism and pervasive developmental disorders.* Edited by D. Cohen and A. Donnellan. New York: Wiley, 61–84.

Piaget, J. 1962. *Play, dreams and imitation in childhood.* New York: Norton.

Pine, F. 1974. On the concept "borderline" in children—A clinical essay. *Psychoanalytic Study of the Child* 29:341–68.

Plummer, D. L., and W. G. Graziano. 1987. Impact of grade retention on the social development of elementary school children. *Developmental Psychology* 23:267–75.

Riguet, C., N. Taylor, S. Benaroya, and L. Klein. 1981. Symbolic play in autistic, Down and normal children of equivalent mental age. *Journal of Autism and Developmental Disorders* 11:439–48.

Rubin, K., G. Fein, and B. Vandenberg. 1983. Play. In *Handbook of child psychology*. Edited by P. Mussen. Vol. 4, *Socialization*. New York: Wiley.

Rubin, S., and D. Wolf. 1979. The development of maybe: The evolution of social roles into narrative roles. *New Directions for Child Development* 6:15–28.

Rutter, M. 1983. Cognitive deficits in the pathogenesis of autism. *Journal of Child Psychology and Psychiatry* 24:513–31.

Rutter, M., and N. Garmezy. 1983. Developmental psychopathology. In *Handbook of child psychology,* vol. 4. Edited by P. Mussen. New York: Wiley, 775–911.

Sackett, G., A. Sameroff, R. Cairns, and S. Suomi. 1981. Continuity in behavioral development: Theoretical and empirical issues. In *Behavioral development.* Edited by K. Immelmann, G. Garlow, L. Petrinovich, and M. Main. Cambridge: Cambridge University Press.

Sameroff, A., and M. Chandler. 1975. Reproductive risk and the continuum of caretaking casualty. In *Review of child development research,* vol. 4. Edited by F. Horowitz. Chicago: University of Chicago Press.

Schneider-Rosen, K., K. Braunwald, V. Carlson, and D. Cicchetti. 1985. Current perspectives in attachment theory: Illustration from the study of maltreated infants. In *Growing points of attachment theory and research.* Edited by I. Bretherton and E. Waters. Monographs of the Society for Research in Child Development, vol. 50, nos. 1–2, serial no. 209:194–210.

Schneider-Rosen, K., and D. Cicchetti. 1984. The relationship between affect and cognition in maltreated infants: Quality of attachment and the development of visual self-recognition. *Child Development* 55:648–58.

Sigman, M., and P. Mundy. 1987. Symbolic processes in young autistic children. In *Symbolic development in atypical children.* Edited by D. Cicchetti and M. Beeghly. San Francisco: Jossey-Bass, 31–46.

Simon, H. 1962. *The architecture of complexity.* Proceedings of the American Philosophical Society, vol. 106:467–82.

Spiker, D., and M. Ricks. 1984. Visual self-recognition in autistic children: Developmental relationships. *Child Development* 55:214–25.

Sroufe, L. A. 1979a. The coherence of individual development. *American Psychologist* 34:834–41.

———. 1979b. Socioemotional development. In *Handbook of infant development.* Edited by J. Osofsky. New York: Wiley.

Sroufe, L. A., and J. Fleeson. 1986. Attachment and the construction of relationships. In *Relationships and development.* Edited by W. Hartup and Z. Rubin. Hillsdale, N.J.: Erlbaum.

Sroufe, L. A., and M. Rutter. 1984. The domain of developmental psychopathology. *Child Development* 55:1184–99.

Stern, D. 1985. *The interpersonal world of the infant: A view from psychoanalysis and developmental psychology.* New York: Basic.

Stipek, D. J. 1981. Children's perceptions of their own and their classmates' ability. *Journal of Educational Psychology* 73:404–10.

———. 1984. Young children's performance expectations: Logical analysis or wishful thinking? In *The development of achievement motivation*. Edited by J. G. Nicholls. Greenwich, Conn.: JAI.

Tager-Flusberg, H. 1981. On the nature of linguistic functioning in early infantile autism. *Journal of Autism and Developmental Disorders* 11:45–56.

Thompson, R., D. Cicchetti, M. Lamb and C. Malkin. 1985. The emotional responses of Down syndrome and normal infants in the Strange Situation: The organization of affective behavior in infants. *Developmental Psychology* 21:828–41.

Trickett, P. K., and E. J. Susman. 1988. Parental perceptions of child-rearing practices in physically abusive and nonabusive families. *Developmental Psychology* 24:270–76.

Varela, F. J. 1976a, fall. Not one, not two. *Co Evolution Quarterly*.

———. 1976b, summer. On observing natural systems. *Co Evolution Quarterly*.

———. 1981. Describing the logic of the living. In *Autopoiesis: A theory of living organization*. Edited by M. Zeleny. New York: North Holland.

Vondra, J., D. Barnett, and D. Cicchetti. 1989. Perceived and actual competence among maltreated and comparison school children. *Development and Psychopathology* 1:237–55.

Weiss, B., M. Beeghly, and D. Cicchetti. 1985. *Symbolic play development in children with Down syndrome and nonhandicapped children*. Presented at the biennial meeting of the Society for Research in Child Development, Toronto.

Werner, H. 1948. *Comparative psychology of mental development*. New York: International Universities Press.

———. 1957. The concept of development from a comparative and organismic point of view. In *The concept of development*. Edited by D. Harris. Minneapolis: University of Minnesota Press.

Werner, H., and B. Kaplan. 1963. *Symbol formation: An organismic-developmental approach to language and the expression of thought*. New York: Wiley.

Wolf, D. 1982. Understanding others: A longitudinal case study of the concept of independent agency. In *Action and thought: From sensorimotor schemes to symbol use*. Edited by G. Forman. New York: Academic.

Zahn-Waxler, C., and M. Radke-Yarrow. 1982. The development of altruism. In *Development of social behavior*. Edited by N. Eisenberg. New York: Academic.

Zimet, S. G., and G. K. Farley. 1986. Four perspectives on the competence and self-esteem of emotionally disturbed children beginning day treatment. *Journal of the American Academy of Child Psychiatry* 25:76–83.

15 Young Children's Self-Conceptions: Origins in the Natural Discourse of Depressed and Normal Mothers and their Children

MARIAN RADKE-YARROW, BARBARA BELMONT,
EDITHA NOTTELMANN, AND LESLIE BOTTOMLY

The natural discourse of mothers and their young children is the focus of this investigation. Mothers' verbal behavior is examined as a potential contributor to young children's expressions of self-knowledge and self-conceptions. Mothers' comments to and about their young children may supply information, confirm or disconfirm ideas that children hold, and convey messages of values and feelings. It is likely that in these communications, children have some of the experiences out of which a sense of self develops (in this volume, see also Bates; Cicchetti et al.; Snow; Wolf).

Although the hypothesis of parental labeling as a source of children's self-definitions is easily accepted, unqualified this view of transmission is unrealistically smooth and simple. In it, the child is viewed as absorbent. But left out of consideration is the child as a selective recipient, an active and developmentally changing creator and interpreter of experience. Also, the self-defining process involves the influences of both parent and child. Here, because we are focusing on the mothers' input and its influence on children's self-references, some part of this process admittedly is being ignored. It might be argued, however, that at the toddler age level, maternal influences may be of critical importance in interpreting to the child the world of self and others.

There is an extensive history of interest by theorists in how the self entity evolves. Long influential have been the "looking glass" self theory of Cooley (1902) and the symbolic interactionist position of Mead (1925), both of which assume that self-evaluations and self-conceptions develop on the basis of

This work was supported by the National Institute of Mental Health, Bethesda, Maryland, and by the John D. and Catherine T. MacArthur Foundation, Research Network Award on the Transition from Infancy to Early Childhood, Chicago, Illinois. For their help in transcribing and coding the data on which this report is based, we thank Rochelle Levin, Mary Ross, Susan Staib, and Ona Brown. We express our appreciation to Dr. Ruth Wylie for the development of the coding system for mothers' verbalizations and for her thoughtful comments in the preparation of this manuscript. We wish to thank Tracy Sherman for comments and ideas that contributed to this paper.

input from "significant others." Empirical researchers on the self have been less concerned about process than about the nature and content of self-evaluations and self-concepts, and etiological processes have generally been broadly formulated.

Thus, investigators of adult self-concepts have assumed (without supporting empirical studies) that early socialization experiences are significant factors in determining an individual's self-perceptions. Bem (1978), for example, is quoted (Harter 1983, 301) as saying that parents comment on and label children's feelings, attitudes, and behaviors and that children learn these labels and apply them to the self. A somewhat similar yet different emphasis has characterized sociological literature. It has been taken for granted that any "superiority" or "inferiority" in social status, by virtue of race, sex, appearance, economic class and the like, will be reflected in an individual's self-esteem. When findings in a large sociological study of school-age children (Rosenberg and Simmons, 1972) failed to confirm this assumption, by revealing that the self-esteem of black and white children did not reflect societal status appraisals, speculative explanations were offered to revise the explanatory hypothesis. Self attributes, it was hypothesized, must be strongly determined early, within family and neighborhood, with the result that later contrary societal evaluations have muted effects (e.g., Rosenberg and Simmons, 1972; Wylie 1979). These speculations have been endorsed by developmental psychologists. For example, in her comprehensive review of child development research on the self, Harter (1983, 301) concluded that "more attention must be paid to the role of socializing agents whose labeling of the child's behavior becomes a source of self-descriptors."

The natural discourse of parents with their young children generally has not been included among the investigated dimensions of child-rearing. There has been little systematic monitoring of what parents say to their children and what young children say to their parents. When the content of verbal behavior has been investigated, the focus has tended to be on specific classes of verbal behavior, such as positive reinforcements or use of reasoning in situations of discipline. That parents' verbal rearing patterns have not been more extensively examined in relation to children's self-conceptions is especially surprising.

The role of familial factors, with few exceptions, has fallen outside the empirical work on the child's emerging and changing self, except in infant research. Sander (1975) and Lewis and Brooks-Gunn (1979), for example, stressed qualities of caregiver-child interaction early on as critical in the process of children's emerging self-definitions. But studies of the self-conceptions of older children have focused on the child per se. These studies have been mainly of children age six years and older, when self-reports can be obtained through interview or questionnaire. This source of data is not well adapted to providing information about self-attitudes and self-concepts in younger children (Harter 1983). Thus, the developmental period from age two to five has been neglected, even though one would expect it to be a critical time for the laying down of the foundations of self-conceptions and feelings. The marked and rapid growth in the comprehension and use of language during these years should make the mother's verbalizations very special experiences for the child's learning about self. In a few studies (e.g., Clark and Clark 1947; Harter 1983; Keller, Ford, and Meacham 1978); aspects of self in preschool-age children have been investigated projectively, through doll play or with pictures. They have not been concerned with processes through which the child acquires self descriptors and attitudes.

The present study was undertaken to learn what parents convey in natural discourse with their young children and what young children might be learning from mothers' verbal behavior. This is an observational study in which mothers' and children's verbal behavior is examined.

The first set of research questions is descriptive; it concerns the kinds of child-self relevant information that mothers impart to their toddler-age boys and girls: What aspects of the child's self are addressed? How is the information adapted to the developmental tasks and characteristics of the child? Is there a common core of information from socializing agents to toddler-age children, and what are the individual differences in these verbal communications?

The second research question asks whether there are responses from the children that are linked with mothers' verbalizations. Although it is not assumed that mothers' comments are always comprehended or immediately matched or internalized, it is assumed that the natural discourse samples represent the mother's and child's history of similar discourse that has cumulative communication value and that we may therefore be tapping some cumulative effects.

A third set of questions concerns the communication of clinically depressed mothers. Are symptoms of adult depression (self-demeaning attitudes; sad, angry, and anxious feelings; apathy; and absorption in oneself) manifested in depressed mothers' comments to their children? Are these behaviors exaggerated or muted in the caregiver role? Do mothers' verbal communications with their children provide some clues with regard to the environmental transmission to children of depression-related attitudes and feelings about self?

Sample

The participants were thirty-five middle-class mothers and their toddler-age children (twenty-five to thirty-six months of age), nineteen girls (mean age = 31.1 months) and sixteen boys (mean age = 31.6 months), recruited in the first two years of a larger longitudinal study of child-rearing and child development in families of well and depressed parents (Radke-Yarrow 1989).

Mothers were screened by a psychiatric interview, the Schedule for Affective Disorders and Schizophrenia (SADS-L), for RDC diagnoses (Spitzer and Endicott 1977). Eighteen mothers were without past or present psychiatric disorder. Seventeen mothers had a diagnosis of depression and had had depressive episodes in the lifetime of the toddler; all met criteria of a major affective disorder: thirteen had a diagnosis of unipolar depression, four of bipolar depression (with only episodes of depression in the child's lifetime). The mother's most severe episode in the child's lifetime (Global Assessment Scale [GAS] by Spitzer, Gibbon, and Endicott 1978) was used as an index of severity of depression.

Procedure

Mother and toddler were observed together on two occasions, approximately a week apart, each time for 2 ½ hours. The setting for their interaction was a comfortable research apartment (living room, kitchenette, bathroom). After the mother and child received an orientation to the surrounds, the apartment was turned over to them, initially with relatively little structuring of their time. However, each session was scripted as a series of situations that follow smoothly one upon another, incorporating experiences and demands that simulate everyday events in a toddler's life. Seven situations were sampled for study of mother-child discourse: (1) a potentially pleasant routine, eating lunch together (five-minute sample), (2) the mother engaged in teaching a block task (five minutes), (3) a mild stress involving a period preliminary to mother's brief departure from the apartment (two minutes), (4) the reunion, followed by free time (eight minutes), (5) a period after mother is informed that child will be measured by a ''doctor'' (an anthropometric examination) (five minutes), (6) a waiting period after the white-coated examiner arrives (five minutes), and (7) the examination (five minutes). The sampling was weighted for mildly stressful situations, which were assumed to magnify demands for verbal interaction that focus on the child.

All sessions were videotaped. Transcripts were made of the speech of mother and child, including paralinguistics (voice tone, facial expressions, laughing and crying, gestures). Coding was done by viewing videotapes along with the written transcripts. Additions and changes could be made in the transcripts at this point. Transcribers and coders were blind to mothers' diagnoses.

Mother's Speech

Mothers' relevant verbalizations were those directed to the child or made about the child in his/her presence and which explicitly labeled some external, behavioral, or inner characteristic of the child or implied such characteristics.

Mothers made statements to a child with very explicit attributions: "You're a boy," "Stop being a crybaby," "You feel tired?" Mothers also labeled the child's behavior in ways that implied some assessment of it (i.e., "The little chair is the right size for you," "Can't you make up your mind?"; or after the child does something helpful, the mother says, "Thank you").

Coding of mothers' speech content was based on a system developed by Wylie (1984) that requires a detailed scanning of mothers' words and phrases. In Wylie's system, substantive content is coded in fifty-one specific categories. For the present analyses, these categories were grouped into twelve broad domains: (1) physical and developmental qualities ("You have a wide hand," "Are you trying to eat like a baby?"); (2) individuality (name, gender, and family membership); (3) physiological drives ("Do you need the potty?"); (4) volitional properties—wishes and preferences ("I know you like hot dogs," "That's your favorite"); (5) instrumental/motor competencies ("You're good at legos," "She has no trouble getting out of her booster seat."); (6) cognitive properties of knowing, remembering, language abilities ("You have a good memory," "Yes, that's yellow"); (7) self-determination ("I let her choose what to put on in the morning," "What do you want to do?"); (8) self-control ("You're not paying attention," "Are you making a mess?"); (9) emotions ("Do you love your sister?" or "She had a tantrum when I told her she couldn't take the doll home"); (10) prosocial/moral characteristics ("He helps me with the dishes at home," "Are you telling the truth?"); (11) sociability ("She plays by herself a lot," "You're silly"); and (12) acceptability or lovability ("I love you," "You're terrible"). Reliability was based on these twelve categories.

The evaluative tone of mothers' comments was rated as positive or pleasant, neutral, or negative or unpleasant. Mother's verbal behavior also was coded at a more global level. For each of the seven situations sampled, ratings were made (0,1,2) of the quality of mother-child dialogue: Is there a dialogue between mother and child in which there is turn-taking and some continuity in a topic to which they both contribute, as if they are listening to each other? Mothers' speech was also scanned for references made to her own feelings, on the assumption that such comments might influence the child's own feelings.

Intercoder agreement for each of the coded aspects was obtained from two pairs of independent coders. The agreements, based on thirteen cases, were 78 percent and 79 percent on identifying mothers' labeling statements, 92 percent and 95 percent on the implicit-explicit distinction, 85 percent and 85 percent on evaluative quality, and 91 percent and 87 percent on substantive content. A single pair of coders coded dialogue (79 percent agreement) and mothers' references to their own feelings (91 percent agreement).

In assessing mothers' comments, we were concerned with (1) the number of her explicit attributions and her implicit labelings and (2) the content of her verbalizations with respect to their positive or negative evaluative quality and their substantive areas.

Children's Speech

Children's language was examined for possible mothers' labeling. All comments by the child that contained a self-reference—that is, a personal pronoun (I, me, mine, my, we, ours)—(e.g., "I know how") or the child's own name ("Debby's doll") were noted. Their substantive content was coded in the twelve categories used for mothers' comments, plus a category to cover the children's verbalizations about their own activities ("I'm playing with Bob"). (Reliabilities ranged from 85 percent to 100 percent; an exception was 50 percent agreement on the prosocial category, which occurred only twice in the reliability sample.) Children's self-referencing comments were rated also for evaluative quality: (*a*) pleasant or favorable to self (in state or trait), (*b*) neutral, or (*c*) unpleasant or unfavorable to self. Examples of pleasant comments were "I can make a lot of bubbles" and "I'm not scared now." Examples of unpleasant references were "I'm scared" and "I don't like dolls." Neutral comments were "That's my sister's doll" and "I'm coloring the house." The context in which the comments occurred, as well as the tone of voice and body gestures, entered into this coding. Intercoder reliability was 82 percent.

Findings

Frequency of Mothers' Labeling of Child and Child Behavior

We began with two expectations regarding mothers' implicit and explicit labeling of their children: (1) that the frequency would be high, in accordance with Wylie's (1987) findings and (2) that the frequency of labeling would be lower in depressed than in well mothers, in line with depressive symptomatology of apathy, sadness, and absorption in self.

The first expectation clearly was fulfilled; the second was not. The children were bombarded with many bits of information about themselves. In the thirty-five minutes of sampled discourse, the mean number of implicit labelings was 330 ($SD = 128$) by well mothers and 307 ($SD = 104$) by depressed mothers, and the means of explicit attributions were 66 ($SD = 28$) by well mothers and 74 ($SD = 34$) by depressed mothers (nonsignificant group differences). The range in total comments was 150–676. There were no differences by gender of child.

In comments to their children, mothers were much more inclined (four to five times so) to edit or verbally monitor the child's ongoing behavior ("That *was* hard," "That will make a mess," "You can stand very tall") than to make direct explicit declarations (e.g., "You are very silly"). These "editorial" comments have an informational quality, although their messages may require many repetitions before the child arrives at their underlying sense. Thus, if the mother supports the child's choices over and over again or repeatedly affirms his or her problem-solving ability, the child may arrive at generalizations about the self, such as, "Mommy thinks I'm good at choosing" and "I'm good at naming colors." As the data indicate, mothers do indeed supply repetition. Overall, these very high rates of comments would indicate that children have available, through their mothers, a tremendous source of information about themselves.

Depression and Mothers' Frequency of Implicit and Explicit Attributions

The unexpectedly high frequencies of verbalizations by the depressed mothers prompted further examination. The first exploration was of the number of attributions in relation to the severity rating of the mother's depression. Mothers with the more severe depressive episodes (GAS score < 50) were compared with mothers with less severe episodes (GAS ≥ 50). Mean frequency for the more severely depressed mothers was 362, compared with 402 for less severely depressed mothers and 396 for well mothers; the differences were not significant.

A second exploration of the high frequencies by the depressed mothers was suggested by findings of an earlier study of the total amount of speaking time by depressed and normal mothers when in partnership with their children (Breznitz and Sherman 1987). These authors reported that when mother and child were interacting in a nonstressful situation, the amount of time in speaking was significantly less by depressed mothers than by normal mothers. However, in situations of stress, talking increased dramatically in depressed mothers and decreased slightly in normal mothers. Since the sampling of situations in the present study, as noted earlier, has a preponderance of time spent in potentially stressful situations, it was reasoned that perhaps the high frequencies that we were seeing in the depressed mothers reflect stress-related behavior.

To test this hypothesis, mothers' speech was reexamined, taking into account the relative calm and stress of the situations. Lunchtime was taken as a sample of calm, and waiting for the doctor's examination as a sample of stress. Analyses by situation did not show differences in the frequency of attributions in well and depressed mothers' speech.

Content of Mothers' Comments

Maternal comments next were examined for their substantive content and their evaluative quality (positive, neutral, negative).

Substantive Content

The content of mothers' discourse is presented in table 1, with categories entered in the rank order of frequency of implicit labels by well mothers. Mothers' labeling predominantly was feedback about the children's ongoing activities ("Yes, that is yellow," "Your tummy is full," "That's a better way to do it," "That will make your sweater messy, you know"). Apparently, mothers were translating the child's behavior into aspects or dimensions that they wished to accent. Mothers also were tuned into their children's developmental tasks. The top-ranking categories reflect developmentally and culturally salient issues in the toddler years; namely, cognitive advances, increased instrumental competencies, movement toward autonomy (self-determination), and increasingly differentiated identity (gender, family membership, etc.). There was a remarkable contrast in the frequency of comments in these categories compared with categories of feelings and social interaction. Mothers infrequently commented to their child about the child's feelings and social qualities.

Table 1   Substantive Content of Well and Depressed Mothers' Comments (in mean percents)

	Implicit Labeling		Explicit Labeling	
Substantive Category	% Well Mothers (N = 18)	% Depressed Mothers (N = 17)	% Well Mothers (N = 18)	% Depressed Mothers (N = 17)
Cognitive characteristics	36.0% (4.2)[a]	35.0% (7.6)	46.8% (12.0)	47.8% (13.2)
Instrumental competence	18.3 (4.6)	19.8 (6.5)	27.7 (9.7)	27.2 (12.9)
Self-determination	22.3 (4.8)	21.9 (4.9)	.2 (1.0)	.3 (1.1)
Individuality	10.6 (4.5)	6.6 (3.5)	4.4 (5.1)	2.8 (2.9)
Physical development	3.0 (2.0)	3.4 (2.0)	8.6 (4.7)	6.9 (4.8)
Self-control	2.1 (1.6)	2.9 (2.4)	5.2 (4.6)	10.0 (14.2)
Prosocial and moral characteristics	2.0 (1.9)	3.1 (3.7)	.9 (3.1)	.7 (1.1)
Emotions and feelings	1.5 (1.3)	2.3 (2.1)	1.4 (1.8)	1.2 (1.5)
Physiological state	1.8 (1.3)	1.6 (1.8)	2.2 (3.3)	.2 (.6)
Acceptability	1.4 (1.0)	2.2 (2.0)	.2 (.6)	.4 (.7)
Volitional properties	.7 (.8)	.9 (.9)	1.3 (1.3)	1.6 (3.2)
Sociability	.4 (.4)	.2 (.3)	.9 (1.6)	.9 (1.7)

[a]Standard deviations are in parentheses.

The directness of mothers' comments varied with the content category. Comments concerning the child's autonomy were indirect more often than direct. Comments regarding self-control or lack of it tended to be direct and explicit.

There were few differences in substantive content relating either to mothers' diagnostic status or to the gender of the child. Well mothers were significantly more likely than depressed mothers to explicitly monitor children's physiological states, $F (1,31) = 5.80, p = .02$, and to implicitly accent the child's individuality (family member and gender), $F (1,31) = 4.02, p = .01$. Based on cultural stereotypes and expectations, two gender-linked differences regarding the content areas in mothers' speech were predicted: that mothers would emphasize the domain of competence (cognition and instrumental competencies) more for boys than for girls and would emphasize the broadly affective domains of prosocial and moral behaviors and emotions more for girls than for boys. The hypothesis for cognition and competencies was not confirmed ($F < 1$). Likewise, mothers of girls were no more likely than mothers of boys to make comments concerning prosocial and moral behavior ($F < 1$). However, the expectation of mothers' differential emphasis on emotions was supported. Mothers of girls in both diagnostic groups made significantly more comments about emotions than did mothers of boys, $F (1,31) = 4.36, p = .04$. This finding replicates the data reported by Dunn, Bretherton, and Munn (1987), who also found that mothers talked to girls about emotions approximately twice as much as to boys. The content of mothers' comments revealed no other gender differences.

While stressing the similarities across mothers, we would also caution against generalizing too broadly. The mothers in this study were seen under similar, controlled circumstances. In real life, families have different life circumstances; the life situations in which they interact provide very different contexts, which we would assume are likely to have significant influence on the content of discourse.

Evaluative Tone

Most of mothers' comments were positive (mean percent $= 68$), supplying supportive and affirmative information to the children, either implicitly or explicitly. There were no significant differences by gender of child or psychiatric status of mother. However, when we examined negative evaluations, we found significantly more explicit negatives made by depressed mothers (mean percent $= 23$) than by well mothers (mean percent $= 16$), $F (1,31) = 5.07, p = .03$. This relatively high use of explicit negatives was even higher in the small subgroup of mothers ($N =$ seven) who have been depressed for most of their lives.

Evaluative Tone in Relation Substantive Content

When mothers' evaluations were considered in relation to substantive comments, we found that the specific content category made a difference in how much children were told their behavior was good or wanting. Dimensions in which mothers' attributions were overwhelmingly positive (mean percent = 75) were cognition, instrumental competence, and prosocial behavior. In other words, these developmental competencies were nurtured by a dependable flow of favorable recognition from mothers. In contrast, some domains had a high proportion of critical comments. This was the case for children's self-control ("You're *not* supposed to touch"), in which the mean percent of mothers' comments rated negative or affectively mixed was 72. Similarly, comments concerning the child's self-determination or autonomy ("Can't you make up your mind?") were frequently (41 percent) negative or mixed. Well and depressed mothers were similar in these respects. Concerning autonomy, there were differences in comments to boys and girls: Purely negative comments were directed more often to boys (mean percent = 34) than to girls (mean percent = 24), $F (1,31) = 6.38$, $p = .02$; and purely positive comments, more often to girls (mean percent = 29) than to boys (mean percent = 23), $F (1,31) = 4.51$, $p = .05$.

Gender of child made a difference also in the positive and negative tone of mothers' verbalizations about emotions. Statements in the negative tone were frequently (mean percent = 33) directed to girls and infrequently (mean percent = 11) to boys, $F (1,27) = 4.50$, $p = .04$. Mothers' depression also made a difference in attributions concerning emotions: more negative labeling about emotions was given by depressed (mean percent = 35) than by normal (mean percent = 11) mothers, $F (1,27) = 5.46$, $p = .03$. Although mothers rarely commented explicitly to their children on their own emotions, negative comments about their own feelings were made significantly more frequently by depressed than by normal mothers (mean percent = 71 and 28, respectively), $F (1,31) = 4.85$, $p = .03$. Well mothers' evaluative comments about characteristics coded as individuality (comments regarding gender and family membership) were more often positive to girls (mean = 82 percent) than to boys (mean percent = 60), while depressed mothers were less positive to girls (mean percent = 56) than to boys (mean percent = 71), $F (1,31) = 9.24$, $p = .01$.

Dialogue in Mother-Child Discourse

From word-by-word analyses, we did not get a picture of the quality of dialogue between mother and child. Did mother and child engage with each other? Did the content of one partner follow from the content of the other? Therefore, ratings of (0 to 2) of dialogue quality were made on each of the seven behavior samples and summed across samples (0 to 14). Although the mean level of dialogue was rated as moderate (mean = 6.7, *SD* 2.8) for well mothers and only slightly less (mean = 5.8, *SD* 2.1) for depressed mothers, individual differences in quality were considerable, reflecting differences in mothers' investment and availability. The result sometimes was a lack of connectedness, as in the following example:

Child	Mother
I scare.	Here you go look. Ha? Surprise.
I scare.	All right, turn the page. Car.
Mommy's car, right?	No that's a red car. I have a blue car.
I scared.	Oh, Dan, you're brave.

In other instances, there was effective thematic communication:

Child	Mother
Doesn't hurt.	Yeah, there aren't going to be any hurts. No hurts.
Uhh.	He's just going to measure how big you are.
Doesn't hurt.	Yeah.
It doesn't hurt.	No. He doesn't. He's nice, like Dr. John. Do you like Dr. John?
I like Dr. John.	I know you do.
I like Santa Claus, too.	
I like my Daddy.	Who? Oh, your Daddy. I like your Daddy too.

These contrasting kinds of discourse provide children with quite different settings for learning from their mother and with differing textures of relationships. Over time, the quality of dialogue may be expected to be a critical variable in determining the impact of mothers' verbal comments on children's self-conceptions.

Children's Self-References and Affect in relation to Mothers' Verbal Behavior

Mothers' verbal behavior provided a barrage of information for their children. In describing mothers' speech, we have emphasized central tendencies, but it should be noted that there were large individual differences as well (e.g., the range in frequency of implicit labeling, sixty-eight to ninety-seven; in explicit attributions, three to thirty-two). The tone of some mothers was negative in 4 percent of their comments; in others, it was negative in 28 percent of their comments. These variable maternal qualities of communication were examined in relation to children's self-references and their general affective state.

The number and variety of self-references made by the child are interpreted as indicators of self-knowledge. The pleasantness or unpleasantness of the states to which self-references referred are interpreted as evidence of the child's feelings about the self. Each of these indicators was examined in relation to variations in the frequency, variety, and tone of mothers' comments and to the quality of the mother-child dialogue.

Children's Self-Conceptions

It was hypothesized that children's self-knowledge is fostered by mothers who provide many labels and attributions in their comments to the child and who make such comments in good dialogue. These predictions were upheld. The number of self-references made by the child was significantly positively related to *(a)* the number of mothers' implicit and explicit attributions, $r(35) = .47, p = .002$; *(b)* the variety in mothers' attributions, $r(35) = .37, p = .01$; and *(c)* the quality of dialogue, $r(35) = .64, p = .001$. The associations were similar in the well and depressed groups. The variety of content areas in children's self-references was positively related only to the quality of dialogue, $r(35) = .36, p = .02$, and this association was primarily in the well mother-child dyads.

The children of well and depressed mothers did not differ in frequency and variety of self-references. Children of well mothers, on average, made thirty-two self-references $(SD = 19.7)$; children of depressed mothers made thirty-five self-references $(SD = 16.9)$. The mean variety in self-references was 5.9 $(SD = 1.7)$ and 6.3 $(SD = 1.7)$ by children of well and depressed mothers, respectively.

In order to determine whether children were saying the same things about themselves as their mothers, mothers as a group were compared with children as a group in terms of the relative emphases on different substantive categories (see table 2). The categories are entered into the table in the rank-ordering of categories in mothers' use, as in table 1. Mothers' labeling was, on the average, more than ten times the frequency of child self-references, which is not surprising given the age of the children. At first glance, it appears that children's and mothers' priorities are not at all the same; but on closer inspection, a certain convergence is apparent. Toddlers' self-references, like their mothers' comments, revolved around immediate activities (e.g., cognitive events and instrumental competencies: "I'm going to color now," "I have some gum," "I did it"). Like mothers' comments, children's references fairly often involved self-determination ("I'm not going to eat it"). Children's comments frequently concerned what is liked or wanted or wished for

Table 2 Children's Self-References (in mean percents)

Substantive Content	Children of Well Mothers (N = 18)		Children of Depressed Mothers (N = 17)	
Negative self-references	33.6	(18.1)[a]	34.9	(21.2)
Cognitive characteristics	5.1	(5.7)	6.1	(7.2)
Instrumental competence	4.2	(3.6)	5.0	(6.7)
Self-determination	14.9	(15.8)	16.5	(14.6)
Individuality	19.4	(16.2)	11.5	(9.7)
Physical development	2.9	(.04)	4.5	(5.3)
Self-control	.1	(.6)	.5	(1.3)
Prosocial and moral characteristics	.2	(.9)	.2	(.8)
Emotions and feelings	.1	(.4)	2.4	(7.0)
Physiological state	14.0	(10.3)	7.2	(7.0)
Acceptability	.00	(.00)	.3	(1.2)
Volitional properties	23.5	(11.7)	25.9	(9.0)
Sociability	1.1	(2.3)	.8	(1.6)
Activity	14.5	(9.2)	19.2	(12.7)

[a]Standard deviations are in parentheses.

(e.g., "I wish I had that doll at home," "I want an orange," "I don't want to go in there"). The children did not define themselves in terms of possessions or appearance, qualities that young school-age children often give in response to direct questions about self (Damon and Hart 1982). Like their mothers, these children made few references to social or emotional qualities; but they referred to their physiological feeling states more than their mothers did.

The children seldom used words referring to positive states. The words that occurred were *happy, glad, excited, love, like, (feel) better,* and *good.* There were more negative inner state words (*need, tired, hurt, hungry, cold, hot*) and negative emotions words (*angriest, mad, sad, cry, scared, don't like, hate, sore, miss you*). Except for the word *like,* all of the feeling words were rare in the toddlers' speech.

The low total frequency of children's references involving feeling and emotions did not provide a basis for matching with mothers' words. However, suggestive of a process is a case between a depressed mother and her daughter in a somewhat unusual interaction pattern. This child used nine different emotion words, the largest number and variety of feeling words in the group. The mother, too, was well above average in the number of feeling words. Their interactions were in a game, which the mother indicated is a regular part of their playing together: mother and child reverse their roles. The child is mother to one of the dolls, and the mother plays baby.

Mother Acting as Baby	Child Acting as Mother
The baby is crying, "Kate, wah, wah, wah."	Baby, stop; you can feed yourself.
I want my bottle. [Cries.]	[Feeds and pats baby.]
Thank you, Mommy, that makes me feel better.	Does that make you not cry anymore?
That makes me feel better. I love you, Mommy.	I love you, too.
You're a nice Mommy.	I yelled at her.
She cried a lot when you yelled.	And that made me have a headache.
You didn't like that?	I had to yell 'cause she was bad.
You hurt my feelings.	[Pats, feeds doll; laughs.]
Thank you.	Does that make you laugh, baby?
That made me feel better.	

To assess further possible associations between mothers' speech and children's self-references, mothers' and children's comments were compared for affective tone. Child self-references were coded as unpleasant, pleasant, or neutral in state. The distinction between neutral and pleasant is often slight; unpleasant tone is unambiguous. The mean percent of unpleasant child references was 34. Significant associations were found between the frequency of self-references that concerned unpleasant or unfavorable content and the frequency of mothers' total negative or disapproving comments and the frequency of mothers' explicit negative comments. The correlation between number of children's negative self-references and mothers' total negative comments was $+.55$, $p = .001$; between children's negative self-references and mothers' explicit negative comments, it was $+.50$, $p = .001$. The correlations within groups of well mother-child dyads and depressed mother-child dyads were similar. It seems reasonable, at this age level, to interpret the association as reflecting an influence of mothers' labeling.

Conclusions and Comments

Maternal influences on the formation of children's early self-conceptions and self-evaluations have been the focus of this study. Detailed analyses of mothers' and children's discourse have provided descriptive accounts of a dimension of socialization that has not been much explored and of a stage in the development of self-knowledge about which there is little information. The natural verbal interaction between mothers and toddlers was observed in comparable situations for all of the dyads.

The analyses of verbatim accounts document an extraordinary amount of self-relevant information coming to toddlers in their mothers' everyday speech. Extracted from context, the content of mothers' speech appears somewhat trivial and not very informative. However, in the context of the child's ongoing behavior, the functions of mothers' verbalizations become evident. The mother's labeling clarifies, verifies, and evaluates, piece by piece, the behavior in which the child is engaged.

Mothers also explicitly attribute qualities to the child. They sum up their views of their children in words such as, "You are a brave girl" or "You are a kind boy." However, these labels, which occur relatively infrequently, are probably not the primary source of self-knowledge for children. These direct messages must compete with the repeated, more implied, but specific attributions that constitute the vast majority of maternal verbal messages.

Mothers are selective in the aspects of child behavior about which they comment to the child. As we have seen, children's cognition, competence, and autonomy are favored, probably because they involve salient developmental tasks and undergo considerable change in the toddler period. Buy why are they so favored over children's social and emotional qualities? Regulation of emotions and development of social relationships are also developmental tasks. Although mothers contribute to their children's social and emotional self-conceptions through nonverbal behavior—moods and emotions they express, models they furnish, and feelings they create in their children by the experiences that they provide—the fact remains that there is very little verbal reference to the socio-emotional domains.

As we have seen, emotion words have meager representation in toddlers' speech, unless expressions of wanting and liking ("I don't like") are included. However, with these latter words, the child efficiently defines aspects of self. There is also an element in toddlers' self-references that seems to suggest their sense of more enduring cognitive self qualities ("I can't do that" or "I can sing"). The latter is particularly interesting, if our interpretation is correct, in showing very early forerunners of the kinds of self-evaluations of stable psychological qualities that enter into self-conceptions of older children (Damon and Hart 1982). On the purely affective side, few self-references by the children are strong self-derogations. However, negative references on average account for a third of the "I" and "me" statements by the children.

The strong associations found between quantity and variety in mothers' attributive comments to their young children and the quantity and variety of children's self-references are consistent with an interpretation that mothers' negatively toned comments influence children's negative self-references. This association is of special interest with regard to depressed mothers and their children. Depressed mothers, as compared with well mothers, provided significantly more negative attributions to their children and negative labeling of their own and their children's emotions. Depressed mothers thus appear to be verbally transmitting the negative feelings characteristic of depression. Depressed and well mothers directed informing comments to their toddlers with similar frequency and in similar substantive areas, but affective tone differed.

The equal frequencies of attributions by well and depressed mothers were unexpected. Several post hoc interpretations suggest themselves: (1) Mothers and children were observed in a laboratory, which, though informal, confined and structured their activities. Under the structure and stress involved, the depressed mothers may have expressed their best and not their modal behaviors. On the other hand, well mothers may have felt freer to behave as usual. (2) One might hypothesize that the bond of mother to young child is very resistant to effects of mother's pathology, that a mother's ability to orient to her child and to respond in a child-referential way may not suffer impairment.

We have seen these children with their mothers at a very young age. As their cognitive and language abilities develop, we would assume that the attributions by their mothers, including the evaluative quality of these attributions, would contribute increasingly to children's self-conceptions and feelings.

In the present analyses, verbal interaction has been extracted from the contexts of activities and relationships in which it is occurring. Therefore, these analyses only begin to characterize the important verbal aspect of rearing behavior. In further research, two extensions are particularly indicated. A more functionally oriented analysis is needed to assess when and how mothers' comments, whatever their content, are used in ways that nurture, intrude, undermine, support, and regulate their children. A second worthy research extension would be to follow the cumulative impact of verbal discourse over time and to probe in more detail into what the child is incorporating into his/her self-concept.

References

Bem, D. 1978. Self-perception theory. In *Cognitive theories in social psychology.* Edited by L. Berkowitz. New York: Academic, 1–62.

Breznitz, Z., and T. Sherman. 1987. Speech patterning of natural discourse of well and depressed mothers and their young children. *Child Development* 58:395–400.

Clark, K. B., and M. P. Clark. 1947. Racial identification and preference in Negro children. In *Readings in social psychology.* Edited by T. M. Newcomb and E. Hartley. New York: Holt, 602–11.

Cooley, C. H. 1902. *Human nature and the social order.* New York: Scribner.

Damon, W., and D. Hart. 1982. The development of self-understanding from infancy through adolescence. *Child Development* 53:841–64.

Dunn, J., I. Bretherton, and P. Munn. 1987. Conversations about feeling states between mothers and their young children. *Developmental Psychology* 23 (no. 1):132–39.

Harter, S. 1983. Developmental perspectives on the self-system. In *Handbook of child psychology.* Edited by P. Mussen. Vol. 4, *Socialization, personality, and social development.* Edited by E. M. Hetherington. New York: Wiley, 275–385.

Keller, A., L. Ford, and J. Meacham. 1978. Dimensions of self-concept in preschool children. *Developmental Psychology* 14:483–89.

Lewis, M., and J. Brooks-Gunn. 1979. Toward a theory of social cognition: The development of the self. In *New directions in child development: Social interaction and communication during infancy.* Edited by I. Uzgiris. San Francisco: Jossey-Bass, 1–20.

Mead, G. H. 1925. The genesis of self and social control. *International Journal of Ethics* 35 (no. 3): 251–73.

Radke-Yarrow, M. 1989. Family environments of depressed and well parents and their children: Issues of research methods. In *Aggression and depression in family interactions.* Edited by G. R. Patterson. Hillsdale, N.J.: Erlbaum, 169–184.

Rosenberg, M., and R. Simmons. 1972. *Black and white self-esteem: The urban school child.* Washington, D.C.: American Sociological Association.

Sander, L. W. 1975. Infant and caretaking environment: Investigation and conceptualization and adaptive behavior in a system of increasing complexity. In *Explorations in child psychiatry.* Edited by E. J. Anthony. New York: Plenum, 129–65.

Spitzer, R. L., and J. Endicott. 1977. *The Schedule for Affective Disorders and Schizophrenia: Lifetime version.* New York: New York State Psychiatric Institute, Biometrics Research.

Spitzer, R. L., M. Gibbon, and J. Endicott. 1978. *Global Assessment Scale.* New York: New York State Psychiatric Institute, Biometrics Research.

Wylie, R. C. 1979. *The self-concept: Theory and research on selected topics.* Rev. ed., vol. 2. Lincoln: University of Nebraska Press.

———. 1984. Characteristics of mothers' verbal attributions to their children in a semi-naturalistic research setting: Guide to identifying and coding maternal attributions. Manuscript.

———. 1987. Mothers' attributions to their children. In *Self and identity: Perspectives across the lifespan.* Edited by T. Honess and K. Yardley. 77–92. London: Routledge & Kegan Paul.

16 The Concepts of Self: A Dialogue of Questions Without Answers

Jerome Kagan

The initial phase in the development of most empirical sciences relies on ideas whose presumptive validity is based on a broad intuitive appeal. Examples of concepts which seemed to earlier scholars to be obviously correct include the beliefs that all objects in the world have unchanging essences, every event is determined by some prior causal force, the infant's organs are present in miniature from the beginning of the embryo's growth, the brain registers a veridical image of what the eyes perceive, and women are weaker than men. Each of these ideas was treated as true because it seemed to match experience or was an obvious deduction from the premises underlying available knowledge. I believe that the concept of self, which is phenomenologically compelling to Western minds, may be another flawed construct. I am skeptical of the assumption of an essential process with some components that do not change over time, the practice of using introspective self-report as the major source of information about the self's characteristics, and the belief that an individual's voluntary actions are unpredictable because they are monitored by the self (hence, each person is morally responsible for his or her behavior).

A serious problem with the construct *self-concept* is that it is not always treated in an objective frame of description. When most investigators write that children who are rejected by their family behave aggressively because of a poor self-concept, they are using the term to refer to hypothetical states that may or may not be available to the child's consciousness. This frame, which is appropriate, is identical with that of a sensory physiologist who explains the perception of color as due to opponent processes in the thalamus. Such an epistemological stance has consensual validity in the scientific community, whether or not the construct of self-concept is valid. However, some social

Preparation of this essay was supported, in part, by grants from the John D. and Catherine T. MacArthur Foundation and the National Institute of Mental Health, U.S. Public Health Service. Reprinted from *Unstable Ideas* (Cambridge, Mass.: Harvard University Press, 1989), with permission.

scientists use the idea of self-concept to refer to a person's conscious evaluation of his or her qualities. The basis for this claim comes from the fact that the most popular procedure involves direct questioning of children or adults about their personal characteristics and associative evaluations. This referent for the idea of self-concept assumes that the theoretically most profitable meaning of the construct involves the person's subjective beliefs.

A few psychologists go further and write as if the contents of consciousness should be a primary criterion for judging the validity of all procedures: if a corpus of evidence indicates that a particular group of children has weak or poor self-concepts in the objective frame but report positive self-concepts on a questionnaire, then the former evidence is suspect. I believe this second view is mistaken. Human consciousness is a natural process to be understood as we understand other psychological processes, including depression, separation anxiety, growth of retrieval memory in infancy, and learning sets in monkeys. Although each of us may feel that our consciousness is among our most significant characteristics and the most important determinant of our behavior, such an assumption is neither empirically proven nor logically commanding.

My own belief is that because our consciousness is perceptually salient to each of us as acting agents, we have exaggerated its psychological significance. If I could enter the mind of a dog and perceive the world as it does, I would probably conclude that olfaction was the most important psychological process in the dog's existence, even though scientists who study dogs award considerably more theoretical significance to their social behavior than to smell. I intend this hypothetical example to be serious, not frivolous. Because so many significant biological and psychological processes occur outside of conscious awareness, theorists would be extremely limited in their imaginative scope if they always had to accommodate to a person's consciousness. We have learned that adults are usually unable to describe how they solve a particular problem (computer programs that simulate human problem solving ignore consciousness). Second, adult consciousness is evaluated by asking a person for a symbolic description presented in the form of sentences that must be grammatical. This procedure imposes serious constraints on the person's output. For example, self-reports rarely contain inconsistency: no sane person would say both, ''I am afraid'' and ''I am happy,'' because the two concepts refer to inconsistent ideas (even if we, in the objective frame, have good reason to suspect that person felt both anxiety and happiness because he was about to initiate an illicit rendezvous). Finally, objective signs of mood and feeling tone usually have very little relation to self-reports. Thus, scientific statements about self-concept in the objective frame must be treated with great caution.

Although this chapter is not the place to consider philosophical views in any depth, I suggest that some of the paradoxes philosophers have encountered are due to a confusion of objective and subjective frames. Such confusion is common in philosophical essays on morality. G. E. Moore suggested that good and bad must be defined by each person's conscious attitudes and feelings. Many years later, John Rawls stated that each person's rational decision in moral situations should be the criterion for morality. Both Moore and Rawls implied that elements of consciousness participate in the idea of moral choice. However, these philosophers, along with many others, also want to believe they are writing rules for morality in the objective frame. Their essays were persuasive pleas to the community to adopt into consciousness the elements of the scholars' objective argument, so that subjective and objective frames would be congruent. Unfortunately, the behavior of most people in situations with moral choice reveals the failure of this assumption. Many terrorists who kill feel moral in their subjective frame, even though we, in the objective frame, regard them in quite the opposite way. By contrast, when a mother offers love to her child, we are prone to declare her moral, even though her private motive may have been to win the child's affection away from an estranged but devoted father. Despite the fact that on occasion the two frames coincide, they are incommensurable.

I do not know if a concept of self will survive the next fifty years of research, and I bear the currently popular idea no prejudice. Should it persist, however, I suspect its primary referential meanings will not be the self-report indexes that often provide its current operational form, and its sense meaning will emphasize a family of processes rather than a unitary one. The tightly reasoned essay is the preferred strategy of scholars who write critiques of controversial themes. However, such essays have become so common that not all are read with care. For that reason, I have chosen to present the controversies that surround the concept of self within a hypothetical dialogue between a young philosopher and an older woman who is his tutor, on the premise that a discrepant style might provoke a more attentive reading. I am not certain that the dialogue will change any attitudes, but I hope it will be enjoyable.

A Dialogue

Scene: A small lake in Northern Italy.

Participants: Simpliciter (S), a young student of philosophy who has just joined the academy, and Reflectiva (R), an older philosopher who has become Simpliciter's teacher and friend.

Time: A morning in May, between past and present.

S: What a beautiful spring morning we are able to enjoy!

R: What nonsense are you speaking?

S: What do you mean, "nonsense"? Is this not a beautiful morning that gives each of us much pleasure?

R: How do you know this moment gives pleasure or the day is beautiful?

S: You are always such a skeptic. Consult your consciousness. If your consciousness feels it is beautiful and you experience pleasure, then my statement is true.

R: But how do I know my conscious feelings are pleasant? All I know is that I feel something. Why are you so certain that pleasure is the proper word to describe these feelings?

S: There is no talking with you when you are in such a mischievous state of mind. Do you not believe that there is a difference between feeling good and feeling poor?

R: Yes, of course. But tell me how I can know the difference?

S: By consulting your self-awareness, your consciousness. What would you suggest we do to determine if you felt good or poor?

R: By deciding first what events defined feeling good and feeling poor.

S: What would you pick?

R: Well, I might measure my pulse and see if it was different when I ate sweet foods than when I ate bitter ones. If my pulse rates were different when I ate the two kinds of foods, then at least I would have a clue as to which foods gave me pleasure and which did not. If my pulse always had a similar value when I was eating sweet foods but was of a different value when I was eating bitter ones, I would know when I was feeling pleasure and when displeasure.

S: But your pulse has nothing to do with how you feel. Feeling is in your consciousness, not in your pulse.

R: I do not understand. You claim that there exist in my conscious mind some events that are best called "feeling good." On the surface, that seems like a reasonable idea. But shouldn't we first determine if these words refer to a similar class of events in all people? I am certain you agree that not all of the words people use have the same referent. I am told that in some islands in the far East, when people say they feel sad they intend to imply that they are wise. Surely we can't rely only on someone's verbal statement about how she or he feels to decide on the state of that person's consciousness. Both of us know many people living under conditions neither you nor I could tolerate for a moment, who would reply that they felt good if someone asked them. Insane patients in our asylums tell visitors they feel happy on days when they look as pale as ghosts. Isn't that sufficient evidence for you to acknowledge that we can not decide if a person is feeling good simply by asking, "How do you feel?" That is why I insisted we need some other evidence.

S: What you say has merit and gives me pause. But your solution is obviously incorrect. Will you grant me that the state I call feeling good must be part of a person's consciousness?

R: In order to hear you out, I will accept that premise; but I warn you, only temporarily.

S: Fine. Well, if feeling good is a property of a person's consciousness, that is where we must search for evidence as to its actualization, not in the beating of the heart.

R: But how do you know what events are in a person's consciousness?

S: By asking, "What do you feel?" The coordination of all the information that contributes to the feeling state is in the self, and the only way to discover it is to ask the person to describe his or her state with the best words possible.

R: I think I see the flaw in your strategy. You believe that the words a person uses to describe his or her feeling state correspond to that person's true state of consciousness.

S: Of course. People will not say they feel fine if the sensations in their consciousness do not match that feeling.

R: That is precisely why I gave you the earlier examples, which you agreed were reasonable. I do not think we can assume that people's statements about their feelings, even if intended to be honest, are always in close correspondence with the state of their consciousness. People will say they feel calm when their hearts are racing, their muscles are stiff as boards, and they show irritation to the slightest frustration. Some people will say they don't recognize a familiar person, although the muscles of their face and the perspiration on their palms reveal that they do. Some unfortunate individuals with lesions in their spinal column, whose brains and consciousness are unable to experience any sensory feedback from their body, will say they feel as anxious as you and I when an accident has occurred. I cannot believe that their statements are faithful to their consciousness, unless you simply assert that the state of consciousness is defined by the sentences a person speaks. Let me try another approach. Please pick up that stick from the ground. Now, close your eyes and move the stick around in this hole in the ground. Good. What does your consciousness feel?

S: I feel intermittent pressure on my hand as the stick hits the side of the hole.

R: Good. Now put the stick in that opening in the tree. Keep your eyes closed. What do you feel?

S: The same feelings, intermittent pressure on my hand.

R: One last request. Hold the stick loosely in your fist, with your eyes closed, while I move it back and forth. What do you feel?

S: Well, the same sensation. I feel the pressure of the stick against my hand.

R: Let us think about this simple experiment. In all three cases, you reported that your consciousness experienced the same sensations, the intermittent pressure of a stick against your hand.

S: Yes, that's true.

R: But wouldn't you have used very different words to describe the three experiences?

S: What do you mean?

R: Well, if someone saw you poking a stick in a hole in the ground and asked you what you were doing, what would you say?

S: I'd say I was exploring a hole.

R: But if someone asked you the same question as I was moving the stick in your hand, what would you say?

S: I would say you were moving the stick in my fist.

R: So, even though your conscious experiences were similar, you would have used very different words to describe them. That is my point. The words people use are not faithful to what their consciousness is experiencing.

S: Then how shall we treat a person's statements about his or her feelings? Shall we ignore them?

R: No. We should treat what people say about their conscious experience as we treat their pulse rate. It is a fragment of information, a small, fallible clue to help us diagnose the state of a person's consciousness. How do you feel at this moment?

S: Confused, a little troubled, and a bit peeved with you.

R: But you seem to me to be much more relaxed than you were when we first met. Your body is less tense, your voice lower in pitch and less strident, and your face almost has a smile. I am certain you are actually feeling much better now than you did earlier, when you commented on the beauty of the morning.

S: You are a devil with words. Let's forget about feeling good or poor and talk about the entity that monitors the thoughts in our minds and the sensations in our bodies—the self. Will you grant me that each person possesses a self that is aware of the quality of its feelings and the content of its thoughts and contains some parts that are continuous throughout life?

R: I'm afraid that, once again, I do not understand. My reply is the same I gave to your statement about feeling good. How can we know if a unitary self exists? And even if such an idea referred to an event in nature, it is unlikely that its components would be constant from day to day, certainly not from year to year.

S: Well, of course, the self exists. What mental entity is it that is aware of pain, knows one's name, decides what sentences to speak, holds opinions about the world, and selects and reflects on actions? I trust you agree that we need to posit some entity that participates in and monitors these processes.

R: I only agree that those events you describe may occur. I am not certain that it is useful to posit a single hypothetical entity that is responsible for all of those functions. I grant you the utility of the word *self*, but I suspect that there is one self that monitors our feelings, a different self that evaluates our virtue, a third self that monitors actions, and perhaps a few more selves that are necessary to cover all the important domains of experience.

S: This time, I will win the argument. Look, you will acknowledge that each of us can relate what we know now with what we have learned in the past and, in light of both sets of knowledge, decide to act in a particular way. If there were not a single entity, that sequence would not be possible.

R: I disagree. A computer in Rome contacts a computer in Milan via a mainframe in Florence, which transfers information to a machine on Lake Como that prints a letter. There is no unitary computer, just connections among separate entities.

S: But those are mechanical objects. You cannot invent a similar analogy for biological phenomena.

R: I believe I can. When I have not eaten for a day, I become hungry. But we know that my hunger is not a single unitary process. My hypothalamus reacts to the drop in blood sugar, the walls of my stomach to emptiness, the receptors in my mouth to dryness. Surely, you will grant that the state of hunger is not a unitary event in a particular place. Why, then, assume that the state we call the self is any different?

S: If the self were not a single coordinated entity, how could you explain that a criminal act committed during adolescence will, twenty years later, lead the person to feel shame or prompt the self to do penance? If the self were many fragmented selves, we would not have access to despair from the deep past, fragrances of earlier springs, or the shiver of last winter's chill. You are simply not willing to acknowledge these facts we know to be true.

R: I do not understand why integration of experiences over time requires us to assume there is a unitary self that does not change. I understand from some of our friends at the academy that if white blood cells are stimulated to make antibody against measles during early childhood, the adult will have white blood cells twenty years later that have the potential to produce antibody to the measles germ. But the white blood cells that existed in childhood are gone; the adult has a totally new set of white blood cells. Even though the fragrance in a flower garden on a May afternoon can evoke the thought of a similar garden experienced ten years earlier, that fact does not require us to assume that the two sensory experiences are part of a unity. You are being unduly influenced by your subjective intuition. But our subjective intuitions are often notoriously poor indexes of what is true in nature. My subjective consciousness tells me that the sun moves and the earth stands still, the ocean ends at the horizon, and water and ice must be composed of different substances. Moreover, new knowledge changes our intuition. For ten years, whenever I met Bruno on the street, he would smile and greet me with a warm voice; and my intuition told me he was my close friend. I then learned he voted against my brother for an academy assignment. Now, although he greets me in exactly the same way, my intuition about the smile and greeting has changed. Further, before our astronomers discovered the distances of the sun and the moon, our intuitions were that both were equally far away. Now that we know the sun is much more distant, our intuitions have changed, and we have the feeling that the moon is closer. No, my friend, you are too trusting of your conscious intuitions. I suspect I have one self that talks to you, a different self that greets a stranger, and a third self that writes my diary at sunrise. You forget that Oriental philosophers assume that there are at least two selves. One self monitors encounters with strangers, the other monitors family and close friends. They even give the two selves different names. When we smile to a neighbor whom we dislike, how can one entity mediate the two inconsistent moods? I appeal to your logic. There cannot be one self that is both friendly and hostile to the same person at the same time. When you are lecturing in the morning to students on philosophy, does your self believe it is wiser than the students?

S: Of course.

R: But you have told me that when you attend the seminars at the academy, you feel intellectually inadequate when the older members are talking.

S: Yes, but they know more about the topic.

R: But how can there be one self that feels intelligent and wise in the morning but unintelligent in the evening of the same day? Surely, that is not logical.

S: But the context has changed. My self is comparing my qualities with those of others and comes to different conclusions, depending upon the target of comparison.

R: But look at what you have just admitted. You have said that you do not have any unitary idea of your wisdom. You have different ideas, depending upon the social situation. That is exactly what I suggested. We have different selves in different contexts.

S: That conclusion does not follow. I do not have to assume one brain when I am talking and another when I am painting.

R: Watch out. We are told that the metabolism of the brain is different when we are engaging in different activities. There is no unitary brain state either, but many different states.

S: But there is one brain that is the site of these different states, regardless of the activity engaged in.

R: You forget that last month we heard a lecture describing the important changes that occur in our brain over a lifetime. This unitary entity you call the self must derive its form, in part, from the synaptic connections in our brains. Yet, these connections are not static. Over a twenty-year period, they must change a great deal, and so the selves of today cannot be identical to the selves of childhood. If they were, they would be the only human qualities that never changed. Although nature is occasionally mischievous and creates unique exceptions to general principles in order to keep us humble, I am not persuaded that the self is that special exception. Let me try a simple thought experiment with you. If your self were a single entity that integrated information from your feelings, thoughts, and actions, then you should be able to tell me how your body felt several minutes ago when you were arguing with me about the meaning of feeling good. Can you do so?

S: No I can't, but how is that question relevant?

R: It is relevant because if you had a single self, it should be able to know what you felt, as well as what you said. If you had several selves, however, and only one was executive at any moment, you might be able to report the question you had asked me but be unable to say how your body felt.

S: But I wasn't paying attention to how I felt when I asked the question.

R: But isn't the entity that was not paying attention one of the selves I am arguing for? It was the self that monitors your feeling states. These separate selves compete; at the time your executive self was composing questions, this self was subordinate. This competition among the selves is not completely under your control, you know.

S: I am beginning to suspect that you secretly agree with the new, radical philosophers who claim that humans do not have a self that is free to select an action. Do you believe that if a team of scholars measured all of my past experience and had access to all of my brain states, they could have predicted my decision to come and talk with you this morning? I don't believe so. That is one reason why we need a unitary concept of self.

R: You seem to be upset by the possibility that some observers might be able to predict your decision to visit with me. Why?

S: It is disconcerting because I have always assumed that one of the central attributes of self is the capacity to make conscious decisions that are not predictable by others.

R: Let us play a little. Suppose it were possible for some omniscient group of experts, who had all the information on your past and current states, to predict most of the time when you would walk, eat, play, or work. But you were completely unaware of these expert predictions. You would still experience a sense of choice and, in that sense, would have a self with free will.

S: No, if my past were controlling my current behavior, then in actuality I would be a partial prisoner of my past. I would not have free will. It isn't just what I believe to be true.

R: But each of us must be a partial prisoner of our past. I cannot help but get upset when a woman is treated unjustly, yet that is not true of all citizens. I cannot help but be polite to an old person, but not all are equally civil. These seemingly spontaneous reactions are determined by my past, even though I have the feeling that at the moment when I criticize someone who has been unfair or I offer an old man assistance in crossing the street, I issued those acts freely. I never feel that my self was coerced by my past.

S: But if your past influenced your behavior, then you are deceiving yourself. You did not have complete freedom of choice.

R: I think I see the problem. Consider a spider constructing a web. Do you agree that it has no consciousness of what it is doing?

S: Yes.

R: Because experts can predict when the spider will build a web and the form of the web, the act of web building is determined, and the spider is not free.

S: Yes, that is true. But spiders have no consciousness. Humans are different.

R: Wait a moment. Let's move up to a chimpanzee, our close relative. We are told that chimpanzees are very similar to us in treatment of their young and how they feed, sleep, and mate. Do you agree that chimpanzees do not have freedom of choice for many significant behaviors?

S: Yes. But suppose they don't have self consciousness, either.

R: Now consider your nephew Damon who, I believe, is three years old. You agree that he has consciousness, don't you?

S: Yes, he does.

R: But can't you predict better than chance when Damon will get upset, what he will say to you when you visit, the games he will play, the length of his sentences, and on, and on? Can't you predict a great deal of Damon's behavior even though he has consciousness and free will?

S: Yes. But not all of his acts.

R: Wait a minute. Let us first agree that a person can have consciousness and yet a great deal of that person's behavior is determined in some way.

S: Yes, I see that. But what about the many times that Damon is unpredictable?

R: For example?

S: Well, last week, he did something uncharacteristic. He went to his room, saying he wanted to play alone. He stayed there for three hours, and he has never done that before.

R: Do you think he decided that act freely, with no incentive? Was there no information you could have gathered that would have helped you to predict that act, even though it was displayed for the first time?

S: I thought a bit about it the next morning. He had been punished for spilling honey over the table and felt ashamed. I think his decision to be alone was a reaction to the spilling of the honey.

R: Well then, it was partially determined by the past and was partially knowable, wasn't it?

S: Yes, I guess so.

R: Give me an example of an act Damon might issue for which you are certain that no information would allow you to predict it better than chance.

S: Well, if he suddenly put on his mother's shoes and took scissors and started to cut up curtains in the house. He is a good boy and would never do that.

R: But suppose he did? Do you believe he would have acted that way independent of any of his past experience—a totally spontaneous act of free will?

S: No, I guess not.

R: Then you agree that no person can perform an act that is totally independent of the past.

S: I admit that. But why then do we have the compelling sense that we choose to behave the way we do?

R: You phrased it correctly: we have a feeling that our choices are free. It is not possible to predict every act a person might display; there is a window of unpredictability. But that is true of every natural event. No expert can predict exactly where a particular leaf in a forest will fall at a particular moment. But the expert can do pretty well at predicting where most of the leaves will fall. We have partial freedom, while our consciousness has a sense of complete freedom. That is the critical point. Free will is an idea of subjective consciousness. From that perspective, it is valid, even though no one has complete freedom of choice from the perspective of another.

S: Wait, I don't understand that last statement. What does it mean for you to say that from your perspective I do not have complete freedom of choice, yet I believe I do? How can both of those statements be true?

R: Let me explain. Each agent has a private consciousness that is not available to others, but others try to understand these private states of agents. Let us call each agent's consciousnesses "subjective understandings," and the beliefs others hold about the agent "objective understandings." I do not claim that the objective understandings are more profound or more valid, only that the two understandings need not be consistent and often are not. They have different meanings because of their separate origins. Do you agree with the zoologists who claim they know why female turtles bury their fertilized eggs in the sand several hundred feet from the shore line?

S: They do so to protect the eggs from predators.

R: Good. Does that explanation have a clear meaning?

S: Yes.

R: Suppose we could enter the mind of the turtle and determine her consciousness. Do you agree that she would have no conception of the purpose of her behavior?

S: Yes.

R: So the objective understanding of the observer has no relation to the subjectivity of the turtle.

S: Yes. But you keep on using animals, who don't have subjective consciousness. Use humans as examples.

R: I will. Do you remember that last month you told me that your wife was rude to your sister Penelope when she visited from Atlantis? Yet, when you told her about her behavior, she said she did not realize she had been rude. She said she was tired and not feeling well and that is why she may not have been as friendly to Penelope as she is normally. Yet, when you reminded her that she was peeved because Penelope had not sent a birthday greeting to you, your wife acknowledged that perhaps she had been irritated at Penelope at the time, but claimed she had no awareness of anger during the visit.

S: Yes, I recall, and I am certain that my wife was rude because my sister forgot to send a note on my birthday.

R: That is a good example of the two perspectives. In your wife's subjective consciousness, she was tired. In your objective understanding, she was angry and therefore impolite. Do you see that the two understandings need not be in accord?

S: Yes. But in that case, I was right and my wife's understanding was wrong. There may be two understandings, but one is correct.

R: Not so fast. How do you know you were right?

S: One explanation of an event has to be correct. We can't have two different, but correct explanations of the same event.

R: But we can, if one is in the subjective frame of the actor and one is in the objective frame of the observer. Only when both explanations come from the same frame must one be correct.

S: I don't see why the frame of understanding makes any difference.

R: Consider a man who believes he is unworthy of any happiness because he has failed at every important task he has undertaken and has tried to commit suicide. But his friends and family see him as a successful professional who is well liked by everyone. We know this is true of our friend Paulo.

S: Yes, that's true.

R: A man who tries to kill himself represents pretty good evidence of someone who believes he is unworthy, or at least unhappy. But no one knew that was true about Paulo. For a man cannot be both sad and happy, worthy and unworthy at the same time. Yet, because one source of unworthiness was in the subjective frame and the other in the objective frame, the statements are not inconsistent.

S: I am beginning to understand.

R: Consider someone who believes he is Homer and plans to rewrite the Odyssey. If we are certain he holds that belief, we take him to a physician for treatment. We would not do that if we were not certain that in his subjective frame he believed he was Homer. Do you agree that the two understandings are complementary? Each has a meaning, but each meaning is derived from its own frame.

S: Now you are going to say that the self's sense of free will has meaning in the subjective frame but not in the objective frame.

R: Precisely. Every Saturday, I note that you will take a walk before lunch but only if you have been reading for most of the morning. Yet, you are certain your walk is a spontaneously chosen act.

S: I believe there is a significant exception to the separation of subjective and objective frames.

R: What is that?

S: The motive of self-interest. In the subjective frame, my self always protects its access to sensory pleasures and power first. And that idea is also regarded as true in the objective frame of our scholars who study human nature. They, too, say that humans have evolved so that they are always trying to maximize their own welfare, power, and economic gain first.

R: I am not certain I agree. Haven't you picked up a piece of glass from a path because you thought that a person might not see it and may step on it? Did you move the glass away because you were self-interested? I don't think so. Last night, around midnight, I took a walk before retiring and saw Ignatio looking at Michael's freshly painted fence. You remember that Ignatio is angry with Michael and has been so since the time Michael flirted with his wife at their anniversary party five years ago. Michael had left his purse on top of the latch by mistake, and Ignatio knew that Michael prized that purse very much. Ignatio looked at it and, to my surprise, took the purse off the post and put it on the threshold of the door so that it would be less visible to passersby, and then left. That was clearly an act of charity. There was no one on the street, and Ignatio had the opportunity to get even with someone he does not like; yet he performed an act of kindness that took effort. He did so because he could not do otherwise.

S: What do you mean, he could not do otherwise? Ignatio is a sane, mature person with free will. If he chose to, he could have done something to hurt Michael.

R: I suggest that Ignatio's feelings at that moment prevented him from doing so.

S: That makes no sense to me. Each of us controls our feelings every day. We are angry with someone, and we greet them politely; we feel sad and yet are able to smile to a friend; we feel attracted toward a lovely woman we do not know, yet act with indifference. We have absolutely no problem controlling our feelings. So why do you say that Ignatio did not steal the purse because he could not control his feelings?

R: In every example you posed, a person would have yielded to feelings that are violations of what he or she might view as proper behavior.

S: Yes, that's true. So what?

R: What emotion do we feel when we act improperly?

S: Self-reproachment. But that is a timid feeling, compared with anger or sexual arousal. How could it overpower such strong competitors?

R: It does so because it is linked to the most important belief each of us trys to maintain.

S: What is that?

R: The belief of the evaluative self that it has virtue because the executive self has acted in accord with what is proper and right.

S: That is nonsense. How can you explain the violent or corrupt behavior of so many people who know that they are not acting in accord with what they believe is right and good? If your hypothesis were correct, most people would behave in a civilized way, and thievery, lying, and corruption would be rare.

R: That is a forceful reply. Let me try to answer it. We have agreed that in the subjective frame each of us feels we can decide how to act.

S: Yes.

R: Will you also grant that our evaluative self wishes to be judged as good?

S: I will for now, but I am not certain of the correctness or utility of that idea. Proceed.

R: If you grant those two assumptions, you may be forced to agree that most of the time we will behave properly, as Ignatio did. He knew that if he stole the purse or let it remain prominent, he would later feel that he was not a good person. What I must explain, therefore, are the far less frequent times when people behave improperly. Let me begin with a stark example. A man kills a traveler in the woods and steals his gold. He knows he is acting immorally and knows he will suffer some guilt. He killed because he believed his emotions—be they greed, a desire for momentary power, or anger at the traveler—could not be suppressed.

S: That was my earlier point. Ignatio felt strong anger toward Michael, but we couldn't understand why that anger didn't influence him last night.

R: Anger did not dominate Ignatio's actions because, at that moment, the executive self was in control of Ignatio's behavior. The feeling self could not deceive the executive self into believing that the anger at Michael was so intense it was not responsible for his actions. If the feeling self could have done so, he might have stolen the purse. Moral behavior protects the evaluative self from reproachment. If the executive self decides it is not responsible for an improper act, no blame is imposed by the evaluative self, and the improper act becomes more probable.

S: But what conditions allow a person to conclude that the self is not responsible?

R: Strong emotions. We give in to what we regard as immoral temptations because the feelings associated with the immoral urge are so strong that the feeling self can persuade the executive self it is not responsible for the act.

S: I don't find that argument persuasive. I know many people, as do you, who are emotionally indifferent, cold as fish, who act immorally with ease and often on impulse. They seem to experience no struggle with responsibility for the act. How can you explain their behavior?

R: I fear you will accuse me of inconsistency. For reasons that I do not completely understand, their evaluative self uses different evidence to affirm its virtue then do you and I. Their acts, which seem immoral to us, symbolize a form of virtue to them.

S: Virtue! Stealing, corruption, murder? Surely you are joking.

R: I realize that statement sounds ridiculous. But wait. Suppose your life history was such that you felt uneasy, anxious, unloved, afraid, or helpless much of the time. Throughout your youth, some of these feelings dominated your consciousness. I suspect you would be tempted to do something to alter this dysphoric mood. Unfortunately, many of the acts you and I regard as immoral have, as a consequence, a temporary sense of elation, efficacy, or potency. An act of vandalism, corruption, intimidation, or murder is an assertion of temporary effectiveness. Through their display, a person is able to mask, temporarily, the feeling of incompetence or impotence; and as a consequence, the evaluative self feels some virtue.

S: That is a poetic statement. What evidence can you supply to support such a speculative and counterintuitive notion?

R: Just a little. Why is it that crimes are most common among the youth who failed in their early studies in school?

S: I don't know.

R: I suspect that their failure at this important assignment made them feel less effective and, therefore, less virtuous. But the major rationale for my position is a logical argument that begins with one significant fact. It is this. Do you agree that of the many, many opportunities that people have to steal, lie, insult, bully, or commit acts of destruction every day, only a tiny number of such acts actually occur? Indeed, the ratio of such immoral acts committed to the total number of opportunities in our entire community on a single day approaches zero. It seems odd, but immoral acts are freak events statistically.

S: I had never thought of improper behavior that way. But on reflection, I suspect you may be right.

R: Do you also agree that, much of the time, those who behave morally despite an easy opportunity to commit an improper act are not restrained by fear of being noticed or punished? Often, the person is alone, and no one could possibly know about the crime. This was true of Ignatio last evening.

S: Yes.

R: Well then, it must be that most of the time human beings behave morally because they have a natural bias to do so, and I suggest that this bias originates in the continuous wish to affirm the evaluative self's virtue. Why else would most people behave properly despite a temptation to immoral behavior without obvious risk? Our task is to explain the aberrant times when a person does act immorally. Take thievery. Let us exclude those who steal because their material needs are strong and consider only those who steal something they do not actually need. Why would they do so unless that act had a symbolic meaning? I suggest that one symbolic meaning is a sense of effectiveness or potency.

S: Why don't you say people steal because they enjoy it? Why do you have to bring in the idea of effectiveness or virtue? You are twisting words to serve your position, when it seems that we have a much less tortuous explanation. They enjoy stealing.

R: Why should anyone enjoy stealing? It is not a sensual act. If it is enjoyed, it must be because of its symbolic value. I grant there are many symbolic prizes other than a feeling of effectiveness, but such a feeling could follow an act of thievery.

S: Why do you make feelings so important to morality? Such a position is not in accord with the writings of our philosophers, who treat moral behavior as a consequence of logic and rationality. They claim that most persons refrain from stealing because they do not want others to steal from them. Because each of us is compelled to be logically consistent, we do not steal, for we have no right to ask of others what we do not demand of ourselves. Of course, these philosophers also have trouble explaining the habitual thief, who is supposed to be logical, too. Although they say that thieves do not reflect upon the logic of their actions, that argument is not less credible than your claim about stealing in order to feel effective. It seems to me we have two weak explanations of the thief. Personally, I have always believed that the thief failed to learn that stealing was wrong or perhaps was not punished for stealing when she or he was a youth, and hence did not experience fear when planning or executing the act. What is wrong with that simpleminded, straightforward explanation of the thief?

R: The first premise in that explanation is clearly wrong. Ask any thief if stealing is wrong, and he will tell you so without equivocation. He knows that stealing is wrong. The second premise is harder to refute, but I appeal to your sense of reasonableness. Think of Aristo's upbringing. His father and mother were upstanding citizens who must have punished him for stealing; yet, he is serving two years in exile for stealing from his father-in-law. He knew stealing was wrong, and he felt anxious about the act. He told us that when we were with him the night he was caught. No, your explanation will not work for him. Thieves know they are behaving improperly and know their behavior is disapproved by friends and society. They steal because it reassures self of a feeling of effectiveness which, in turn, permits the thief to feel some virtue.

S: You are using nonsensical words. Now I shall adopt your skeptical position. What do virtue, potency, and worthwhileness mean? How do I know if a person feels virtue, or the lack of it?

R: Yes, I have lapsed into loose talk. Mea culpa. We are told that humans are the only species with the symbolic categories "good" and "bad." Unlike the categories of furniture and food, whose exemplars I can point to in a room, I cannot point to anything in the world and say that it belongs to the category of either good or bad. That is why some of our philosophers have concluded that morality belongs to esthetics. Good and bad are evaluative terms whose meanings rest with our feelings, and one source of these feelings is part of our nature. I trust you agree that the emotion of empathy emerges in all children by the second birthday.

A second source of these feelings is more complex, and I am less certain of its origins. All children seem to appreciate the actions and qualities their community classifies as good or bad. If they act in a way that deviates from their understanding of the community's belief, the evaluative self feels a lack of virtue, and the person will to try to behave in a way that will enhance the sense of virtue. So each person looks for opportunities that will permit the evaluative self to come to the judgment that it is good.

We celebrate Gando's birthday each year and erected a statue of him in the Common. You will remember that he was incompetent in school, a poor athlete, and he stammered at group meetings. I suggest that he had a sense of being ineffective as a young man and therefore felt minimally virtuous. He became our most moral citizen to enhance his virtue. He defended the rights of slaves against a vocal majority and fasted for three months to gain their eventual freedom. Our community was so moved by that act of sacrifice that they insisted on the legislation honoring him. I do not wish to minimize Gando's accomplishments, nor do I impugn his moral intentions when I suggest that those moral behaviors were attempts to persuade the evaluative self of its virtue. Perhaps he had to behave more morally than his peers because he was less effective than they in the domains that, as a child, he had learned were valued by our community. I am not suggesting that his moral actions were not issued out of honest care for others. He chose to help those in need because, like Ignatio in front of Michael's fence, he could not do otherwise. But he felt that strongly because his evaluative self demanded affirmation of its virtue.

Let me give you a second example. You must remember our revered scholar Wigetto, who confided to a friend that he had committed two crimes for which he felt guilty. As a school teacher in one of our rural districts, he once struck a girl who was a pupil in his classroom. Initially, he denied the act to the authorities and felt badly about that lie. More seriously, he let his friends believe that he had no barbarian blood, when he knew that one of his grandfathers had been a northern barbarian. He felt guilty over permitting that deceit to persist and experienced a lack of virtue. In order to relieve the guilt, he gave away most of his money and worked without stipend for years. As you know, he wrote a long treatise about morality in which he attempted to place it on a transcendental plane. I suggest that his behavior during most of his adult life was an attempt to affirm the evaluative self's virtue.

S: But that argument makes the absurd prediction that the more effective, talented, or potent a person is, the more virtuous he will feel and therefore the less moral he will be in a conventional sense. We both know that is not true. The peasant is not more honest or loyal than the artist. According to your argument, peasants should be our most moral citizens because they have minimal effectiveness in other domains we value.

R: And they may be. If we equated the opportunities to commit the same immoral acts for our peasants and our statesman, I am not certain who would emerge as more moral. But you will recall that this discussion arose because you claimed that self-interest was an exception to my insistence that the subjective and objective frames should be distinguished. I am suggesting that the evaluative self has a continual desire to affirm its virtue. If that victory occurs in one domain of living, there is a less urgent need to affirm it in another. But this desire usually takes precedence over all other interests of our many selves. It is our most important interest.

S: I believe you choose words to suit your argument. I claim that the self's attempt to prove it is virtuous is simply a derivative of self-interest, and self-interest is always primary. Reassuring the self that it is virtuous permits it to conclude it is better than others and therefore entitled to more privilege.

R: Slow, you run too fast with that idea. I don't think you are right when you say people are always comparing their self with the self of another. Yes, we do compare ourselves with others for some qualities and on some occasions. But we do not do so when we remove a piece of glass from a path. The new idea that humans always act in the service of self-interest has created serious mischief. So many scholars have come to accept the truth of that assumption about human nature, the average citizen now treats it as a law. And because they believe they should not violate a natural law, they try to obey it. Indeed, some of our citizens feel uneasy when they do not act in self-interest, even at times when they do not wish to. This so-called law is simply an ethical statement with no more scientific validity than the proposition "Poseidon rules the oceans." What worrys me is that the presumptive validity of the law of self-interest is becoming a self-fulfilling prophecy. Let me remind you of a current problem in our society where the desire among some citizens for virtue appears to subdue their self-interest.

S: I don't believe you can do so.

R: Some citizens in our community have become upset by the fact that some of our naturalists are doing experiments with small animals, usually rabbits, to find out how our bodies work and to discover ways to cure our serious diseases. These discoveries will surely benefit the entire community. Yet, this vocal group claims that the work is cruel to the animals, and they insist that the research be stopped, even though cessation of the work is opposed to their own self-interest, for it will delay the time when these common diseases will be cured.

S: Well, isn't it cruel to cut up a rabbit's body?

R: No more cruel than what our butchers do to prepare a holiday meal. Why is it not cruel to kill a pig for a wedding feast but cruel to kill a rabbit to learn more about human diseases?

S: Well, we must eat meat.

R: That is not true. You know we could survive on plants. It is possible to live a healthy life and never eat animal flesh. No, I don't believe these people care deeply about an animal's feelings. Their deep motive, and I doubt they are aware of it, is to impugn the moral authority of the naturalists. Those who study nature are highly respected by most citizens in our community. They have secure positions and are well financed; and each year, many are publicized and received state honors. But they talk to each other about their work in technical language most of us do not understand, and they are beginning to probe phenomena we believe are sensitive and private. As a result, the average citizen has become threatened by their work and would like to reduce their power and virtue. A good way to accomplish this goal is to challenge their morality by accusing them of being cruel to animals. That is a serious charge, for it implies that our naturalists have less virtue than they and the majority of the community believe.

S: How can you be certain of that counterintuitive explanation? Do you have another example?

R: I do, but it is even more speculative. You will remember from your study of ancient history that the Brehwins were poor shepherds in the desert, surrounded on one side by the Potomies and on the other by the Tyleptians—two groups with much secular power and wealth.

S: Yes, I do remember.

R: Well, suppose the Potomies and the Tyleptians were like our naturalists, and the Brehwins were the citizens attacking them. The Brehwins were threatened by the power of their two neighbors and therefore were motivated to find a way to reduce the authority of both. Unconsciously, the Brehwins looked for some accusation that would impugn the Potomies' and Tyleptians' morality.

S: What did the Brehwins do? I forget.

R: You will remember that the Potomies and the Tyleptians believed in local gods—a god for the wind, a god for the sun, one for the earth. These gods were unpredictable and not always on the side of humans in times of crisis. Wouldn't it be clever to invent a god that was superior to all these local gods, a god who was in charge of the sun, the earth, the water—a god who controlled all the gods? It would also be wise to make this god a trusted, gentle being who was always man's friend. That is exactly what the Brehwins did. You will remember that they claimed their god was superior to the many gods of the Potomies and the Tyleptians. They even declared that the gaining of wisdom and honesty—two qualities they as shepherds could attain—as morally superior to the accumulation of wealth and power, which they felt they were unable to attain. They impugned the moral authority of the Potomies and the Tyleptians, as some of our citizens impugn the morality of our naturalists.

S: That is an extremely speculative argument.

R: I agree that it is. But I believe in the principle it illustrates. The evaluative self is made uneasy by any person or group that has more of some quality it regards as symbolic of virtue. So it tries to get the executive self to denigrate those people in some way. If it can't take away their secular signs of virtue—be they power, wealth or status—it can suggest that they are immoral.

S: It seems now that you agree with my view of the primacy of self-interest. Since most societies believe that poverty, low status, or being dominated by others leads the evaluative self to feel a lack of virtue, doesn't it follow that in order to avoid judging the self as bad such persons would seek to gain more wealth, status and power? You must agree that such motives and actions are self-interested.

R: That is very clever of you.

S: And since more rather than less wealth, status, and power bring better health and the ability to resist exploitation and coercion, it is unlikely that any society would, for very long, hold the belief that these qualities were bad. And if I am right in that assertion, then self-interest would be universal in both the objective and the subjective frames.

R: You catch me without an immediate reply, but your argument only holds for societies with variation in wealth, power, and status.

S: But you will acknowledge that such variation exists in all societies we know anything about.

R: Will you accept a compromise? If self-interest refers to desires for sensory pleasure, power, wealth, and status, then can we agree that self-interest is only a primary preoccupation of human beings when there is variation in these prizes? However, the evaluative self's preoccupation with affirming its virtue is salient under all societal conditions. You and I can imagine conditions in which self-interest was not a foremost concern but cannot imagine conditions in which affirmation of virtue was not.

S: Yes, in a mood of wild fancy, I might imagine such a hypothetical community. But because its realization is impossible, my claim that self-interest is a universal characteristic of our species is, for all practical purposes, true. Do you appreciate that this is the first time in our many discussions that you have become the idealist and I the skeptic? How did that happen?

R: Yes, I did note that change in our positions, and my feeling self is troubled. My executive self shall brood on it this afternoon and give you a reply when we meet tomorrow morning.

Index